SERIES III   CYCLE A

LECTIONARY
PREACHING WORKBOOK

SERIES III   CYCLE A

LECTIONARY
PREACHING
WORKBOOK

FOR USE WITH ROMAN CATHOLIC, EPISCOPAL,
LUTHERAN, AND COMMON LECTIONARIES

GEORGE M. BASS

C.S.S. Publishing Co., Inc.

Lima, Ohio

Library of Congress Cataloging-in-Publucation Data

Bass, George M., 1920-
Lectionary preaching workbook.

1. Preaching. 2. Bible—Liturgical lessons, English. 3. Bible—Homiletical use. 4. Sermons—Outlines, syllabi, etc. 5. Church year—Prayerpbooks and devotions--English. 6. Common lectionary. I. Title
BV4211.2.B267   1989   251   89-9971
ISBN 1-55673-135-3

Table of Contents

Preface

As the third person asked to prepare this preaching workbook, it became obvious to me that it had to be done differently than the other two series. The "key" to such an effort found direction in a book written by the late Harry F. Baughman; it was called *Preaching from the Propers*. This writer rejected its thesis in *The Renewal of Liturgical Preaching*, which is what Baughman was addressing. His theory was, simply, that the preacher should exegete each item of the propers (Introit, Old Testament, Lesson, Epistle, Gradual, and the Gospel) for any given day, make a comparative and combined study of them, and the *theme for any given Sunday — and the sermon — would emerge*. Baughman's theory was sound; the problem was in the propers themselves; they had been moved about from Sunday to Sunday and seldom harmonized with each other in any given set of pericopes. For a few Sundays of the church year, the theory was valid; it would work, but for most — *because the theological content of the Sundays and the theological framework of the church year were not taken into consideration* — the theory didn't apply. *But it is acceptable today, because it can be operative in the new liturgies and lectionaries of the churches.*

In this study, commentary is provided on the three lessons for each Sunday, as is standard practice for commentaries, but *the richness of the other appointed propers — the Prayer for the Day, the appointed Psalm, the Psalm Prayer,* all of these from the *Lutheran Book of Worship,* — will also be explored for their contributions to the content of the sermon. The theological clue provided by the kerygmatic framework of the church year, which determines the scripture readings assigned to the first half of the year and all major and minor festivals, will also be examined for its relationship to sermon themes. This theory does not apply to the second, or Pentecost, portion of the year to the same degree as it does to the first half of the year — Advent to Pentecost — with some exceptions. The second half has a kerygmatic framework, but the Sundays really are "ordinary" rather than "extraordinary," as in the festival portion of the year.* Accordingly, the second section of this study is done a bit differently than the first half. Therefore, the Advent to Pentecost half of the book is a kind of "Baughman revisited" effort, because his theory will work for most of the assigned lections and propers; the Pentecost Season cannot fall under the same rubric because the second lessons are *almost always* out of synchronization with the other two readings.

The homiletical material is meant to take the shape of *suggestions or sermon ideas*, something of how this preacher would approach the task of preaching from Sunday to Sunday. Sermon *Outlines and Plans* are meant to get the preacher started on his/her own development of sermon or homily, *which might not resemble what is in the workbook when it is done. Pastoral exegesis of the local situation determines what the preacher will emphasize in a text as it speaks in love and grace, sin and judgment, law and gospel, to a particular congregation, and how the sermon will be shaped.* Occasionally, a sermon plan of a well-known preacher will be included in the homiletical materials to highlight the content or the shape — or both — of a sermon.

This study also includes some examples of what I call *Impact Material*, stories and other illustrations which make sermons interesting and memorable, and make connections with contemporary life. Most of these are from my own experiences, observations, and writings. For a fuller understanding of what this is attempting to do in this area, the preacher might read Chapter 6 of *The Song and the Story*, which is titled "Sermon Illustration in the Story Sermon."

The parish pastor, in the final analysis, has to do the difficult and critical work of preparing and preaching the Sunday sermon to any given congregation. This workbook, from this perspective is *incomplete*, because the *applications have to be made by parish pastors; no one else can do this work.* This workbook, therefore, has been prepared to assist in this *momentous* — and *vital* — *and most important ministry of the parish preacher, the proclamation of the good news to the faithful in the Sunday assembly.* It is meant to *enrich, not replace,* other workbooks and homiletical commentaries, and it is offered in the hope that it will be helpful to those who have *the most important job in the world, the preaching of the Gospel.*

George M. Bass
St. Matthew's Day
September 21, 1988

Introduction

1. The preacher's task — the preparation of the weekly sermon.

Over the past three decades, preachers have been heard to make two complaints about preaching: First, it is extremely difficult to find sufficient time to properly prepare the sermon for next Sunday; and second, the finding of suitable illustrative material is a frustrating task for every single week of a preaching ministry. The *Lectionary Preaching Workbook* is addressed to the first of these two problems, but it will also suggest some ways in which the second problem may be resolved.

Forty years ago, Andrew W. Blackwood addressed the business of sermon preparation in a book called *The Preparation of Sermons.* He touched on all aspects of the preparation and production, including the business of planning. He believed, as does this author, that an organized effort at planning and preparing sermons is requisite to consistent quality and excellence in parish preaching. It always will be. A systematic plan is, if done well, an approach to the solution of the difficulty preachers claim to have in finding time to prepare each week's homiletical effort. Blackwood suggested that preachers needed a long-term plan, and he once taught a course on "Preparing a Year's Preaching." His concern was not simply for the pastor's use of time, but for his perception, borne of years of the study of preaching, preachers, and sermons, that good sermons have to have an incubation period; he spoke of "a homiletical seed-plot" — a kind of synonym for a long-term plan — that almost every pastor needs to become an effective preacher. However, the complexities and demands of contemporary parish ministry consume so much of the pastor's time that such planning is a luxury that few preachers can afford. The *Lectionary Preaching Workbook* is conceived to encourage and assist pastors — through the development of a long-term plan for preaching — to make the best use of their homiletical time by suggesting an approach to the development of such a program.

2. The ready-made Long-term Plan for preaching in the liturgy and the church year.

The liturgy, through the church year and its lectionary, offers busy parish pastors a ready-made plan for the preparation of sermons. In this edition of the workbook, the plan will follow the comprehensive structure of the church year as it is arranged in three cycles — Christmas, Easter, and Pentecost (The Time of the Church in the LBW) — rather than the seasons alone. The first two cycles represent about one half of the year; Pentecost fills out the other — or last — half. Each of the first two cycles is about one quarter of the year. (Easter, composed of two seasons, Lent and Easter, is always exactly thirteen weeks in length). By dividing Pentecost in two at the end of August, so that there is a summer quarter and a fall quarter, the church year may best be utilized in long-term planning. This parallels — from the perspective of the church year — Perry Biddle's suggestion that preachers ought to plan thirteen weeks ahead in their preaching ministries.

3. A Short-term Plan for preaching.

Effective preaching also requires a short-term plan that calls for intensive work on one or two sermons soon to be preached. The detailed studies for each of the Sundays of the cycles and seasons will illustrate one way of developing and actualizing such a plan. It will include: a list of lessons, Prayer of the Day, Psalms, Psalm Prayers, other liturgical details, such as assigned/suggested hymns, comments on the Gospel, theological motifs, possible pastoral exegesis, sermon ideas, plans, plots, shapes, as determined by the text. (The plan, or plot, of a sermon by an effective preacher may be included on some occasions to stimulate the preacher's imagination in this stage of the process.)

4. *The homiletical use of the lectionary.*

To make the most of the lectionary — any of the variations of the lectionary in use today — a comprehensive reading of Scripture is necessary. This is where the plan finds its foundation and the source of "sermonic seeds" (H. Grady Davis, *Design for Preaching)* that may germinate and become useful sermons in due time. Such Bible reading calls for reading of the Gospel for the Year — Matthew, this year — in its entirety *as a first step* in this process. Once that is done, the pastor ought to read the other assigned pericopes along with the Gospel of the Day. This will allow time for the preacher to absorb the lessons and let them come to life within the mind, imagination, and heart of the pastor. Such reading opens the way for developing the long-term plan, including the nuclear work on the sermons, and it also prepares the preacher for the intensive and specific work that must be done to develop effective sermons.

5. *The role of John in the lectionary.*

The Gospel of John, preachers should remember, finds its way into all three cycles of the church year, which is a variation of ancient liturgical tradition; John was the main Gospel for Lent and, especially for Easter. Although John does not have a "year of its own," it is the most frequently used of the four Gospels. As the Gospel of the Easter cycle, it displaces the Gospel of the year on many Sundays and, thereby makes a unique impact on the story of Jesus' passion, death, and resurrection; the various lectionaries use no less than ten readings from St. John during Lent and Easter. An annual reading of John ought to be a *second step* in the homiletical life of the parish pastor, especially during Epiphany, as the church approaches Lent and Easter. This will give the preacher a different perspective on the redeeming events in the life and ministry of Jesus and will prepare the preacher, when supplementary study of John is done, for preaching during the Easter cycle.

6. *A supplementary reading program.*

The parish preacher needs to develop some sort of a supplementary reading program. Concomitant reading greatly enriches the exegetical and homiletical efforts of the preacher. Much of this, too, should be done during the summer as a follow-up to the reading of the gospel and the other appointed lections. Obviously, one needs to read commentaries, volumes on the theology of appointed books, and various homiletical articles, journals, and contemporary theories for preaching the gospel. Summer, in most parishes, is a time when the pastor might catch up on non-theological reading — fiction, biography, autobiography, drama, poetry, short stories, and anything else that is of interest and *makes contact with contemporary life.* Joseph Sittler used to save time during the summer to go to plays and movies, as well as read materials that might have been crowded out during the academic year. When the preacher does this, with a preliminary plan in place and some sort of system for recording excerpts from such reading (file system, computer disc, journal, or whatever the preacher may best use), the secondary problem — finding illustrative materials — may also be addressed and, at least, partially solved. Such reading generates homiletical ideas and aids in the actual development of sermons.

7. *The function of the church year in lectionary and liturgical preaching.*

To employ a lectionary in one's preaching ministry often gives rise to a misconception: the preacher is doing liturgical preaching simply by concentrating on the message of the appointed texts. Nothing could be farther from the truth; the system is more complex — and much richer — than that. It is of utmost importance for the parish preacher to comprehend, first and foremost, the relationship of the church year to the lectionary, and then, of course, to the proclamation of the gospel.

a. The church year is the *calendar* of the church. It signals the church about its worship celebrations and festivals. It announces the important events in the life of Christ that are remembered and commemorated. It establishes the rhythm of public and individual worship in the perspective of the gospel. The central focus of the year is on the death and resurrection of the Lord — in light of his promised return. Easter is the essential festival and, also, the primary season of the church year. Every Sunday carries the mark of the loving grace of God in Jesus' death and the mighty power of God in the Lord's resurrection; each Sunday, regardless of cycle or season, is a celebration of this saving event, a "little Easter." For example, the *Book of Common Prayer* of the Episcopal Church contains this prayer called "A Collect for Sundays:"

> O God, you make us glad with the weekly remembrance of the glorious resurrection of your Son our Lord: Give us this day such blessing through our worship of you, that the week to come may be spent in your favor; through Jesus Christ our Lord. Amen

b. The church year is a *theological framework for worship and preaching.* This framework is *kerygmatic and eschatological,* spelling out the future in terms of past and present experience with the gospel. Each cycle of the year has specific kerygmatic motifs which fit within the theological/eschatological framework of the church year. The church year also functions on a different level, acting as a kind of prompter for preachers, reminding them that the proclamation of the gospel is the very heart of their "homiletical business." *The church year, when understood as a theological framework, is a guarantee that the gospel will be proclaimed — by the preachers — from the perspective of the redeeming events: "Christ has died! . . . Christ has risen! . . . Christ will come again!"*

c. The church year provides *theological clues* for the gospel content and themes of preaching (and worship).

In the first, or festival, half of the year, *the first hermeneutical clue to the theme of the day is given by the cycle, the season, and the Sunday, or festival, of the year.* The Sundays of Advent, for example, have the same themes in all three cycles, spelling out the various dimensions of eschatology — past, present, and future — in the New Testament; *their biblical/kerygmatic content is set from one year to the next.* Together, they establish the theology and the preaching themes for the season before Christmas, while clarifying the basis on which exegesis of the appointed readings should begin. When the preacher comprehends the biblical and theological content of cycle, season, and Sunday, the exegetical and hermeneutical task is given an important assist.

d. The church year and the selection of the gospel and the other readings.

The church year functions in two different ways in the choice and appointment of the biblical readings used in the worship and preaching of the church. In the first half of the year, the festival portion, and for major and minor festivals, too, the content of each Sunday, within the season and cycle, determines the selection *(Lectio Selecta)* of the Gospel until the second Sunday after the Epiphany (when semi-continuous reading begins). The first and second readings (with the exception of most of the Epiphany season) are selected to harmonize with the gospel for the day. In both halves of the church year, the Old Testament reading is chosen to complement the Gospel for the day.

In the second half of the church year, Pentecost season, most of the Sundays do not have clearly established themes, as do the Sundays of the first part of the year. The Gospel for the year is read semi-continuously (a modified *Lectio Continua system),* with the exception of a few Sundays (The Holy Trinity, Reformation Sunday, All Saints Sunday, and Christ the King). The Gospel in the non-festival section of the church year, determines the biblical content and the kerygmatic theme for the day. The Second Lessons are also semi-continuous readings from various New Testament books.

Summary: The public life of the church in worship, and particularly the preaching, is, therefore, under the aegis of the gospel-oriented church year. It informs preachers about the content of the sermons which they deliver to the people. The church year context calls for kerygmatic preaching that announces anew and freshly the very heart of the gospel, Jesus' death and resurrection and his promised return at the end of the age. For the first half of the church year (except for part of the Epiphany season), the Sundays have "set" biblical content and theological themes; these control and determine the choice of the lessons and the other liturgical elements for the Sundays of Advent, Christmas, Epiphany (to a lesser degree), Lent, and Easter, as well as major and minor festivals throughout the entire year. Because the content of the Sundays is kerygmatic, the proclamation of the gospel is guaranteed, at least in the biblical readings, and virtually demanded of the preaching that is undertaken on the assigned Gospels and other scriptural readings.

8. Other homiletical clues offered by the liturgies of the church.

Preachers will avoid homiletically short-changing themselves, if they recognize the importance of other liturgical and biblical elements that are set alongside the lessons of the liturgical churches. The first thematic clue to any Sunday's biblical content, beyond the title of the Sunday in the cycle and season of the church year, usually comes in the Prayer of the Day. The prayers for Advent illustrate this beautifully. These prayers are, most often, revisions of the ancient, and classical, Collects of the church; some are newly prepared for contemporary worship books. More than anything else, in its address and/or petition to God, the Prayer for the Day announces the biblical and kerygmatic theme of the day to the people, replacing the ancient Introits of liturgical worship, which, theoretically, were supposed to function that way.

Second, the psalmody "responds" to the first reading while, also, connecting the first two lessons to each other and supporting the Gospels for the Day. The "responsory psalms" vary from denomination to denomination to a considerably greater degree than the lessons, therefore only the psalms appointed in one liturgical book (the LBW, with which the author is most familiar) are included. (Reginald Fuller deals with the responsory psalms of the Roman lectionary in his *Preaching the New Lectionary;* the *Prayer Book Studies* of the Protestant Episcopal Church considers the psalms used in their liturgy).

Third, the LBW prints, in the *Ministers Desk Edition,* a Psalm Prayer, which puts each psalm in kerygmatic perspective. For example, Psalm 98, which begins, "Sing to the Lord a new song, for he has done marvelous things, with his right hand and his holy arm has he won for himself the victory," has this prayer attached to it:

Lord, we sing to you a new song, for your victory is ever new. In the empty tomb you have given us a glimpse of your future, and in your victory over death you have shown us how we shall overcome the last enemy. As the seas roar and the hills sing together, we too will praise you for your great triumph, Father, Son, and Holy Spirit, now and forever. (LBW)

These prayers, therefore, provide additional hermenteutical and homiletical clues to the preacher.

Fourth, most liturgical books include in their propers a *verse,* which gives biblical and/or kerygmatic *focus* upon the gospel to be read; such "verses" tend to be overlooked or dropped in many non-Roman congregations in favor of a set sentence or verse, that is said or sung between the Second Lesson and the Gospel. Offertory sentences, too, which are also listed in the propers for each Sunday, suffer the same liturgical fate as the verse, but seasonal and Sunday prefaces usually are included in liturgical worship. Homiletically, these are important liturgical elements, which not only work to keep the worship itself unified, but also assist the preacher in working with the preaching text(s) for the day. In general, these parts of the propers are *not* included in the commentary and suggestions for the Sundays.

9. A word about contemporary homiletics.

The pastor, today, must be conversant with the contemporary homiletical discussions that are being carried on among homileticians, theologians, and various preachers, especially in the areas of theology, the content, and the shape of the sermon. Most attention, these days, tends to center on the shape of the sermon with the intention of making preaching more palatable to the people. In the past two decades, homiletics has run the gauntlet of emphasis on liturgical preaching (Reginald Fuller, David Babin, William Skudlarek, and, among others, myself), communication (Reuel Howe, Clyde Reid, and others), experimental preaching (William Thompson, John Killinger, and others), the listeners ("Overhearing the Gospel" — Fred Craddock), oral writing and style (Clyde Fant, Lowell Erdahl, and others), narrative preaching (Fred Buechner, Edmund Steimle et al; Charles Rice was the first among many proponents of story preaching), and, most recently, "homiletical moves" (David Buttrick). This much is manifestly clear: literary style is passe, textual and expository sermons seem to be outmoded, and "nothing of yesterday preaches" (Gerard Sloyan's title for a book of meditations; he is also the author of *Worshipful Preaching).*

It is the conclusion of this writer that preachers need to learn some kind of oral style to assist their delivery of the sermon (see Richard Lischer, *A Theology of Preaching).* Preachers ought to master at least two different types of sermons (Richard Jensen suggests three in *Teaching the Story)* that will function as "meat and potatoes" styles of proclamation (John Killinger, *Homiletics,* and GMB both use this term) for regular preaching. One type of sermon that fits into this category is the *thematic* sermon (Elizabeth Achtemeier calls this the basic type of sermon preached in the "main line" denominations); it is really one kind of modern expository or, even, of a textual, sermon. If the thematic sermon is prepared in an oral style, with "chunks of thought," interesting impact material (graphic illustrations and stories), it can avoid the "dull and deadly" denunciation of expository preaching. It is an invaluable style of preaching for some Gospels, most epistles, and other kinds of texts.

The other type of sermon that is especially useful for regular preaching of the gospels is Edmund Steimle's *Biblical Story Sermon* (Steimle, Neidenthal, and Rice, *Preaching the Story,* among others, GMB, *The Song and the Story).* This, too, is a type of modern expository sermon which is built upon the *plot or story-line* of the text, unlike the thematic sermon that is constructed on the *theme* of the text.

The third type of useful sermon I, with Achtemeier, Jensen, and others, call *experimental.* This may include: dialogue sermons, "pure narratives" and modern parables (Walter Wangerin and others), children's sermons, object lessons, "visually assisted" sermons (the use of TV monitors, video tapes, etc. — Robert Schuller and others), poem sermons, sermons in song, and others. Such sermons are strictly *occasional* types of preaching that offer variety, renewed interest, and imaginative communication of the gospel in the sermonic diet that preachers feed to their people. Most of the sermon suggestions in this volume will fall into the first two categories.

A Preacher's Introduction to the Gospel of St. Matthew

1. The importance of the Gospel of Matthew for preachers and preaching during Year A.

Matthew appears to have written his Gospel, which is, in part, a revision of the Gospel of Mark, to meet the changed needs of a congregation of Jewish Christians living in the environs of Antioch, in Syria. These people were aware of the destruction of the Temple some fifteen to twenty years before this Gospel was written. They knew the story of the death of nearly one thousand Jewish patriots on the low mountain — Massada — overlooking the Dead Sea. They not only were aware of the execution of Paul and Peter and others of the disciples, but they themselves had experienced first-hand the harsh persecution by Gentiles and by Jews as well. There are indications, too, that this was an affluent congregation, assaulted by the temptations of wealth and a certain degree of comfort, if not luxury. No doubt, they did not expect the Lord's promised return to be imminent any longer. It was a congregation of Christians whose faith needed renewed *eschatological direction and expanded ethical dimension*. In many respects, the church for which Matthew wrote his Gospel was not unlike numerous contemporary American congregations; this makes it especially appropriate for contemporary preaching.

Despite the fact that this Gospel was written almost exactly 1900 years ago, it is remarkably contemporaneous in its theological orientation and its comprehensive message. To be sure, the world has changed radically over these nineteen centuries; life will never again be what it was at the close of the first century A.D. Few contemporary Christians will ever experience the kinds of persecution known to the members of the early churches; very few, if any, will know death as the result of their faith that Jesus is Lord. Persecution is more subtle today, consisting of direct and indirect attacks on the spirituality and the values of believers by the media, satire and ridicule, a pervasive secularism, and a high-technology, profit-oriented society that has no deep need of God. Science, technology, and the expansion of the economy seem to be all that most people think they require to live rich lives today.

But the Gospel of Matthew speaks a positive message to twentieth-century Christians. *It tells them that Jesus is Lord — and that he will be with them until the end of the age;* it tells them why this is so. It speaks to their faith, or the lack of it, and does so in the context of the encounter with God that occurs in the birth, life, death, resurrection, and the promised parousia of Jesus Christ.

2. The author and the dating of this Gospel.

There is little likelihood that the author of the Gospel of St. Matthew was actually the disciple of Jesus mentioned in the catalog of the apostles. Over half a century had elapsed by the time ''Matthew'' wrote and published his version of the story of Jesus; he would have been a very old man. Chances are that he had been dead for some years by A.D. 85-90, when St. Matthew was written. The original Matthew might have known some Latin that could have been necessary to his business as a tax collector, but it is highly improbable that he knew enough Greek to compose a Gospel in Greek. This author could have been another man named Matthew, or he might have simply appropriated the name of Matthew to give more credibility to his Gospel.

3. The structure of the Gospel of Matthew.

Matthew, most scholars contend, is divided topically into three main sections: first, Jesus is introduced as the Son of God, the long-promised Messiah who has come at last to usher in the age of salvation (1:1—4:16); second, Matthew tells the story of Jesus' life and ministry, along with the reaction of the religious leaders to his preaching, teaching, and healing

(4:17—16:20); third, he tells the story of Jesus' suffering, death, resurrection, ascension, and his projected return to glory, and judgment to usher in the fullness of the new age (16:21—28:20).

It has been said that Matthew wrote his Gospel so that he could tell the pivotal part of the story in some detail, which is why almost half of the Gospel has to do with the events leading up to, and including, the death and resurrection of Jesus. As is typical of ancient biography, there are many gaps in the story that Matthew spins; most of Jesus' life before he was baptized by John and began his ministry is completely omitted, but the essential ingredients that spell out the nature of the Christian faith are delineated for all time.

The structure of Matthew, despite the lectionary's two-fold system for reading the Gospel (selective reading in the festival cycle, semi-continuous reading in Pentecost), does fit into the rationale of the church year quite well. The important details of the first section of the Gospel (1:1—4:16) are prescribed for the Christmas cycle (selections for two Sundays in Advent, the first Sunday after Christmas, the Epiphany, Epiphany 1 and 3). Jesus' public preaching and teaching (4:17—16:20) are introduced in the middle of Epiphany (Fourth Sunday of Epiphany through Transfiguration) and is continued, after Lent and Easter, in the first half of Pentecost. The last half of Pentecost (16:21—28:20) deals with matters related to the passion, death, and resurrection that are not assigned to Lent or Easter, but are critical to a full comprehension of the story of Jesus.

4. Matthew's theological motifs.

Matthew wrote this Gospel so that people might know that God had entered the world in his Son, Jesus Christ, to accomplish the salvation of his people and, in the risen Lord, to abide with his people to the end of time. He spells out his *christology* by showing how Jesus is the Son of David and, also, the Son of God, the Messiah whom God had promised to Israel. God himself identifies Jesus as his Son at his baptism and his transfiguration, and Jesus accepts this identification in his address to God as "Father." The demons recognize him as the Son of God, and so do the Roman soldiers at his execution. But Satan, the "Evil One," tempts him in the wilderness with "If you are the Son of God . . ." Jesus is to prove it by a miracle. The crowds taunt Jesus to "come down from the cross, if you are the Son of God!" In the face of all of this, Jesus proves himself to be the only-begotten and unique Son of God, because he obeys God perfectly even in the face of death itself, trusting that God will vindicate him by raising him on the third day. This Jesus, therefore, is the One who has saved God's people from their sins and delivered them from death. He is the One they call "Lord." *The focus of the Gospel is, from this perspective, "anastasial;" the resurrection, with the promised presence of the Lord, is the climax of it all.*

The Evangelist also sounds an *eschatological* note that delineates the nature of the Kingdom of God, or the Kingdom of Heaven, as the rule of God over the affairs of humanity. In Jesus, the Kingdom has come to earth, broken into time, and takes dominion over the lives of people in Jesus' death and resurrection. One canticle (LBW) says it this way, "This is the feast of victory for our God. For the Lamb who was slain has begun his reign. Alleluia." He also shows very clearly that the fullness of the Kingdom has yet to come; it is an *eschatological* Kingdom, because it has invaded time in Jesus' life and ministry, but has yet to reach the culmination that God has planned for his people at the end of the age.

Matthew's Gospel incorporates *ecclesiology,* addressing the ethical nature of the lives of people who are subjects in the Kingdom of God, members of the church. In response to God's grace in Jesus Christ, they are called to repentance and the new life in Christ, and are expected to live out the gospel in deeds of love, mercy, and kindness. Those who believe and confess that Jesus is Lord become, through baptism, his disciples — servants, as their Lord demonstrated himself to be — and are expected to proclaim the gospel by their manner of life, as well as by their words. Jesus, he makes it clear, has fulfilled the Law for them, but calls upon them, at the same time, "Be perfect, therefore, as your heavenly Father is perfect.'' (5:48 NIV) As disciples of Jesus, they are not free to live any way that they please; Matthew has no place for antinomianism in his theology of the Christian life, summing up all of "the law and the prophets" in two commands that reflect the nature of the new life in Christ — love — that should be peculiar to Christians. He makes it perfectly transparent that what Jesus has to say about life in the Kingdom of God is valid for all people, for all time. The community of believers, the church, conscious of the presence of the Lord, is called upon to be faithful to the Lord and God "until he comes again" at God's appointed time.

The heart of Matthew's theology is that God has come to his people in Jesus, his Son, and will empower his disciples, the church, to do his will until the end-time. Through Jesus, he has instituted the Kingdom — his rule or reign — over the earth, and he has promised that his kingdom will fully come "at last."

5. *Preaching Themes in the Gospel of St. Matthew.*

a. The Gospel of St. Matthew elucidates and expands the several themes of the Christian year. Matthew identifies Jesus as the "Coming One," the Christ of Advent, Christmas, and Epiphany, God's *Messiah* and the *Savior* of the world. He is to be proclaimed as *Lord and Savior of all.*

b. Matthew also depicts Jesus as *Redeemer* in his suffering and death, the One whose last journey to Jerusalem was undertaken with full knowledge that his fate had been sealed by the repudiation of him by the "Jews." He is to be preached as the Christ of Lent and of Easter, the Day of Resurrection.

c. Jesus, according to Matthew, is the *ascended and reigning Lord,* who is to be proclaimed as *Christ the King,* the One who will return at God's appointed time to judge the world and usher in *the fullness of God's Kingdom.* The second coming, the *parousia,* of Christ must still be announced to the world as the culminating event of the Gospel. In the meantime, this theme, when articulated in church year preaching, creates an "Advent Church," a church that continues to expect Christ's return and, in the interim, seeks to demonstrate that it is "of God" as it reflects the "servant-form" of discipleship.

d. Matthew depicts Jesus as the *teacher* of the church, who informs his disciples about life in the Kingdom of God through his sayings, parables, and merciful and self-sacrificial deeds. Preaching from this *ethical* perspective in pentecost shapes and reshapes the church, the disciples, into a *community* that is profitable to the Lord and God's Kingdom.

e. The concluding note of the Gospel determines the *evangelistic and missionary* nature of *discipleship* for all believers, and until the end of this age. The ever-living Lord will be present with his people as they live as his disciples and do his work in the world. To be true to the Gospel of St. Matthew, preaching must always *proclaim the Good News* to all people.

The Church Year Calendar

The Christmas Cycle

Advent
First Sunday in Advent — blue or purple
Second Sunday in Advent — blue or purple
Third Sunday in Advent — blue or purple
Fourth Sunday in Advent — blue or purple

Christmas
Christmas Eve — white
The Nativity of Our Lord — white
First Sunday after Christmas — white

Epiphany
The Epiphany of Our Lord — white
The Baptism of Our Lord (First Sunday after the Epiphany) — white
Second Sunday after the Epiphany — green
Third Sunday after the Epiphany — green
Fourth Sunday after the Epiphany — green
Fifth Sunday after the Epiphany — green
Sixth Sunday after the Epiphany — green
Seventh Sunday after the Epiphany — green
The Transfiguration of Our Lord (The Last Sunday of Epiphany)— white

The Easter Cycle

Lent
Ash Wednesday — black or purple
First Sunday in Lent — purple
Second Sunday in Lent — purple
Third Sunday in Lent — purple
Fourth Sunday in Lent (The Annunciation of Our Lord) — purple
Fifth Sunday in Lent — purple
Sunday of the Passion (Palm Sunday) — scarlet or purple
Holy Thursday — scarlet or white
Good Friday — black or no paraments
Holy Saturday — white

Easter
The Vigil of Easter — white or gold
The Resurrection of Our Lord (Easter) — white or gold
Second Sunday of Easter — white
Third Sunday of Easter — white
Fourth Sunday of Easter — white
Fifth Sunday of Easter — white
Sixth Sunday of Easter — white
The Ascension of Our Lord — white
Seventh Sunday of Easter — white
The Day of Pentecost — red

18

The Pentecost Cycle (The Time of the Church)

The Season After Pentecost
The Holy Trinity (First Sunday after Pentecost) — white
Second Sunday after Pentecost — green
Third Sunday after Pentecost (The Nativity of St. John the Baptizer — white) — green
Fourth Sunday after Pentecost — green
Fifth Sunday after Pentecost — green
Sixth Sunday after Pentecost — green
Seventh Sunday after Pentecost — green
Eighth Sunday after Pentecost — green
Ninth Sunday after Pentecost — green
Tenth Sunday after Pentecost — green
Eleventh Sunday after Pentecost — green
Twelfth Sunday after Pentecost — green
Thirteenth Sunday after Pentecost — green
Fourteenth Sunday after Pentecost — green
Fifteenth Sunday after Pentecost — green
Sixteenth Sunday after Pentecost — green
Seventeenth Sunday after Pentecost — green
Eighteenth Sunday after Pentecost — green
Thanksgiving Day, Canada — white
Nineteenth Sunday after Pentecost — green
Twentieth Sunday after Pentecost — green
Twenty-first Sunday after Pentecost (Reformation Sunday — red) — green
All Saints Sunday (Twenty-second Sunday after Pentecost — green) — white
Twenty-third Sunday after Pentecost — green
Twenty-fourth Sunday after Pentecost — green
Thanksgiving Day, USA — white
Christ the King (Last Sunday after Pentecost) — white

Preaching Resources for Series A

Commentaries on the Gospel of Matthew
Edwards, Richard A., *Matthew's Story of Jesus,* Fortress, 1985.
Kingsbury, Jack Dean, *Matthew,* Fortress, 1986.
Kingsbury, Jack Dean, *Matthew as Story,* Fortress, 1986.
Patte, Daniel, *The Gospel According to Matthew,* Fortress, 1987.
Schweizer, Edward, *The Good News According to Matthew,* John Knox, 1975.

Other Commentaries
Achtemeier, Elizabeth, *Proclamation 3,* Fortress, 1984.
Achtemeier, Elizabeth, *The Old Testament and the Proclamation of the Gospel,* Westminster, 1982.
Craddock, Hayes, and Holloday, *Preaching the New Common Lectionary,* Abingdon, 1984
Reginald Fuller, *Preaching the New Lectionary,* The Liturgical Press, 1974.
McCurley, Foster, *Proclaiming the Promise,* Fortress, 1975.
Proclamation (various volumes), Fortress.
Sloyan, Gerard, *A Commentary on the New Lectionary,* Paulist Press, 1975.

Church Year
Board of Discipleship, United Methodist Church, *Seasons of the Gospel,* Abingdon.
Gibson, George A., *The Story of the Church Year.*
Nocent, Adrian, *The Liturgical Year* (Four volumes), The Liturgical Press, 1977.
Rochelle, Jay, *The Revolutionary Year,* Fortress, 1971.

Other Church Year Preaching Aids
Augsburg Sermons (annual)
Concordia Pulpit (annual)
C.S.S. (Lectionary sermon sets)
Emphasis, C.S.S.
Homily Service, Liturgical Conference, Washington, D.C.
Preaching Helps (published formerly by Seminex)

Liturgical Preaching
Babin, David, *Week in — Week out,* Seabury, 1976.
Bass, George M., *The Renewal of Liturgical Preaching,* Augsburg, 1967.
Bosch, Paul, *The Sermon as Part of the Liturgy,* Concordia, 1977.
Fuller, Reginald, *What is Liturgical Preaching?,* SCM Press, 1957.
Lischer, Richard, *A Theology of Preaching,* Abingdon, 1971.
Skudlarek, William, *The Word in Worship: Preaching in a Liturgical Context,* Abingdon, 1981.
Willimon, William H., *Preaching and Worship,* Westminster, 1984.

Contemporary Homiletics
Achtemeier, Elizabeth, *Creative Preaching: Finding the Words,* Abingdon, 1980.
Achtemeier, Elizabeth, *Preaching as Theology and Art,* Abingdon, 1984.
Bass, George M., *The Song and the Story,* C.S.S., 1984.
Buechner, Frederick, *Telling the Truth: The Gospel as Tragedy, Comedy and Fairy Tale,* Harper and Row, 1977.
Burghardt, Walter, *Preaching: The Art and Craft,* Paulist Press, 1987.
Buttrick, David, *Homiletic: Moves and Structures,* Fortress, 1987.
Carl, William J., *Preaching Christian Doctrine,* Fortress, 1984.
Cox, James W., ed., *Biblical Preaching: An Expositor's Treasury,* Westminster, 1983.
Craddock, Fred B., *Preaching,* Abingdon, 1985.
Craddock, Fred B., *As One Without Authority,* Abingdon, 1979.
Craddock, Fred B., *Overhearing the Gospel,* Abingdon, 1978.
Crum, Milton, *Manual on Preaching,* Judson, 1977.

Ellingsen, Mark C., *Doctrine and Word,* Westminster, 1983.

Erdahl, Lowell, *Preaching for the People,* Harper and Row, 1978.

Fant, Clyde E., *Preaching for Today,* Harper and Row, 1987 (revised).

Fuller, Reginald, *The Use of the Brain in Preaching,* Fortress, 1981.

Halvorson, Arndt, *Authentic Preaching,* Augsburg, 1982.

Jensen, Richard, *Telling the Story,* Augsburg, 1980.

Keck, Leander E., *The Bible in the Pulpit,* Abingdon, 1978.

Killinger, John, *Fundamentals of Preaching,* Fortress, 1986.

Lowry, Eugene, *Doing Time in the Pulpit*, Abingdon, 1985.

Lowry, Eugene, *The Homiletic Plot,* John Knox, 1983.

Marquart, Edward F., *Quest for Better Preaching,* Augsburg, 1985.

Mitchell, Henry M., *The Recovery of Preaching,* Harper and Row, 1977.

Nichols, J. Randall, *Building the Word: The Dynamics of Communication and Preaching,* Harper and Row, 1981.

O'Day, Gail R., *The Word Disclosed: John's Story and Narrative Preaching,* CBP Press, 1987.

Patte, Daniel, *Preaching Paul,* Fortress, 1984.

Rice, Charles A., *Interpretation and Imagination,* Fortress, 1970 (reprinted, 1987).

Salmon, Bruce C., *Storytelling in Preaching,* Broadman Press, 1988.

Sanders, James A., *God Has a Story Too: Biblical Sermons in Context,* Fortress, 1979.

Sleeth, Ronald E., *God's Words and our Words,* John Knox, 1986.

Steimle, E. A., Neidenthal, M., and Rice, C., *Preaching the Story,* Fortress, 1980.

John R. Stott, *Between Two Worlds: The Art of Preaching in the Twentieth Century,* Eerdmann's, 1982.

Thompson, William, *Preaching Biblically: Exegesis and Interpretation,* Abingdon, 1981.

Tribble, Phyllis, *God and the Rhetoric of Sexuality,* Fortress, 1978.

Wardlaw, Don E., *Preaching Biblically: Creating Sermons in the Shape of Scripture,* Westminster, 1983.

Williams, Michael E., *Preaching Peers,* Discipleship Resources, 1987.

Williams, Michael E., *Preaching Pilgrims,* Discipleship Resources, 1988.

The Christmas Cycle

The Christmas Cycle is composed of three integrated seasons: Advent, Christmas, and Epiphany. It might better be called the Advent, or the Parousia, Cycle, because it centers on the return, the Second Coming, of Christ in judgment rather than, as popularly believed — and even suggested by the title of the cycle — on the birth of Jesus as the First Coming of our Lord. It establishes an *eschatological* perspective for the entire Christian year, not only in the season of Advent, but in Christmas and Epiphany, as well, reminding the faithful that the full plan of God's redemption of the world will not be initiated until the time comes that God has determined for Jesus' return in glory. The cycle varies, in most years, from twelve to fourteen weeks in length, so that it is approximately one quarter of the calendar. This is important for planning one's preaching ministry; the very nature of the season seems to suggest that coherence and unity in the reading of the Gospel (and supporting lessons) might best be achieved if "inclusive planning" — for all three of the seasons — is done before one begins to preach on any of the Sundays of Advent.

Advent, consisting of the four Sundays immediately preceding Christmas, emphasizes the presence of the Lord in the proclamation of the Word and, especially, in the celebration of the Eucharist. The Sundays have the same basic content in all three series of Gospels, Matthew (A), Mark (B), and Luke (C):

1st Sunday in Advent — "A time of expectation and prayer for the Parousia;"

2nd Sunday in Advent — "A time of preparation for the Second Coming, as well as for Christmas;"

3rd Sunday in Advent — "A time to rejoice in the presence of the Lord;"

4th Sunday in Advent — "A time to announce Messiah's birth *in proper perspective ("He will come again, as he said.")."*

Advent, therefore, is oriented, as these themes recur and are expanded in the Gospels and the other lessons assigned annually to the Sundays of Advent, to the three "comings" of Christ. *Advent does not exist primarily to prepare the church for the celebration of Christmas; it has an ultimate purpose — to prepare the people of God for the Parousia.* Advent was probably a kind of "winter Lent" that was connected to Epiphany, a baptismal festival in the early Church (see my book *The Renewal of Liturgical Preaching* for additional information about the relationship of Advent to Epiphany. Adrian Nocent, in *The Liturgical Year,* treats Advent in significant detail.) Compared to Advent, in this respect, Christmas was a "liturgical latecomer."

Liturgical colors for Advent: blue or violet.

Christmas, despite the fact that it is popularly observed as a one-day festival, is a twelve-day season that finds popular — and almost singular — expression in the familiar carol, "The Twelve Days of Christmas." It is quite probable that that one day festival will be shifted to December 24th in 1989, inasmuch as Christmas Day falls on a Monday this year. Twelfth Night, the eve of Epiphany, which really concludes the Christmas season, is given some expression in the controlled burning of Christmas trees and, rather rarely of late, in the worship plans and patterns of various congregations. (Epiphany, unless it occurs on a Sunday, tends to be omitted from worship plans and sacramental practices, as well as popular piety. The Church has nearly forgotten that Epiphany was a reserve day for baptisms in the earlier history of the Church.) The other problem, which is equally serious for the worship life and spiritual growth of the faithful, is the reality that *Christmas is really celebrated popularly during Advent; the festival is — popularly — the end of the Advent season rather than the beginning of a twelve-day celebration* of the birth of Jesus that finds ultimate expression in his death and resurrection and the promise of his coming to the world a second time. *Christmas — in the Christ Mass — finds eschatological orientation* in the Holy Communion, which always is a celebration of the Parousia: "as often as you eat this bread and drink the cup, you proclaim the Lord's death until he comes (again)" (1 Corinthians 11:26); and his *redemptive presence,* too. Thematically, the proclamation of the Gospel needs the twelve-day Christmas season to reestablish annually the full meaning of Christmas in the life of the Church.

Liturgical colors for Christmas: white or gold.

Epiphany is, in many respects, a season that is "up for grabs." While the churches agree on how the Gospel should be read in all three years — semi-continuously, beginning with the Epiphany account of Jesus' birth (Matthew 2:1-13) — they don't agree on the naming of the Sundays after Epiphany. The Roman *Ordo* of the post-Vatican II liturgical reforms names the Sundays after Epiphany as Sundays "in Ordinary Time;" the Sundays after Pentecost were given the same "Ordinary Time" designation. Episcopalians, Lutherans, and others decided to call the same Sundays "after Epiphany" (the First Sunday after the Epiphany is celebrated as the Baptism of Our Lord") and "after Pentecost." When seen the latter way, and despite the fact that the same Gospels and most of the other lessons are assigned to these Sundays by Roman Catholics and non-Romans, the Lutheran arrangement has more eschatological content — *realized eschatology* — stressing Jesus' manifestation to the world at his birth, his Baptism, ministry, and at his Transfiguration. Lutherans in the United States have celebrated the Transfiguration on the last Sunday after the Epiphany, partly as an echo of God's announcement at Jesus' Baptism ("you are my Son"), and also to serve as a climax to the Epiphany season and a bridge into the Easter Cycle (Lent and Easter seasons). The Gospels of Epiphany amplify the announcement of the Coming of the Christ to the world that was made at Jesus' birth. This remains the *manifestation* of the Messiah to Israel and, then, to the Gentile world, as well, and it completes the Christmas Cycle.

Liturgical colors for Epiphany: white (Epiphany, The Baptism of our Lord, and the Transfiguration) and green for the other Sundays.

Preaching in the Advent Season

Preaching the Advent themes is not easy, simply because it is eschatological preaching and such preaching is always difficult. Some preachers dodge the eschatological note on the First Sunday in Advent, the Second Coming of the Christ, by preaching on the "new church year." A quasi-liturgical "new year's sermon," which has no foundation in the lections for the day and is, therefore, topical, is the result. The context for preaching the Parousia during Advent is always *eschatological* — the birth, life, ministry, death, resurrection, and ascension of the Lord. When one's Advent sermons are oriented primarily toward the historical birth of Christ, rather than the fuller theological meaning of the *incarnation*, the theological orientation of the entire church year is in jeopardy. *Christ doesn't come at Christmas any differently than he comes to us at any other time of the year; he comes in the word and the sacraments of Baptism and the Eucharist. Every eucharistic celebration has the quality of future eschatology, because Christ is not only present in the meal through the Holy Spirit, but God's promise is proclaimed and renewed that the risen, ascended Lord will come again.*

Advent establishes the kerygmatic perspective for Christian preaching for the entire year by sounding the note of future eschatology — Christ will come again! This, of course, complicates the preaching task of the pastor, demanding that pastoral preaching and teaching be done within this theological agenda. Christians are in the same predicament that Israel was in as they awaited the coming of the Messiah; nearly two thousand years have passed and he has not returned as he said he would. Will he come again? Can he keep his promise to the church? Is it possible for the Lord to return in glory to judge the world at the end of the age? Those are more likely to be the questions asked by contemporary Christians rather than *"when* will he return to the earth?" Too much time has elapsed since the Lord ascended to heaven; Christmas, as the loveliest and most hopeful time of the year, is more likely to be the main item of theological concern during Advent. People are more apt to listen to sermons on "preparing for Jesus' birth at Christmas" than they are to sermons that declare "prepare for the Day of the Lord."

Sermons during Advent should:

1. *Proclaim* the expected return of the Lord at some time in the future that is only known by God; *he is with them while they wait* (Matthew);

1. *Call* upon people to prepare as though the Lord were to return today or tomorrow; he will come at God's appointed time — unexpectedly;

3. *Tell* Christians to prepare through repentance and prayer, by dying and rising — as renewal of their baptism covenant — and living the new life in Christ;

4. *Assure* Christians that they have nothing to fear in the judgment of the Second Coming; they can look forward to Christ's return with confidence and, in the meantime, serve him with joy;

5. *Announce* that the Christ who was born as a real child at Christmas is actually present as his birth is remembered and celebrated throughout the Christmas season.

Advent establishes and programs the preaching agenda for the entire church year when it is properly understood and allowed to influence and determine the theological mind-set of the preacher. Preaching during Advent is a complicated business, at best, but it is of critical importance to the person attempting to "preach through the church year" *to discern the eschatological themes of Advent and to proclaim the fullness of the gospel* to the faithful people of God.

First Sunday of Advent

Roman Catholic	Isaiah 2:1-5	Romans 13:11-14	Matthew 24:37-44
Episcopal	Isaiah 2:1-5	Romans 13:8-14	Matthew 24:37-44
Lutheran	Isaiah 2:1-5	Romans 13:11-14	Matthew 24:37-44
			or Matthew 21:1-11
Common	Isaiah 2:1-5	Romans 13:11-14	Matthew 24:36-44

The church year theological clue

The risen, ascended Lord, Jesus Christ, whose reign has begun, will return at the end of this age, to bring in the fullness of God's Kingdom and reign over all of the affairs of the earth. Be prepared! Wait! Watch! Wonder! Work! Walk!

The First Sunday in Advent is the theological/thematic key to the entire year's preaching from the lectionary; it sets the stage, as it were, by directing the attention of preacher and people upon the completion of God's business with the world in Jesus Christ, the Parousia. By announcing that Christ will come again in glory and judgment, the church year and the liturgy/lectionary remind people that the church is to live as if the Lord were to return to-day; Christians, who are nourished by the Word as they wonder about the Second Coming of Christ, will develop *"The spirit of waiting."* (Adrian Nocent, O.S.B., in *The Liturgical Year,* volume one) as they respond to the Good News by living out their covenant, their baptism, in Jesus Christ, in expectation and repentance. Therefore, while the lessons all point to the future, they make it clear that the Christ, who was born in Bethlehem long ago, is the *Lord God Incarnate* in his only Son, the ever-living, ever-present, and ever-available Savior of the world. *Because believers live in the hope that the Lord lives and reigns and will come again, and because they know that they can do nothing but wait for the appointed time of the Christ's return, they are able to wait hopefully and, thus, are fully prepared for the Parousia.*

The Prayer of the Day is one of the so-called "stir up" prayers of Advent, as they were known in the Anglican tradition:

> *Stir up your power, O Lord, and come. Protect us by your strength and save us from the threatening dangers of our sins, for you live and reign with the Father and the Holy Spirit, one God, now and forever.*

The Psalm of the Day (LBW) is Psalm 122 — This is one of the psalms sung by pilgrims as they "went up to Jerusalem" for the Passover celebration. By striking the notes of expectation, as they go up, and excitement, as they enter the city, the psalm serves admirably as a response to the First Lesson and a bridge to the Second Lesson and the Gospel. The church, ever since it began building shelters for the believers to worship in, has seen itself as pilgrim people who, like the Israelites, were on their way to the Holy City — not just Jerusalem, but heaven itself. Thus, with the risen, ascended Lord seated on a throne and waiting for the signal from God to return, the believers gathered around his feet *to give thanks to God for their Lord while they, too, waited for the time of the Lord's return*. The promise of the Parousia was precious to them, and they tenaciously held on to it, even in the face of suffering and death. Christ was all that they had, their only hope in a hostile world. As time runs out for us, it becomes clear that he is our only hope, too, and knowing that, we can wait in hope and with thanksgiving.

The Psalm Prayer (LBW)

> *Lord Jesus, give us the peace of the new Jerusalem. Bring all nations into your kingdom to share your gifts, that they may render thanks to you without end and may come to your eternal city, where you live and reign with the Father and the Holy Spirit, now and forever.*

The readings:

Isaiah 2:1-5

Isaiah's vision is of a future time that will see all the nations of the earth "flowing" toward the "mountain of the house of the Lord" to learn the ways of God and to begin living by "the word of the Lord." This is an *eschatological vision* that looks, as do the Second Lesson and the Gospel, to the end of the age, of history. At that time, God will judge the nations and all people, ushering in an era of peace when instruments of war will be converted into tools for the blessing of humanity. Only then will war finally be exterminated and, in the new age, will people live together in peace. The last verse establishes a theme for Advent which puts Christmas in proper perspective — "O house of Jacob, come, let us walk in the light of the Lord."

Isaiah's theology is truly *eschatological,* not simply pointing to the future but delineating a new age only God can — *and will* — inaugurate beyond human history. It is only by this action that the terrible scourge of war can be eliminated and a genuine era of everlasting peace begin. That will be the day of God's summit meeting, the great day of judgment and grace, when his plan *for a new act of creation* will be put in place and made operative for all nations. *Then, and only then, will people fully "walk in the light of the Lord."*

Romans 13:11-14

This lesson speaks of the expectation held by the Church of Rome that the Lord would soon return to the world as he said he would; the Second Coming, Paul believed, was imminent. Believers *know* the time — "the night is far gone" and "the day is at hand" when this will occur, thus they are to turn their backs on darkness and live in ("put on") the "armor of light;" it is their business to live responsibly as Christians should by "putting on the Lord Jesus Christ" — in other words, living out their baptismal promises and covenant with God in dedication and singular devotion and fidelity to the Lord rather than living licentiously, as though God did not even exist. One difficulty the preacher faces in this text is that Paul's sense of timing was wrong. How, then, does one proclaim this message to people today?

Paul's eschatological theology reflects that of Isaiah and, certainly, that of Jesus Christ, but the timing of his prediction of a proximate Parousia was also wrong; Christ didn't return in the first century A.D. But Paul was correct when he said that his coming is always near, "at hand." He knew that the Lord is present, through his Word and the Holy Spirit, when the church gathers, when the Word is proclaimed, and when the sacraments are celebrated. Paul was fully convinced that the risen Christ would finally return and bring in the full and complete reign of God's kingdom. Although the timing of his expectation was incorrect, he was absolutely right in his insistence on an *eschatological faith* as the heart of the Gospel.

Matthew 24:37-44

The context for this pericope is Jesus' discourse on the Second Coming. He teaches that the Parousia will come suddenly, unexpectedly, totally without warning. People will be "taken" at their daily tasks, but he does not indicate on what basis they will be selected. His admonition is to "Watch therefore, for you do not know on what day your Lord is coming," emphasizing the urgency to watch with his parabolic saying about the householder and the thief. Again at the end of the lection, he warns them, "Therefore, you also must be ready; for the Son of man is coming at an hour you do not expect."

The Second Coming — "Christ will come again" — is articulated in many contemporary eucharistic prayers; people voice that response, but one question the preacher must answer before a sermon can be composed on this text, even for this Sunday, is whether or not anyone actually expects Jesus to return today. Has the church waited too long for the Second Coming of the Lord and become spiritually and mentally exhausted by the delay? And if people continue to believe that Christ will come again, why has God delayed so long in allowing it to happen? What people do believe in is that, for all practical purposes, the world might very well end quickly through nuclear accident or nuclear war. Could this kind of an end fit into the plan of God for bringing this age to a close? If so, what would remain for Christ to judge and reign over? How is the preacher to make theological sense out of all of this? Is there any hope for humanity and the world?

Matthew's *eschatological theology* of the age of salvation, when viewed from the perspective of his entire Gospel, provides a fitting conclusion to his version of the Good News and positively shapes the liturgical season of Advent that begins the church year. What he writes in chapters 24 and 25 about the end of the world and the Second Coming of Jesus Christ is an integral part of the gospel story; the Kingdom had only been inaugurated in Christ's death and resurrection, and Jesus promised to return, as Matthew recounts in his story, to complete the work on behalf of God. *That Christ,* whose birth is recorded in the Gospels for all time, *will also be with his church in the meantime, and until he comes again.* This must be told to all of the world as the climax of the Gospel story.

A sermon suggested by the Gospel (Matthew 24:37-44)

The preacher's task is to "make sense" of the gospel (Clement Welsh, *Preaching in a New Key)* for contemporary — and secularly oriented — Christians living in a scientific and pragmatic age that faces the possibility of an "end-time" through self-destruction. The headlines, as I write this, announced, "Train blast stirred fears of nuclear war, Pravda says." On June 4, 1988, three cars loaded with industrial explosives blew up in Arzamas, 240 miles east of Moscow, killing at least 73 people, wounding an unknown number, destroying 150 homes, leaving 250 families homeless, and severely damaging 250 buildings. One witness, who saw the explosion and the mushroom cloud, said, "The first thing that came to my mind was, 'Has it started?' " — a reference to a nuclear attack.

That reaction might have occurred under similar circumstances, almost anywhere in the northern hemisphere. Some Christians believe that one final war will bring judgment and total destruction upon the entire human race; there is no hope. God has a different plan in mind, and it needs to be spoken to the people in a sermon, or sermons, on the business of waiting for the Lord's return in genuine Christian hope.

A sermon plan: "Christ Will Come Again — Believe it or Not!"

1. The long *wait* of the people of God for a better day (Advent is a time of waiting for the "Day of the Lord," and we acknowledge that it has been an interminably long wait, but Christ will return, as he said, when God gives the signal) is a *hopeful wait,* because *all fear will be banished on that day.*

2. Faithful believers *watch* — always — as if the Lord were to return today. Advent is the season when people are called upon to prepare for the end of the age and the Parousia. Confident *prayer*, coupled with daily repentance and renewal, is one way to watch, living out our baptismal faith and the resurrection hope of the Gospel in daily life.

3. Christians, who perceive the grace of God at work for the benefit of the world, *wonder* at the patience, love, and goodness of God. God has his own good reasons for the long wait. He does indeed have a plan to save us from ourselves and to deliver us from destruction and despair, as well as the domain of the devil, in the Second Coming of our Lord. He alone knows the timetable for activating the last act of his drama of salvation. No one on earth can predict when Christ will come again, and nothing on earth can deter that return when God sets the plan into action.

4. In the meantime, true believers will do the daily *work* that the Lord has called them to do, trusting that the Lord is as good as his word. The work of the Kingdom is serving God and people, preaching the good news to all the world, and witnessing in deeds as well as words to the Lordship of Jesus Christ.

5. For now, "come, let us *walk* in the light of the Lord," with confidence in his word, giving thanks to God for the presence of the risen Christ, who "walks" with us until his return at the appointed time to judge the world and bring in a "new heaven and a new earth" on God's great day.

An Old Testament Advent sermon series

1st Sunday in Advent: Isaiah 2:1-5 — "God's Summit Meeting."
2nd Sunday in Advent: Isaiah 11:1-10 — "God's Spirit-annointed Savior."
3rd Sunday in Advent: Isaiah 35:1-10 — "God's Day for Rejoicing."
4th Sunday in Advent: Isaiah 7:10-14 (15-17) — "God's Promise to become Immanuel."

A Sermon on the First Lesson, Isaiah 2:1-5 — "God's Summit Meeting."

1. God has revealed the final stage of his plan for the earth centuries before Christ was born; God plans a *summit meeting.*

2. At the end of the age, God will gather all people at his "mountain" — his *summit meeting* — to teach them his ways and enable them to "walk in his paths." *God will dictate the terms of the summit.*

3. Humanity, instructed by the law of God and brought under his judgment, *will witness the end of war and the beginning of everlasting peace in a new age,* beyond recorded history.

4. Those who live in this hope are able to "walk in the light of the Lord" right now, even when they are surrounded by seemingly total darkness. *The future summit meeting gives them that hope.*

A Sermon on the Second Lesson, Romans 13:11-14 — "Living an 'Advent' Life."

Two of my good friends understand what Paul was talking about when he said, "You know what hour it is, how it is full time now for you to wake from sleep." Both friends have had heart attacks and live with potential "time-bombs" in their chests. One believes that he has less than ten years to live; the other, not yet forty years of age, hopes to live long enough to see an infant child grow up. Both know that death could come at any time; they *know the time and are making the most of it.* Actually, all of us are in the same predicament; time is running out on the human race, and the end-time is nearer than we may know, or as Paul says, "nearer than when we first believed." This is a time to be wide-awake, alert to the message of the gospel and its meaning for us right now.

1. Time is running out on the human race. With each passing day, the **time** for Christ's return draws nearer. He will come again to usher in a new era, *the day of salvation,* in God's good time; the gospel tells us about that.

28

2. That's why we, like the people Paul addressed, need to be **awake**, anticipating the return of the Lord, and *living in the light of the new day, rejecting all of the works of darkness.*

3. This is the time of **living out our baptismal relationship** with the Lord by dying daily to sin and rising to live the new life in Christ.

4. The new life of Christ enables us to pray, "Come, Lord Jesus! Come quickly!"

Other preaching suggestions

1. Develop a three-text sermon — "God's Great Day:"
   a. God has planned a *great day* for all people. (Isaiah)
   b. The *great day* will come suddenly and unexpectedly. (Matthew)
   c. Christians respond to God's *wake up call* in the gospel and *watch* for the *great day*. (Romans)
   d. Meanwhile, as we look and as we listen, "Let us walk in the light of the Lord."

(Note: Should the preacher develop each of these excerpts from the lessons very much, it is obvious that an extremely long sermon would result; this is one of the problems with multi-text sermons. Therefore, exposition and explanation must be limited and the most important portion of each text should be highlighted through imagery and illustration. David Buttrick's homiletical rule of only one illustration for each "move" or main idea in the sermon is helpful here; only the key thought or concept in each section should receive a major illustration. This not only controls the length of the sermon, but it also adds narrative quality to the proclamation of the gospel, allowing the people to use their imaginations to isolate the good news as they listen to the Word.)

2. A "variant" sermon on the first lesson, Isaiah 2:1-5 — "A vision of a New World."
   a. An ancient vision with contemporary significance.
   b. A vision of a day when war will be abolished and permanent peace established.
   c. Through deeds of love and mercy, our business is to proclaim Good News of this New World to all people.
   d. Jesus will come again as Lord and rule as the Prince of Peace forever.

3. A "variant" sermon on the second lesson, Romans 13:11-14 — "God's Wake-Up Call."
   a. Christ's "wake-up call" is an announcement that his return in imminent.
   a. By renouncing darkness and turning to the light, his followers respond to the "wake-up call."
   c. They wear the uniform of the day — their baptismal garb, "the armor of light," and live the life of God's faithful people.
   d. So they — we — are ready for anything this world may hold for us, even for the Second Coming of Christ.

4. A suggestion for an Advent series on the Psalms:
   a. First Sunday in Advent (LBW) — Psalm 122 — "Pilgrim People."
   b. Second Sunday in Advent (LBW) — Psalm 72:1-14 — "Long Live the King's Son."
   c. Third Sunday in Advent (LBW) — Psalm 146 — "A God Who Can Be Trusted."
   d. Fourth Sunday in Advent (LBW) — Psalm 24 — "A Welcome for the King of Glory."

A "sermon-starter" for preaching on Psalm 122 — "Pilgrim People."

This Psalm, in context of Advent and the Gospel, makes *pilgrim people* of all who believe and confess that Jesus is the coming Lord. Christians are continually "on the move" toward that "mountain" where they will be met by God on the last day. Theirs is a joyful journey, because they know that God has already revealed himself to the world in Jesus Christ and has taken extreme measures — in the death and resurrection of Jesus Christ — to reconcile the world to himself; they know they have nothing to fear as they go, for Jesus travels with them and will support them to the end of the age.

Pilgrim people are:

1. Expectant people
2. Hopeful people
3. Prayerful people
4. Prepared people

These ideas illustrate a few of the possibilities in the pericopes of any single Sunday of the church year in the hope that pastors will use their intellect and imaginations to discover the wide variety of sermons that might be preached on any given Sunday. Time and space do not allow the homiletical possibilities to be exhausted for any given Sunday.

Second Sunday of Advent

Roman Catholic	Isaiah 11:1-10	Romans 15:4-9	Matthew 3:1-12
Episcopal	Isaiah 11:1-10	Romans 15:4-13	Matthew 3:1-12
Lutheran	Isaiah 11:1-10	Romans 15:4-13	Matthew 3:1-12
Common	Isaiah 11:1-10	Romans 15:4-13	Matthew 3:1-12

The church year theological clue

The Second Sunday in Advent is clearly oriented toward *preparation for the coming of the Lord.* This preparation has two dimensions: to prepare "our hearts" — which God is constantly attempting to do through his Word and Spirit — for the Second Coming of the Lord; and, to "prepare our hearts" for his *incarnation,* as he comes to us through Word and Spirit at Christmas and every day of our lives. This much ought to be evident to us; that if our hearts are prepared for his *eschatological coming,* they will certainly be perfectly attuned to his *incarnational advent* right now. The expectation of the eschaton is, from one perspective, *realized eschatology;* from a second point of view it is *future eschatology,* while from a third position it is an exercise in what might be called *immediate eschatology;* he is constantly coming to us in Word and sacrament.

All elements of the liturgy for the Second Sunday in Advent make it announce or support the theme for this Sunday's worship as *preparation for the coming of the Lord.* The clue is both eschatological and incarnational. It emerges as eschatological in Isaiah 5: the reading from Isaiah anticipates the future advent of the Messiah and describes his attributes; the psalm acts as a kind of antiphon to Isaiah's description, detailing the nature of his reign and the benefits that will be bestowed upon the earth. The excerpt from Paul's letter to the Roman Church is incarnational, as well as eschatological; it urges the people to read the Old Testament as "Advent preparation," especially those parts — the context implies — that anticipate the coming of Christ as the "root of Jesse" and glorify the crucified and risen Lord who will come again. The Gospel — for the other two years of the lectionary cycle, as well as Year A — brings all of this into sharp focus through John's announcement and exhortation, "Prepare the way of the Lord, make his paths straight." Matthew 3 articulates the message in this total context. The bottom line, for the faithful, is one of expectation and hope.

The Prayer of the Day — Another of the Advent "stir up" prayers related to the Lord's advent and, this time, asking God to prepare our hearts to receive him:

> *Stir up our hearts, O Lord, to prepare the way for your only Son. By his coming give us strength in our conflicts and shed light on our path through the darkness of this world; through your Son, Jesus Christ our Lord, who lives and reigns with you and the Holy Spirit, one God, now and forever.*

The petition of the original collect points more to God's purpose for our lives, that is, to love and serve him as long as we live: ". . . so that by his coming we may be enabled to serve thee with pure minds . . . ." The intent of both prayers is initially the same, asking God to do for us what we cannot do for ourselves — "to stir up our hearts . . . to prepare (make ready) the way for your only begotten son."

The Psalm of the Day (LBW) — Psalm 72:1-14(15-17) — This psalm enunciates and echoes the themes that emerge from the pericopes appointed for the Second Sunday in Advent, because it is a prayer for a king who will be instructed in the duties of his office by God himself. Scholars contend that it is a prayer for the rulers of the house of David, and also a prayer for the messianic king who is yet to come. That the church sees this as a messianic psalm is rather evident by its selection for this Sunday. As a response to the First Lesson, it is most appropriate, and functions almost as the ancient graduals did in the movement from one lesson to another. The Psalm Prayer ties it into the gospel of the Lord, as well as the Gospel for the Day.

The Psalm Prayer (LBW)

Almighty God, you gave the kingdom of justice and peace to David and his descendant, our Lord Jesus Christ. Extend this kingdom to every nation, so that through your Son the poor may receive justice, the destitute relief, and the people of the earth peace in the name of him who lives and reigns with you and the Holy Spirit, one God, now and forever.

The readings:

Isaiah 11:1-10

This has been called one of the great messianic prophecies attributed to Isaiah. He paints a picture of the ideal ruler from the line of kings begun by David, noting that he is to be blessed with "the Spirit of the Lord" and other special gifts from God. Isaiah lists these in three pairs, which describe his intellectual gifts, his practical wisdom, and his spiritual relationship with God. The prophet describes the rich benefits of his rule, which never came to realization in an earthly king; fulfillment of the prophesy is realized only in the coming of the Messiah, who comes for all people and to rule over every nation. Note that when Psalm 72 is used as a responsory to the first reading, it provides what might be termed a "natural bridge" from the Old Testament lection to the Pauline pericope and the Gospel for the Day. Most congregations tend to use the Psalm this way.

Romans 15:4-13

Paul's first words in this pericope, "for whatever was written in former days was written for our instruction," prompted some American Lutheran bodies (the ULCA, for example) to follow the lead of the Anglican communion and designate the Second Sunday of Advent as "Bible Sunday," a day to promote the regular reading of the Bible. This emphasis, which is sorely needed in the contemporary church, is an appropriate exercise as part of the spiritual discipline connected to Advent, but ought to be questioned if only general reading of scripture is involved. By reading the daily lessons from a church year lectionary of the several liturgical churches, the devotions of the faithful are oriented toward the themes of Advent (and the rest of the year). Christians should find their faith renewed by Old Testament passages that give both promise and hope for the coming of the Messiah, and as, in the readings of the New Testament, hope and promise are confirmed in conjunction with the Second Coming of Christ. So Paul writes, quoting Isaiah, "The root of Jesse shall come, he who rises to rule the Gentiles; in him shall the Gentiles hope." This theme is omitted in the Roman Lectionary which ends at verse nine.

Matthew 3:1-12

Those who conceive of Advent as a time to prepare for Jesus' incarnation, particularly in Jesus' birth at Christmas, will be disappointed with this Gospel as they are with the

Matthew 24 reading for the First Sunday in Advent. Matthew presents John the Baptizer as the preacher and prophet described by Isaiah, "The voice of one crying in the wilderness: Prepare the way of the Lord, make his paths straight." John demanded that people "Repent, for the kingdom of heaven is at hand." This included the Pharisees and Sadducees, who apparently were hedging their religious "bets" by coming to John for baptism. He thundered a bold message to the "brood of vipers," as he called the Pharisees and the Sadducees, declaring that the day of God's wrath and judgment was upon them. Advent is a time to prepare for the coming of Christ — now, as well as in the future — by repenting of one's sins and actually changing one's ways of living.

John's proclamation points beyond himself to Jesus Christ, who comes after John but is superior, as the Baptizer admits, to himself. John the Baptizer holds such a high opinion of the Christ that he sees himself as a humble slave who is not even worthy of carrying Jesus' sandals. Jesus will baptize with fire and the Holy Spirit, not simply with water for repentance, as John did. And John declares that he will come in judgment and "gather the wheat into the granary, but the chaff he will burn with unquenchable fire." Christ, as John perceives him on the basis of his knowledge of Scripture, is a stern, severe sort of Savior, who doesn't seem to have empathy and compassion for a hurting humanity. There is little or nothing of Isaiah's "Suffering Servant" in John's Messiah, but there is no doubt that, in John's mind, he is the unique and holy one sent by God to save and redeem his people.

In this scene, Matthew reveals the theological stance of John the Baptizer as eschatological; John is still looking for the Coming One, although it is rather evident that he believes that the Messiah's advent is imminent. But his theology is also incarnational, by-passing any mention of Jesus' birth or formative years and dwelling, instead, on his life and ministry as his incarnation. This Gospel, therefore, serves as a corrective to people who limit the incarnation to the nativity story, while reducing the eschatological sweep of Advent to a singular celebration of Christmas. Jesus' incarnation includes all dimensions of his life and ministry — birth, ministry of preaching, teaching, healing, suffering and death, resurrection and ascension — and, in another perspective, his Second Coming. John's eschatological theology has nothing to do with Christmas, but it has everything to do with the incarnation and with Advent.

A sermon suggested by the Gospel (Matthew 3:1-12)

A contemporary setting for a sermon on Matthew 3: Two young boys were recently expelled from their school in North Carolina because they refused to stop preaching the Gospel as their parents had taught them to do. One of them is about ten years old, the other is five. They stand outside their school, holding up what could be a Bible alongside their faces to act as a megaphone, and they shout verses of Scripture, calling on all who pass by within earshot to repent of their sins before it is too late. When the school principal ordered them to enter the school building and go to their classes, they refused and continued to "preach" their version of the Gospel; their father does the same thing. The story made national news, including several of the prominent news programs.

The five-year-old has received the most publicity, probably because he is so young, and he could pass for a young John the Baptizer. He and the other members of his family could be transported to the church of St. John the Baptist, St. John's University, Collegeville, Minnesota, and placed alongside the sculpture of the Baptizer, which stands by the baptismal font in the atrium/narthex of the church. The sculpture is stark and severe in every detail, and is completely black; without saying a word, the message the statue symbolizes is transparently clear, "Repent (you who have been baptized in the name of the Lord), for the kingdom of heaven is near. Prepare the way of the Lord." No one is emotionally disturbed or upset by the sculptured figure of John the Baptizer, but they would be if the boys and their father were allowed to speak for him. Even a recorded message, not unlike those in the Hall of the Presidents in Disney World, would move more than a few people to call for the removal of both message and sculpture. John's message continues to move people to hear and repent or reject it and be condemned.

A sermon plan: "Prepare the Way of the Lord — Today."

The setting above — or something similar — could provide, when constructed with imagination, an inductive introduction to the sermon. John has been dead for almost twenty centuries, but his message is critical for all advent, or Christian, people.

1. The "bad news" — "Repent" (all of you who know yourselves to be sinners); the "good news" is "the kingdom of heaven is at hand" (in the Messiah, Jesus Christ) right now. Both are meant for everyone, saved and unsaved.

2. The "mightier one" — Jesus the Messiah — has come, is coming constantly, and will come again at the end of the age.

3. No one is exempt from the call to repentance as a changed life that will "bear fruit" appropriate to a Christian life-style. Good works cannot provide people with the assurance of salvation; people are saved by God's grace and initiative in his redeeming action in Jesus Christ.

4. Repent, but rejoice, for Jesus, who baptizes with fire and the Holy Spirit, is with you now and forever (the central message of Matthew). Believe and hope in him.

A homiletical suggestion for an alternate way of shaping this sermon

Employ Milton Crum's technique (in *Manual for Preaching,* and employed by Reginald Fuller in *The Use of the Bible for Preaching*) for developing one type of a biblical story sermon. The three-fold technique finds natural expression in this text: situation, complication, resolution.

1. The situation: John the Baptizer, according to Matthew, comes on the Judean scene more as a preacher than a baptizer; he "does" baptisms, but they seem to be secondary to his preaching in this Gospel.

2. The complication: his message, "Repent, for the kingdom of heaven is at hand," is popular to the crowds of people, but offensive to the religious leaders of the people. The tone of the judgment he declares threatens not only their personal sense of worth before God, but also stirs up self-righteous indignation over the threat that he represents to their legalistic religious system of sacrifice and good works.

3. The resolution: John "gets off the hook" with the Pharisees and Sadducees, to some degree, by proclaiming the advent of the "mightier one," the Messiah, who has the very power of God at his disposal to bring judgment upon — and salvation for — the entire human race. "Prepare the way of the Lord, make his paths straight."

A sermon on the First Lesson, Isaiah 11:1-10 — "God's Spirit-Anointed Savior."

1. God's *promise:* to send a kingly one who shall bring all people to God.

2. His *character* will be formed by the Spirit of the Lord — wisdom and understanding, counsel and might, knowledge of the fear of the Lord, his delight.

3. His *actions* will take the shape of righteous judgment and compassion for all people.

4. The *result:* He will restore peace and harmony on the earth and "a little child shall lead them."

5. The *reality:* The church's prayer, "come, Lord Jesus, come, quickly!"

A sermon on the Second Lesson, Romans 15:4-13 — "Living by the Book."

(Note: this epistle has been in the lectionary of the Holy Catholic Church since A.D. 602, first on the Third Sunday in Advent, and then on the Second Sunday in Advent since 1570. Vatican II and non-Roman lectionaries support its use on this Sunday.)

The late and renowned preacher and Brown Professor of Preaching at Union Seminary, New York City, Dr. Paul Scherer, preached on this text not long before he retired. He determined it to be so important that he devoted two sermons, on a Tuesday and a Thursday of the same week, to a single verse of the text, verse 4:

> *For whatever was written in former days was written for our instruction, that by steadfastness and by the encouragement of the scriptures we might have hope.*

> Jerusalem Bible: *And indeed everything that was written long ago in the scriptures was meant to teach us something about hope from the examples scripture gives of how people who did not give up were helped by God.*

Inductive introduction: I learned the importance of this pericope from my grandfather, a devout Methodist, who lived in our home for the last fifteen years of his life. He had lost almost everything — his beloved wife, two of his three children, his source of income, his independence; and a crippling fall saw him confined to his bed and a nearby chair for the last three years he lived — but he never lost his faith or his hope in Christ. When he died, I received two of his Bibles, the family Bible, in which he kept the records of births, deaths, baptisms, marriages, and other significant events, and also his personal, devotional Bible. The latter was virtually worn out; the leather cover was worn and rounded at the corners, the gold on the edges had been rubbed off by loving hands, and every page seemed to have something underlined or comments written on the borders — some in pencil, some in black ink, some in blue ink. From him and his Bible, I learned how important the daily reading of scripture can be in the life of a person who seems to be running out of hope. *The Bible is a book of hope, a precious gift from God.*

One could readily expand this topic of story-experience into a complete textual or thematic — *and narrative* — sermon. It might not be any of the expository types of sermons, but it could be very biblical in context. My title might be, "My Grandfather's Bible" and could follow the text very closely.

1. This book — the Bible — makes *learners* out of those who read it faithfully. Sunday worship, with the reading of Scripture, preaching, and the sacraments, is not sufficient to teach and help us appreciate the Story.

2. Those who truly love God come to *love* the book, which strengthens their faith, nurtures their love, and kindles the flame of hope in their lives when it is read devotionally and diligently in times of private worship and study, because the Bible tells the whole Story of God and his people.

3. That Story, accompanied by the Holy Spirit, enables the faithful to *live* by the book — not legalistically or by the letter of the law, but in the freedom that the Good News offers in the culmination of the Story, Jesus Christ. *The Bible assures the world that God always keeps his promises to his people.*

4. *Living by the book assures genuine quality of life to the children of God.*

Psalm-series Sermon — Psalm 72:1-14 (15-17) — "Long Live the King's Son!"

1. His reign shall be determined by *God's righteousness* and shall be marked by *justice for the poor* and *prosperity for the people.*

2. He will be an *advocate* and a *deliverer* of the poor and oppressed people of the earth, a *blessing* to the whole world.

3. He will *rule* as *redeemer* over the humble and all of the exalted rulers of the nations.

4. He will *live forever* and all nations will finally call him *blessed.* Come, Lord Jesus!

Third Sunday of Advent

Roman Catholic	Isaiah 35:1-6a, 10	James 5:7-10	Matthew 11:2-11
Episcopal	Isaiah 35:1-10	James 5:7-10	Matthew 11:2-11
Lutheran	Isaiah 35:1-10	James 5:7-10	Matthew 11:2-11
Common	Isaiah 35:1-10	James 5:7-10	Matthew 11:2-11

The church year theological clue

The liturgical/homiletical purpose of this Sunday is to deal with a question that is fundamental to the incarnation, Jesus' identity as the Messiah, who has come to God's people and who will come again. The focus of the gospel shows how Jesus' word and works identified him as the Messiah, the incarnate Word, giving a better understanding of the incarnation as it was revealed in his life and ministry to the church that is about to celebrate his birth. The Gospel also points to John the Baptizer as the forerunner of Christ, who prepares the way of the Lord, and is also a model of godly service and witness for all believers.

The lessons for this Sunday make it a Sunday of transition between the first two Sundays in Advent, which are oriented to the Second Coming, and the Fourth Sunday in Advent, which offers final preparations for the joyful celebration of the birth of Christ. In this respect, it enriches the Christmas worship by reminding the church that Christ is present in the world through his Word, the sacraments, and the Holy Spirit, *and that the one whose birth will be observed in about a week will come again at the end of the age.*

The Prayer of the Day — The only Advent collect which does not begin with "stir up . . . ." The prayer appears to have been inspired by the appointed — and traditional — Gospel, because it suggests that John the Baptizer had the biblical knowledge and necessary wisdom to understand the answer Jesus gave to the delegation John sent asking him, "Are you he who is to come (the Messiah)?" The church prays for such wisdom in order to witness to the Christ and prepare his way in the world.

The Psalm of the Day — Psalm 146 was selected because it centers on Jesus' answer to the disciples of John who asked him, "Are you he who is to come, or do we look for another?" — and is a fitting response to the First Lesson, Isaiah 35:1-10. It asserts that people who know and trust the Lord are happy and hopeful because they depend on the Lord God, "who made heaven and earth, the seas, and all that is in them," and *keeps his promise forever.* He is a God who gives justice to the hungry and oppressed, sets the prisoners free, opens the eyes of the blind, lifts up those who are bowed down, cares for the stranger, sustains the orphan and widow, *but frustrates the way of the wicked. Praise the Lord, O my soul!*

The Psalm Prayer

> *God of glory and power, happy indeed are those who have put their trust in you. Shine the brightness of your light upon us, that we may love you always with a pure heart and praise you forever; through your Son, Jesus Christ our Lord.*

The readings:

Isaiah 35:1-10

Isaiah's prophecy in this chapter has to do with the return of the Israelites from the Babylonian captivity, which he sees as a repetition of the exodus from Egypt. Their trust in the Lord will be rewarded and their hope will at last be realized; the people of Israel will return to Zion and the glory of their nation will be restored. Rather than sustaining his people with manna, as in the exodus, God will bless the poor and the oppressed, work miracles among the blind, the lame, the dumb and others, and he will not only restore the glory of Zion but establish a highway — the Holy Way — for "the return of the ransomed of the Lord."

Isaiah's eschatological theology here is consistent with his vision of a faithful God, who keeps promises to his people and, therefore, can be trusted. He has the power to rescue and restore his people Israel and return them safely to Zion. That, Isaiah declares, will be a great day. The prophesy also provided Jesus with a biblical answer to John's question, "Are you he who is to come?" That is the main reason it was selected to complement Matthew 11, the Gospel for the Day.

James 5:7-10

This epistle is an echo of the type of eschatology that predominates on the First Sunday in Advent; it looks to — and anticipates — the return of the Lord. It is "out of sync" with the other propers for this day, probably because it was taken from a ninth century lectionary (Murbach, France), which appointed this lesson for a weekday reading for Advent. The lesson was moved to Sunday in the post-Vatican II lectionary and, thereby, found its way into contemporary lectionaries.

James has a well-developed eschatology, which looks for the Parousia and prompts him to urge the people to be "patient (like a farmer waiting for the harvest) until the coming of the Lord." He also believes that the Second Coming is "at hand" and "the Judge is standing at the door." In a time of persecution that causes suffering, the patience of godly people should be like that of the prophets. The note of *patience* speaks directly to contemporary Christians and addresses the fact that Christ will come when God gives the signal; the church must continue to wait *expectantly* — and patiently.

Matthew 11:2-11

Anyone who is familiar with the relationship of John the Baptizer and Jesus has to wonder what prompted John to send disciples to Jesus to ask, "Are you he who is to come, or do we look for another?" It is a preposterous question, one which he should have asked Jesus when he appeared for baptism at the River Jordan; it comes too late in the story and readers are hard-pressed to arrive at a satisfactory reason for John's question. Nor does Matthew tell how John received Jesus' answer, "Go and tell John what you hear and see" — the mighty works he does among the hopeless and helpless people of Israel. Either the answer was satisfactory, or John was beheaded before another scene in this drama could be orchestrated.

Christ's speech about John the Baptizer, culminating in his assertion that John the Baptizer is the Elijah figure whom the prophets declared would appear in connection with the coming of the Messiah, is almost like a *eulogy,* as though Jesus knew that John would soon die, and wanted to set the record straight about John for all time. John was the one he said he was, the one who came to prepare the way of the Lord and make his paths straight.

The theology spelled out in this Gospel is *realized eschatology,* in that it has to do with the First Coming, the appearance in the flesh, the incarnation, of Jesus as the Messiah of God. The crux of the matter for us is whether or not John's question is ours; do we believe that Jesus is the Messiah? Or, could our question be even more fundamental, "Just who are you, Jesus?" — or even "Who does this Jesus think he is, anyway?" If we can't perceive from Jesus' answer that he is the Messiah, we have no reason to celebrate Christmas or simply to go through the motions of observing Advent.

A biblical story sermon suggested by the Gospel, Matthew 11:2-11 of the Steimel model in **Proclaiming the Story** *— "A Surprising Question and a Strange Answer."*

The setting: John, in prison, sends his disciples to Jesus with what is for him a surprising question, "Are you he who is to come, or do we look for another?" It is surprising, not simply because John has already encountered Jesus as the one sent by God, his beloved Son, but because it is a terribly contemporary question and it needs to be answered in a satisfying way. Was Jesus really the Messiah? John's question was serious; he really wanted to know what Jesus' answer would be. It really was the *right question for him to ask!* Don't we tend to ask the wrong question much too often?

In the movie, *Desperately Seeking Susan,* it is not really Susan, a veritable free spirit, who is being sought by her friends and lovers, but Roberta who is doing the desperate seeking. Roberta is the wife of a very successful spa and tub salesman; she lives in a luxurious apartment, has almost everything she could want. At the same time, she really has nothing, not even the love of her husband who, she finally realizes, is more in love with himself than he is with her; his greatest pleasure is to watch the commercials he has made of himself. Roberta manages to change places with Susan and, in this process, she finds a man who loves her very much. She is not looking for a person with whom to have an affair; she is really, the movie makes clear, looking for herself, asking that contemporary question that is so common, "Who am I?" John might tell us that we are searching for our own identities when we ought to be asking a question about Jesus: "Are you the one who is to come, or should we look for another?" (adapted from *The Cradle, the Cross, and the Crown,* C.S.S., 1986)

The unfolding story: Jesus' answer, too, is strange, because he makes no direct assertion of his identity nor does he refer to their encounter at the Jordan. He replies to the question by pointing out what he is doing in his ministry. Jesus' answer, when it was relayed to John by his disciples, must have brought peace and blessed assurance to his soul. Truly, it is when people, through faith, perceive the full scope of Jesus' life and ministry, the fullness of the incarnation, including his suffering, death, and resurrection, that they identify him as the one to whom they can entrust their very lives while they are living and their eternal destiny when they die.

The climax of the story: When Jesus preached John's "funeral sermon" he emphasized, in his reply, that service to God and people was a sign that he was the Messiah. Service is also the nature of the life that believers are to live in imitation of their Lord. Serving people in the name of Jesus the Christ is the only way to find full favor with God; it is the secret of genuine greatness in the eyes of God; it does not win eternal life for anyone — that comes through the grace of God in Jesus Christ — but it does give comfort and assurance to the person who faithfully serves the Lord.

Jesus' sermonette for John functions as a reminder that we were all ordained for service, in the Sacrament of Baptism. The Lord has come! Serve him as long as you live — and know when you do so, you prepare the way of the Lord in the world.

(Note: in this type of sermon, which follows the plot, or the story line, of the text, two other stories — the preacher's and those of the people — need to be interwoven with the biblical story, as in the first part of the sermon. This technique is more one of integration of biblical and contemporary story than it is a matter of illustrating the truth of the gospel. By themselves, the contemporary stories a pastor interweaves with the story may be in the form that could be called illustrations, but the Steimle technique as demonstrated in "The Stranger," in *God, the Stranger,* turns the entire sermon into a complete story.)

Old Testament sermon series, Isaiah 35:1-10 — "God's Day for Rejoicing."

1. The Lord God is one who comes with majesty, glory, and power to save and restore his people.

2. His coming will work miracles that will rejuvenate his people; he will free them from their enemies (especially sin and death, in our case).

3. He shall "rework" the earth and establish a holy way back to him which finds its culmination in Christ.

4. Because Christ came as Messiah and opened up the way back to God for all people, this is a day of rejoicing and praying, Come, Lord Jesus! Come quickly!

A Sermon on the Second Lesson, James 5:7-10

Paul Scherer, in one of the two sermons on Romans 15:4 which he preached in Union Seminary chapel, said, "There was a tugboat that for fifty years sat moored to her dock in the River Thames. She had been set there by an act of Parliament under Queen Victoria to be a ready help in time of trouble, if any ships should get into difficulty with the Tower Bridge, which had just recently been built. Now, no ship ever had, and it was unlikely that any ship ever would, but for fifty years she sat there — captain and a crew of six, 27 tons of coal in her bunkers, steam going day and night, ready to dash out at a moment's notice on her great adventure. That, you say, is patience."

1. Christians, like the Jews who awaited the coming of the Messiah before them, live in the expectation that Christ will come to earth a second time, this time as judge.

2. His Second Coming is taking an even longer time than his appearance as Messiah, but he will come again when the Lord God determine that the time is ripe.

3. Impatient though they may be for the Parousia, Christians have to learn to live in hope as they wait patiently (as the tugboat did) for the Lord's return.

4. For now, Christians wait patiently for the Parousia by doing the Lord's work in their daily lives.

Psalm-series sermon — Psalm 146 — "A God Who Can Be Trusted."

1. God, in all he has done in the past, has revealed himself to be trustworthy; he keeps his promises to his people. *The faithful can depend on God to keep his word* (as he has done in the coming of the Messiah).

2. In his life and ministry, Jesus has *verified God's reliability* by doing the same things that God has done since the beginning of time; opens the eyes of the blind, sets the prisoners free, cares for the stranger, orphans, and widows, etc.

3. God also reveals his trustworthiness by his stance against sin, evil, and wicked people, *frustrating those who refuse to listen and obey him.*

4. "The Lord shall reign forever . . . throughout all generations" and he can be trusted to reign, in Jesus Christ at the last day, with justice and mercy and love.

Fourth Sunday of Advent

Roman Catholic	**Isaiah 7:10-14**	**Romans 1:1-7**	**Matthew 1:18-24**
Episcopal	**Isaiah 7:10-17**	**Romans 1:1-7**	**Matthew 1:18-25**
Lutheran	**Isaiah 7:10-14(15-17)**	**Romans 1:1-7**	**Matthew 1:18-25**
Common	**Isaiah 7:10-17**	**Romans 1:1-7**	**Matthew 1:18-25**

The church year theological clue

A quarter of a century ago, there was a movement in Great Britain by the Joint Liturgical Group to move Christmas (and other festivals, too) to a Sunday to encourage greater attendance and participation in the festive worship. This did not happen formally (in fact, the anticipated 1980 merger of the Anglican Church with several Protestant communions did not occur, either), but the Fourth Sunday in Advent, through liturgy and lections and popular piety, has clearly taken the shape of "Christmas Sunday" in many parts of the church. At the least, another proposal (to name the Sundays of Advent as Sundays before Christmas) did not reach full fruition, because there is really only one Sunday *before* Christmas." This should preserve the purposes of Advent and, at the same time, give Christmas its due.

The theological/homiletical clue, from the perspective of church year and liturgy, is to focus the proclamation of the gospel on the incarnation of Jesus Christ, the Son of God, as the *beginning* of the drama of salvation. The readings support and substantiate this liturgical view of the Fourth Sunday in Advent as the time to anticipate the proximity of Christmas and to prepare for the celebration.

The homiletical problem in preaching is that the content of this Sunday is what most people in our congregations already have been celebrating, rather than waiting for. Advent has become so secularized, with early emphasis on the "commercial countdown" (so many shopping days left until Christmas, etc.), that the Fourth Sunday in Advent and Christmas, too, are practically over by the time they arrive. Therefore, the other two themes of Advent — the Parousia and the present Advent of the Lord — need to find emphasis alongside the historical coming of Christ in his birth if pastors are to preach on the full meaning of the incarnation, which finds expression in the twelve day Christmas season, the Epiphany season, and beyond.

The Prayer of the Day — The third, and last, of the "stir up" prayers, which begins exactly as did the prayer for the First Sunday in Advent: "Stir up your power, O Lord, and come." it continues, oriented to Christmas:

> *Take away the hindrance of our sins and make us ready for the celebration of your birth, that we may receive you in joy and serve you always; for you live and reign with the Father and the Holy Spirit, now and forever.*

The petition, in the light of the address that asks the risen and reigning Lord to stir up his power and come to us in the celebration of his birth, is an expression of repentance by those with contrite hearts so that our rejoicing might be full and complete, and our lives be dedicated to Christian service.

The Psalm of the Day — Psalm 24 — When sung to a psalm tone, this psalm could serve nicely as an entrance hymn:

> *Lift up your heads, O gates;*
> *lift them high, O everlasting doors;*
> *   and the King of glory shall come in . . .*
> *"Who is he, this King of glory?"*
> *   "The Lord of hosts,*
> *   he is the King of glory."*

The one who was in the creation and to whom all people and all things belong, is about to enter the world through the king, his Son, to give God's blessing to his people. Long sought by his own, he comes at last to them, whose hands have been cleansed and whose hearts have been purified through repentance and repudiation of sin. With heads lifted high, the people of God ready themselves to receive him with joy as they celebrate the feast, his birth.

The Psalm Prayer

Lord God, ruler and guide of heaven and earth, you made your Son a priest and brought him into your everlasting temple. Open our hearts that the King of glory may enter, and bring us rejoicing to your holy mountain, where you live and reign, one God, now and forever.

The readings:

Isaiah 7:10-14

A one-level exegesis of this passage throws it into the past — and stormy — history of Israel and Judah, when Ahaz, King of Judah, was caught in a political and military squeeze by an allegiance between the northern kingdom of Israel and then-powerful Syria. King Ahaz didn't really want to hear Isaiah's prophesy that all would be well, but he couldn't ignore it, especially when Isaiah spoke his familiar word, "Behold, a young woman shall conceive and bear a son, and shall call his name Immanuel." This was not intended to be a messianic reference, at that time, but an announcement that the queen would become pregnant and bear a son who would be a political savior for Judah. Early in the history of the New Testament church, the reference to Immanuel was connected to the Christ; Hezekiah, the "Immanuel" of whom Isaiah was speaking, was put in the background. Jesus was Immanuel, no question about it, partly because he came from the house of David, but also because there were special signs and events connected with his birth. It is from this perspective that this text is assigned to the Fourth Sunday in Advent.

The Roman Catholic lectionary reading ends at verse 14, but the other three in this study include verses 15 through 17, which describe how "the land will be deserted," as well as the special character and characteristics that this child-king will have. He will know "how to refuse the evil and choose the good" and will usher in restoration of a bygone era. But the liturgical/homiletical intention in assigning this reading to this Sunday remains in the connection that Christians make of "Immanuel" to Jesus Christ. In actuality, a single verse, 14, could be employed as the First Lesson: "Behold, a young woman shall conceive and bear a son, and shall call his name Immanuel." (The *Jerusalem Bible* reads: "The Lord himself, therefore, will give you a sign. It is this: the maiden is with child and will soon give birth to a son whom she will call Immanuel." This translation "fits" more accurately Joseph's dream in the Gospel). This is *realized eschatology* for the church.

Romans 1:1-7

This epistle summarizes the heart of the gospel, much as Paul does in his other epistles — but with some differences — so that the church in Rome would understand that his kerygmatic theology was identical to that which the people had been taught. He emphasizes that Jesus "descended from David according to the flesh" and was "designated Son of God in power according to the Spirit of holiness by his resurrection from the dead . . . ." The reading seems to have been selected primarily because it asserts that Jesus/Immanuel comes from the Davidic line and thereby substantiates the interpretation that Isaiah's prophecy may be applied to Jesus Christ. Interestingly, what he has to say about himself, the gospel, and the church at Rome, precedes his familiar apostolic greeting, "Grace to you and peace from God our Father and the Lord Jesus Christ." The epistle also serves to tie the Isaiah reading to the Gospel for the Day.

Matthew 1:18-25

A portion of the Christmas story is read annually on the Fourth Sunday in Advent; in this case, it is the story of Joseph's dream about his pregnant fiancee and the son she soon would bear. This is the first of three dreams in which an angel came to Joseph and gave him a message; this time the angel told him the incredible tale that Mary was pregnant by the Holy Spirit and her son would "save his people from their sins." Who can say what Joseph might, or might not, have done had the angel not come and spoken to him? He, too, was a special person — compassionate, for his concern for Mary and his unwillingness "to put her to shame," but also godly in an even deeper sense, because he accepted and obeyed without question — on this and the other two occasions when an angel visited him — what he perceived to be the will of God and married Mary. *He,* says Matthew, *called his name Jesus.* And although Joseph disappears from Jesus' story between his youth and the beginning of his ministry, he will always be remembered for his part in the Christmas story.

Matthew 1, therefore, serves to announce to the people that the Christian celebration is at hand, and to affirm that Jesus Christ is the One named Immanuel; in him, God comes to, and is with, his people. He will be with them to the end of the age when, as other parts of the story inform us, he will come again in glory and judgment. Connected, as it is in the lectionary, to the readings of Luke 3 and John 1, the celebration of Jesus' birth is given proper emphasis so that Christmas worship will have some depth to it. This is the story, indeed, of how the incarnation took place by the will and action taken by God.

A sermon on Matthew 1:18-25 — "A Dream — and the Incarnation."

The homiletical lesson that the late Peter Marshall left as a legacy to the church is that *The Jesus story is most effective when it is told as a story.* His example has rubbed off on many preachers and their preaching in the four decades since his death, and preachers would do well to give narrative expression to the Christmas story *as story* in their planning and sermon production for the end of Advent and Christmas. This Gospel, in particular, begs to be preached as a biblical story sermon; such a sermon is built into the text and highlights, on this Sunday, the important role that Joseph plays in the Christmas story. He is not the physical father of Jesus, nor has his marriage to Mary been finalized, but he saves her from shame or worse and even gives Jesus his name.

A story sermon sketch: The good and gentle Joseph was faced with a crisis; Mary was pregnant and he had the power to determine her future. Joseph had to make the most important decision of his life, although he probably didn't look at it that way; he had to decide whether or not he should break the engagement and abandon Mary to scorn and shame, letting her suffer the consequences of her "sin." That's the complicated situation in which Matthew begins to tell his version of the Christmas story. Even if Mary had told him that she was pregnant "by the Holy Spirit," his dilemma would not have been solved. Clearly, his was a far more critical decision than he could possibly imagine. (Note: the "complication" in this plot comes at the very beginning of the story, and finds ready expression in numerous contemporary stories. One of these might be used to ground the situation and the gospel in life today.)

Joseph's dream provides additional complication to an already complicated situation; it must have been vivid — and memorable (so many dreams are dreamed and forgotten or ignored!); later, he must have told the dream to Mary, and after Jesus' birth, he might have told it again and again (but that's only conjecture!). What matters, in the story, is that *the dream was real for Joseph;* it was just as if God were speaking to him in person and making the decision for him. In essence, that's what happened; the angel sent by God gave him such an incredible message that he knew it had to be true, and truly to be from God. His role in the drama of Messiah's birth was communicated to him so that he could not mistake the purpose and will of God in the pregnancy of Mary; the child was "conceived in her of the Holy Spirit; she will bear a son, and *you shall call his name Jesus* (which was done, according to Luke 2:21), for he will save his people from their sins."

When Joseph awakened from his dream, he had already made his decision; he would obey the command of God that came to him through the angel, take Mary as his wife, and name the child Jesus after his birth. Jesus was born into a family, a holy family, and saved from illegitimacy, or worse, by the loving and compassionate obedience of a God-fearing man. And that's a lesson for us as we are about to celebrate Christmas once more. (Note: The secret of developing the text into a biblical story sermon, as does the late Edmund Steimle, is in interweaving the three strands of story: the story in the text, the preacher's story, and the people's story. See his *Proclaiming the Story* or his one page article in *Partners*, June 1979, for additional details. Two examples — one by Steimle and the other by me — are in my book, *The Song and the Story*.)

A possible three-text sermon — "What It Means to be a Servant of the Lord"

Paul Tournier once wrote about dedicated service to Jesus Christ: "We surrender our whole being to the authority of Jesus Christ. This means that we must let God direct us in the use of our body and goods, our work and our money . . . . This means that devotion to Jesus Christ turns over to him not only our inner life but also our social life."

1. The prophet Isaiah was completely dedicated as a servant of the Lord, demonstrating the graciousness of God in his prophecy, but he spoke of a child he would never see. God has a way of bringing about surprising results to the efforts of his faithful servants. (First Lesson)

2. The Apostle Paul as a servant of the Lord, saw himself as an "apostle," set apart for the gospel of God, which he promised beforehand through his prophets, the gospel concerning his Son . . . ." His surrender to God was so complete that he not only preached the gospel fearlessly, but was beheaded for his faith in Jesus the Christ, and the Christ he preached has become known throughout the entire world. (Second Lesson)

3. Joseph, as the dedicated servant of the Lord God, who dared everything — ridicule from his neighbors, scorn from his friends, possible boycott from his customers — awakened from his dream and accepted the pregnant Virgin Mary for his bride. Believers will be faithful to God, even when common sense, or injured pride, tells them to live as they think to be best for them. (The Gospel Lesson)

4. Few people will become prophets after the order of Isaiah, and fewer will become actual martyrs, but all of us can express our sainthood, as did Joseph, in full and complete surrender to God of all we have, all we are, and all we hope to be in life and in death.

An Old Testament sermon, Isaiah 7:10-14 (15-17) — "Immanuel — God's Word to the World."

1. The word God spoke to Ahaz — Immanuel — has been heard, not by Ahaz alone, but all over the world.

2. Immanuel is a word of blessed assurance; God is with the people who will have him as their Son.

3. Immanuel is the name of One, Jesus Christ, who saves the entire world in his death and resurrection.

4. Immanuel is the name that is above all other names, not only at Christmas, but for all time.

Psalm-series sermon — "We Believe in God, Our Creator and Redeemer."

1. Like it or not, believe it or not, the God who created the world and everything in it is still in charge of human events in time and eternity.

2. Those who declare, "I believe in God, the Father Almighty," in true repentance and faith, "shall receive a blessing from the Lord." He gives them his son and the Holy Spirit to establish, strengthen, and confirm their faith.

3. Christmas tells us that the king of glory "has come into the world" and calls upon us to "lift up our hearts" as we celebrate his coming again.

4. Tell the story so that the entire world may be filled with his glory! He will come again! That's a promise — from God himself.

(Note: This is the sort of personal story I like to use in the sermons that I write and preach: A couple of decades ago, my son and I made a Saturday afternoon trip into Barcelona, Spain, from the Costa Brava, where we were staying for a few days. The most memorable sight for me was the Church of the Holy Family, planned and begun by Antonio Gaudi, the "father" of contemporary architecture. The church was begun in 1895, but it was not finished when we were there, nor is it completed now; it is being built in the time-honored tradition of the great cathedrals of Europe, and its completion is still in the future. Despite the fact that there is no roof, no windows, and a tremendous amount of work to be done, a sculpture of the Holy Family had been executed and placed on the facade. Mary, Joseph, and the baby Jesus were there — and an angel, with trumpet raised, not merely to announce the birth of the Christ child, but ready to signal the return of the risen Lord at the end of time. But there was a problem: The trumpet, somehow or other, had been bent downward, as if the angel (Gabriel?) had been waiting so long to blow his horn that the metal of the horn had lost its strength and partially collapsed. For me, this has been a parable of the problem that we, who celebrate the birth of Jesus, have in regard to his Second Coming. How long, O Lord? How long must we wait?)

The Nativity of Our Lord

Roman Catholic	Isaiah 9:2-7	Titus 2:11-14	Luke 2:1-14
Episcopal	Isaiah 9:2-4, 6-7	Titus 2:11-14	Luke 2:1-14, (15-20)
Lutheran	Isaiah 9:2-7	Titus 2:11-14	Luke 2:1-20
Common	Isaiah 9:2-7	Titus 2:11-14	Luke 2:1-20

The church year theological clue

As one of the major festivals of the Christian church — and probably the most popular — Christmas liturgies were shaped by gospel tradition and worship practices in the early church. In Jerusalem, by the fourth century, there were three masses of Christmas: the first was at midnight in the Grotto of the Nativity at Bethlehem, the second took place at dawn, after the faithful had walked back to Jerusalem, in the Church of the Resurrection, and, later in the day, a third and solemn mass was celebrated. The nature of these eucharistic services informs us that "Christmas was never meant to be the *object* of the festival. Rather, it is the *occasion* of the feast of thanksgiving, which commemorates Jesus' entrance (incarnation) into the world." That's why the John 1 Gospel was included in the propers for Christmas Day.

The biblical and liturgical content of Christmas insists that the grace of God in Jesus' birth needs to be proclaimed, not simply by a retelling of the story as though the birth of Christ were the saving event in its entirety and, therefore, can be recreated and relived through a kind of "born again in the babe of Bethlehem experience" (as in Phillips Brooks' much loved carol, "Be Born in Us Today"), but in preaching and in the Christmas Eucharist, which proclaim and commemorate the *redeeming event in the cross and tomb and anticipate his Second Coming to the world*. In the meantime, Christ first comes to each of us in baptism and gives us new birth through water, the Word, and the Holy Spirit; he does, of course, renew that gift in every celebration of the Eucharist, including the Christ Mass (the hymn might better read, "cast out our sin, and enter in. Be reborn in us today"). The initiation of God's reign that will finally bring lasting peace to the earth is highlighted, and/or implied, in the context of the Christmas liturgy. As he said to the disciples after the resurrection, "Peace be with you," repeating the angels' Christmas greeting, "Peace on earth among people of good will," which is God's benediction in Christ for the whole world.

The Prayer of the Day — Most of the liturgical churches provide two or three prayers for Christmas, which are to function as the ancient collects did. For example, the LBW provides two prayers for the three sets of propers (for three different services, not for three different years. The lections for years A, B, C are one and the same in the lectionary.) The first prayer acknowledges that the brightness of Christmas comes from the true Light, Jesus Christ, and takes an incarnational stance, asking God to help his people walk in the "light of Jesus' presence" in addition to an *eschatological position* that they may "in the last day wake to the brightness of his glory." It is truly in harmony with the ancient celebration of Christmas as the Christ Mass with its "as often as you eat this bread and drink this cup, you proclaim the Lord's death until he comes."

The second Prayer for the Day in the LBW, which is really provided for the first Christmas worship service, on Christmas Eve at midnight, is more generally used in parts of that church. It complements the Luke 2 Gospel and emphasizes God's *revelation* of himself in his son, Jesus Christ, petitioning the Lord God to "set us free from the old slavery of our sin" through his incarnation. Birth and incarnation, in this prayer, are presupposed to include the content of Jesus' death and resurrection, because Jesus is called "the redeemer of the world." Redemption from sin and death comes through the cross and the empty tomb experience that Jesus accepted in order to accomplish God's will in the world. The identification of Jesus at his birth as the Son of God and Savior of the world prefigures his death and resurrection.

The Psalm of the Day (LBW) — Psalm 96 — It is impossible to determine for what occasion this psalm was composed, but it is obvious why it was selected as the responsory psalm, the Psalm of the Day, for Christmas services; it has an almost transparently *eschatological* theme to it, anticipating the coming of the Messiah-like King, who will bring salvation to the people. It promises a king unlike any who has reigned up to this time, one whose coming has consequences for the entire world. Thus, at the birth of the King of Kings, it is right and proper that the people should:

> *Sing to the Lord a new song;*
> *sing to the Lord,*
> *all the whole earth.*
> *Sing to the Lord and bless his name;*
> *proclaim the good news*
> *of his salvation from day to day.*

The Psalm Prayer

> *Lord Jesus, the incarnate Word, when you consented to dwell with us, the heavens were glad and the earth rejoiced. In hope and love we await your return. Help us to proclaim your glory to those who do not know you, until the whole earth sings a new song to you and the Father and the Holy Spirit, one God, now and forever.*

The readings:

Isaiah 9:2-7

This pericope contains one of the loveliest and perhaps most-loved of the prophecies in all of the Old Testament. The reading is most appropriate for Christmas with its declaration, "The people who walked in darkness have seen a great light; those who dwelt in a land of deep darkness, on them has light shined." It also spells out the reasons for rejoicing at Jesus' advent, announcing, "For to us a child is born, to us a son is given; and the government will be upon his shoulder." It also describes Jesus Christ perfectly, because he fulfills the description of the prophecy in a manner and degree never seen in the kings of Israel — "his name will be called 'Wonderful Counselor, Mighty God, Everlasting Father, Prince of Peace.' " Whether or not the author had any messianic intentions when he wrote this beautiful prophecy does not matter; it fits the Christmas celebration perfectly and prepares the people for hearing the Christmas Gospel as it is read and preached and lived out in the Eucharist.

Titus 2:11-14

In the context of instruction to believers of all ages, Titus writes of two advents of the Lord, one in the past — "for the grace of God has appeared for the salvation of all men" — and the other in the future — "awaiting our blessed hope, the appearing of the glory of our great God and Savior Jesus Christ." He speaks of the cross-event — "(he) gave himself for us to redeem us from all iniquity" — the Christ's intention in that act — "to purify for himself a people of his own who are zealous for good deeds." Accordingly, this lesson does not fit the sentimental and dominant conceptions that many persons hold toward Christmas, that celebrating the incarnation of Jesus means centering worship and hope on the birth of the

Christ child, rather than on his birth as the first part of the drama of reconciliation with God in his death, resurrection, and Parousia. The importance of this lesson, therefore, is that it clarifies our theology in view of the saving events in Jesus' life and the culmination of it all that will take place in his glorious return that is called the Parousia. It means that both the promise of the Messiah in the First Lesson and Luke's beautiful story of Jesus' birth in his Gospel — and the celebration of Christmas — are kept in proper kerygmatic perspective — death/resurrection and Parousia — by this pericope.

Luke 2:1-20

For the first time in Series A, another gospel — Luke, in this instance — is assigned to the worship on a specific day, Christmas. The Christmas Gospel belongs to Luke (and to John, when a separate set of lections is provided for the worship on Christmas Day); Matthew has his chance to tell his version of the story of Jesus' birth on the Epiphany of Our Lord, January 6.

Luke's story is full of exegetical holes, because most of the quasi-historical details — the details about the census, the governorship of Quirinius, Bethlehem as the actual location for Jesus' birth, for example — are possibly, even probably, inaccurate. But the symbolism of the story is valid, using the shepherds to portray how Christ came to minister to and save the lowly and despised of the earth. Shepherds, in that time, were on the same level as prostitutes and tax-collectors; little of the Good Shepherd image was evident in their lives and lifestyles. Some had given their business a bad name, because they were thieves and robbers. It is also fitting that Luke should speak of a whole host of angels announcing the birth of Jesus and giving him the glory due unto his name. Angels, again, play out their appointed role as messengers in the revelation of God to human beings; they announce what is going to happen and proclaim what is taking place through God's graceful and glorious acts in his only son, Jesus. Luke makes it manifestly clear that this is the *beginning* of the story of Jesus' incarnation, hardly the whole tale. God has moved into the world and human experience in the birth of Jesus Christ; the rest of the story is yet to come.

A sermon on the Gospel, Luke 2:1-20 — "The Reason for Our Rejoicing."

Among all the sermon titles that I have composed for sermons written and/or preached, there is one that I will never forget, "Our Cause for Rejoicing." On the Saturday before our first Palm Sunday, as it was called in those days, and in our first parish, my wife, Doris, was cutting stencils for that service and the services of Holy Week. She went into labor for the birth of our first child, but finished the task before I took her to the hospital. It was a long and arduous delivery, which finally occurred at 2:20 a.m. on Palm Sunday morning. I didn't get to see her and the baby for a couple of more hours, and then I drove the forty miles from Philadelphia to our home in Chester County. There was barely time to make the necessary telephone calls to family and close friends, and to shower, shave, have breakfast, pick up my sermon manuscript, and go to church to make final preparations for Palm Sunday's festive worship service. Not until I checked the bulletin for the day did I recall the title of the sermon my wife had typed; it was, "Our Cause for Rejoicing." It was meant for Palm Sunday's theme, but a son had been born, mother and child were well, and I could announce it to both congregations of the parish in conjunction with Christ's entrance into Jerusalem. The only thing that would have made the title more appropriate to the day were if our son had been born on Christmas Day rather than Palm Sunday.

1. Christ's birth is a cause for rejoicing. God has moved into human history to take a hand in the affairs of humanity here on earth.

2. Jesus' birth caused a celebration in heaven and, on a limited basis at that time, on earth. That celebration has spread from the Middle East to the ends of the earth; it finds expression in the Gloria in Excelsis of the Sunday liturgy and especially in the festival we call Christ Mass, or Christmas.

3. We rejoice because God, out of love, compassion, and grace, sent Jesus into the world to save people from sin and deliver them from death.

4. God will make our joy complete, ushering in his promised "peace plan" that will surpass the efforts of nations to establish "peace on earth" and bring in the age of peace that all sensible and caring people hope for.

5. At Christmas, Jesus was born and we really have a cause for rejoicing.

A three-text sermon — "God Makes and Keeps His Promises."

1. *God's promise of a Messiah-deliverer gave hope to his people.* A promise always gives hope to those who receive it. When it is made by God, it makes present life bearable and the future positive, as Isaiah points out in his prophecy.

2. *A promise — God's — became reality* when Jesus was born, as Luke tells us, in Bethlehem of Judea. Christmas becomes, from the perspective of Isaiah and Matthew, a day of thanksgiving (a Eucharist) and praises to Father, as well as to the Son whose birth we celebrate.

3. God's promise has a *future dimension,* as Titus affirms, because the resurrected and ascended Lord will return at the end of time to finish the work that he began during his earthly life and ministry.

4. Hope in the Lord God, who keeps all of his promises to his people.

An Old Testament homily — "A Light for the Darkest Night."

1. The Light, of which Isaiah spoke, surely shines upon the earth, *penetrating* the darkness in people's hearts and giving them light to live by. The birth of the Promised One, Jesus Christ, brings that light into the world.

2. Jesus *illuminates* the world as the Wonderful Counselor, the Mighty God, Everlasting Father, and Prince of Peace. He lights up the earth by who he is, as well as by what he does as the Son of God.

3. The light will continue to *shine* on the earth, through the Word and Holy Spirit, until God brings in the fullness of the kingdom in Jesus' Second Coming, which will completely *eradicate the darkness.*

4. Be assured that "the zeal of the Lord of hosts will do this."

A homily on the Second Lesson for Christmas, Titus 2:11-14 — "A Way to Celebrate Christmas."

1. Our Christmas celebration is a *thanksgiving* to God because the Christ, the Son of God, who was born so long ago, came as Lord and Savior of all people.

2. He came in human form *to free us from sin and death,* and also to "purify for himself a people of his own who are zealous for good deeds." *He came to make servants of God of us all.*

3. Christmas is *really and fully celebrated* when those who have blessed the Lord at his birth *continue to live thankfully and obediently, serving God by serving his people* in the manner he prescribes for believers.

4. At the table-feast, at which he is the ever-present host, Jesus blesses and renews people and assures them that he will be with them in the Holy Spirit until he comes at the last day.

First Sunday after Christmas

Roman Catholic	Sirach 3:2-6, 12-14	Colossians 3:12-21	Matthew 2:13-15, 19-23
Episcopal	Isaiah 61:10—62:3	Galatians 3:23-25, 4:4-7	John 1:1-18
Lutheran	Isaiah 63:7-9	Galatians 4:4-7	Matthew 2:13-15, 19-23
Common	Isaiah 63:7-9	Hebrews 2:10-18	Matthew 2:13-15, 19-23

The church year theological clue

The liturgical function of this Sunday is that, practically, it becomes a kind of Octave of Christmas. As the first Sunday in the twelve days of the Christmas season, it continues the celebration of Jesus' incarnation with more of the details of the Christmas story, and encourages the church to worship the Messiah who has come in the name of the Lord. The homiletical clue, from the very nature of the Sunday's purpose and readings, is to tell the story more completely and with more depth, so that it will be clear to the church that God broke into the world to save his people at any cost. What he has begun in Jesus' birth will be completed according to plan, for he is the God and Father of all.

The Prayer of the Day (LBW) — A reworked collect that highlights the incarnation in the context of the birth of Jesus Christ, expanding the scope of the incarnation by observing how God "wonderfully created and yet more wonderfully restored the dignity of human nature" in Jesus' life, death, and resurrection. The petition asks, "In your mercy, let us share the divine life of Jesus Christ who came to share our humanity." This means, in the light of the full Gospel, that the effect of the Fall has been reversed; human beings no longer are at the mercy of Satan because their status has been restored to the level of full communion with God. The petition is a fitting response to the fuller meaning of incarnation as encompassing the totality of Jesus' life from his birth to his ascension, as well as his continuing incarnation through the Word and Holy Spirit.

The Psalm for the Day — Psalm 111 — A song of thanksgiving for all of the wonderful works that the Lord God has done; "He makes his marvelous works to be remembered." Among these unforgettable actions of God is, of course, the birth of Jesus, which is being remembered and celebrated; "He sent redemption to his people; he commanded his covenant forever; holy and awesome is his name." This collect is also a way of reminding the church that the Christmas celebration continues for twelve days, the Christmas Season; it concludes with the Epiphany, the Twelfth Night of the joyful festivities generated by the nativity of Christ. Subsequently, as the last verse proclaims, "The fear of the Lord is the beginning of wisdom; those who act accordingly have a good understanding. His praise endures forever."

The Psalm Prayer

> *Merciful and gentle Lord, the crowning glory of all the saints, give us, your children, the gift of obedience, which is the beginning of wisdom, so that we may be filled with your mercy and that what you command we may do by the might of Jesus Christ our Lord.*

The readings:

Isaiah 63:7-9

This word from a "later Isaiah" is tailor-made for the First Sunday after Christmas, praising God for "all that the Lord has granted us (in Jesus' incarnation, the church implies), and the great goodness to the house of Israel." The Lord "claims" those he has made in his image as his people, affirming that he (the Messiah) "became their Savior." Jesus entered into all levels of human experience, suffering as all humans suffer, yet *redeeming* humanity through his affliction, rather than withdrawing from the pain and anguish that had to be his in his efforts to loose people from sin, death, and the strangle-hold that Satan has had on humans and their destiny. Isaiah puts it so beautifully:

> *The angel of his presence saved them; in his love and in his pity he redeemed them (obviously not in his birth, but in his life, death, and resurrection); he lifted them up and carried them all the days of old.*

Theologically, this text makes a *kerygmatic connection* with the incarnation event, preparing people for the Galatians reading and Matthew's story about the flight to Egypt.

Galatians 4:4-7

This pericope offers an "amen" to the reading from Isaiah, bringing the Old Testament perspective into the sharp focus of the gospel of Jesus Christ:

> *When the time had fully come, God sent forth his Son, born of woman, born under the law, to redeem those who were under the law, so that we might receive adoption as sons.*

Paul reminds us that the birth of Christ assures us that we have been freed from the bondage we have been in and are empowered through the Holy Spirit to join Jesus in addressing God as he did, "Abba! Father!" Because he has set us free from all that has enslaved us, he has claimed us as his children and made us inheritors of the kingdom through Jesus Christ. Jesus and the kingdom are the gifts that God gives us at Christmas. In this reading, therefore, is the reminder that we are continuing the Christmas celebration this day.

Matthew 2:13-15, 19-23

Matthew is the only one of the four gospel writers to include this lovely, but terrible and puzzling, tale that finds its origin and impetus in another dream that Joseph had and another message delivered to him by an angelic visitor. When the whole story is told (including verses 16-18, which briefly sketch out the gory details of Herod's slaughter of the male children in Bethlehem), it takes on a paradoxical character; God saves his son but, at the same time, allows innocent children to die. If Matthew's purpose were merely to show how Old Testament prophecies found completion in Jesus' incarnation, why didn't he omit this part of the story? Surely, he didn't need to make this connection with the Old Testament reference (Exodus 1:16, 22) to Pharoah's command to the midwives, "throw all the boys born to the Hebrews into the river, but let the girls live." Herod's command to kill all the boy babies under two years of age is a continuation of the Epiphany story when the Wise Men from the East were warned in a dream to avoid Herod on their return journey because he wanted to kill Jesus. Since Matthew was telling this story to a largely-Jewish congregation, it had to stand on historical facts, which attested to the fulfillment of scripture in the early life of Jesus Christ.

Theologically, the dreams of the Wise Men and Joseph, together with the visits by the angels, are indications that God was at work in all that happened when Jesus was born, and that the plan he had put into action would succeed, no matter what forces were arrayed against him. It can be argued that the seeming paradox of Jesus' escape and the death of the boys in Bethlehem is a sign of the kind of trouble that his presence arouses in the world. It is also an indication of the manner in which God will use the death of other innocent persons to accomplish his purposes in the world, just as his plan calls for the sacrifice of the innocent one, his Son, to die to save all of the world. This part of the story declares, when Jesus comes into the world, that God's intentions will be accomplished, no matter what may happen.

A sermon on the Gospel, Matthew 2:13-15, 19-23 — "Refugee Family."

It is always the First Sunday after Christmas, Year A, in our living room. A painting hangs on the north wall of the room, done in batik by a Chinese artist who escaped from mainland China to Taiwan; it tells the Epiphany story. A walled Chinese city forms the background, the landscape is bare and sparse, and the trees have no leaves; it is a stark winter scene. Two figures, one a woman on a donkey, are traveling away from the city; they look like Mary and Joseph — and the child the woman seems to be holding in her arms — as they flee the environs of Bethlehem and Jerusalem to take refuge from Herod in Egypt — is, for us, the baby Jesus. Whether or not this was the intent of the artist, I do not know; it might be a rendition of his own escape from a city in China, his way of telling part of the story of becoming a refugee. But I do know that everyone who sees it is immediately reminded of the familiar biblical story of the "Flight to Egypt." The painting tells the beginning of the story; it does not, cannot, of course, tell the whole story that Matthew relates.

1. The birth and early life of Jesus were surrounded by as much intrigue and tragedy as was the culmination of his life when he was plotted against, betrayed, put on trial for his life, and executed. Wise men, who followed a star to Bethlehem were innocently involved in the plot to kill the baby Jesus by Herod. The very life of Jesus was put in jeopardy by a puppet-king who believed that Christ was a threat to his throne; he ordered the death of all young boys in Jerusalem, hoping to kill Jesus in the process.

2. God took a hand in all of this; he would not, could not, allow his plan for delivering and saving his people to be overturned. He warned the Magi, through a divine visit to them as they dreamed in Bethlehem after they had found the Christ child, to return to their homeland by a different route to avoid Herod. He warned Joseph in another dream that Jesus' life was in danger, and to take Mary and Jesus to Egypt, where — as refugees — they would be safe. He visited Joseph in another dream and told him that it was safe to return to their homeland, guiding him to settle in the town of Nazareth. That's where Jesus was reared as a faithful Jew, the son of Mary and Joseph.

3. God, you see, was the real "star" of the show, the central figure in the story — not the star in the sky that the Wise Men saw and followed, not Joseph, who obeyed God, not the Egyptians, who provided refuge for Joseph, Mary, and Jesus (Matthew tells us nothing at all of the details of their life in Egypt), and certainly not the infamous Herod, whose intention to remove this threat to his reign was totally thwarted. God was the one who engineered the escape to Egypt and caused it to happen according to his plan, which was to protect the life of the Christ child at any cost.

4. That same God is still in charge of the world and all that happens, and he will see to it that the risen Christ is with us, guiding us, protecting us, and giving us salvation, no matter what the cost. No matter how brightly the stars shine at night, God is the "star" of the story of Jesus and all of us.

Note: Preachers seldom have the opportunity to preach the entire story that Matthew tells in any given year. In 1989-90, the Festival of the Holy Innocents occurs on the Thursday

52

before the First Sunday of Christmas and Epiphany comes on the Saturday following this Sunday. Therefore, it seems like good strategy to combine in one sermon the three different Gospels from Matthew 2:1-23 that have been chosen for the three occasions (for the First Sunday after Christmas, the Holy Innocents, Martyrs, and the Epiphany of Our Lord) in order to tell the entire story. Theologically, God is at the center of the entire chapter; he is the protagonist of the story, which raises some questions that are difficult to answer.

Arthur Clarke's classic science fiction story, *The Star,* is a retelling of part of the Matthew 2 story in a futuristic space voyage to the distant star-planet — 3000 light years from earth — that shone in the sky when Jesus was born and led the Magi to the Christ child. When the space explorers landed on the planet and discovered the charred remains of a beautiful civilization, they were able to date the explosion that created the "star of Bethlehem" as 4-6 B.C.; an entire race of intelligent beings and their advance civilization were destroyed by the blast, prompting the Jesuit priest-scientist on board the space ship to ask, as he stands in front of a crucifix: "O God, there were so many others stars you could have used. What was the need to give these people to the fire, that the symbol of their passing might shine above Bethlehem (when Christ was born)?" If God is the author of this story, why didn't, why couldn't, God save the baby boys of Bethlehem? That seems to be Clarke's question, doesn't it? I suggest that the whole story should be read and told in the sermon on the First Sunday after Christmas.

A sermon on the Gospels for Holy Innocents Day and the First Sunday after Christmas, Matthew 2:1-23 — "Long Live the King of the Jews."

1. The star was real; "The Gleam of a Star Was There" a poem by an unknown poet:

What of the night, was the moon adrift,
Was the galaxy unveiled or fair?
Only this man knew of that sky long ago,
The gleam of a star was there.

And it did its work, leading the Magi to Jerusalem — and Herod — and then to Bethlehem, where the baby Jesus was located.

2. Herod, the insecure king, decides that Jesus must die. *That was when Jesus was actually condemned to death, although it took thirty-three years before the death sentence was executed* outside Jerusalem, only a few miles from where he was born. God stepped into the picture and intervened in the person of an angel who told Joseph what was about to happen and what to do. Joseph obeyed and took Mary and Jesus to Egypt.

3. The atrocity committed by Herod — having all boy babies in and around Bethlehem killed in order to protect his insecure hold on the throne — makes God out to be something less than God. He is more like an earthly parent intent on protecting his or her own offspring, regardless of how many other children may be lost to whatever threatens their existence. Is this, too, a foreshadowing of the death of the innocent victim, Jesus Christ? Is it a sign of the rivers of innocent blood that will be spilled so that the gospel might be preached throughout the world? This much we know: awful as this episode is, it is an integral part of the story and has been duplicated in the noble army of martyrs in every century of the Christian era. (The Arthur Clarke story could be used in this section of the sermon.)

4. God provided for the Holy Family and protected them until Herod died (he apparently was never punished for his crime) and it was time to bring them back to their homeland. Again, God employed a dream and an angelic visit to get his message to Joseph. And, once more, Joseph obeyed in true faith and took his family to Nazareth, which became the place where Jesus was reared. God's word gives us protection and guidance to live faithfully and safely as his people.

An Old Testament sermon, Isaiah 63:7-9 — "In Memory of God."

1. The God of the Christmas story is a *caring and concerned God,* who sends his Son, Messiah, into the world to redeem his people.

2. He is a *God of love and mercy,* who will go to any lengths in order to save the world through his Son. In his incarnation he entered into "their affliction (and) he was afflicted" — suffering death on the cross on their/our behalf.

3. As God "he lifted them up and carried them" through the Exodus into the Holy Land and, now, through the death and resurrection, he transports believers into new life in Christ.

4. Psalm 111 offers a fitting conclusion for a sermon on this reading:

Hallelujah!
I will give thanks to the Lord
with my whole heart,
in the assembly of the upright,
in the congregation.

(Note: This psalm virtually begs to be combined with the First Lesson and allowed to become a full-blown sermon for this day.)

A sermon on the Second Lesson, Galatians 4:4-7 — "No Accidental Birth."

1. The pregnancy of Mary and the birth of Christ were no accident; God had planned this, according to Paul, from the beginning of time (he says, "But when the time had fully come, God sent forth his son, born of woman.").

2. Christ had to be born under the law — as a human being — in order to accomplish God's purpose, "To redeem those who were born under the law." This, Paul knows, will cost him his life.

3. Believers become "sons," or "children," of God by the sacrifice of Christ, and they are no longer slaves to Satan and sin. They are heirs, through Christ, of the Kingdom of God, and they are able — through the Holy Spirit — to dare to address their God and Father, "Abba! Father!", in confidence and faith, as Jesus did.

The Epiphany of Our Lord

Roman Catholic	Isaiah 60:1-6	Ephesians 3:2-3a, 5-6	Matthew 2:1-12
Episcopal	Isaiah 60:1-6, 9	Ephesians 3:1-12	Matthew 2:1-12
Lutheran	Isaiah 60:1-6	Ephesians 3:2-12	Matthew 2:1-12
Common	Isaiah 60:1-6	Ephesians 3:1-12	Matthew 2:1-12

The church year theological clue

The Epiphany was originally a unitive festival, an observation of Jesus' birth, his baptism, and the first miracle he performed at Cana; Coelius Sedulius' fifth century hymn, "When Christ's Appearing Was Made Known," (Hymn 85, LBW) illustrates this three-fold nature of the Epiphany. Twelfth Night now concludes the Christmas season, the First Sunday after the Epiphany commemorates the Baptism of Our Lord, and the first miracle at Cana is assigned to the Second Sunday after the Epiphany only in Cycle/Year C. As it is now constituted, the liturgical function of this festival, which brings the lections into homiletical focus, is to celebrate Jesus' incarnation as God's revelation as Messiah and to affirm that he came into the world for the benefit of all people; he comes to do for humanity what persons cannot do for themselves, to win salvation for them.

The Prayer of the Day — A classic collect that has again been modernized in language ("nations" instead of "Gentiles," "glory" rather than "beauty," etc.), but retains the basic theme and evangelical theology of Epiphany ("revealed your Son by the leading of a star") and its eschatological thrust ("to know your presence in our lives" and "bring us at last to the full vision of your glory"). Hence, the collect puts the Nativity and details of the infancy story of Christ into proper perspective by addressing the prayer to the "Lord God."

The Psalm of the Day — Psalm 72 — This psalm was first used on the Second Sunday in Advent, but for a slightly different purpose. Verse 7 is highlighted during Advent, "In his time shall the righteous flourish; there shall be an abundance of peace till the moon shall be no more," but verse 11 is emphasized for the Epiphany, "All kings shall bow down before him, and all the nations do him service." When these verses are used as antiphons on the Second Sunday in Advent and for the Epiphany of Our Lord, respectively, they accent different themes in the psalm by bringing them into sharp relief. The first reveals what the reign of the "king's son" will be like, while the second points out the scope of his reign. It should also be noted that verses 15-19 are optional in the Advent selection, but the whole psalm is appointed for Epiphany.

The Psalm Prayer

> *Almighty God, you gave the kingdom of justice and peace to David and his descendant, our Lord Jesus Christ. Extend this kingdom to every nation, so that through your Son the poor may receive justice, the destitute relief, and the people of the earth peace in the name of him who lives and reigns with you and the Holy Spirit, one God, now and forever.*

The readings:

Isaiah 60:1-6

The church has taken this pericope, which originally referred to Israel's return from the exile in Babylon, and put it into a Christian context. Jesus, to the church, is the "light (that) has come," and in him God's "glory is rising on you (and the whole world." Christ is the light that shines in the darkness and the one to whom all nations shall come. He has staked his claim in the world; all people and all things are his, gold and incense will be brought to him, and the name of God will be praised. After all, it is God who delivered the Israelites from the captivity in Babyon, and it is God who has sent Jesus into the world to free all people from sin and bring to the earth the kingdom of God. (Note: In the older Roman missal, as well as some Lutheran lectionaries, this reading was employed as the epistle for the Epiphany. Archbishop Cranmer was probably the first one to replace this lesson with a New Testament epistle. His choice was Ephesians 3.)

Ephesians 3:1-12

Paul makes the connection between Isaiah 60 and the Epiphany itself clear, and he understands his mission to be to communicate the good news of God's revelation, his light, in Jesus' advent, and to declare to the "nations" — Gentiles, as well as Jews — that salvation has come through the grace of God in Christ and that it is meant for all. Just as John the Baptizer was close to death when he sent his disciples to Jesus, asking, "Are you the one who should come, or should we look for someone else?", so Paul was close to death when he sent this letter with one of his disciples to the church at Ephesus. The difference between them — and both of them died the same way, by being beheaded — was that John was uncertain about the identity of Jesus Christ while Paul was absolutely positive that Jesus was the Christ of God, the long-awaited Messiah. He had not only been party to the establishment of the church, but he had also witnessed to the now-elusive unity of the church that brought Jew and Gentile into the body of Christ.

The Gospel — Matthew 2:1-12

This is the third section of Matthew 2 to be used in the lectionary but, chronologically, it is the very beginning of the Epiphany story. In Matthew's year, it is used with about the same frequency as the pericope for the Holy Innocents Day; the reading (verses 13-18) for the First Sunday after Christmas is read every three years, and is, therefore, treated homiletically more often than the other two parts of Chapter 2. Matthew incorporates the various signs — the star that led the Magi to Jerusalem and Bethlehem, the gifts they brought and presented to the Child, Bethlehem, Herod, etc. — and divine visitations, replete with angels who give warnings and guidance to the Magi and, later, to Joseph. The point of the story is to show how Jesus *is* the Epiphany, God's revelation of himself and his intentions for the entire world.

A sermon on the Gospel, Matthew 2:1-12 — "The Star that Shines Forever."

Phyllis McGinley, in *Stones from a Glass House*, published a poem which, despite some biblical inaccuracies, demonstrates that she understands what the Epiphany is all about:

In Palestine, in Palestine,
The flocks unsheltered sleep.
Though night-long still,
On every hill,
A watch the shepherds keep.

And people walk with living fear,
Lest singing as it fell,
Should shine upon some midnight clear,
The star that is a shell.

Hanging on the wall beside my desk, is a painting by a former student, Pastor Ron Bock, showing a shepherd on a very dark night, with sheep gathered around his feet, his shepherd's crook over his head, looking up, obviously in wonder, at a single bright star in the sky. Epiphany is real and true — the star is no "shell" — because God sent Jesus into the world to fulfill his long-standing promise of a Messiah. The story of the star, which was the same star the shepherds had seen, inspired and led the Magi "from the east" to Jerusalem and an audience with King Herod, finally directed them to Bethlehem, where they found the baby Jesus, worshipped him, and gave him gold, frankincense, and myrrh. That it was God's will that they should have a part in this drama receives impetus from God's intervention by way of a dream that sent them home by a route that would avoid another meeting with Herod, in order to protect the Christ child from a jealous, if not mad, despot. Our spiritual stance, for Epiphany and its season, is that of those who watch, wonder, and worship.

1. The Epiphany Star is no "shell;" through it, God beckoned Magi "from the east," not merely as star-watchers who might only wonder about it, but to travel to Jerusalem/Bethlehem to find and worship the child born as "the King of the Jews."

2. The star continues — through the Word — to shine in the darkness of the world to light up the way out of earth's night into the new day, through Jesus Christ, which brings believers to full communion with God, the Father.

> *As a star, God's holy Word*
> *Leads us to our King and Lord;*
> *Brightly from its sacred pages*
> *Shall this light throughout the ages*
> *Shine upon our path of life.*

(Verse 6 of Nikolai Grundtvig's hymn "Bright and Glorious is the Sky," Hymn 75, LBW).

3. In the full light of the day, "the star that is no shell" shines and makes the day brighter as it reflects the glory of the Lord God in Jesus Christ so that as we worship him, we give him the gift of ourselves.

4. The church exists as a fellowship of believers who worship Jesus Christ, their Lord and Savior, but who also tell the story of Jesus to others so that the star might also shine upon them and light up the darkness of their lives.

An Old Testament sermon, Isaiah 60 — "The Son and God's Morning."

1. In Jesus Christ, the light of the Lord has surely come upon the earth; a new day is dawning.

2. Sin has been defeated by Jesus' perfect obedience, but its darkness has yet to be eradicated from the world.

3. As the Good News is told to all people, more and more will turn and "come to Christ," their Lord and God.

4. That great day is coming when everyone who exists will bring gifts to Christ and sing praises to the God who is Creator and Father of all.

A Second Lesson sermon, Ephesians 3:1-12 — "The 'Swan Song' of a Faithful Apostle."

1. The mystery of the gospel was incarnate in Paul. Probably a prisoner facing execution in Rome, he sings his "swan song" about the glorious gospel which has been entrusted to him. He is faithful to Christ, when a word or two of denial could save his life.

2. With the revelation of God's mystery in the person of Jesus Christ, the secrets of God's plan of salvation are made known to all who hear the gospel; Christ came for the sake of the whole wide world.

3. Through the grace of God, all who believe are made members of the church, the body of Christ, and come to know how great God really is.

4. Epiphany teaches us to sing a new song, even a "swan song," if we must.

The Baptism of Our Lord
First Sunday after the Epiphany
First Sunday in Ordinary Time

Roman Catholic	Isaiah 42:1-4, 6-7	Acts 10:34-38	Matthew 3:13-17
Episcopal	Isaiah 42:1-9	Acts 10:34-38	Matthew 3:13-17
Lutheran	Isaiah 42:1-4	Acts 10:34-38	Matthew 3:13-17
Common	Isaiah 42:1-4	Acts 10:34-38	Matthew 3:13-17

The church year theological clue

The theological intention in giving the baptism of Jesus its own special day, the First Sunday after the Epiphany, rather than attempting to restore it to January 6 and reconstruct Epiphany as a unitive event, is several fold: first, it is an important part of the incarnation, as a reaffirmation by God that this man was the Holy Child born in Bethlehem three decades or so in the past; second, Jesus has come to bring in the Kingdom of God and save all people through the forgiveness of their sins by his perfect obedience to the Father; and, third, the church intends the faithful to gain better comprehension of the meaning and importance of baptism in their lives. God claims us, as he did Jesus Christ, by assuring those who have been baptized "in the name of the Father, and of the Son, and of the Holy Spirit," "You are my beloved children." He also forgives our sins in Jesus, delivers us from Satan, and promises us eternal life.

The Prayer of the Day (LBW) — This collect compresses the details of the story of Jesus' baptism into a single sentence, "at the baptism of Jesus in the River Jordan you proclaimed him your beloved Son and anointed him with the Holy Spirit." It proceeds, then, to connect our baptism with that of Jesus Christ, asking God to "make all who are baptized into Christ faithful in their calling to be your children and inheritors with him of everlasting life." It makes Jesus' baptism a present reality that has implications for our baptisms and our baptismal lives, not simply something that occurred in the past and might be easily forgotten.

The Psalm of the Day (LBW) — Psalm 45:7-9 — Here is a song that the Christian — or the Jew, for that matter — can come to love because it sets one to singing and speaking the praises of the Anointed One of God. For Luther, it had implications for the oral nature of preaching the Word; he said, of himself and with the psalmist (v. 1), "My tongue shall be the pen of a skilled writer." The LBW excises the very heart of this psalm (vv. 7,8) and appoints it as a responsory to the Old Testament reading, focusing attention upon God's presence and actions in Jesus' baptism:

Your throne, O God,
endures forever and ever,
    a scepter of righteousness
    is the scepter of your kingdom;
    you love righteousness
    and hate iniquity.

Therefore God, your God,
has anointed you
    with the oil of gladness
    above your fellows.

The psalmist comes close to saying, "This is my beloved Son, with whom I am well pleased."

The Psalm Prayer

> *Lord God, you have formed the holy Church to be the bride of Christ. Grant to your Church the faith and peace she will need to do your will and to show your glory, through your Son, Jesus Christ our Lord.*

The readings:

Isaiah 42:1-9

This passage sets forth the first two of the "servant songs" that are the work of the writer known as Second Isaiah. They speak of an unknown servant of God who is a "type" of Jesus the Messiah; the content of these two songs quickly found its way into the New Testament writings, particularly the accounts of Jesus' baptism. Although there is controversy about the translation of key portions of this text (as in verse 1, "my servant whom I uphold, my chosen one in whom my soul delights;" some would prefer "son" to "servant," or insist, at least, that one is equivalent to the other), there is general agreement that Isaiah 42 speaks pointedly to Jesus' baptism by John in the Jordan. Isaiah believes that Yahweh's "servant" will be endowed with God's Spirit and will bring God's justice to all nations; he has come — in Jesus — to be related to all people, not just to the Israelites. All of this speaks to the baptismal scene in which Jesus seeks baptism from John "to fulfill all righteousness" (or justice) and is identified by the Spirit of God "descending on him" and a voice from heaven, "This is my beloved Son, with whom I am well pleased." The theology of Christian baptism is here, and the concept of the baptismal covenant finds its origin here, too, in "I have given you as a covenant to the people, a light to the nations." Verses 6b and 7 have found their way into Matthew 11 in Jesus' answer to John's question, "Are you the one who is to come, or shall we look for another?"

Acts 10:34-38

This text was appointed for this day to underline the fact that God had actually anointed Jesus when the Spirit descended upon him after he came up out of the Jordan. In response, Jesus "went about doing good and healing all that were oppressed by the devil." Peter understood that Jesus was Lord of all and, as such, was a historical personage as well as the "Jesus of faith." This text, as an integral part of Cornelius' baptism, clearly implies that Christian baptism conveys the forgiveness of sins upon those who receive it. It grounds baptism in our lives as an action of God that is intended for all people, and which is validated by Jesus' death and resurrection. The church accepts Peter's speech about Jesus' baptism and, especially, his anointing as the Son of God, and allows him to speak about baptism to the faithful on this occasion when the Baptism of Our Lord is celebrated.

Matthew 3:13-17

This pericope is Matthew's version of the Baptism of Jesus in the Jordan River by John the Baptizer. The story causes consternation, at first, because it seems to suggest that if Jesus sought baptism, he must be a sinner, too. The dialogue between John and Jesus corrects any misapprehension that people may have about this matter; Jesus' baptism really represents his "oneness" with the Father and his sinlessness in all things. The uniqueness of his baptism, in contrast to all the other baptisms — and there must have been many of them done by John — is that "the heavens were opened" and the Spirit of God (descended) like a dove and alighting on him (Jesus)" accompanied by a voice which said, "This is my beloved Son, with whom I am well pleased." For all time and for every person, God identifies Jesus Christ as the one he has sent into the world to initiate the coming of the Kingdom of God and to restore humanity, through the forgiveness of sins in his death and resurrection, to a right relationship with God, creator and loving Father.

A Sermon on the Gospel — "Not a Silent Sacrament."

It happens with some regularity in our neighborhood. We live across a lake from a Baptist-oriented college which sponsors several religious conferences during the summer. Their beach area on the lake is used for several purposes — swimming, canoeing, fishing, and, on some occasions, even for baptisms. At the annual neighborhood summer picnic held recently, one of the hosts suddenly ran into his home and reappeared with a couple pairs of binoculars. "There was a baptism over there last week," he declared, pointing to the beach that was about a quarter mile away, "and it looks like another is going to take place today." Sure enough, a considerable crowd had gathered and, as we watched — most of us without binoculars — several people went into the water. We could hear nothing, but we could see almost everything that occurred, even from that distance. But we didn't have to hear because we knew what the minister was saying when he immersed several people, one by one, in the lake; "I baptize you in the name of the Father, and of the Son, and of the Holy Spirit. Amen." After the baptisms were completed, the baptismal party walked out of the water and the newly-baptized persons were greeted by the onlookers with obvious joy and celebration.

In the congregation of which I am a member, one can determine when baptisms are going to be administered without looking at the Sunday bulletin. All one has to do is look at the pulpit, and if the small baptismal banner is hanging there, a silent signal announces that the sacrament will be an integral part of the worship service. The banner has a place to display the name, or names, of the one, or ones, to be baptized that day, plus the wording of the baptismal declaration, "(Name) _____, child of God, you have been sealed by the Holy Spirit and marked with the cross of Christ forever." The Sacrament of Baptism, in that building, is, quite often, anything but silent. The words can be heard all over the building and the congregation is usually aware of the sound of the water being poured on the head of the person being baptized. And the silent announcement on the baptismal banner becomes a spoken word for all of the baptized when the minister says, "You have been sealed by the Holy Spirit and marked with the cross of Christ forever."

1. Jesus' baptism seems to have been a silent baptism; John is reported to have said nothing during the baptism itself. He "had his say" before the baptism when he said to Jesus, "It is I who need baptism from you." John recognized Jesus as the Messiah, the one who was coming to Israel, and confessed his sinful nature to the sinless one. Sinners are the ones who need baptism, or need to have their baptisms renewed through confession and communion at the table of the Lord.

2. But Jesus' baptism was not a silent one. God was the one who spoke when our Lord was baptized; he was the only one who had the right to say anything. He declared to the world, "This is my beloved Son, with whom I am well pleased," and by that revelatory action turned the baptism into an epiphany, a manifestation of Christ as God's Son to the world. It is always God who does the speaking in baptism; he claims us through the ancient formula and, without speaking a word audibly in the service, announces, "You are my son, my daughter" to every person who is baptized. ("_____, child of God, you have been sealed by the Holy Spirit and marked with the cross of Christ forever.")

3. God speaks and sets us apart for himself and his purposes in our baptism, and he offers us the strength to live in this vital relationship with him and the Son through the power of the Holy Spirit working in our lives. Precisely because we, too, are the sons and daughters of God, temptation will come our way in powerful and insidious forms that seek to turn us from the way of the Lord, but God offers help to resist the temptation to fall away from him and to remain faithful as long as we live. (Note: Verse 1 of chapter 4 of Matthew's gospel is necessary to the completion of this sermon, especially in the light of Satan's word to Christ, "If you are the Son of God," followed by the three "temptations.")

4. The baptismal font stands always as a silent witness to the sacrament in which God has spoken and claimed us as his people. It reminds us that we live by the power of the Holy Spirit, allowing God to allay any doubts we may have that Jesus really is the Son of God and has taken away the sin of the world — of each one of us — and has promised to be with us all until the end of time. (The central theme of Matthew.)

A First Lesson sermon — "A Son and a Servant."

1. The sending of a servant in whom the Lord God delights (over against the Word spoken at Jesus' baptism, "This is my beloved son, in whom I am well pleased.") is good news, indeed. Humanity needs divine help to cope with sin and death — and live the godly life. *God's son will come as the servant* of God and his people.

2. God has announced these things through his prophet before they are to appear. He has brought them into reality in the appearance of Jesus Christ of whom he said, "This is my beloved Son." *His baptism is the sign that the Son has become a servant* and will do God's bidding on earth.

3. *The servant comes to establish justice on the earth.* This is the work that God has determined that his servant/son shall do in the world. And God will see to it that the work gets done. The servant is certain to suffer, even die, despite all the good that is done for people.

4. *The servant/son is God's covenant with all nations;* as their light, he will open the eyes of the spiritually blind, free captives from the prison that sin is, as well as those who live in darkness of death. That is the description of the Christian life, as well as the life of Christ.

A Second Lesson sermon — "Synopsis of a Sermon."

1. *Jesus is the anointed one of God,* sent into the world to bring into reality God's plan for dealing with sinful humanity.

2. *Jesus is the man for all people;* God intended his ministry to be a saving work for every creature who ever lived on earth.

3. *Jesus restores goodness to the world* by refusing to do evil, going about doing good, and blessing all with whom he comes into contact by his gracious words and compassionate deeds.

4. *Jesus' good intentions and obedience cost him his life,* but the Lord God raised him up so that the work he came to do might ultimately be finished.

5. *Jesus is the Lord of all,* and he, the resurrected and ascended Lord, has begun his heavenly reign, which will be extended throughout all the world at God's signal. Come, Lord Jesus!

Second Sunday after the Epiphany
Second Sunday in Ordinary Time

Roman Catholic	Isaiah 49:3, 5-6	1 Corinthians 1:1-3	John 1:29-34
Episcopal	Isaiah 49:1-7	1 Corinthians 1:1-9	John 1:29-41
Lutheran	Isaiah 49:1-6	1 Corinthians 1:1-9	John 1:29-41
Common	Isaiah 49:1-7	1 Corinthians 1:1-9	John 1:29-41

The church year theological clue

A careful examination of the readings appointed for this and the other Sundays of Epiphany in the three-year cycle reveals that something is different; a radical change has been made; the three lessons are not in harmony, because the Corinthian letters make up the Second Lessons for virtually all of the Sundays after the Baptism of Our Lord. This same pattern of readings is picked up again on the Second Sunday after Pentecost, so that in the other Sundays of Epiphany and Pentecost the church year theme is muted more or less. But on the Sundays after the Epiphany, the theme of Jesus' *manifestation and identity* is expressed in the first readings and the Gospels, is quite clear. On this particular Sunday, the intention of church year and the liturgical material is to announce that Jesus Christ came into the world to save all people from their sins. This is the theological and, therefore, the liturgical/homiletical clue for the Second Sunday after the Epiphany.

The Prayer of the Day (LBW) — This is a genuine Epiphany prayer, which emphasizes the continuation of the manifestation theme in the worship during the Epiphany season — "Lord God, you showed your glory" (in Jesus Christ) — and introduces the ministry of Jesus in the world by mentioning its results — "and led many to faith by the works of your Son." The second sentence of the prayer reverses these, speaking of Jesus' work today in relation to his work before his suffering, death, and resurrection — "As he brought gladness and healing to his people, grant us these same gifts." The climax of the prayer asks for another gift — "and lead us also to perfect faith in him."

The Psalm of the Day (LBW) — Psalm 40:1-12 — If nothing else, this psalm offers the people of God a pattern for prayer that is worth adopting. The faithful begin their prayers with praise to God for all he has done, then offer thanksgiving for his goodness and grace, and only then do they offer their petitions to God for the needs of all people and themselves. At the time the Bible was written, the psalm was considered to be more than a model for public and private devotions; it had messianic implications for the Hebrew nation, hence the incorporation of verses 7-9 in the book of Hebrews (10:5-10). The psalm contains a picture of the "rescue God," as God is called in a novel by Robert Flynn, *The Sounds of Rescue, the Signs of Hope* — "I waited patiently upon the Lord; he stooped to me and heard my cry. He lifted me out of the desolate pit . . . he set my feet upon a high cliff and made my footing sure." Surely, the church can sing with the writer of the psalm, "He put a new song in my mouth, a song of praise to our God . . . . Happy are those who trust in the Lord."

The heart of the song suggests to Christians that Christ will replace the sacrificial system of the Temple with himself and his own sacrifice ("the Lamb, who will take away the sin of the world"). No doubt about it, the church has long considered this to be a messianic psalm that is suitable for use during the Epiphany season.

The Psalm Prayer

Lord Jesus Christ, you became obedient to death and your name was exalted above all others. Teach us always to do the Father's will, so that, made holy by your obedience and united to your sacrifice, we can know your great love in times of sorrow and sing a new song to our God, now and forever.

The readings:

Isaiah 49:1-6

This is the tenth pericope in a row that has employed Isaiah for the First Lesson, which means that Isaiah is used more in the first two thirds of the Christmas cycle than is the Gospel of the year, Matthew. The several lectionaries assign readings from Isaiah to the third, the fifth, and the eighth Sundays after the Epiphany while the Lutheran and Common lectionaries celebrate the Transfiguration on the Eighth Sunday after the Epiphany (the Last Sunday after the Epiphany this year), rather than on August 6.

This reading from Isaiah is the second "servant song," which continues to speak, from the Christian point of view, of Jesus' manifestation to the world as one called by God before his birth who could say, "from the body of my mother he named my name." Later in the prophet, he says, "And now the Lord says, who formed me from the womb to be his servant, to bring Jacob back to him, and that Israel might be gathered to him." But this "servant," whose work in the world is to restore the Hebrew people to a right relationship to their God, is to become a "light to the nations, that my (God's) salvation may reach to the end of the earth."

1 Corinthians 1:1-3

After his customary greeting to the church at Corinth, which has some misconceptions, even delusions of grandeur, about itself as *the* church, Paul reminds the Corinthian Christians that they are part of a larger fellowship than the one they enjoy in Corinth; their ecclesiology was flawed and their polity was deficient. But Paul also reminds them of the grace they have received in Jesus Christ, of the fine and faithful preachers and teachers they have had, of the gifts of the Holy Spirit, which will strengthen their faith and give them hope as they await the return of the Lord. In conjunction with the gifts of the Holy Spirit, he remarks, "the testimony to Christ was confirmed among you." Despite the independent way that the Corinthian correspondence is read during Epiphany, this Epistle is tailor-made to fit between the reading of Isaiah and the Gospel for the Day, John 1:29-41, and it is especially suited for congregations which consider themselves to be independent churches who have no connections with, or need of, the rest of the holy catholic church.

The Holy Gospel, John 1:29-41

Here is additional evidence that the child born at Christmas, who was baptized as an adult by John the Baptizer, is the Messiah. John the Evangelist gives no details about the baptism of Jesus, any more than he does about the birth of Christ, but he does supply more of a narrative as he shows John the Baptizer as a witness to the coming of Christ to the world and to his identification as Messiah. The Baptizer declared, "Behold, the Lamb of God, who takes away the sin of the world." Jesus is the one John preached, "After me comes a man who ranks before me." He was also witness to the fact that Jesus came to him for baptism, that he knew him because God had informed him that "He on whom you see the

Spirit descend and remain . . . baptizes with the Holy Spirit.'' (John 1:33) John declares that he had actually seen this man anointed by God, and he is convinced that Jesus is the Messiah. The purpose of this Gospel is to encourage the church to reflect once more, with some theological comprehension, on the birth and baptism of Jesus the Christ, and to comprehend that confessing Christ as the Son of God places the demands of the faith — following Christ obediently and as a servant — upon believers. That's what happened to two of John's disciples, when John pointed ''the Lamb of God'' out to them; they became disciples and followed him.

A sketch that, with work and prayer, could become an effective Sermon on the Gospel, John 1:29-41 — "Testimony Time."

''Testimony time'' is a device that several of the television evangelists use when they develop their programs; a guest will be invited to testify to his or her experience of Jesus Christ. It is apparently quite effective, because it brings the gospel into the realm of human experience and builds up the faith by making it concrete and incarnate, in a person. In this gospel, ''testimony time'' it is presented in biblical perspective; John the Baptizer is the one who testifies. It takes the shape of a compelling drama.

The setting: A delegation of priests and Levites, dispatched by the Pharisees to question John the Baptizer, confronts him at Bethany, ''on the far side of the Jordan.'' John testifies, first, about himself in answer to their question, ''Who are you?'' He tells them that he is not the Christ, nor Elijah, nor the Prophet, but a ''voice'' crying, ''Make straight the way for the Lord.'' He also has to answer their second question, which was about his business, ''Why are you baptizing, (then)?'' His answer: ''I baptize with water; but there stands among you — unknown to you — the one who is coming after me; and I am not fit to undo his sandal.''

Scene one: The next day — Jesus appears and is identified, apparently, to the priests and Levites as ''the Lamb of God, who takes away the sin of the world.'' John's speech:

1. ''This is the one I spoke of . . . .''

2. ''(He) ranks before me because he existed before me.''

3. ''I did not know him myself, and yet it was to reveal him to Israel that I came baptizing with water.''

4. ''I saw the Spirit coming down on him from heaven like a dove and resting on him.'' This was how John knew Jesus' identity (''He who sent me to baptize with water had said to me, 'He on whom you see the Spirit descend and remain is he who baptizes with the Holy Spirit.' '')

5. ''I have seen and I am the witness that he is the Chosen One of God.''

(Develop the Law/Gospel dialectic in this text. John didn't forget his role as ''witness'' to the coming of Christ, ''the Lamb of God, who takes away the sin of the world;'' he never once sought to play God or thought himself to be the Lord's anointed one. He went about his business for God and waited for the Father to reveal his Son to him. Don't we, too often, confuse our identities, our roles and work in the business of Christ and the church, let alone forget that Jesus came ''to take away the sin of the world?'' Don't we, too often, forget that we are sinners in need of forgiveness and deliverance from death and the devil?)

Scene two: The next (third) day — Jesus appears again, this time to John and two of his disciples, to whom John says, ''Behold, the Lamb of God.''

1. The disciples desert John the Baptizer and follow Jesus Christ.

2. Jesus asks them, ''What do you want?''

3. They answer, ''Rabbi, where do you live?'' (Seeking an invitation to spend some time with him?)

4. ''Come and see,'' Jesus replies. They do and spend the day with Christ.

5. The evangelist doesn't report what happened, only the result: they became Jesus' disciples, and Andrew, one of the two, went to find his brother, Simon, and told him, "We have found the Messiah."

The homiletical development begs the preacher to correct Andrew's theology — "We have found the Messiah" — for contemporary believers, because we never "find" Christ; we are always "found by him," as in the hymn:

I sought the Lord, and afterward I knew,
    He moved my soul to seek him, seeking me.
It was not I who found, O Saviour true;
No, I was found of Thee.

The final scene: Christ comes to us in the witness of John the Baptizer, the Evangelists, and other New Testament witnesses, through the testimony of the church triumphant and militant, through family, friends, and people we don't really know. And he most certainly comes to us in his precious Word and in the blessed sacraments of the church. He is indeed the Lamb of God, who takes away the sin of the world. *Epiphany is all of the different ways that Christ comes to us to make us his own people.*

A multi-text sermon — *"The Singers of Servant Songs."*

1. Isaiah sings of a person who was *born to be God's servant in the world,* and a light to the nations of the world. The course of his life was determined and charted by God before his birth. He could have been singing about the Chirst, couldn't he? His song "fits" Jesus.

2. Paul writes of the savior, Jesus Christ, who has appeared, and is Lord of the church here on earth. Jesus is God's gift to the church and the world. Our business is to respond to God's grace, as Paul did, with thanksgiving and dedicated service to God and his people.

3. John the Baptizer testifies that Jesus is the one sent by God who comes after him. He alone is the holy one, whose sinlessness and perfect obedience to God cause us to cry out, "Lord, have mercy and forgive our sins." (Lavin, in Tolstoy's *Anna Karenina,* when his wife is ill and her life is in jeopardy puts that emotion in our hearts and the words in our mouths. He reminds us, as he cries out a "Kyrie, Eleison," that we are the ones who are "sick" and need Christ's deliverance.)

4. The Christ we need has come to us in the only way that will be beneficial to humanity — he comes as a servant, the servant of God — to save us — and, we know, he suffered for taking up the servant's role.

A sermon for the First Lesson, Isaiah 49:1-6 — *"The Song of the Savior."*

1. Put into the mouth of Christ, this is the antiphonal response of Jesus to Mary's lovely song, "The Magnificat" — "My soul magnifies the Lord . . . henceforth all generations will call me blessed." Jesus answers, "The Lord called me from the womb, from the body of my mother he named my name."

2. Christ was called to be a servant, and he knew that that was his God-given destiny. But at least once in his life, he wondered, with Isaiah, if he had "labored in vain" and "spent my strength for nothing and vanity," when he cried out from the cross, "My God, why have you forsaken me?" That gives us cause for reflection and repentance, doesn't it?

3. In the guise of a servant, Christ became a light to the nations to take salvation to the ends of the earth. He called himself a servant but also said, "I am the light of the world."

4. Jesus had to serve by dying on the cross in order to fulfill his mission and bring light and life to all people.

A sermon on the Second Lesson, 1 Corinthians 1:1-9 — "The Communion of Saints."

1. *Every congregation is a communion of saints.* Despite their theological problems and practical difficulties, many of which are not unknown to contemporary congregations, the church at Corinth was really a communion — *a community* — of saints. So is every Christian congregation.

2. *God, in Jesus Christ, is a saint-maker.* No believer becomes a saint on his or her own merits; saints are made by the grace of God, who calls people to Jesus Christ and incorporates them into the church, the communion of saints. God sanctifies his people in Jesus Christ.

3. God keeps his saints alive in the faith, so that they may face anything in life knowing that they are not on their own, but that Jesus Christ knows and is always with his own saints.

Third Sunday of the Epiphany
Third Sunday in Ordinary Time

Roman Catholic	Isaiah 8:23—9:3	1 Corinthians 1:10-13, 17	Matthew 4:12-23
Episcopal	Amos 3:1-8	1 Corinthians 1:10-17	Matthew 4:12-23
Lutheran	Isaiah 9:1b-4	1 Corinthians 1:10-17	Matthew 4:12-23
Common	Isaiah 9:1-4	1 Corinthians 1:10-17	Matthew 4:12-23

The church year theological clue

The liturgical/homiletical clue provided for the Third Sunday after the Epiphany combines *manifestation and ministry* within the overall Christmas Cycle clues of *incarnation* and *Parousia.* Jesus comes as the light of the world in his ministry. As the Epiphany Season progresses, however, some of the sharpness of definition is lost, not so much because the theological framework of the church year is blurred, but mostly because the *lectio selecta* method for the selection and reading of the Gospels changes to a modified *lectio continua* — semi-continuous system on this Sunday in the Second Lessons. The preacher ought to be aware that this Sunday's second reading begins where last Sunday's lesson left off, and that next Sunday's text skips from the twentieth verse of 1 Corinthians (the end of today's reading) to 1 Corinthians 1:26-31. This same pattern of reading lessons continuously, or semi-continuously, from 1 and 2 Corinthians applies to Years A, B, and C. This is related to the Roman Catholic usage of naming these Sundays *Ordinary Time.*

The Prayer of the Day (LBW) — This prayer highlights the "ministry motif" in the preaching and teaching dimensions at the beginning of Jesus' public life; he came to call people to repentance and proclaim the imminence of the Kingdom of God. It is also a prayer of *involvement,* which asks God to anoint us so that, we, too, might carry on that ministry by taking good news to the afflicted, ministering to the broken-hearted, and proclaiming liberty to the captives. The Prayer of the Day seems to suggest a tropological treatment of the Gospels by the preachers, wherein the Word is turned toward the people. Of course, preaching always must face up to that task, if it is to be effective proclaimation of the Word.

The Psalm for the Day (LBW) — Psalm 27:1-9 — "The Lord is my light and my salvation" is at once a title but also expresses the theme of the entire psalm and of Epiphany, as well. For the whole world, as well as for Christians, the coming of the Christ means that light has entered into the realm of human experience. David, who probably wrote this psalm, was in obvious difficulty (fleeing from Absolom?), but (because he has "seen the light"?) he knows that God will see him through his difficult time. Countless saints and martyrs have recited this psalm, turning it into a prayer when life-threatening situations come upon them. It also expresses the longing that spiritually-sensitive people, who have experienced the "graceful" support of God in their trials and tribulations, have for permanent fellowship with God, and the confidence they have that God will sustain them forever. "Therefore," says the psalmist — and Christians and Jews, too — "I will offer in his dwelling an oblation, with sounds of great gladness; I will sing and make music to the Lord."

The Psalm Prayer

> *Gracious Father, protector of those who hope in you: You heard the cry of your Son and kept him safe in your shelter in the day of evil. Grant that your servants who seek you face in times of trouble may see your goodness in the land of the living, through your Son, Jesus Christ our Lord.*

68

The readings:

Isaiah 9:1b-4

This is, of course, in part, the Old Testament reading for the first service of Christmas. On that occasion, the passage, as the church interprets it, was connected to the birth of Jesus Christ; the light came into the world, because he was, and is, as John the Evangelist reminds us, the light of the world; Christ's nativity portrays this as the *dawning* of the light in the world. When Jesus began his ministry, the light really began to shine into the darkness of people's lives, as Matthew suggests by incorporating most of the first part of Isaiah 9 into this Gospel, which tells about the light dawning as Jesus began to preach, "Repent, for the kingdom of heaven is at hand. Despite the fact that the light came into the world at Jesus' birth, it was only when he preached, taught, and healed people that the light really began to shine in the darkness. The darkness will never be able to overcome that light; even death, when his enemies attempted to put out the light, failed, for Christ rose on the third day and the light will shine forever.

1 Corinthians 1:10-17

The Christian congregation at Corinth was in something of a spiritual shambles; its problems were apparently practical but they were really theological. The congregation had developed factions within it — not unlike those one might encounter today — simply because the people had placed their loyalties in Paul, or Apollos, or Cephas, rather than — as the true saints did — in the Christ. Of course, the latter were the ones who understood the nature of the gospel and were standing on solid ground. Paul wrote to the entire congregation to help them comprehend that they were not saved by him, or Apollos, or Cephas, but by Jesus Christ — and on the cross. He also suggests that no matter who baptized them — some by Cephas, some by Apollos, a couple by Paul — that it was in the name of Jesus that they were baptized; they all belonged to Christ. Accordingly, Paul was writing to them so that theological light would shine into the darkness of their dispute and restore unity to their disrupted congregation. Homiletically, the pericope is very useful when congregations are celebrating the Week of Prayer for Christian Unity; it speaks to the entire church, as well as to any and all congregations.

Matthew 4:12-23

The arrest of John the Baptizer marks the beginning of the earthly ministry of Jesus Christ; his first act was to move from Nazareth to Capernaum which, from Matthew's perspective, was the fulfillment of Isaiah 9:1, which Matthew quotes, rather loosely, in his account of the ministry of the Lord. Jesus broke into public view in Galilee, preaching, "Repent, for the kingdom of heaven is at hand." He immediately began to gather a band of disciples, of whom two fishermen, Simon and Andrew, were the first pair to be enlisted by Christ. Charismatic and authoritative person that he was, Jesus had no difficulty in getting them, along with James and John, to follow him. All four left their nets and their boats and went with Jesus. Matthew indicates that, at this time, Jesus began his Galilean ministry with only these four disciples; the others he called, as Matthew gives the account, as he went about preaching, teaching, and "healing every disease." This Gospel, therefore, because Jesus' ministry starts in "Galilee of the Gentiles," speaks to the universality of the gospel; the good news is meant for all people, for every nation. It also outlines the nature of the Christian response to Christ in the preaching and teaching of the gospel, the delineation of the nature of mission and discipleship, and the care of the poor, the sick, and the disadvantaged people of the world.

Sermon on the Gospel, Matthew 4:12-23 — "The Man — His Mission, Message, and Ministry."

1. The silent signal to God's anointed, Jesus, the light of the world, came when John the Baptizer was imprisoned; Jesus knew it was time to begin his God-given work — to bring light to the darkness — on earth. He probably didn't know it, but he had only three short years to change the course of events in this world. He did — through his mission, message, and ministry.

2. *The mission* — to preach the gospel to — and *light up* — all the world. His move from Nazareth to Capernaum sent a strong signal to the world; he had come for the benefit and blessing of all people, not simply for the sake of Israel. God's intention was that Christ would save all people and restore them to communion with the Father.

3. *The message* — "Repent, for the kingdom of heaven is at hand." The light uncovers sin and sinners cannot remain in the darkness. Matthew reports that Jesus began his itinerant preaching ministry with a message that was identical to that of John the Baptizer. Later, of course, he expanded it into the full-blown version of the good news that we call the gospel.

4. *The ministry* — preaching the gospel of the kingdom, teaching in the synagogues, and healing every disease. These constitute the full scope of Jesus' ministry and represent a balanced ministry. He supplemented his good words about God's love with a demonstration of genuine compassion for the sick and infirm, and provided the reality of God's love in the healing process.

5. He began in Galilee, but the ministry of his gospel is going into the whole world, just as he intended it to at the beginning through men and women whom he calls to follow him today.

A multiple-text sermon — Isaiah 9 and Psalm 27 — "God Turns on the Light of the World."

1. The "lights" went out in all the world when Adam and Eve disobeyed the Lord God in the garden; no one, except God, could turn them on again. We live — and walk — more in the "land of deep darkness" than we do in the light.

2. When the time was right, God turned on the light in the world by sending Jesus, his Son, to save the world. Up to that point, people had seen, through his servants and the prophets, glimmers of light, but in Jesus *the world was illuminated forever.* (Suggestion: Read the story of "Mr. Electrico," in Ray Bradbury's introduction to *The Stories of Ray Bradbury,* a man whose magic set sent out sparks and streaks of light. When he touched the twelve-year-old Bradbury on the shoulder with a kind of "flaming sword," he said, *"live forever."* Bradbury says, "I decided that was the greatest idea I had ever heard.")

3. To know and believe that Jesus is God's Son, our Savior, is *living in the light.* Believers are the ones who "have walked in darkness (and) have seen great light . . . those who dwelt in a land of deep darkness, on them has light shined."

4. Let your light shine in the dark places of the world, because it is the business of Christians to reflect the light by what they say and the way they live. That is the measure of our discipleship and our ministry. We become "fools for Christ" because we are insomniacs; the light will not let us go to sleep when there is so much to do. (Note: Preachers would do well to read Loren Eiseley's autobiographical story, "One Night's Dying," in *The Night Country,* which contains an account of a firefly that got into his near-dark study one light, landed briefly on several different books, then stayed on one book, with his "light" flashing on and off as if to draw attention to it. When the firefly flew away, Eiseley got up, took the book, opened it and reports, "I came immediately upon these words from St. Paul: 'Beareth all things, believeth all things, hopeth all things, endureth all things. ' " After another involved and mystical experience, he wrote: "As I went toward my plane the words the firefly had found for me came automatically to my lips, 'Beareth all things', believe, believe. It is thus that one night's dying becomes tomorrow's birth. I, who do not sleep can tell you this."

70

A sermon on Christian unity — 1 Corinthians 1:10-17 — "Paul's Appeal for Christian Unity."

Some years ago, I had the opportunity to get to know a Roman Catholic priest/professor, Domenico Grass, S.J., who taught at the Pontifical Gregorian University in Rome. I was apparently only the second or third Protestant pastor/professor he had ever known. One day, in a conversation about the gospel, he said to me, "Why, professor, you and I believe the same things about Jesus Christ!" He had realized, probably for the first time in his life, that we had a basis for unity in the gospel of our Lord. Later that year, he sent a Christmas card to my wife and me, adding after his signature, as a kind of afterthought, "I will remember you both in the Christmas mass." For him, and us, unity had been established in our Lord, Jesus Christ. Paul was saying something like that to the people who belonged to the church at Corinth.

1. The church is *one in Christ;* it cannot be otherwise, whether we know it, or not, like it, or not. The church is his, not ours.

2. *Division in the church is of the devil,* who persuades people to place their loyalty in human pastors and charismatic religious leaders rather than in Christ.

3. *Baptism creates unity in Christ,* because it marks us with the cross of Christ forever. There is only one baptism and one Lord (as Paul told the Ephesian congregation).

4. As we gather round the table of the Lord, *The Table of Unity,* we pray that God will help us resolve theological differences between the different parts of the body of Christ, so that the unity we have in Christ will be complete in his church. Then, the heart of God will be made glad. (For nearly a whole year, my family and I heard Dr. Harry Whitley, the former pastor of St. Giles Cathedral, Edinburgh, Scotland, make an announcement that went something like this: "The Holy Communion will be celebrated in the Murray Aisle Chapel at 12:15 p.m. We cordially invite our Christian guests to join us [in the Lord's Supper], remembering that this is the table of the Lord and not the table of any one denomination.")

Fourth Sunday after the Epiphany
Fourth Sunday in Ordinary Time

Roman Catholic	Zephaniah 2:3, 3:12-13	1 Corinthians 1:26-31	Matthew 5:1-12a
Episcopal	Micah 6:1-8	1 Corinthians 1:(18-25) 26-31	Matthew 5:1-12
Lutheran	Micah 6:1-8	1 Corinthians 1:26-31	Matthew 5:1-12
Common	Micah 6:1-8	1 Corinthians 1:18-31	Matthew 5:1-12

The church year theological clue

Manifestation and ministry continue to be the dominant theological and liturgical themes for this Fourth Sunday after Epiphany, which provide the homiletical clue to the selection of readings and the sermon itself. The theological framework of the church year is quite "thin," almost indiscernible in the middle of Epiphany; actually, the beginning and ending of the season keep the manifestation/ministry themes in focus. The celebration of the Transfiguration on the Last Sunday after the Epiphany, as it is built into the Common and Luthern lectionaries and church years, strengthens the theological framework of the season. 1 Corinthians and Matthew continue to be read in semi-continuous manner throughout the season. The ministry of Jesus reveals who he is; it makes the incarnate Christ manifest to the world as the light for disciples to live by. The manifestation theme is clearly connected to the Christmas/incarnation theme and cycle.

The Prayer of the Day
— This is a prayer that might be used on any Sunday or other worship occasion; it could be a post-confession prayer, because it acknowledges human frailty and vulnerability to sin, and prayers for strength "in body and spirit so that, with your help, we may be able to overcome the weakness that our sin has brought upon us." It has little to do with the Epiphany season or, specifically, with the Gospel for the Day.

The Psalm of the Day
— Psalm 1 — As a responsory to the second reading, the Epistle to the Corinthians, and as an introduction, it works better than most of the ancient graduals did. The key verse is, "Their delight is in the law of the Lord," because it tells why the people of God are happy; they have heard and obeyed the Word of the Lord their God. Those who stay close to God, place their faith in him, and continually allow God to nurture their relationship with him through his Word and Spirit, are "like trees planted by streams of water." On the other hand, the psalm warns, the wicked are like "chaff which the wind blows away;" they are doomed before the judgment seat of God. God will bless the righteous, but the wicked are already condemned. The psalm accommodates, thematically, the second reading and the Gospel for the Day, as well.

The Psalm Prayer

> Lord God, in your loving wisdom you have set us beside the fountain of life, like a tree planted by running streams. Grant that the cross of your Son may become our tree of life in the paradise of your saints, through Jesus Christ our Lord.

The readings:

Micah 6:1-8 (Lutheran, Common)

This is another of those places where an earlier Old Testament reading (Zephaniah 2:3, 3:11-13) has been replaced because another text is believed to be in closer harmony with the other lessons, especially with the Gospel. Micah portrays God as puzzled by Israel's ingratitude and unfaithfulness, in view of all that the Lord God has done for his people; God has been just and gracious in all of his dealing with Israel, but Israel has separated itself from him. The life-style — of nations or individuals — that is acceptable to God is one that is marked by *doing justice, loving kindness, and walking humbly with God.* Sacrifices, even the sacrifice of one's first-born, cannot affect reconciliation between human beings and their God, except in the case of God's Son, who is obedient in doing justly, loving mercy, and walking humbly with his God. The reading highlights the utter and abject spiritual poverty of people before God, because those who know themselves to be poverty-stricken before the Lord are the ones who do justice, love kindness, and walk humbly with God.

1 Corinthians 1:26-31

The first problem in the congregation at Corinth was their factionalism and divided loyalties toward the religious leaders who had delivered the gospel to them; the second difficulty was their spiritual pride. They thought themselves to be saved on their own account, because they knew themselves to be worthy of grace, which was not only deserved but largely won because they saw themselves to be superior in all things to other Christians. Therefore, Paul makes it clear to them — and parallels Micah 6 in this respect — that *all people are poor before God;* no one deserves the gift of grace God gives freely to the world in Jesus the Christ. People's spiritual confidence must be in God the Father and their Lord, Jesus Christ, not in themselves. Only when they know their poverty are they rich, when they know their foolishness are they wise, and when they know their weakness are they strong. God is really God and the only God, good and righteous, loving and gracious. "If you have to boast about something, *boast in the Lord.*"

Matthew 5:1-12

This, of course, is the Gospel that is read annually on All Saints' Day, which tends to be celebrated on the first Sunday of November rather than on November 1. It poses some preaching problems for All Saints' Day, which preachers might carry over to the Fourth Sunday after the Epiphany; it almost appears that this Gospel was intended to be read with brief comments made on each of the Beatitudes spelled out in the pericope; a full-blown running commentary sermon, or a "primitive" expository homily, for that matter, would be much too long for today's congregations to endure on either occasion. This gospel emphasizes the nature of the Christian life, according to Jesus' authoritative teachings; the "crowds" had followed Jesus, primarily because he had worked incredible healings, but instead of seeing him work more miracles, they, along with the disciples, discovered the power of his teaching. Jesus taught them — and us — about the dimensions of abject spiritual poverty, the spiritual conditions that are acceptable to God in those who know themselves to be unworthy of his grace and helpless to win their own salvation. (Note: This gospel is best "preached" in the form of a thematic sermon that spells out the basis for true happiness in life and after death through God's gifts of grace as they are spelled out in the Beatitudes.)

A sermon on the Gospel, Matthew 5:1-2 — "He Taught It On a Mountain."

In his book, *Jesus the Magician,* Morton Smith contends that there were many magicians roaming about the world in Jesus' day; some of them did astounding acts of magic, and they drew considerable crowds. There can be no doubt that many people in the crowd that followed Jesus and his disciples to the mountain did so in the hope of seeing even greater miracles than he had previously performed. They went there to see a show; instead, they were given a lesson. They were taught, or overheard, a lesson taught by a master teacher.

They discovered that Jesus spoke with a level of authority unknown among the scribes and Pharisees of the day. What has happened to the authority of his teachings today?

1. *Jesus' preaching and teaching are more important* to us than are the miracles that seem to be promised in the New Testament. If miracles could be guaranteed, it is highly probable that many more people would be Christians; but they are not. A couple months ago, a young man and his wife were jogging fairly late at night; a pickup truck came along and hit him, throwing him forty feet and leaving him paralyzed. Just yesterday the headlines of a local newspaper read, "Hit-run victim's recovery 'remarkable.' " The accompanying story told how the man had two vertebrae damaged, but was only paralyzed for five weeks. He is still recovering from his injuries, but his wife says, "The doctors don't say (his recovery) is a miracle, but we think we've received a miracle. If they're (miracles) out there in the world, we've gotten one. The odds were against us." The people following Jesus not only wanted to see a magic show miracle; they wanted to see instantaneous healing actually occur; they witnessed a miraculous exhibition of another kind, Jesus' teaching, which is meant for us, too.

2. Repentance, which Jesus had been preaching, along with "the kingdom of heaven is near," calls for a radical change of life-style by those who respond to this demand. The true Christian is one who is aware of his/her poverty — spiritual poverty — in emotions, in attitude, in hunger and desires, in relationships, in intentions, in complete and utter devotion to God. This person knows the meaning of sin and repentance — and discipleship. Discipleship means living a sub-servient life, poor in spirit, not simply living in physical poverty, although there may be benefit in that, but of knowing one has no standing before God aside from the sacrifice of Christ. One has to know that to be a true follower and disciple of Jesus Christ.

3. True happiness comes to those who know they have no spiritual worth of their own, but who live the life of Christ instead in total dependance upon him, not to gain the rewards he has promised — the kingdom of heaven, inheriting the earth, being comforted and satisfied, seeing God, becoming children of God — but, at the same time, knowing that Christ has promised these things to the suffering faithful.

In my wife's home congregation, there was a woman who was everybody's "Aunt Lena." She was, economically, a poor woman, but she never knew it; she believed that she was a rich person through her faith in Jesus Christ, and indeed she was. She lived on a meager pension, but whenever she received any money, she filled her offering envelopes first; she gave away most of the rest. But she knew spiritual need, and was in church at least once every week. She was "mother" to many, comforter to the bereaved, counselor to countless children, and willing worker whenever anything had to be done in her neighborhood, her church, or her town. She was the sort of person about whom Jesus was talking in the Sermon on the Mount, a true believer and genuine disciple of the Lord.

4. Listen to, and live by, the Word of the Lord, as he first taught it on a mountain.

A Sermon on the First Lesson, Micah 6:1-8 — "Priorities for Godly Living."

Verse 8 of this text is so familiar to people.

> *He (God) has showed you, O man, what is good; and what does the Lord require of you but to do justice, and to love kindness, and to walk humbly with your God?*

So the obvious sermon — even expected message — is textual in its shape and form as it deals with this particular verse.

1. Priority number one: not just the love of justice, *but the active pursuit of justice* for all people who are victims of any injustice. Christians have to be involved in setting things right in the world. It is the business of Christians to seek for others what they alone might have — security, freedom from fear, hunger, and poverty, equal rights in matters of race, economics, religion, and political significance. Justice for all is the active concern of God's people.

2. Priority number two: adopting a Christian life-style whose foundation is love for all people, as well as for God. The Jerusalem Bible translation of verse 8 is "to love tenderly." This is echoed in Jesus' command, "Love one another as I have loved you." Jesus expects his disciples to live this way; it was not simply a request on his part. Love is the basis for kindness to others, genuine concern for people which recognizes that one must live a "life of love" that reflects genuine affection for the Lord in one's life style. It is passing along to others the treatment one has received from God, love, mercy, kindness, as totally unmerited grace.

3. Priority number three: to respond to God's mercy with genuine humility, knowing that without the grace of God you have no hope. A Christian prays, because it is true, "God, have mercy upon me, a sinner." Such a person knows that God alone is the righteous one, and in Jesus he gives us forgiveness of our sins and the blessed hope of eternal life. Those who know their true spiritual condition apart from God, along with God's merciful deliverance in Jesus Christ, can do no other than to "walk humbly with (their) God." Not even the "best" of us can save ourselves from sin and death; only Christ can do that.

4. Consider these requirements of godly living in the light of the cross of Christ, and ask the Lord to make them priorities in your life.

A sermon on the Second Lesson, 1 Corinthians 1:26-31 — "The Call to be Christian."

1. We need to remember that *people are called to the faith by Christ,* and by him alone. Though baptism makes us children of God and members of his body, the church. Jesus has done the entire work of salvation for us. Our business is to know this and believe it.

2. Like the Corinthians, when given time we become impressed with our own importance to Christ and his church. This is one of the hazards in being members of Christian congregations which has to be avoided at any cost, or we lose all that has been given to us. Boasting is a manifestation of pride, our fiercest spiritual enemy. Repentance is a sign of faith received through grace.

3. *Jesus is the source of true humility.* All that is good and permanent in our lives — righteousness, sanctification, redemption, and the like — comes from him. Knowledge of what he has done for us, which we could not do for ourselves, makes us truly humble and contrite.

4. *Christians praise the Lord* — "Let him who boasts, boast of the Lord," says Paul — and avoid self-praise. Not only is this pleasing to God, but it is effective evangelism — "This is what the Lord has done for me . . . ." — know it and say it with boldness and confidence.

Fifth Sunday after the Epiphany
Fifth Sunday in Ordinary Time

Roman Catholic	Isaiah 58:7-10	1 Corinthians 2:1-5	Matthew 5:13-16
Episcopal	Habakkuk 3:1-6, 17-19	1 Corinthians 2:1-11	Matthew 5:13-20
Lutheran	Isaiah 58:5-9a	1 Corinthians 2:1-5	Matthew 5:13-20
Common	Isaiah 58:3-9a	1 Corinthians 2:1-11	Matthew 5:13-20

The church year theological clue

The theological framework provided by the church year for the Epiphany season throws light upon this Sunday primarily in the incarnational/manifestation scope of the season. By this time in Epiphany, the preacher may well have the same reaction that is often felt in the Pentecost Cycle; there seems to be little theological help for the preacher in the church year or the liturgy. One has to keep in mind that the readings emphasize the early stages of Jesus' ministry in the world. In this ministry, his manifestation on earth deepens the mystery of the incarnation by concentrating on his authoritative teaching. By struggling with the type of thematic preaching done in the Epiphany Season, the preacher is also learning how to preach in the Pentecost Season.

The Prayer of the Day (LBW) — This is a prayer that is radically different from the older collects used in liturgical churches, but one that is obviously oriented to the Gospel for the Day, Matthew 5:13-20, and beyond it to the one who is the Word incarnate, therein sounding again the Epiphany themes of manifestation and light: "Almighty God, you sent your only Son as the Word of life for our eyes to see and our ears to hear." The second sentence speaks to the sinner's response to the word Jesus spoke as supreme teacher: "Help us to believe with joy what the Scriptures proclaim . . . ." It is a prayer that places us on the "mountain" where Jesus teaches us as he taught the people long ago.

The Psalm for the Day — Psalm 112 — This psalm was obviously selected because it announces the "light" theme of Epiphany, "Light shines in the darkness for the upright." Actually, it is a psalm that has had a variety of interpretations — as a glorification of the law, a psalm of comfort, the strength and power there is in trusting God — which are all secondary, from the perspective of the church, to emphasis upon the light, Jesus Christ. It functions well as a responsory psalm, picking up the heart of the Old Testament reading, "Then shall your light break forth like the dawn, and your healing shall spring up speedily" (Isaiah 58:8), and moving into the Second Lesson, where Paul says, "For I decided to know nothing among you except Jesus Christ and him crucified." (1 Corinthians 2:2) He is the light of the world; he is the light of love.

The Psalm Prayer

Lord Jesus, you are the light shining in darkness for the upright. Teach us to love one another as you love us, that we might bring peace and joy to the world and find the happiness of your home, where you live and reign with the Father and the Holy Spirit, now and forever.

The readings:

Isaiah 58:5-9a

This is a pericope that might well be employed as a reading for Ash Wednesday or some other time during Lent; it directly addresses fasting, one of the three traditional disciplines of Lent, and expands the horizons of a second, alms giving (but it omits the third, prayer). The primary reason this reading is selected for Epiphany comes in verse 8, "Then shall your light break forth like the dawn," which at once affirms that Epiphany is a season of *light* that is reflected in the lives of believers, as well as directly in the life and ministry of Jesus Christ. The light of which Isaiah speaks is a consequence of the quality of their lives; their actions toward those who are oppressed, hungry, homeless, and poor cause the "light to break forth like the dawn." This theme is more fully developed in the Gospel for the Day, Matthew 5:13-20. But this message could stand by itself; religious actions, such as fasting, which are directed to God alone and have no external expression in daily life are worthless; genuine devotion to God always issues in acts of love and compassion toward people. The two are inseparable: to assert one's love for God in any form requires affirmation of that expression in the contacts one has with others in this world.

1 Corinthians 2:1-5

This passage should make preachers stop and reexamine the content of their preaching. Paul makes it clear that the proclamation of the gospel is not a philosophical system that is articulated in Christian pulpits; Christian preaching is theological, the announcement of what God did — and is still doing — in Jesus' death and resurrection. Paul knew this and, therefore, preached "Christ crucified," positive that the power of God, which reaches, touches, and converts people to Jesus Christ, is active in such preaching. God cannot be fully found in philosophical systems or through human wisdom alone; he reaches out to people in his Word, Jesus Christ, and turns their hearts and lives to himself through the Holy Spirit and the power of the cross event. There are implications in this, of course, for the Christian's life; the children of God are to allow the power of the Lord God to change their lives so that they witness to the love of God by the good works they do in his name. The cross lights up the world and those who live in it. Paul wants no one ever to forget this essential and theological truth.

Matthew 5:13-20

This selection, gleaned from Jesus' authoritative teaching on the mountain, is well-suited as a reading for Epiphany and, also, for developing the *Godly life-style* theme of Isaiah. Jesus was actually informing the disciples as to what they had actually become because they had answered his call and followed him; they are to be like salt, a city on a hill, and a light in the world. The works that they do in the name of Jesus Christ ("Let your light so shine before men, that they may see your good works and give glory to your Father who is in heaven") will have the effect of "salt" on the quality of life, will be as evident to others as a "city on a hill," and will shine as a floodlight in the world. In the middle section of this Gospel, Jesus also makes it perfectly clear that the law has not been abolished by his coming; he came to fulfill it through perfect obedience to the Father, which meant his death on the cross. The law still crushes human beings, because even the most sincere believer cannot live sinlessly and thereby fulfill it; the law kills, but Jesus offers forgiveness and frees us from the destructive power of the law, and renews the lives of his saints.

A sermon on the Gospel, Matthew 5:13-24 — "Salty Christians."

Numerous sermons have been preached upon the theme of "Salty Christians" in verse 13 of Matthew 5; it is a textual choice some preachers may still want to make, partially because it can stand by itself, and also because there are complexities in this pericope. It has been argued by at least one liturgical/homiletical scholar, that verses 13 through 16 should have sufficed very nicely to articulate the Epiphany "light" theme; verses 17 and 20 could be counted as superfluous. One of the reasons for the inclusion of this section might also be that there is a connection here with the beginning of Jesus' ministry. Twice the phrase, "kingdom of heaven," is used in conjunction with Christian living: First, "whoever then relaxes one of the least of these commandments and teaches men so, shall be called least in the kingdom of heaven; but he who does them and teaches them shall be called great in the kingdom of heaven;" and, second, "unless your righteousness exceeds that of the scribes and Pharisees, you will never enter the kingdom of heaven." A separate sermon, too, might be preached on verses 21-24, on reconciliation. However one chooses to approach this text homiletically, one has to do so in the knowledge of its richness and preaching possibilities.

One approach — thematic — "Good Works — the Life-style of the Kingdom of Heaven."

1. The natural expression of the Christian faith in daily living is "good works," which should be *the believer's response* to the good news in Jesus Christ. They are part and parcel of our ministry. These works function like salt, adding "flavor" to life, as well as preserving it. The "good life" of the Christian, therefore, functions as light in the world; it can't be hidden, nor can it — or should it be — covered up. It is the incarnation of the gospel in the lives of those whom Christ has claimed as his own. *A Christian life proclaims the gospel to the world through deeds of love and mercy.* ("They will know we are Christians by our love." I know a person who lives that way, manifesting genuine love and concern and care for other people. She is always ready to help people, to give comfort, to write notes of sympathy and concern — not one, but many — to those who are hurting. She seems always — and in all ways — to be doing things for others, not to gain praise or reward from people or God, but because this is the nature of her life in Christ. Such people are a real delight to our Lord, because they live the way they do and do good works as a consequence of salvation, not to win it. See Herman G. Stuempfle's *Preaching Law and Gospel* for more on good works — obedience — as the "consequence of salvation" on the part of the believer.)

2. People whose lives might be counted as good, because of the sincere servant quality of their lives, are all too rare, however. The way too many persons live doesn't measure up to their professions of faith; theirs is a "scribe-Pharisee" religious mentality, built around knowledge of the Bible, theological pride, religious ritualism of a kind, and strict self-righteousness. Because such people believe in their own goodness, they may think they have open-access to God and have no need to foster right relations with other human beings. For them, reconciliation is a one-way street, going only toward God and moving away, rather than toward, other human beings. No one, Christ teaches us, can be an island of righteousness, because all are sinners and need the faith, forgiveness, and freedom from fear and death that only he, through grace, can give.

I live on a rather isolated street with sixteen houses; and believe it or not, all of the families are active church members of one denomination or another. Two families are Presbyterian, two are Methodists, one is Roman Catholic, one is Mormon, one is Congregational, one is Episcopalian, one is United Church of Christ, one is Baptist, five are Lutheran, and one is a combination of the Roman Catholic and Presbyterian. Indeed, this is an ecumenical mix, but a neighborhood with some real care and concern for others in it, and a good neighborhood to live in. But there are two families who seldom participate in any of the activities of the neighborhood; they might be the "most religious" in church attendance, participation,

78

and support of their congregations. Both belong to denominations that have little ecumenical concern or contacts with other churches, and these families seem to mirror that attitude. It is difficult to resist the feeling that they think themselves to be superior — religiously — to the rest of us, that their life-styles are more pleasing to God, their righteousness is more Christ-like than ours, when it may just be that they are not as socially involved with their neighbors as the rest of us happen to be. Don't you know people like this, who seem to consider themselves to be Christians *par excellence?* And doesn't our tendency to judge them place us in, possibly, more spiritual jeopardy than we suppose them to be in?

3. God has reclaimed us in Jesus Christ and made us his own people again by forgiving our sins, reconciling us to himself through the cross of Christ, and giving us new life in the resurrection of our Lord. He has made us what we are — children of God — so that his light may shine into the world, not only by the preaching of the Word and the administration of the sacraments, but also by the way we actually live.

4. In the Epiphany of our Lord, God caused light to shine into the darkness of the world. In us, that light still shines and lights up the darkness. The bottom line in all of this, according to Jesus, is that (only?) those who let their lights shine so that others see their good works and give glory to God are the ones who can have any thought that their lives resemble the life to which God has called them.

A sermon on the Old Testament Lesson — "God Provides the Glory." (The *Jerusalem Bible* translates Isaiah 58:8b — "your integrity will go before you and the glory of Yahweh behind you.")

1. God loves acts of piety and devotion, including fasting, by his people, as long as they are directed either toward God or neighbor. Prayer, praise, and thanksgiving are always welcome to God, when they point beyond self and spill over into the arena of everyday life. This lesson sounds the note of spiritual discipline usually associated with Lent; it tends to point the faithful toward Lent and Easter.

2. Self-denial, as in fasting or any other form of spiritual exercise, has to be balanced by concern and care for the poor and hungry, or it takes the shape of self-condemnation. Self-denial, in the hope of winning, or solidifying, one's salvation, may well be an act of spiritual selfishness, rather than an expression of grace.

3. The *true light of God* shines in the world through our lives and ministry when works of love and piety include people as well as God.

4. The glory in good works belongs to God, for he provides it.

A sermon on the Second Lesson — "Lift High the Cross!"

1. The cross-event is the *very heart of the good news* of Jesus Christ. The cross throws the light of God's love into the world. It represents a concrete act of love on the part of God, absolute and faithful obedience on Jesus' part.

2. The death of Jesus on Calvary has power to bring people to God more than any system of wisdom or philosophy. Not even theology can save sinners; the cross alone brings salvation ("And I, when I am lifted up from the earth, will draw all (people) to myself").

3. Christians cling to the cross in faith with one hand, while using the other hand to do God's works in the world. That is the way, the only way, that Christians really can be faithful and actually "lift high the cross!"

Sixth Sunday after the Epiphany
Sixth Sunday in Ordinary Time

Roman Catholic	Sirach 15:15-20	1 Corinthians 2:6-10	Matthew 5:17-37
Episcopal	Sirach 15:11-20	1 Corinthians 3:1-9	Matthew 5:21-24, 27-30, 33-37
Lutheran	Deuteronomy 30:15-20	1 Corinthians 2:6-13	Matthew 5:20-37
Common	Deuteronomy 30:15-20	1 Corinthians 3:1-9	Matthew 5:17-26

The church year theological clue

By the Sixth Sunday after the Epiphany, as happens rather quickly in the Pentecost season, the season has pretty much lost its theological "shape" and impact; the lectionary and the lessons take over and seem to indicate that there has been a movement away from the several theological implications *(the incarnation and manifestation* of Jesus in the Epiphany season) to a concentration of the ethics of those who belong to the kingdom of heaven. Liturgically, the Epiphany theological frame still surrounds this Sunday and its ethical implications with the manifestation and the light of Jesus Christ in the world.

The Prayer of the Day (LBW) — The prayer looks to the Gospel for the Day, as well as the other readings, where Jesus is the supreme teacher, and suggests the basic Epiphany theme once more: as the Word, Jesus *lights up the world*, and as teacher of the word, Jesus *lights up the hearts and minds of people* so that they will understand what they see and hear, especially in their obedience to the word of God. The last phrase recognizes that no one can keep the word of life and live a life pleasing to God — a life of obedience — without the grace and power of God, therefore the prayer concludes with a petition for these gifts of God.

The Psalm of the Day (LBW) — Psalm 119:1-16 — This psalm was chosen to accent the theme of *obedience to the word:* "Happy are they who observe his decrees and seek him with all their hearts!" It also elaborates on the difficulty of obeying the statutes of the Lord, along with the necessity of learning them "with an unfeigned heart" — with sincerity and good intentions. The psalmist asks, "How shall a young man cleanse his way?", and answers his own question, "By keeping to your words," praying, "With my whole heart I see you; let me not stray from your commandments" and "instruct me in your statutes." And he speaks of a devotional attitude, "With my lips will I recite all the judgments of your mouth . . . . I will meditate on your commandments and give attention to your ways . . . . I will not forget your word." He begins the next portion of the psalm with a prayer for grace, "Deal bountifully with your servants that I may live and keep your word. Open my eyes, that I may see the wonders of your law . . . . Do not hide your commandments from me."

The Psalm Prayer

> *Lord, you are just and your commandments are eternal. Teach us to love you with all our hearts and to love our neighbors as ourselves, for the sake of Jesus our Lord.*

The readings:

Deuteronomy 30:15-20

This speech of Moses contains a promise and a warning — good news and bad news. The promise is that if the Israelites obey God and keep his commandments, they will live and

80

prosper in the promised land. But if they disobey — and thereby deny the primacy of their God in their lives — they will perish and enjoy only limited occupation of the land. Moses makes it clear that they must *choose life* for themselves and their descendants:

> *Loving the Lord your God, obeying his voice, and cleaving to him; for that means life to you and length of days, that you may dwell in the land which the Lord swore to your fathers, to Abraham, to Isaac, and to Jacob, to give them.*

1 Corinthians 2:6-13

It is Paul's strong belief and continuing conviction that the *role of the spirit* in our lives is crucial, because the Holy Spirit enables us not only to see, but also to understand, what is in the heart of God. The Spirit alone is able to penetrate the mind of God, and the Spirit alone can reveal those thoughts to human beings. Without the ministry of the Holy Spirit, no one can really comprehend the meaning of the Word that comes to people. Human wisdom cannot invent the intentions of God, nor fathom the Father's forthright declarations without the work of the Holy Spirit; the will of God remains a mystery to people who have not received the ministrations of the Holy Spirit; the Spirit alone penetrates this mystery for the believers. Therefore, this reading adds yet another dimension to the Epiphany theme — *The Holy Spirit lights up the darkness of human minds and hearts so that all people may come to comprehend the mind of God for themselves.*

Matthew 5:20-37

Once more, Jesus the teacher touches the themes of Epiphany, throwing direct light upon his *uniqueness and authority among religious teachers* and, from Matthew's perspective, demonstrating how the teachings of Jesus offer new light to mere mortals. Jesus updates the commandments of God and some of the teachings of Holy Scripture by using a device: "You have heard that it was said (of old) . . . . but I say to you . . . ." He gives new interpretations to murder (anger and hatred are just as evil as the killing of people, because they are a type of bloodless destruction); to adultery (lust is an inward form of adultery); to marriage and divorce (divorce forces people into a type of adultery); and to lying and perjury ("swearing falsely" is an invasion of the rights and privileges of God). The problems for preachers are several: how can one speak convincingly of the contemporary applications of any of these ethical pronouncements of Jesus? Who actually believes them, let alone observes them today? And also, the make-up of this pericope is such that one discovers at least three, maybe four, sermons in the pericope. How can one do justice to this complex assortment of ethical and moral themes? How should the preacher deal homiletically with this passage?

A sermon on the Gospel, Matthew 5:20-37 — "Jesus on Ethics and Morality."

Some years ago, Peter Mattheissen wrote a novel, *At Play in the Fields of the Lord,* which has been called a minor classic; it makes contact with the gospel at several points. A young North Dakota farmer, Martin Quarrier, believes he is called to become a missionary, receives a limited theological education, and sets off for South America, where his assignment takes him into a remote part of the continent; there he makes contact with a band of primitive natives. Despite his zeal and his genuine concern for these people, he is killed by a native with one of the cross-marked machetes he had given to them. The reason they turned on him was a theological one; he forgot about the uniqueness of Jesus Christ and taught them that Jesus was actually their god, Kisu, not knowing that their god was an evil deity who was responsible for many of the catastrophes, especially great rains and floods, that came into their lives. Instead of raising the natives' theological perceptions to new and higher levels — as an epiphany should do — Jesus became the incarnation of evil for them and was destructive to their faith. In his life, Jesus brought light into the world into a new ethical and moral awareness that can be obtained only with the help of God.

1. "It has been said of old . . . *'the demands of God's law are clear and unbending —* "Do not kill," "do not commit adultery," "do not swear (God's name is holy)." ' " These constantly remind us of what God expects of his people, and they condemn us when we break God's commands. But we have been affected by, and have bought into, the residue of Joseph Fletcher's situation ethics. His theological system was not devised as much for the age we live in as it was by the theological mind-set of people living in this era. What remains of the older and time-tested moral and ethical standards of the Bible? Is there any such thing as sin anymore? Are most preachers like Phyllis McGinlely's Dr. Harcourt in the poem, "This Side of Calvin":

And in the pulpit (he) eloquently speaks
on diverse matters with both wit and clarity.

All things but Sin. He seldom mentions Sin.

2. "But I say to you . . . ." brings a new and more demanding interpretation of the commands of God. Jesus shows how evil thoughts, hatred, lust, and taking God's name in vain are spiritually destructive. Sin always destroys our relationship with God and other human beings, too. Jesus teaches what sin really is and how it destroys human and divine relationships in our lives.

3. The resolution of this problem comes with the recognition of one's utter helplessness in purging oneself of such inward sins, aware of one's desperate need for forgiveness, and of one's absolute dependence upon the power of God to stand any chance of being called righteous. Jesus alone has perfectly obeyed God's law. All that humans can do, who see their lives through God's eyes, is cry out, "Mea culpa, mea maxima culpa" in true repentance, adding, "Kyrie eleison," — "Lord, have mercy" — to our confession of our sin.

4. Jesus' ethical and moral teachings constantly make it clear to us that we have to depend entirely on him — and the grace of God — for our salvation. The law, especially as Jesus gave it new interpretation, will always be beyond our ability — or even our will — to fulfill it. Jesus' teachings about the law, ethics, and morals, in this light, turn us toward the Gospel and Jesus only, if we are to have any hope at all.

A sermon on the Old Testament reading, Deuteronomy 30:15-30 — "God's Idea of 'the Good Life.' "

1. *Obedience is the key to the "good life."* The really "good life" is attended only by those who "love the Lord," "walk in his ways," and "keep his commandments and his statutes and his ordinances." They know the "joy of the Lord" and what the "good life" is all about.

2. *Disobedience is destructive* of any right and lasting relationship with God, and also of any real quality of life. The disobedient not only defy God by the way they live, but they destroy themselves in the process. Seeking out the "good life," as the world defines it, is a way of losing the really "good life."

3. *Jesus lived the "good life" — perfectly;* He is the only person to do so. He is our role model, and our hope when we discover that we cannot keep all of God's Commandments.

4. *Walk in the light of the Lord* — and celebrate Epiphany every day of your life, and know the joy of the "good life" as God prescribes, orders, and supports it.

A sermon on the Second Lesson, 1 Corinthians 2:6-13 — "The Holy Spirit — Our Teacher."

1. True spiritual maturity means that people are ready for learning the *truth about the wisdom of God.* Such persons know that they have much to learn about God's mysteries.

2. The church has been given *the light of the Holy Spirit,* so that "What no eye has seen, nor ear heard, nor the heart of man conceived, what God has prepared for those who love him" may be perceived and understood by believers. Such wisdom comes as "gifts of the Spirit."

3. To take us to spiritual maturity, the Holy Spirit becomes our teacher at the express orders of the risen and ascended Lord. As teacher, the Holy Spirit turns on our spiritual "lights" so that we might know how to live in "the wisdom of the Lord." Note: One of the loveliest festivals celebrated in this country takes place for two weekends early in December, in San Antonio, Texas. Luminaries are placed about every four feet on both sides of the entire River Walk. The trees are festooned with colored lights. The entire scene speaks of light — and hope — and peace. The sight-seeing boats, which take visitors and tourists up and down the length of the River Walk, are crowded with people who spontaneously and enthusiastically sing the lovely carols of Christmas. Special Christmas displays and goods line the River Walk, too. The spectacle might be even more meaningful if the luminaries were also used during Epiphany, or for the entire Christmas cycle, lighting a few more of the weeks of Epiphany until, at last, the entire River Walk would be illuminated. Of course, anyone who suggested such a procedure would be told of its impracticability, but — with some imagination and ingenuity — a congregation might be able to plan and achieve something similar and of symbolic significance that would heighten the meaning of the Season of Light for the believers.)

Seventh Sunday after the Epiphany
Seventh Sunday in Ordinary Time

Roman Catholic	Leviticus 19:1-2, 17-18	1 Corinthians 3:16-23	Matthew 5:38-48
Episcopal	Leviticus 19:1-2, 9-18	1 Corinthians 3:10-11, 16-23	Matthew 5:38-48
Lutheran	Leviticus 19:1-2, 17-18	1 Corinthians 3:10-11, 16-12	Matthew 5:38-48
Common	Isaiah 49:8-13	1 Corinthians 3:10-11, 16-23	Matthew 5:27-37

The church year theological clue

As the Epiphany season nears its conclusion, the homiletical framework of the season continues to thin out and the role of the readings becomes more important for the establishment of the theme for the day. Under the older church year, this would be Sexagesima Sunday, the second of the "three-to-get-ready for Lent" Sundays. They were removed from the church year's "Pre-Lent" and added to Epiphany simply because they had become part of Lent, making Lent, in effect, nine and a half weeks long. If there is any value in extending the length of Epiphany, it is simply that the second readings from 1 Corinthians and the gospel from Matthew are given the task of establishing the theme of the day. At best, the theological clue, *manifestation/ministry,* is indistinct on this Sunday from the standpoint of the church year.

The Prayer of the Day (LBW) — Here is another prayer that might well — or better — be used in conjunction with the Prayer of the Church. It asks the Lord God: to keep "your family, the Church, always faithful to you"; and, "that all who lean on the hope of your promises may gain strength from the power of your love"; concluding, "through your Son, Jesus Christ our Lord." The second part is clearly gospel-oriented (God's promises) and cross-centered, suggesting that in the Gospel for the Day "the power of your love" in Jesus Christ is given very practical and ethical expression.

The Psalm of the Day (LBW) — Psalm 103:1-13 — This beautiful psalm of thanksgiving and praise has been one of the most-used of all the psalms, finding its way into regular use as, at least, the introduction to table prayer. Two portions of the psalm are also assigned to table prayer. Two portions of the psalm are assigned to the Seventh Sunday after the Epiphany, verses 1-5 and 5-13; verses 14-22 are not included for liturgical use on this occasion. The first section of the psalm enumerates the blessings of God that the psalmist has personally experienced as gifts from the Lord — forgiveness, healing, deliverance from destruction, steadfast love, and mercy, and the good things that satisfy people's hunger. In the second part of the psalm he reminds Israel of God's blessings to the nation and to his people — justice for the oppressed, self-revelation, mercy, and grace, patience with perverse people, withholding his anger, compassionate toward sinful human beings, steadfast in his love, and, like a father, he pities his children. The church sees that most of this latter list has been repeated in the experience of Christian congregations; the former list continues to be verified in individual lives.

The Psalm Prayer

> *Lord, you have compassion for the sinner, as a father has compassion for his children. Heal the weakness of your people and save us from everlasting death, that with the saints and angels we may praise and glorify you, Father, Son, and Holy Spirit, now and forever.*

The readings:

Leviticus 19:1-2, 17-18

This pericope is probably the source of the "you have heard it said" parts of the Gospel for the Day, spelling out how one should comport oneself in relationships with one's neighbor. First of all, one should not hate one's neighbor, regardless of what the person might have done that is offensive and even extremely harmful to a person. Second, one should confront the neighbor with the offense committed by that person, thereby avoiding the commission of sin by the one who has been offended. Retaliation compounds sin by repeating the original offense, perhaps in a different way; one cannot take vengeance on an offensive neighbor and hope to be an innocent victim in the eyes of God. Fourth, a grudge must not be extended into a feud that begins with one person and then involves that one's children and, ultimately, the whole family. Sixth, the gospel note is sounded, "You must love your neighbor as yourself." The conclusion, "I am Yahweh," indicates that these, indeed, are authoritative commands and ethical precepts because they come from God himself.

1 Corinthians 3:10-11, 16-23

What the Apostle Paul says to the church at Corinth, wherein the people are confused theologically about a number of matters, needs to be spoken in congregations of every age. Loyalty to leaders is often intense and long-lived. If there are several strong leaders in a congregation, dissension may destroy the unity of the church; some support one leader, others someone else, and still others yet another person. The divisive claims to follow Apollos, Cephas, and Paul signal this leadership and loyalty crisis. Regardless of who founded, or led the congregation, Jesus is the only foundation for the church; the church is built upon him.

The second section of this pericope, verses 16 and 17, have been cut off from its context and inserted here to remind Corinthian-like churches of the workings of the Holy Spirit, and to warn them about impending disaster and destruction. The last verses speak to the members of congregations who think that they are approved by God through their wisdom, but that won't work. God knows the thoughts of even the wisest person, "He catches the wise in their craftiness," and "The Lord knows that the thoughts of the wise are futile." He concludes with a reminder to all Christians, not simply to the Corinthians, "For all things are yours, . . . and you are Christ's; and Christ is God's."

Matthew 5:38-48

With this pericope, the readings from the 5th chapter of Matthew are concluded, but the "I tell you" teachings are carried over into the 6th chapter of Matthew. Leviticus 19 furnishes the "you have heard it said of old" references in Jesus' teachings, which give rise to his "but I say to you" authoritative statements that give new twists to the older commands of God. Again, the emphasis continues on Jesus' *manifestation* by pointing to the new light he brought into the world in his teaching ministry. Specifically, he laid the foundation for contemporary non-violent attitudes and actions by radically changing the "eye for an eye" ethic of the past into caring responses (turn the other cheek; give your coat as well as your shirt, etc.) for someone who has wronged you. And love for one's enemy, which God required in the Old Testament, is elevated into positive action, which most of the martyrs took literally, "love your enemies and pray for your persecutors." Jesus was deadly serious, when he said in the last verse of the chapter, "You, therefore, must be perfect, as your heavenly Father is perfect." That's how we all are to live in this world as the children of the heavenly Father.

A Sermon on the Gospel, Matthew 5:38-48

On one level, this Gospel almost implores the preacher to speak about the new — and highly impractical — ethics of the kingdom of heaven. Jesus revealed that God's kingdom has a higher ethical standard than those of the world. He replaced the revenge/vengeance ethic with a love/forgiveness ethic. An offended public rages in objection to the light sentence imposed upon a convicted criminal who, they believe, deserves a far more severe punishment; the criminal ought to be punished, not forgiven. When the United States cruiser U.S.S. Vincennes brought down an Iranian civilian plane, with 290 people on board, there were immediate cries for retaliation and revenge; the deaths of the people killed, in what was explained as a correct defensive action, had to be paid for. It has been suggested that more than a few Americans, still remembering the deaths of nearly 300 Marines in Beirut, Lebanon, when their living quarters were blown up in a terrorist incident supposedly orchestrated by Iran, were thinking, if not saying, "Well, that repays them, in part, for what they did in Lebanon." Some list the string of international crimes of terror, including the imprisonment of the embassy workers in Tehran, and call for even more direct action against the government of Iran for their evil deeds. On almost every level of human relationships, we continue to perpetuate the revenge motif in our attitude and actions toward our enemies.

1. Jesus not only initiated the kingdom of God here on earth, but he also spelled out a higher love/forgiveness ethic for that kingdom. Christians are to love one another as part of the body of Christ, but they are also expected to love their enemies, and forgive them for their evil deeds and actions, instead of attempting to get even with them by doing things similar to what has been done to them. "An eye for an eye and a tooth for a tooth" ethic is not acceptable in the kingdom of God; that is a human standard, based on a "revenge motif." If God operated that way, not a single human being would have a chance of belonging to the kingdom and receiving the hope of heaven.

2. *Jesus expects his followers to act toward others the way that God is toward them.* He knew there would be opposition and persecution, even martyrdom, of the disciples and others who believed in him, and actively participated in the work of the kingdom; some would be imprisoned, others would be tortured, more than a few would be executed for their faith. Jesus backed up his ethical teaching about love and forgiveness by the first word he spoke when he was hanging on the cross, "Father, forgive them, for they know not what they do." If he had done the human thing, he would have been cursing his tormentors and the ones who betrayed, judged, and condemned him, just as the thieves — one, at least — were doing beside him. And while all human beings are imperfect and no one can attain sinlessness, there is one way to approach God's perfection, and that is by forgiving one's enemies as God forgives us. "Forgive us our sins, as we forgive those who sin against us" is the prayer of those who know their imperfection, but who may approach the "mercy seat" of God draped in more than a modicum of perfection, because forgiveness has replaced revenge in their lives and actions toward others.

The most remarkable letter I have ever read was written by a woman who now runs the housing office in the seminary where I teach; her name is Mary Ehrlichmann, and she wrote the letter three days after her husband was shot and killed by a young hitchhiker he had picked up. What compounded the tragedy was that her husband was a teacher and counselor who worked with high school students, always trying to help them. This is what she wrote, in part:

> *During the past three days my grief and desolation have been eased and comforted . . . by the love and faith of so many wonderful friends and relatives. But in the midst of all of this, and especially in the quiet moments, my thoughts keep turning to three . . . . I wonder to whom you are turning for comfort, strength and reassurance . . . .*

86

I suppose I will never know what motivated your actions that night, but if the shots were fired out of sheer panic, my heart aches for you and I wish there were only some way I could help you in what you are suffering now. If hate made you pull the trigger, I can only pray that you can come to know the love of God that fills the heart and leaves no room for hate. If you were under the influence of drugs, please, for my sake and your own, don't waste your lives, too. Get help and rid yourselves of that stuff. Please, if you see this, find a church some place where you can be alone; then read this again. Know that God forgives you and that my family and I forgive you (emphasis, mine); then go out and make something worthwhile out of the rest of your lives. God bless and keep you.

That letter spells out so clearly "Father, forgive . . . ." and "Forgive us as we forgive," doesn't it? "Be perfect as your Father in heaven in perfect!"

3. Concealed in this combination of the "But I say to you" teachings of Jesus is what amounts to a forecast of his fate. He knew that he was ultimately going to face suffering and death, as would his disciples, too, but Jesus was ready to pay the price. His life was sinless, but that sinlessness only received final expression when he was nailed to the cross on Calvary. The gospel itself, as the good news of deliverance from the devil, sin, and death, is in Jesus' "But I say to you" — words about vengeance, non-violence, compassion and generosity, prayer that expresses love for one's enemies, and genuine love for all people. The cross is the ultimate expression of love — and Jesus had to die on the cross to make that love concrete in human experience. In this combination of teachings, Jesus was preparing his disciples so that they could understand his death in the light of the ethics of the kingdom of God. Matthew passes this teaching along to us, too.

4. The bottom line for us is to try to *be perfect as Jesus was perfect*, no matter what it may cost us. Who is willing to pay that price by forgiving one's enemies instead of calling for their destruction? Jesus was, are we?

A sermon on the First Lesson — "Love My Neighbor? Who Says So?"

Most of this lesson interfaces nicely with the Gospel for the Day. It sounds the same note as the gospel, "You must love your neighbor as yourself." Many years ago I read a story about the archbishop of a third-world country in Africa, who was asked to bless some tanks for the country's military forces. The reporter covering the story, who was insulted by his assignment, could not understand why the archbishop would do such a thing. He met a native, as he was waiting for the ceremony to begin, who responded to his perplexity by explaining that "if you have to bless, you bless." He said that his neighbor's dog would come over to his garden and do considerable damage; asking the neighbor to restrain the dog did no good. He said, "I either have to bless him, or curse him, so I bless him." His response to the archbishop's perplexing action was this: "If you have to bless, you bless." God said something like that, through the author of Leviticus, to his people, when he declared, "You must love your neighbor as yourself."

1. Who says so? God says so. He is the one who has decreed that people should love other people as they love themselves. "My ways are not your ways," says God — but they should be!

2. God desires to eliminate hatred from the human vocabulary and from interpersonal relationships, as well. I was associated with a junior high school's girls' basketball team and overheard many of the comments the girls made about other people. So often, they said, "I hate her," or "Don't you hate him?" One had to wonder if they were serious, realizing that their attitude was damaging to team morale and, more importantly, destructive of developing character in these young people. And one also had to hope that they were simply going through a phase. Unfortunately, in most of us, that phase too often is life-long in nature.

3. God reserves vengeance for himself; " 'Vengeance is mine,' says the Lord." He does not allow human beings, when they are wronged, to take revenge on others, because he is the only one who is in a right position to judge the actions and motives of people. God alone is holy and is able to make right judgments of others.

4. Jesus became incarnate, for one thing, to show the world how this ethic could be fulfilled. His death gives ultimate expression to it. (Note: This lesson may simply be incorporated into the sermon on the Gospel for the Day. It is thoroughly compatible with the theme of the gospel.)

A sermon on the Second Lesson, 1 Corinthians 3:10-11, 16-23 — "On Building the Church."

1. The church of Jesus Christ was built once and for all, but it has to be built-up in every generation and in every place. The work might be begun by one person (Paul, for example), but others build on the work done before them. The fate of the church in China was unknown for several decades; some people thought that the church would have to be built from the ground up once China became an internationally open society again, but that is not so. The church in China is probably stronger, even larger, now than when the missionaries were expelled in the late 1940's. A Chinese Christian in Shanghai, whose congregation was very much alive, told me that the churches don't need missionaries or money from the western churches, because they were able to carry on by themselves, building up the church in a time of persecution. He said that they need contact with other parts of the church to exchange theological and biblical insights, as well as to show the world the inclusive nature of the body of Christ, the church.

2. The church is holy because it belongs to God, not to the people who are members of it here on earth. William Willimon once composed an experimental sermon about worship, in which a "clown" enters a church building and interrupts the worship service by engaging the pastor in a dialogue about what is going on in that place. At one point in the two-way discussion (dialogue sermons, wherein two people talk to each other, are really "double-monologue sermons," because the congregation has no active part in them; the people are spectators, as well they may be in a straight monologue type of pulpit address), the clown asks the pastor, "Who owns this place, anyway?" The pastor responds, "God does." "Who paid for it?" continues the clown. The pastor answers, "They did (the people)." And the clown replies, "Well, if they paid for it, I'll bet they think they own it." Something like that applies to our congregations; we think they are ours, because we belong to them and are engaged in their upbuilding, but every congregation belongs to God as part of the church of Jesus Christ.

3. As we engage in "church building," we are doing the work of God, and building on the foundation that he laid in Jesus Christ our Lord.

The Transfiguration of Our Lord
Eighth Sunday after the Epiphany
Eighth Sunday in Ordinary Time

Roman Catholic	Isaiah 49:14-15	1 Corinthians 4:1-5	Matthew 6:24-34
Episcopal	Exodus 24:12 (13-14) 15-18	Philippians 3:7-14	Matthew 17:1-9
Lutheran	Exodus 24:12,	2 Peter 16-19	Matthew 17:1-9
Common	Leviticus 1-2, 9-18	1 Corinthians 4:1-5	Matthew 5:38-48

The church year theological clue

Most Lutheran, Episcopal, and some other churches celebrate the Transfiguration on the Last Sunday after the Epiphany, rather than on the traditional date of August 6. This tends to give theological definition to the end of the Epiphany season and the entire Christmas cycle, as well. The *incarnation/manifestation* note is sounded again in the Gospel for the Day, "This is my beloved Son, with whom I am well pleased. Listen to him." The word God spoke at Jesus' baptism is repeated here and is meant to provide transition into the Easter cycle and, particularly, to the season of Lent; when the Luke account is used, Series C, the transition is patently clear. The other churches, which simply use the propers for the Sunday which chronologically occurs on this date, do not seem to enjoy the same degree of closure to the season, nor transition to Lent and Easter, either. The theological/liturgical/homiletical clue is not so apparent in their propers.

The Prayer of the Day — The LBW provides two prayers for the Transfiguration of Our Lord; both of them mention the Transfiguration specifically. The first emphasizes the glory of God that was shown — manifested — "in the transfiguration of your Son." The petition is eschatological, asking God to "give us the vision to see beyond the turmoil of our world and to behold the king in all his glory." The second prayer is related to the confirmation of the faith "by the witness of Moses and Elijah," and that "in the voice from the bright cloud you foreshadowed our adoption as your children." The petition sentence asks God to "make us with the king heirs of your glory, and bring us to enjoy its fullness." Both bring Epiphany to a fitting conclusion and, rather subtly, point the church toward Calvary.

The collect for the last Sunday after the Epiphany in the Protestant Episcopal Church prepares the people for Lent even more specifically; "O God, who before the passion of your only-begotten Son revealed his glory upon the holy mountain . . . ." The intention of this collect cannot be missed; it also functions in a two-fold manner, bringing Epiphany to its conclusion and bridging the gap between Epiphany and Ash Wednesday. "Grant to us that we, beholding by faith the light of his countenance," the prayer continues, "may be strengthened to bear our cross, and be changed into his likeness from glory to glory."

The Psalm of the Day (LBW) — Psalm 2:6-13 — Verse 7 makes it absolutely clear why this psalm was chosen for the Transfiguration, "Let me announce the decree of the Lord: He said to me, 'You are my son; this day have I begotten you.' " (Of course, the psalm could also be used for the Baptism of Our Lord). In the early verses of the psalm, the passion is foreshadowed — "Why do the kings of the earth rise up in revolt, and the princes plot together, against the Lord and against his anointed?" The psalmist understands that God will give this son "the nations for (his) possession." Finally, he calls upon the rulers of the world to "be warned," and to "submit to the Lord with fear, and with trembling bow before him," which functions almost like the word in the gospel, "Listen to him." Those who do so will be happy in the Lord; those who do not will perish.

The Psalm Prayer

> *Lord God, you gave the peoples of the world to be the inheritance of your Son; you crowned him as king of Zion, your holy city, and gave him your Church as his bride. As he proclaims the way of your eternal kingdom, may we serve him faithfully, and so know the royal power of your Son, Jesus Christ our Lord.*

The readings:

Exodus 24:12, 15-18

The experience of Moses, when God commanded him to go up Mt. Sinai to receive the tablets of the law, is a type of the transfiguration experience of Jesus on another mountain centuries later. The glory of God took Moses up into a cloud that must have seemed like a volcano to the people who watched and waited below. They must have thought that he had been devoured by the mountain; he stayed there forty days and forty nights (a pattern for Jesus' retreat to the wilderness after his baptism?) before he went down from the mountain to rejoin the people. (If the pastor intends to preach from this text, it would be well to read the entire context of this pericope and approach it from its narrative perspective. It is a story worth telling, especially alongside the Transfiguration of Jesus, over and over again.)

2 Peter 1:16-19, (20-21)

The Christians must have been accused of telling tall tales about Jesus and, apparently, one of the tallest of these was the story of Jesus' Transfiguration on the mountain; it was too much to believe! Had the story merely mentioned what happened to Jesus, and even the voice speaking, "This is my beloved Son," it might not have been too hard to believe. But to talk about the appearance of Moses and Elijah, and to insist that they were actually talking with Jesus, was too much to accept; sheer reason dictated that this was indeed a tall tale. The author of 1 Peter, however, sticks to the story; he insists that human beings did not concoct this event, but that it actually happened. It was orchestrated by God himself, not by the imagination and ingenuity of human minds. He declares,

> *We were eyewitnesses of his majesty . . . when he received honor and glory from God the Father and the voice (said) . . . , "This is my beloved Son, with whom I am well pleased."*

Not only did they see Jesus transfigured, talking to Moses and Elijah, but they also heard the voice that identified Jesus Christ as the Son of God. So theirs was the evidence of sight and of sound and, in the light of their post-resurrection experiences with the Lord, they call upon all people "to pay attention to this as to a lamp shining in a dark place, until the day dawns and the morning star rises in your hearts." This reading, therefore, is especially appropriate for the last Sunday of Epiphany, as well as for the Transfiguration of Our Lord.

Matthew 17:1-9

The Transfiguration of Our Lord is celebrated on three different days in the church year. August 6 is the actual date set aside for this feast/festival, when it receives attention as a separate event in the life, history, and experience of the church. The Episcopal Church observes the Transfiguration as a Holy Day and reads this Gospel on August 6, as well as on the last Sunday of Epiphany. The Roman Catholic Church, which retains the August 6 date in its calendar, really celebrates the Transfiguration on the Second Sunday in Lent. A strong

90

argument can be made for this, especially in the year of Luke, who is the only one of the evangelists to divulge that Moses and Elijah were talking to Jesus about his "exodus" that was soon to occur in Jerusalem. The Common Lectionary also coincides with the Lutheran and Episcopal lectionaries in the appointment of the Transfiguration of Our Lord on the Last Sunday after the Epiphany. All of the liturgical churches tend to celebrate the Transfiguration only once, even if their calendars list the propers on two different liturgical dates.

The argument presented by 1 Peter supports, according to some scholars, the actuality of the Transfiguration, insisting that this event really did occur. Others believe that it is central to Matthew's christological argument, closely paralleling the happenings at Jesus' baptism, while drawing on Exodus 24 for much of its detail. This much is absolutely clear to the preacher: it is the intention of the (Lutheran) Church, at least, that the minister of the Word should grapple with the central truth of this pericope — that Jesus Christ is the Son of God, who came into the world, at the Father's bidding, to turn things around in human affairs, and to bring about reconciliation of God and his people — no matter if it cost him his life. The connection between Jesus' Transfiguration and his crucifixion, which Luke links up on top of the mountain, is made by Matthew as Jesus and the three disciples descend from the mountain and he says, "Tell no one the vision, until the Son of man is raised from the dead." Therefore, when the Transfiguration of Our Lord is celebrated on the Last Sunday after the Epiphany, the gap from Epiphany into Lent is closed by the declaration, "This (Jesus) is my beloved Son, with whom I am well pleased." "Listen to him" moves the church into the season of Lent as part of the Easter cycle. Is it too much to suggest that, since the baptismal pronouncement, "This is my beloved Son," is made in this gospel, that the baptismal content of Lent is thereby rather subtly suggested? This could be another argument for setting the Transfiguration at the end of Epiphany, just three days before Ash Wednesday and the beginning of Lent.

A sermon on the Gospel, Matthew 17:1-9 — "The Spectacle on the Mountain."

St. Paul Outside the Walls is one of the seven pilgrimage churches left in Rome; at one time, there were at least 55 such edifices. Pilgrims, as well as interested tourists, continue to visit this and the other six churches when they go to Rome, mostly to give honor to St. Paul, who is buried there. But the glory belongs to Jesus Christ, as the mosaic in the apse of the church announces. In it, Jesus is "seated in glory, offering his blessings from above the altar." Almost unobserved, a tiny, vested figure kneels by Jesus' foot; he is bent over in a posture which depicts his kissing Jesus' foot. He is a pope, according to his vestments, but which one? Is he the pope who planned the rebuilding of St. Paul's? Has the 13th century (mosaic) simply been altered by a later playful father? Could this be a representation of St. Paul, put there to remind the popes and all Christians of the full glory of Christ. Or could this be a representation of all the popes and people (caught up in this one little figure) to show the brightness of his glory in the world which must fall down and worship him . . . .?" (from *The Renewal of Liturgical Preaching).* The Transfiguration pictures the glorification of Jesus Christ in such godly proportions — "This is my beloved Son" — that those who really hear the story and "see" the transfigured Christ can do no other than fall down and worship him.

1. The retreat to a mountain top was an "invitation only" affair; only Peter, James, and John were allowed to ascend the mountain with Jesus. When Moses went up Mt. Sinai at the command of God, he took Joshua with him; he might have told Joshua that they were going up the mountain to get the stone tablets of the law and the commandments that God had prepared for the Israelites. Matthew doesn't suggest that Jesus went up the mountain in response to a message from his Father; the only clue comes in Chapter 16, where Jesus tells the disciples what is going to happen — including his death and resurrection — at Jerusalem. The import of those words must have taken a spiritual toll upon the Lord, which took him up the mountain, needing not only time with God but the support of his closest disciples, Peter, James, and John. What person can face impending and certain death lightly, without need of comfort and assurance? Death is too much for the best of us, and even Jesus needed company when he faced up to what was to happen to him in the near future.

2. When Jesus was transfigured, Peter wanted to hedge his bets; he wanted to make certain that something good and lasting would come out of this experience — some kind of a memorial or marker — so he blurted out, "Lord, it is well that we are here; if you wish, I will make three booths here, one for you and one for Moses and one for Elijah." Before Jesus could reply, God intervened once more — he "overshadowed all four of them — and thundered, 'This is my beloved Son, with whom I am well pleased; listen to him.'" Who wouldn't do what they did in that situation — fall down on their knees in fear and trembling? And when Jesus reassured them and they "lifted up their eyes, they saw no one but Jesus only." This is what the season of Epiphany has been building up to, the glorification of Jesus Christ the Lord; the word reveals that Jesus is the Son of God and is destined to be the Savior of the world.

3. In the spectacle on the mountain, the glory of the Lord was revealed, not only to Peter, James, and John, but to the whole world. When God spoke at Jesus' baptism, it was largely a matter of identification; on the mountain, God accomplished the *glorification* of the Lord as the one who, when he was lifted up on the cross, would draw all people to himself; it was Jesus' confirmation day. Something like that happened to Moses the second time he went up to the top of Mt. Sinai; God took him up in the cloud, and when he went down from the mountain, there was a radiance about his countenance that told the Israelites that something dramatic had occurred between Moses and the Lord God. The disciples actually saw the transfigured Jesus, witnessed his glory, but completely misunderstood what was taking place, as the evangelist tells us the story.

4. Peter, James, and John probably couldn't wait to get down the mountain to tell the others what they had experienced with Jesus. But Jesus knew what they wanted to do and stopped them in their tracks: "Tell no one the vision, until the Son of man is raised from the dead." How could this come about, that the Son of God, the Jesus they had just seen glorified by the Father, could possibly be put to death in Jerusalem? This much we know; the story of the Transfiguration was not told until after Jesus' death and resurrection. When it is told today, we are made ready to enter into the season of death, Lent, in the hope of receiving some answers on the way to the cross and the empty tomb.

A sermon sketch on the First Lesson — Exodus 24:12, 15-18 — "A Man on a Mountain."

1. Central to the Exodus, as the Israelites moved from Egypt to the Promised Land, is the experience of one man, Moses, with God at Mt. Sinai. (Retell this story, briefly, as a kind of a "Readers' Digest" shortened version of the biblical account of God's giving the Ten Commandments to Moses and Israel. Most "man on the mountain" stories today are about mountain climbers, who battle great odds, display tremendous courage, and superb strength, as they attempt to reach the top of the highest mountains on earth. In this story, God is center stage, the protagonist, in the drama of what happened to the man on the mountain. The story has to be told from this perspective.)

2. God put on a "sound and light" show of his own for six days on top of Mt. Sinai as "the glory of the Lord settled" on the mountain. Apparently, the Israelites couldn't miss the demonstration of God's glory; it must have seemed like a volcano to them; they had never seen anything like it, and had to wonder what was going on up there.

3. On the seventh day, Moses was "captured" by the cloud on top of Mt. Sinai. It apparently took a considerable period of time before God got through to Moses and Moses was ready to receive the law and the commandments for Israel. Moses must have been

92

something of a tough nut to crack, but God got to him at last. That tells me that there is hope for us; God will be patient, taking his time "to get to us" so that we "see" his full glory in Jesus Christ, his Son, and our Lord.

4. Moses, the man of God on the mountain was so overcome by what happened to him that he stayed there for forty days and forty nights. That really is how — and where — Lent began. The man on the mountain was the first penitent; he waits — with Jesus — for us to join him in Lent.

A sermon on the Second Lesson, 2 Peter 1:16-19 (20-21) — "We Were There."

1. Some years ago, Edmund Steimle preached an Easter sermon that he titled, "No Idle Tale." He asserted, by his references to the Easter story and the accounts that substantiate it, that "it is all true." The resurrection of Jesus, he declared, really took place as the evangelists reported it; it is "no idle tale." That's what "Peter" says of the Transfiguration of the Lord; we didn't make it up because "we were eyewitnesses of his majesty . . . when he received honor and glory from the Father and the voice (said) . . . 'This is my beloved Son, with whom I am well pleased.' " The story of Jesus, including this part, is true; no one made it up.

2. The Transfiguration of Jesus is the fulfillment of scripture, as Peter, James, and John perceive it. They know very well what had happened to Moses at Mt. Sinai and, when something like that happened to them when they were with the Lord, they came to understand that this was God's way of fulfilling the words of the prophets about the Messiah. The man who was transfigured in their presence on the mountain could be none other than the Messiah himself. Peter wants us to believe this, too.

3. When one has doubts about this part of the story, or anything else in the gospel, one should ponder the Word and give God time, through the Holy Spirit, to "break through the darkness" within us "until the day dawns and the morning star rises in your hearts." It is in facing up to the mystery of Jesus that God helps us to accept Jesus as the crucified and risen Son of God. We cannot go back to the mountain and be eyewitnesses of the glorification of Jesus, as did Peter, James, and John. But God is with us in this quest for assurance and faith, and he enables us to believe this story and know, as we enter Lent, that Jesus is the Lord, the blessed Son of God.

The Easter Cycle

This cycle is made up of two seasons, Lent and Easter, which together form exactly **one-quarter** of the calendar and church years; the cycle is always thirteen weeks long, having 6½ weeks in Lent and 7 weeks in the Easter Season. Unlike Advent, which could exist on its own as an eschatological season, Lent cannot be separated from Easter. The crucifixion of Christ is the conclusion of Lent; without the resurrection of the Lord, Jesus would only be a martyr, or worse. Since Easter — the great fifty days — is the "essential season" of the church year, it gives its name to the entire cycle. Easter, of course, deals with the redeeming events, the death and resurrection of the Lord. It puts its mark on every Sunday of the year; every Sunday is a "little Easter," a celebration of the cross and the resurrection. In this respect, Easter is a unitive event, always keeping death and resurrection together. But there are practical problems, both in worship and preaching, and one of these problems is that church people don't have a very good grasp of the nature of the Easter cycle, the manner in which Lent and Easter are inextricably bound together, and numerous pastors are not aware of the importance of keeping the two seasons together in their homiletical planning and their preaching. Practically, Lent has almost supplanted Easter as the essential season of the church year; it represents, as celebrated in most churches, a reversal of the practices and the anastasial theology of the early Church.

The Season of Lent

Lent is a period of forty days, penitential in nature, and taking its shape from the forty days that Jesus spent in the desert after his baptism in the Jordan; it has biblical connections with the forty days Moses spent on Mt. Sinai and Elijah's forty-day journey to Mt. Horeb, both of which were forty-day fasts. Actually, it assumed its shape and length gradually in something of an evovlutionary process; at first, it was only a three-day observance, then it took the shape of a three-week period, later it had different lengths in various parts of the church until finally it became the six-and-a-half week season (nine-and-a-half weeks when pre-Lent — the "gesima" Sundays — was added to Lent) that it is today.

Lent apparently did not take the shape of a long preparatory fast until it was expanded from the *triduum* (Good Friday, Holy Saturday, and Easter) to three weeks and then to an actual forty days. At first, that fast began on what is now the First Sunday in Lent — originally known as the *quadrigesima,* or forty days before Easter (actually, before the *triduum).* That is why the First Sunday in Lent always uses the gospel reading that tells the story of Jesus' forty days in the desert wilderness; the model for Lent is found in this forty-day typology. Later, Sundays were removed from Lent and the extra days, Ash Wednesday to the Saturday before the First Sunday of Lent, were added; in some places, the *triduum* now became Holy Thursday, Good Friday, and Holy Saturday. And later on the pre-Lent Sundays were added — the *quinquagesima,* then *sexagesima,* and, finally, *septuagesima,* as fifty, sixty, and seventy days before Easter.

As Lent became longer and the faithful joined the catechumens in the observance of Lent, Lent lost much of its pre-baptismal character and became a season primarily devoted to spiritual preparation for Easter. The Lenten discipline, which was supposed to be undertaken by the faithful for the forty days of Lent, consisted primarily of fasting, almsgiving, and prayer. The traditional Gospel for Ash Wednesday, from Matthew 6, outlines these threefold marks of a faithful "keeping" of Lent that all of the members of the church were to make part of their daily lives; Lent took on the character of a "spring revival" in much of the church. The contemporary world situation that the church finds itself in calls for new interpretations of Lenten discipline which turn the people of God toward the suffering and desperate needs of people today and puts the human predicament before the cross of Christ. Lent cannot be an exclusively "interiorized" spiritual journey; the suffering of Christ does not allow that in light of people's problems today.

Pastors attempting to make the most of Lent should remember that Lent was connected to Easter through the passion and death of the Lord and also in the Sacrament of Baptism. Easter was the principal day for baptism. Lent, in that age, had the character of an educational, as well as spiritual, event for the catechumens; they underwent three "scrutinies," which consisted of exorcisms and instructions in the faith; they were instructed in the secrets of the church (the Creed, the Lord's Prayer, etc.). And, finally, they were baptized on Easter Day. Some congregtions today are returning to the ancient practice of doing the final educational and ceremonial rites of confirmation during Lent, scheduling confirmation on the Sunday of the Passion, if it can't be scheduled for Easter Sunday. The rediscovery and reconstruction of the Easter Vigil has led to the reaffirmation on the baptismal covenant of the believers in attendance at this the first eucharist of Easter. These developments suggest that *the theological framework of Lent is Baptism as incorporated into the death and resurrection of Christ.* In baptismal preaching, the pastor may discover the best way to make the most of Lent and, also, of the entire Easter Cycle. (For examples of such preaching, see *Plastic Flowers in the Holy Water* [C.S.S.], *You Are My Beloved* [with Frederick Kemper, Concordia], and *Is the Cross Still There? Letter to Jennifer,* [C.S.S. to be published in 1991.])

The problems pastors face as they prepare their preaching for Lent may be these:

1. Lent tends to dominate the worship and preaching of the Easter Cycle. Accordingly, Easter has become a one-day celebration instead of the "essential season" of the church year.

2. Lent is really a "Sunday-only season" for most contemporary Christians; A few of the faithful keep the fast by attending and participating in the weekday services of Lent. Preachers, therefore, have to make the most of Sunday preaching during Lent.

3. Lent has become a "bloodless sacrifice" for most, possibly because the almost-exclusive preaching emphasis on the passion and death of Christ has tended to diminish the dimensions of human predicament, sin and death, which are responsible for so much human suffering.

4. Lent has become so cross and Good Friday oriented that the joy of Easter is muted and the theological dimensions of new life in Christ — through baptism, which is the point of participating in the discipline of Lent — are reduced or even lost.

To make the most of preaching during Lent, the pastor must understand the nature of the Easter Cycle and plan before Lent begins the worship and preaching for the entire cycle from both sides of the cross and empty tomb — and with the involvement of the faithful through the renewal of their baptismal covenant. Over against Ash Wednesday's sobering word, "You are dust and unto dust you shall return." The gospel promise of the risen Lord, "Behold, I make all things new" has to be sounded loudly and clearly.

In summary, it remains that Ash Wednesday — over against the Easter event (cross and resurrection) — is the liturgical, homiletical, and theological key to the worship and preaching of Lent. Its *first* word is, "Remember, you are dust, and unto dust you shall return." The Gospel for Ash Wednesday is the traditional one — and only one set of pericopes is prescribed for all three years of the lectionary — Matthew 6:1-6, 16-21; the other readings from Joel 2 and 2 Corinthians 5 and 6 are also traditional. The Ash Wednesday Gospel makes it perfectly clear that Lent is about the human predicament, sin and death, rather than entirely about the passion and death of Christ. Holy Week and Easter inform the church how God has dealt with human frailty and the inability of people to obey his commandments and save themselves from the devil and death in the death and resurrection of Jesus. This predicament — sin and death — finds resolution in preaching in the context of baptism as incorporation into the new covenant in Jesus and the body of Christ, the church. Ash Wednesday's terrifying reminder is answered in baptismal preaching during Lent: *those who die with Christ, in baptism, also share in his resurrection and the new life of the risen Lord.*

In the light of all this, planning for the worship and preaching of Lent is of crucial importance, which many pastors seem to comprehend; Lent is the one time of the year that parish pastors, who may exist on a kind of hand-to-mouth homiletical regimen from Sunday to Sunday, do plan in detail. But most of us plan only for Lent and fail to plan for Easter. I suggest that planning for the entire Easter Cycle is necessary, if one is going to be faithful to the church year themes in the Sunday and weekly opportunities to proclaim the good new to the people. When the congregations perceive how seriously their pastors are taking their preaching ministries during the entire Easter Cycle — and not just Lent — they will most likely respond by attending worship with more regularity and enthusiasm and may even learn to make more out of Lent and Easter, so as to live out their baptism in the world.

Suggestions for a
Mid-Week Sermon Series in Lent

1. Every sermon series for Lent should begin on Ash Wednesday, when the sermon needs to articulate the human predicament, death, with the pronouncement, "Remember, you are dust and unto dust you will return." In congregations where there is no imposition of ashes, the first day of Lent will be *Ashless Wednesday* unless this theme is included in the sermon, either as the introduction both to the sermon and Lent or as the actual theme of the sermon (in which case, one would need to read, and perhaps retell, most of Genesis 3 as the sermon text).

2. Plan the worship and, particularly, the preaching for the entire cycle around a theme that wrestles with the kerygmatic theology of the Easter Cycle; the content of such a series ought to be sound, solid, and evangelical.

3. If a mid-week Lenten sermon series is planned, plan to extend the series — and special worship services — through Eastertide. (When people perceive the importance of the complete cycle, in the light of the human predicament, they just may become more mature in their faith and their daily responses to the Word.)

4. Develop titles that attract people and pique their interest in the sermons, making certain that they say something of importance related to the theme or story-line of the sermon. Avoid catchy titles and spectacular themes that have nothing to do with the business of Lent (and Easter), which is facing up to the human predicament and how God has dealt with it in Jesus' death and resurrection.

5. Create a title for the entire series, which will tell what the theme is for the sermons of Lent. It would be well to do this for Sundays, as well as the mid-week services. Books of sermons for Lent and Easter offer some models for the parish pastor. A list of some of the titles I have used follows to illustrate this point:

The Garden and the Graveyard — Genesis 1-11, Ash Wednesday to Easter Sunday (Augsburg, 1971)

The Pilgrims and the Passion — Psalms of Ascent, Ash Wednesday to Easter Sunday (Augsburg, 1973)

Plastic Flowers in the Holy Water — Baptism, Ash Wednesday to Easter (C.S.S., 1981)

You Are My Beloved Children — Baptism in the Sunday Gospels, series B, Lent and Easter (Concordia, 1981)

The Tree, the Tomb, and the Trumpet — Gospels, series B, Lent and Easter (C.S.S., 1984) This could be adapted to mid-week preaching by developing two-part sermons. Part I would be preached on Sunday; Part II during the week.

Is the Cross Still There? — Baptism, Ash Wednesday to Easter: Letter to Jennifer, (C.S.S., to be published in 1991)

As often as possible, I now attempt to do inclusive planning for Lent and Easter, as two of the above titles indicate, but this is not always possible when one is a guest preacher. More often than not, I preach a series of sermons for Lent, sometimes on Sundays, more often at mid-week services. *Is the Cross Still There?* is a revision and expansion of a Lenten series preached in St. Luke's Lutheran Church, Bloomington, Minnesota, in 1988 and, in revised form, in St. Michael's Lutheran Church, Roseville, Minnesota, in 1989. These are the titles for the nine sermons, seven of which were preached:

1. "Letter to Jennifer" — Romans 5:1-11
2. "Lent Declares, 'The Cross is Still There'" — Genesis 3 and 3:19

3. "Baptism and the Book of Life" — Philippians 4:1-9
4. "The Church — A Special Community" — 1 Corinthians 12:12, 13
5. "The Ministry of the Baptized" — 2 Corinthians 6:3-10 (Luke 3:3-9)
6. "Marked for a Mission" — Mark 16:14-20
7. "Supper Near the Water" — John 13:1-16 (Maundy Thursday)
8. "The Cross: Sign of God's Love" — Luke 23:33-46 (Good Friday)
9. "The Cross Will Always Be There" — Luke 24:1-12 (Easter)

6. Apply the theology of the texts used for the sermons through graphic illustrations and stories which make positive connections with contemporary life. *A sermon always allows the text to speak to people living now and wrestling with life and its predicaments.*

7. Read widely. See with perception what is happening in the world. Reflect on what is read and observed. Then fill files, computer disks, and/or journals with these things and a ready store of illustrations and stories will be available when writing sermons. Avoid, at all costs, the last-minute hunt for impact materials (illustrations and stories, excerpts from plays, movies, books, etc.); too much time is lost in that type of process.

8. Prepare your sermons in time to learn them. Keep in mind that Andrew Blackwood used to say that one's sermon preparation is not finished until the sermon is learned.

Ash Wednesday

Roman Catholic	Joel 2:12-19	2 Corinthians 5:20b—6:2	Matthew 6:1-6, 16-18
Episcopal	Joel 2:1-2, 12-17 or Isaiah 58:1-12	2 Corinthians 5:20b—6:10	Matthew 6:1-6, 16-21
Lutheran	Joel 2:12-19	2 Corinthians 5:20b—6:2	Matthew 6:1-6, 16-21
Common	Joel 2:12-19	2 Corinthians 5:20b—6:2	Matthew 6:1-6, 16-21

The church year theological clue

The title of this day, Ash Wednesday — the rite for the imposition of ashes on the foreheads of the penitents and the central proclamation of the day, "You are dust, and unto dust you will return" provide the theological clue for preaching during Lent and Easter. Every person who is born here on the earth will, sooner or later, be claimed by death. The Genesis 3 story is certainly true in this respect; no one is exempt from death — even Jesus, the very Son of God, had to die, partly because his incarnation caused him to share fully in the human experience of life and death, as well as to atone for the sins of others and bestow salvation upon repentant sinners. The grip of death is destroyed and people are released in the resurrection of Jesus Christ. Easter reverses Ash Wednesday's awful announcement and says, "You are children of God, and through the living Christ you shall live forever." The death of human beings is preached during the season of Lent in the shadow of the cross; Jesus had to die in order to conquer death once and for all. The final and total victory will come with the Parousia; when Jesus returns, death, which has been already conquered by Christ, will be no more. The Second Coming of the Lord will usher in the day of abundant and eternal life for the children of God.

The Prayer of the Day (LBW) — This is simply a revision of the traditional — and classic — Ash Wednesday collect appointed for use in many of the Western churches. God is addressed as a creator who loves all that he has made and forgives penitent sinners of their wrong-doings. The petition for God's grace looks to the cross and the empty tomb, asking God to

> create in us new and honest hearts, so that, truly repenting of our sins, we may obtain from you, the God of all mercy, full pardon and forgiveness; through your Son, Jesus Christ our Lord, who lives and reigns with you and the Holy Spirit, one God, now and forever.

In some parts of the church, this collect may be said as the first collect every day in Lent.

The Psalm of the Day (LBW) — Psalm 51 — is the plea of a penitent (David, it is assumed) who is deeply aware of his sin, has searched his heart, and lifts up his voice to his Maker, pleading for mercy and forgiveness. It is one of the most abject prayers of confession and pardon in the whole Bible. The penitent knows the character of God, because he asks — "in your great compassion" — for ultimate absolution — "blot out my offenses." He knows his own situation perfectly, "I know my transgressions, and my sin is ever before me," and even that "I have been wicked from my birth, a sinner from my mother's womb." The intensity and singular beauty of his plea increases with these words that found their way, for obvious reasons, into the liturgies of the church long ago:

> Purge me from my sin, and I shall be pure;
> wash me, and I shall be clean indeed . . .
> (a baptismal connection?)
> Hide your face from my sins
> and blot out all my iniquities.

Create in me a clean heart, O God,
and renew a right spirit within me.
Cast me not away from your presence,
and take not your Holy Spirit from me.
Give me the joy of your saving help again,
and sustain me with your bountiful Spirit.

As the Psalmist nears the end of his prayer, he cries out the word that all who have heard God's Word in the Garden ("You are dust, and unto dust you will return") need to address to God — "Deliver me from death, O God, and my tongue shall sing of your righteousness, O God of my salvation." When he adds, "The sacrifice of God is a troubled spirit; a broken and contrite heart, O God, you will not despise," there is no mistaking that this is a psalm for Lent, especially for Ash Wednesday.

The Psalm Prayer

Almighty and merciful Father, you freely forgive those who, as David of old, acknowledge and confess their sins. Create in us pure hearts, and wash away all our sins in the blood of your dear Son, Jesus Christ our Lord.

Clearly, this is not only a prayer for Ash Wednesday, but one that is also suitable for the entire season.

The readings:

Joel 2:12-19

In this reading, it is God himself who issues the *invitation* to begin the season of Lent by engaging in the penitential discipline described in this text, which is reiterated in a different form and then expanded in Jesus' teaching in Matthew 6, the Gospel for the Day. The invitation is to "Return to the Lord, your God, for he is gracious and merciful, slow to anger, and abounding in steadfast love." With the invitation, there is also a *command* that is most appropriate for Ash Wednesday and the full season of Lent: "Blow the trumpet in Zion; sanctify a fast; call a solemn assembly; gather the people." Those who respond, or in the case of Christians "keep Lent," tell the world that they know "where" their God is; he is "in Christ, reconciling the world to himself." The final part is a *promise* to the people of Israel: "the Lord had pity on his people . . . and said, . . 'Behold, I am sending to you grain, wine, and oil, and you will be satisfied; and I will no more make you a reproach among the nations.' " God is as good as his promise; the death and resurrection of our Lord tell us that.

2 Corinthians 5:20b—6:2

Paul's plea to the church at Corinth, "we beseech you on behalf of Christ, be reconciled to God," speaks specifically of the mercy God has extended to the world, to all who know themselves to be sinners, in Jesus Christ. Jesus became "sin, who knew no sin, so that in him we might become the righteousness of God." This is almost an accusation of the Corinthian congregation — which might be one of our problems, too — that they have not taken the gospel as seriously as they should have, apparently, not comprehending that their sin separates them from God when it goes unrecognized and unconfessed. Genuinely repentant sinners, who base their hope of forgiveness and new life on Christ, are the only ones who can really be reconciled to God, because reconciliation comes through Jesus' death on

100

Golgotha. His plea, "we entreat you not to accept the grace of God in vain," points to the root of our predicament in our separation from God, assuring us that God will accept us forever in the Lord. Lent, for the Christian, "is the acceptable time; behold, now is the day of salvation."

Matthew 6:1-6, 16-18 (19-21)

The spiritual discipline of Lent is spelled out in detail in this gospel in the context of, as Jesus puts it, "your Father who sees in secret (and) will reward you." In the practice of "piety," Jesus lists almsgiving first and directs that it should be done secretly and without any show of generosity; to advertise one's charity, so that others may see it and praise the giver, is unacceptable to God. To those whose giving has been acknowledged by others, Jesus says, "You have already received your reward." Prayer is the second act of piety that godly persons should practice, but not in ways that bring attention to one's religiosity; such prayer, which is done to gain honor from others and is not really directed to God, is hypocritical and, therefore, worthless. Fasting, which is the last of the three acts of piety in Jesus' teaching, and is almost unknown among Americans, is also a spiritual exercise that has no merit unless it is performed to heighten one's sense of self-denial and the quest for the presence of God. In his forty days in the wilderness, Jesus engaged in two of these disciplines and did so in a one-on-one relationship with his heavenly Father. This, no doubt, sustained him when the tempter tried to win him over to himself. When we follow his example, these devotional actions are not only expressions of penitence and self-denial, but are also signs of our complete dependence upon Jesus Christ for salvation. Our almsgiving, prayers, and fasting are expressions of our gratitude and love, as well as repentance.

One of the puzzles about this traditional gospel is that the Lord's Prayer has been omitted in the Ash Wednesday pericope. Since Jesus gave it to the disciples to teach them how to pray, it might be used for mid-week preaching, or, in some situations that are isolated by pastoral exegesis, as a Sunday sermon series.

A sermon on the Gospel, Matthew 6:1-6, 16-18 (19-21) — "Jesus Tells Us How to Keep Lent."

In the midst of Jesus' teaching on the mountain, there was — from our perspective — a complete time change; suddenly it was Lent. Those who have heard the Word of God; "You are dust, and unto dust you shall return," will be open to what Jesus has to say about piety. Because we know our predicament — impending death — and can do nothing to avoid it, we turn to God for deliverance with a *mea culpa, mea maxima culpa* and *kyrie eleison* in the hope that God will heed our prayers and save us from sin and death. Because we know that we are sinners and will finally get what we deserve — death — we are wont to follow Jesus' spiritual prescription, not to attempt to save ourselves but knowing that he has saved us and will incercede with God his Father — and ours — on our behalf. In the meantime, in the hope that this will become the pattern of our spiritual lives, we seek to do what he tells us to do.

1. Christians are peculiar people, whom God expects to give generously to those in need, because they know that God has given generously to them in Jesus Christ. At the heart of their faith is the knowledge that "God so loved the world that he gave his only Son, that whoever believes in him should not perish but have eternal life." The alms are given to others, but it is only God's business to know the giver and the amount of the gift.

I know of a congregation in which the tithers had different colored envelopes than the non-tithers. When the offering place was passed in that church, it was as if the tithers were standing on their feet and saying to the others, "See what I am doing for the Lord; I am a tither and a better giver than you are. Hey! Look at me!" The most generous giver I ever knew was a lady who lived in almost abject poverty, was house-bound, living in the remnant of an old Pennsylvania farmhouse, who always had a gift for the poor whenever she received private communion. The pastor, the church treasurer, and the Lord were the only ones who knew about her alsmgiving. I'm certain that the Lord was happy; that's how he wants it to be.

2. Jesus couldn't stand hypocrites who prayed for self-glorification rather than to place themselves before the mercy seat of God. He still despises spiritual hypocrites, who may be those singing the hymns and the liturgy the loudest in the churches today. Prayer has both personal and private dimensions, but neither of them should draw attention to the one who offers prayer. While people today are not likely to pray loudly in church or on the street-corners, our sin may just be that the only time we pray is in church in that one hour on Sunday morning. Our prayer for Lent might just be, "Lord, teach us to pray" — privately and devotionally, in your name. Our trouble may be that God can't hear our prayers because we don't pray unless we're in desperate trouble and cannot help ourselves. An unknown author wrote:

> Two went to pray, oh, rather say
> One went to brag, the other to pray.
> One stood up close and trod on high
> Where the other dared not lend an eye.
> One near to God's altar trod,
> The other to the altar's God.

Sincere prayer takes us close to God, who gladly receives the prayers we offer in Jesus' name when we pray, "Lord, be merciful to me, a sinner."

3. As for this third act of piety that Jesus taught about — and which Lent puts before us today — we need to pray even more loudly and spiritedly, "Lord, teach us why we should fast," as well as, "Lord, help us to fast" during Lent. Fasting, in a world where there never seems to be enough food to go around, has practical implications never dreamed of in Jesus' day. They did know about drought and famine, but not in the scope that these are being experienced today, when millions of people are living on the verge of starvation. Fasting ought to take us closer to God so that we might be nearer to our neighbors' impossible situations, in which many people are not just hungry, but are actually starving to death. Fasting, in our world, is not simply a matter of spiritual discipline to be engaged in for forty days; it is a life and death response to Jesus' command "to love one another as I have loved you."

4. The spiritual discipline of Lent teaches us that to stay close to God through almsgiving, prayer, and fasting requires that we also be close to our neighbors in the world. That is the way that Lenten discipline does us some good, teaching us what self-sacrifice, loving service, and Christian living are all about. Above all else, engaging in the discipline of Lent indicates that we really know where our treasure — Jesus Christ — is, and that we cling to him with all our hearts, minds, and strength.

A sermon on the First Lesson, Joel 2:12-19 — "God's Plan for Lent."

1. God calls us in Lent to return to him with acts of repentance and spiritual devotion.
2. God tells us to call a solemn assembly and to gather the people (to the observance of the Lenten fast).
3. God shows us where he is in our world — he is there on the cross of his Son, Jesus Christ.
4. God sends us the riches we need to live, even to overcome death. He satisfies our every need and longing, and expects us to minister to others as he has to us.

102

A sermon on the Second Lesson, 2 Corinthians 5:20b—6:2 — "LENT — A Time to Stand Up and Be Counted."

1. *We "count" to God,* despite the fact that we are helpless and hopeless sinners; the cross of Christ tells us how much we count to God.

2. *To be "counted"* among those in communion with the Lord God, we need to become reconciled to him in Christ. Jesus has brought about reconciliation by dying for us on Calvary.

3. Today is the day that *the "counting" begins:* "Behold, now is the acceptable time; behold, now is the day of salvation."

4. Come and *"be counted"* by Christ, in the name of the heavenly Father.

First Sunday of Lent

Roman Catholic	**Genesis 2:7-9; 3:1-7**	**Romans 5:12-19**	**Matthew 4:1-11**
Episcopal	**Genesis 2:4b-9, 15-17, 25:3:7**	**Romans 5:12-19 (20-21)**	**Matthew 4:1-11**
Lutheran	**Genesis 2:7-9, 15-17; 3:1-7**	**Romans 5:12 (13-16), (17-19)**	**Matthew 4:1-11**
Common	**Genesis 2:4b-9, 15-17, 25—3:7**	**Romans 5:12-19**	**Matthew 4:1-11**

The church year theological clue

The structure of the church year determines, in all three years of the lectionary, that this Sunday is, in part, a "pattern" Sunday; it shows that Lent is a forty-day retreat by the faithful, "patterned" after Jesus' solitary sojourn in the wilderness immediately after he had been baptized in the Jordan. As a spiritual journey, Lent is observed in public and in private, in corporate worship and in individual devotions and actions. But, in the use of the Gospel for the Day, again in all three years, Satan is defeated by Jesus once and for all and the fate of Jesus is sealed; the Evil One has to do everything he can to get rid of him and, as the end of Lent reminds us, he does — but only for parts of three years. The temptation of Jesus gives hope to all who are aware of the consequences of sin — death — because Satan has been overcome and Christ remains the sinless Son of God, the only one who can offer a worthy sacrifice for sin to the Father and, thereby free humanity from sin and death.

The Prayer of the Day — The LBW offers two prayers for this Sunday; the first one would be suitable at the Easter Vigil because it has in it a reference to the Exodus and how God "brought them (Israel) to the promised land." It makes a rather subtle connection with Jesus' wilderness experience, asking God to "guide now the people of your Church, that, following our Savior, we may walk through the wilderness of this world toward the glory of the world to come." The prayer seeks to put this Gospel in its proper perspective. The second prayer addresses God, "our strength," in the face of temptation and the battle between good and evil that Satan wages within all of us. The prayer is realistic, seeking strength to be steadfast in the Word, but asking God to raise us when we fall and to restore us to grace through Jesus Christ. This prayer may be the more fitting and appropriate of the two prayers appointed for the First Sunday in Lent, depending upon the spiritual needs of the local congregation.

The Psalm of the Day (LBW) — Psalm 130 — Most funeral liturgies appoint this psalm as one of the lessons that may be read as part of the worship service. By using this psalm as a responsory, the church essentially puts it into the mouth of Jesus when he has concluded the forty-day fast and is tempted by Satan. He was close to a kind of death — maybe closer to actual death than he had been in the desert — because he would have been separated from God, along with all human beings, by sin. Jesus called upon God silently, no doubt, and he found strength to withstand the onslaughts of the Devil in the Word of God; God did hear his voice and "considered well the voice of (his) supplications." Of the Lord — and, hopefully, of us — it may well be said, "I wait for the Lord; my soul waits for him; in his word is my hope . . . . for with the Lord there is mercy." Part of the prayer is ours, not that of Jesus, although we believe it because he died to gain assurance for us, "If you, Lord, were to note what is amiss, O Lord, who could stand? For there is forgiveness with you, therefore you shall not be feared." Oh, Lord, hear our voices, for we are all close to death.

104

The Psalm Prayer

God of might and compassion, you sent your Word into the world as a watchman to announce the dawn of salvation. Do not leave us in the depths of our sins, but listen to your Church pleading for the fullness of your redeeming grace; through Jesus Christ our Lord.

The readings:

Genesis 2:7-9, 15-17; 3:1-7

The garden story of Adam and Eve — and the serpent — shows us how quickly and how completely human beings got "out of control." They couldn't handle the freedom that God had given them when he created people in his image. The world was too good, contained too much that attracted them and tempted them to disobey the injunctions of the Creator. Because he was — and is — God, the Father knew what was going to happen, but to make humanity in his image meant that he had to give his creatures the freedom to make their own ethical and moral choices. Pride and perversity combine to become the fatal flaw in human character, informing people that they know at least as much as God about what is good, or what is bad, for them. This penchant for disobedience, sin, finds expression in every person's life, so that "all have sinned and fallen short of the glory of God." The story suggests, therefore, that something has to be done to restore fallen humanity to a right relationship with God and to deliver people from sin and death — and, don't forget, the Devil. Jesus had to do two things: live a sinless life of perfect obedience; and restore God's people to their proper relationship with the Father (Adam and Eve knew that something was wrong between them and God — that they were sinners — when the discovered that they were naked), thereby delivering the human race from its fate apart from God. Omitted in this reading is the first word of Lent (v. 19b), "Remember, you are dust, and unto dust you shall return." That part of the story, which is really about the "first exodus," needs to be read, somewhere, sometime, too.

Romans 5:12 (13-16) 17-19b

This part of Paul's letter to the Romans takes up where the Genesis story leaves off; it completes it and clarifies it from the standpoint of sin and redemption. Adam and Eve were the first sinners, and all other human beings born after have become sinners with them and suffer the same fate they experienced, death, separation from God. Paul points out that while Adam's sin resulted in the condemnation of all sinners, Jesus' perfect obedience — his righteousness — gains God's forgiveness and restores fallen humanity to the right relationship with God once more. Jesus is God's gift to the human race, given freely out of love and grace by God, and he had to die that the gift might be delivered to repentant sinners.

It is probably better to read the shorter form of this reading; comprehension will be easier and the point of Paul's argument will be clearer. The longer version, which includes verses 13-17, might best be included in a Bible study of Romans, which could be done during Lent (four of the first five "second readings" in Series A are from Romans), or a more extended sermon series, or a detailed study of the book could be done in Pentecost (sixteen lessons in a row are selected from Romans).

Matthew 4:1-11

There can be little doubt that, as Lent expanded in the early years of its evolution in the liturgy, the forty-day motif — the *quadragesima* — was settled on as a "natural" pattern for Lent. When this Gospel is read, the first thing that strikes the reader is the forty-day fast of Jesus. His baptismal experience must have affected him deeply, especially when the voice declared, "This is my beloved Son, in whom I am well pleased." Jesus knew that his identity was a burden, as well as a delight; up to that time, he had to know that there was something different about him from other people, and at his baptism he discovered what it was, hence the immediate retreat into the solitude of that desert-like wilderness for a month and a third. But nothing is told in the story about what happened during the long fast; perhaps Jesus never told anyone — after all, there were no companions or observers with him — but kept that part of the story locked up in his heart and mind as private business between God and himself! Matthew doesn't fabricate a tale about the forty days, but he does give the detailed picture of what happened as Jesus ended the fast; the tempter appeared in the wilderness just as he had in the Garden and tried, unsuccessfully, in three different ways to get the Christ to do the "human thing" — to give in to temptation and sin, and to obey him and become subservient to Satan, as all other mortals had done. But Jesus resisted and rejected the temptations, for he is the Second Adam, of whom Paul speaks, and he will not give in to hunger, or to doubt, or to the lust for power. God called him his Son at his baptism; he proved to be the Son of God in his temptation.

A sermon on the Gospel, Matthew 4:1-11 — "Temptation, Triumph, and the Tree."

Baptisms are usually times of family reunion, special dinners, video taping of the event, and a great joy and rejoicing as another person — usually a baby in the contemporary church — is claimed and named as a child of God. It was different with Jesus; when God declared, "This is my beloved Son, in whom I am well pleased," he went out to a desert-like wilderness and spent forty days in prayer and reflection on what had just happened. In all the baptisms I have performed in my ministry, only one person — a four-year-old girl — made a response that had any similarity to that of Jesus. She stood up close to the front, heard the explanation about baptism, the water, the Paschal Candle, saw her infant brother baptized, watched and heard as a cross was traced on his forehead with "Scott, child of God, you have been sealed with the Holy Spirit and marked with the cross of Christ forever." As soon as the baptism was concluded, she ran over to one of her grandmothers, lifted up her bangs, and said to her, "Is it (the cross) still there?" She was asking, in a way, "Am I still a child of God?" Jesus knew, at the conclusion of the fast, that he was indeed the Son of God; he probably knew that a cross was there, not on his forehead but in his future. That's where his baptism would actually be completed.

1. *Temptation:* Jesus was really tempted three times — first, to satisfy his hunger by turning stones into bread. As I write this, a local judge, who has been suspended from office without pay for a year as the result of an inappropriate and immoral action, has been on a water fast for more than fifty days. He has lost considerable weight, of course, and no longer appears in public; he may be too weak. He is in grave danger of dying or, at least, of ruining his health. Second, Jesus is tempted to test his faith in God by jumping from the heights of the Temple; and, third, to give in to the temptation to rule the whole world and enjoy everything in it — but he turned his back on temptation — and Satan. For our part, we know that we are more like the first Adam than we are like the second Adam, Jesus, because we fail, and Satan succeeds in seducing us so that we are his. Someone wrote a little verse many years ago:

> *There's nothing in man that's perfect,*
> *There's nothing that's all complete.*
> *He's nothing but a big beginning*
> *From his head to the soles of his feet.*

> *There's something that draws him upward*
> *And something that drags him down,*
> *And the consequence is he wobbles*
> *'Twixt muck and a golden crown.*

The poem is almost right; the whole truth is that we, like Adam, fall into the muck — sin — and are deserving of what is in the future — death.

2. *Triumph:* Think about it; Jesus actually defeated the devil, triumphed over him despite his hunger and weakness, and routed him in his total victory. That was the beginning of the end of Satan — not that he would disappear from the earth and abandon his efforts to deceive people and win them over to his side — but that Jesus sealed his doom by turning down the things that he offered to the Christ; Satan had never known total defeat before Jesus sent him on his way. We know, therefore, that he — before he was nailed to the cross — had won the victory for us; it was inevitable that he should die — Satan would make a comeback by getting the authorities on his side — but God finalized his triumph over death and the devil on the third day, the Day of Resurrection. That we know about, and that's why we're here, sinners still, but forgiven sinners who live in the hope of sharing ultimately in the triumph of Jesus Christ.

3. *The tree:* Jesus, simply put, was too much for the devil and, subsequently, he was too good to live. Satan couldn't have a person like Christ going around preaching that the kingdom of heaven is at hand, calling upon people to repent of their sins and allow God to change their lives, and sharing in their pain and suffering, healing their hurts, instead of inflicting anguish and sorrow upon them. Jesus was just too much for Satan! Satan couldn't handle him. That's why he is just right for us; he has done what we can't do — his obedience affected our restoration to God — and he was willing to go to the cross to accomplish our release from the devil and win for us the victory over death. In this story, his fate was sealed — our future secured — and God gave all of us a new lease on life.

A sermon on the First Lesson, Genesis 2 and 3

"Simply tell the story; tell the story simply" was the sage advice given by a homiletician one time. This dictum certainly applies here. This is a story that needs to be told again — perhaps in contemporary garb — but told so that the hearers grasp the message and comprehend the meaning of the tale.

1. In creation, God changes the dust of the earth into living beings made in his image. Another tall tale? It's as good as any, because the story doesn't tell how God made human beings, but only that he created them out of what was at hand for the task, the dust and dirt of the earth.

2. God's first act of grace toward his creatures was to place them in a garden where they had everything they needed to enjoy life. They thought they needed something more, and, when tempted by Satan, they took what they wanted for themselves, ignoring the command of God. That act, that "fall," has been repeated over and over again in every age, in every human being who has ever lived — save one. By disobeying God, his people defaced the image of God and would never be able to restore it.

3. It was in their act of disobedience that the eyes of Adam and Eve were opened; they saw their nakedness and tried to cover it up and, simultaneously, cover up their sin, but it did no good; they knew right then that they were sinners. Paradise was lost! Expelled from the Garden, — exodus — humanity has had a nearly impossible time trying to make anything really good out of life ever since. Christ, the second Adam, offers hope to repentant sinners, and holds out the possibility of restoration — exodus in reverse — to the garden in a new heaven and a new earth. In that day Jesus will take Satan by the tail and hang him upon the tree to die, and the faithful will live with the Lord forever.

A sermon on the Second Lesson, Romans 5:12 (13-16), 17-19 — "An Amazing Gift of Grace."

1. Every person who ever lived has succumbed to temptation and become a sinner separated from God. Sin is a prison from which nobody can escape without outside help. David Roberts once told the story of a medieval blacksmith, who was not only a man of tremendous strength and a great craftsman, but he was also a leader in his town, which was near the border of the country. One night, an army from the other country invaded the town, took the town's leading citizens, including the blacksmith, and bound them with chains and threw them into dungeon cells. The blacksmith didn't worry; he knew all about chains, and he believed that all he had to do was find the weak link, use his great strength upon it, break free, bend the bars of his cell, escape and lead a revolt to over-throw the invading army. But suddenly a wail of horror came from his cell; as he ran his fingers over the chains, he came across his own trade-mark and he knew that those chains would have no weak link; he had made them himself. He could not escape by himself; he would be there in the dungeon-cell until someone came, removed the chains, and set him free. That, Roberts pointed out, is the human condition.

2. Jesus' obedience — his righteousness — has brought about reconciliation with God, but at tremendous expense; he had to lay down his life so that we could live.

3. Therefore, we rejoice, because forgiveness and deliverance are a free gift of God. And we serve him out of love, not to gain what has already been given to us — forgiveness and eternal life — but because he has given us blessed assurance in Jesus, who is our Lord forever.

Second Sunday in Lent

Roman Catholic	Genesis 12:1-4	2 Timothy 1:8b-10	Matthew 17:1-9
Episcopal	Genesis 12:1-8	Romans 4:1-5 (6-12), 13-17	John 3:1-17
Lutheran	Genesis 12:1-8	Romans 4:1-5, 13-17	John 4:5-26 (27-30, 39-42)
Common	Genesis 12:1-4a (4b-8)	Romans 4:1-5 (6-12)	John 3:1-17

The arrangement of the lessons for the second through the fifth Sundays in Lent is rather confusing; it looks as if all of the pericopes were written on slips of paper and pulled from a hat. There appears to be a haphazard arrangement of the readings; most are essentially the same in the various denominational lectionaries, but they are listed on different Sundays. The reason for the apparent confusion is in the way that Lent is interpreted in the several churches. The Roman Church celebrates the Transfiguration on the Second Sunday in Lent, and employs John 4, John 9, and John 11 for the next three Sundays of Lent. John is the traditional Gospel for Lent and Easter; some Roman exegetes insist that it was written for the instruction of catechumens and the scrutinies of Lent, both of which take different form — again — after Vatican II. In the Roman liturgical scheme, Lent really has five Sundays after Ash Wednesday; Sunday is essentially (and, practically, in the churches of Protestantism) included in Lent; the Week of the Passion concentrates on the final week of our Lord's life, leading up to the *triduum* (now consisting of Holy Thursday, Good Friday, and Holy Saturday), the Easter Vigil, and the Easter celebration. The Episcopal Church assigns the John 4, 9, and 11 Gospels to the same Sundays as the Roman Church, but continues to call the Sixth Sunday in Lent Palm Sunday (with two liturgies: one of the palms, the other of the Word). By putting John 3 (the Nicodemus story) on the Second Sunday of Lent, as does the Common Lectionary, the ancient tradition of reading John during Lent receives additional emphasis. The Lutheran lectionary moves John 4 and John 9 ahead one Sunday, inserts Matthew 20 on the Fourth Sunday in Lent, while retaining John 11 on the Fifth Sunday in Lent; the Sixth Sunday is the Sunday of the Passion and, as in other churches, it ushers in Holy Week.

The church year theological clue

Lent is structured so that those who keep it will go through devotional exercises designed to bring about conversion of the penitent to the life in Christ. Lent is really the altar (font) call of the church, at which the believers will find forgiveness of their sins and renewal of the gifts God gives in baptism to those who will have him as their God in Jesus Christ. Sunday is seen in the Roman Church, as always, from a sacramental perspective; some pastors in other churches approach Lent in much the same way; all see *renewal of the baptismal covenant as the goal of going through Lent to Easter*. The framework is eucharistic and baptismal; this should be kept in mind when preaching through the rest of Lent.

The Prayer of the Day — The first of two LBW prayers for the Second Sunday in Lent, which is quite similar to the single Episcopal collect, strikes the ancient penitential theme of Lent: "Bring back all who have erred and strayed from your ways; lead them again to embrace in faith the truth of your Word and to hold it fast." Repentance, renewal of faith, and obedience on the part of pardoned sinners, are implied in conjunction with this prayer, and mentioned more directly in the Episcopal prayer. The second collect is specifically directed to the use of John 4 on the Second Sunday in Lent, because it speaks of Christ's welcoming "an outcast woman" of faith, asking God to "give us faith like hers" so that we may trust God alone and love one another as we have been loved and accepted by God.

The Psalm for the Day (LBW) — Psalm 105:4-11 — The exhortation of the psalmist, "Search for the Lord and his strength, continually seek his face," suggests that penitents need to be reminded early in Lent that keeping it is a long and arduous task which calls for spiritual strength and perseverence. After reminding people of "the marvels he has done," verse 8 points out the reason that they may have confidence in God; "He has always been mindful of his covenant." By elaborating on how God has kept his covenant with Israel "for a thousand generations," the psalmist's words speak — suggestively — to the Christian of the new covenant in Christ, which God gives in baptism. Christians may search for the Lord in Lent because they know that they have already been found by Jesus Christ.

The Psalm Prayer

> God our Father, through the death and resurrection of your Son you have fulfilled the promise to Abraham, Joseph, and Moses to redeem the world from slavery and to lead us into the promised land. Grant us living water from the rock and bread from heaven, that we may survive our desert pilgrimage and praise you forever; through Jesus Christ our Lord.

The readings:

Genesis 12:1-8

On a superficial level, this reading might be interpreted as a simple story about faith in God and obedience to his commands. Those are central themes in the tale, no question about that, but there is more to it than finding a model for the godly life in this story about Abram, or Abraham. It is basically about the call of Abram by God to become the founder and leader of a nation, to initiate a community that would be known as the people of God. He left Haran, took his wife and others with him and set out for Canaan, at God's direction, went on to Shechem, "to the oak at Moreh," where God visited him and he heard God say, "To your descendants I will give this land." God raised up and called other leaders for Israel, until he finally called his Son, Jesus, to be the one that would lead all of the people of the world into a new and inclusive promised land, the kingdom of God himself.

Romans 4:1-5, 13-17

Paul puts the Abraham story into the framework of law and gospel, insisting that Abraham engaged in a work that was born of faith, not of the law. Abraham believed in God and trusted him; his faith was a gift from God, therefore, he was justified by faith, not by works of the law. The promise to him that Israel should inhabit the promised land and that his descendants should inherit the world came of God's free grace, not from obedience to the law. This beginning of a covenant relationship between God and the people he created was entirely a work of love and grace on the part of God and does not rest on human merit. When the gift of faith through grace is received and the Word is believed by people, works that describe the life of Christ issue forth abundantly. Obedience, acts of love, mercy, and kindness are expressions of faith, not works done to obtain the blessings of God.

John 4:5-26 (27-30, 39-42)

John's accounts of Jesus' encounters with people just beg to be told to people today, partly because they may be too long as readings, when they follow two other lessons. This lovely

110

story, which sees Jesus at the well in Sychar, asking a Samaritan woman for a drink of water, reveals the humanity of Jesus in his weariness and thirst, and his divinity in his consideration of an "outcast" woman. Jesus turns around the woman's question, "How is it that you, a Jew, ask a drink of me, a woman of Samaria?", by telling her that if she really knew who he was — the source of living water — she would ask him for a drink. She didn't understand him until he told her what he knew about her, when she perceived he was a prophet. He not only told her about herself but about things to come "when the true worshipers will worship the Father in spirit and in truth (not on Mt. Gerazim or in Jerusalem)." That she understood because she expected the coming of the Messiah, who, "when he comes, will show us all things." The gospel (short form) ends with Jesus' clear declaration, "I who speak to you am he." The longer reading tells the rest of the story about what happened in Sychar. This ought to be included in a sermon, especially a biblical story sermon, on this Gospel.

A sermon on the Gospel, John 4:5-26f — "A Woman, A Well, and a Man with Living Water."

To appreciate fully the importance of water to one's life, it is probably necessary for a person to come close to dying of thirst, or, at least to live in a land where water is scarce. Antoine de St. Exupery once observed that Arab children of North Africa, where water was in extremely short supply when he wrote *Wind, Sand and Stars,* begged for a drink of water rather than pennies. After he was rescued from certain death after five days under the blazing sun of the desert, he wrote about water:

> *Water, thou hast no taste, no color, no odor; canst not be defined, art relished while ever mysterious. Not necessary to life, but life itself, thou fillest us with a gratification that exceeds the delight of the senses. By thy might, there return into us treasures we had abandoned. By thy grace, there are released in us all the dried-up runnels of our heart. Of the riches that exist in the world, thou art the rarest and also the most delicate — thou so pure within the bowels of earth! . . . A man may die though he held in his hand a jug of dew, if it be inhabited by evil salts. For thou, water, are a proud divinity, allowing no alteration, no foreignness in thy being. And the joy thou spreadest is an infinitely simple joy.*

The Gospel for the Day is a story begging to be expanded into a biblical story sermon by interweaving our stories with the story in this pericope.

Jesus, when he reached the well at Sychar, was not dying of thirst, not even like he must have been at the end of his forty-day fast in the wilderness, but he was thirsty. The woman he asked for a drink of water was not thirsty, but she was *dying of thirst* — and Jesus knew it. After all, her condition was that of all sinners, of everyone who has made the wrong choices in life and wound up alienating himself or herself from communion with God and other people. Jesus knows that most people are really dying of thirst.

Despite the fact that she was one of the despised Samaritans, Jesus offered her the living water that he had to give to spiritually thirsty people. She didn't know what her real thirst was, because she requested, "Sir, give me this water that I may not thirst, nor come here to draw." She thought Jesus was going to provide her with some sort of an artesian well that would never run out and would eliminate some of her daily labor. She was partly right; she wouldn't thirst if she drank the water he offered. He is the living water, and he offers it to people through the gift of himself in his Word and the sacraments of the church.

The woman, after Jesus confronted her with her marital immorality and talked to her about the age when people would worship God "in spirit and in truth," not only demonstrated her belief in God but also revealed her expectation of the coming of the Messiah. Then and there she came to understand what Jesus was talking about all the time, and she received another precious gift when he said to her, "I who speak am he." In and through his word, Jesus actually gives himself to the world.

The rest of the story also needs to be told — and relived by people who have heard the Word and received Jesus Christ, the living water. When the disciples returned and wondered what was going on, she dropped her water jar and ran back into town to tell everyone the good news about what had happened to her at the well. It turns out that there were lots of thirsty people in that city, so thirsty that they invited Jesus to stay with them — and he did, for two days, assuaging their thirst with himself and the water of life. The one who cried out, "I thirst," on the cross, always answers the cries of those who are dying of thirst.

A sermon on the First Lesson, Genesis 12:1-8 — "When God Calls, Some People Obey."

1. That's what Abram did; he heard God's promise of what he would do for the people to be known as Israel — and *he believed* what God told him.

2. He acted on his faith, gathered up his family and possessions and set off for the land God had promised to him and his people. *He obeyed* the call of God.

3. Abram built two altars to God, one on the land and the other on the mountain after God had said, "To your descendants I will give this land; *he claimed* it in the name of God.

4. He *lived by the covenantal promise* God had made to him, much as we are to live out the covenant of our baptism in our lives. Lent exists to get us back on the right path of faith and action when God calls us in Christ.

A sermon on the Second Lesson, Romans 4:1-15, 3-17 — "How Faith and Works Go Together."

1. Abraham is a good example of how faith and works come together and operate in our lives. Abraham had faith; he lived by faith and did the work God assigned to him.

2. His faith was a precious gift from God; it saved him. He was not saved by works but by *sola fides,* faith alone, that was his through God's grace. Don't we always like to believe that we deserve salvation, because we have earned it through our good works? That attitude condemns us as much as any sins we commit.

3. As a forerunner of the old covenant, Abraham shows us how to live as people who abide in the new covenant in Jesus Christ. We, too, live by God's gracious promises, which we try, through the grace of our Lord, to complete in our lives.

4. Jesus, not our works, makes us righteous before God. Lent won't let us forget that. The cross always reminds us that God loves us and blesses us beyond anything we think we deserve or merit.

Third Sunday in Lent

Roman Catholic	Exodus 17:3-7	Romans 5:1-2, 5-8	John 4:5-42
Episcopal	Exodus 17:1-7	Romans 5:1-11	John 4:5-26 (27-38) 39-42
Lutheran	Isaiah 42:14-21	Romans 5:8-14	John 9:1-41 or John 9:13-17, 34-39
Common	Exodus 17:3-7	Romans 5:1-11	John 4:5-26 (27-42)

The church year theological clue

In the pre-Vatican II scheme of the liturgical year, which was employed in the Lutheran and Episcopalian Churches, too, the Sundays of Lent had definite and identifiable themes built into them; these were announced in the Introits of the several Sundays. Thus, the First Sunday in Lent was *invocabit* — "He shall call upon me, and I will answer him;" the Second Sunday in Lent was *reminiscere* — "Remember, O Lord, thy tender mercies and thy loving-kindnesses;" the Third Sunday in Lent was *oculi* — "Mine eyes are ever toward the Lord;" the Fourth Sunday in Lent was *laetare* — "Rejoice ye with Jerusalem, and be glad with her;" the Fifth Sunday in Lent was *judica* — "Judge me, O God, and plead my cause against an ungodly nation" (Passiontide was two weeks long under the old system); the Sixth Sunday in Lent was *palmarum* — a title given it by Jesus' entrance into Jerusalem rather than from the introit. The titles and the clear-cut themes they suggest have been eliminated in the new church year pericopes; the liturgical/homiletical and theological clues now are suggested by the psalms, the lessons, and the gospels, for the most part. Interestingly, the oculi — "eyes/sight" theme — spiritual illumination — is retained in the LBW by assigning the John 9 story about the man who had been blind from birth and was healed by Jesus to the Third, instead of the Fourth, Sunday in Lent. Jesus came to open the eyes of the blind that they might "see" God. The liturgy seems to play a game of "musical Sundays" from one denomination to another during Lent. The ancient themes of Lent and the church year still exist, but the sequence by which they are proclaimed is not rigidly fixed.

The Prayer of the Day — This LBW prayer functions as a reminder to the faithful, as well as a supplication to God, of the role of Christ in God's plan for regaining control of the earth ("Your kingdom has broken into our troubled world through the life, death, and resurrection of your Son."). It also functions to hold together the seasons of Lent and Easter by speaking of the incarnation, redemption, and the resurrection of the Lord. The latter portion is general, although it might fit better with the theme of the Second Sunday in Lent; it pleads, "Help us to hear your Word and obey it, so that we become instruments of your redeeming love." The least that can be said of it, although it doesn't really point to the gospel, is that it is appropriate for the near mid-point of Lent. It may also help to open the ears of people whose hearing has waned a bit and the eyes of those that might have become dim during Lent.

The Psalm of the Day (LBW) — Psalm 142 — Whoever wrote this psalm was really in trouble, perhaps even his life was in jeopardy. Someone — or many persons — is making life so miserable for him that he desperately calls upon God to come to his aid and assistance; God is his only hope, the only one who can deliver him from the enemy. From one perspective, the cry of the psalmist is pathetic; from another, it is absolutely beautiful, because he completely puts himself in the hands of God. It is quite evident from the LBW perspective that the use of this psalm, especially when the psalm prayer is taken into consideration, is connected to the passion of Jesus, particularly to his agony on the cross, despite the fact that this is only the third week of Lent. Such an interpretation affirms once more that Lent ends with the crucifixion and death of Jesus outside of Jerusalem; it keeps the faithful going in the right direction whether they know it or not.

The Psalm Prayer (LBW)

Lord Jesus, hanging on the cross and left alone by your disciples, you called on your Father with a mighty cry as you gave up your spirit. Deliver us from the prison of affliction, and be yourself our inheritance in the land of the living, where with the Father and the Holy Spirit you are blessed now and forever.

The readings:

Isaiah 42:14-21

The church has taken these words from (Second) Isaiah (the chapter which contains the first of the servant songs) and, for liturgical purposes, has put them into the mouth of Christ. The connection to the gospel comes in the middle of the reading, after "Isaiah" has made his plaintive address to God: "And I will lead the blind in a way they know not, in paths that they have not known I will guide them." He speaks of the spiritually blind, of course, and is not pointing to anything like the miracle wrought in John 9, when Jesus opened the eyes of a man who had been born blind. Spiritual blindness is the result of spiritual deafness; those who do not, or will not, hear the Word of the Lord are bound to be blind. So the prophet says: "Hear, you deaf; and look, you blind, that you may see!" The latter third of the passage obviously creates some difficulties for the preacher ("Who is blind but my servant, or deaf as my messenger whom I send? Who is blind as my dedicated one, or blind as the servant of the Lord?"); is the prophet saying that the servant of the Lord is so attuned to the Word of the Lord that he/she does not see the danger before him/her or hear the threats being made against him/her? (This reading, like several others, might best be incorporated into a sermon on the John 9 gospel that shows Jesus to be the light of the world.)

Ephesians 5:8-14

In the centuries when there were numerous station churches in Rome, and a station mass was appointed for every day of the fast, part of this epistle was read at the Church of St. Lawrence-Outside-the-Walls in conjunction with the station mass of the Third Sunday in Rome. Since Lawrence was "one of their own," a convert who had been brutally executed for his faith, and since he was buried in the crypt under the altar, the Romans held this place in high regard, and still do as a holy place. And what they heard in this reading connected them to Lawrence, Paul, Peter, and all the other martyrs who gave their lives for Christ and the faith. Surely, they knew that they lived by the same faith in Jesus Christ; that they were children of light which came from the Lord. It is highly probable — especially in the years when baptism was still an inherent part of Lent — that they knew how they had received the "light in the Lord;" they probably knew the meaning of baptism, and the connection of this epistle to baptism, better than we do today. The last verse is most appropriate for the near-middle of Lent when people are beginning to lose their zeal and enthusiasm for keeping the fast: "Awake, O sleeper, and arise from the dead, and Christ shall give you light." That promise should wake us up and keep us going toward the cross and the empty tomb.

John 9:1-41

The restoration of sight to the blind man is one of the seven signs that point to Jesus as the Messiah, and, in this case, the light of the world. This suggests that in series C, when the Gospel of John is only read on the Fifth Sunday in Lent, that one might do a series of mid-week "word-service sermons" on "The Seven Signs of the Savior." More than a few scholars suggest that much of this story is redaction that occurred in the oral tradition. The heart of it is the incident in which the blind man received his sight by obeying Jesus, whom he later came to recognize as the light of the world. The shorter form (John 9:13-17, 39-42) is claimed to be the original section of the story, and concentration on this part supports the Jesus/light theme in the gospel. The most puzzling part of all of this is why the churches that have used John for Lent for so many centuries could not agree on the Sunday when this gospel is used. The difficulty, most likely, comes from weakening the structural themes, described by the names in the older lectionaries, for Lent. But what matters most is that the theme of the text — Jesus is the Messiah, the light of the world — is proclaimed faithfully and imaginatively to the people in the retelling of this fascinating story.

A sermon on the Gospel — John 9:1-41 — "Blind Man's Bluff."

The man really was blind, you know. And he really had been blind from birth. Not only did he and his parents testify to that, but he knew his way around the city of Jerusalem and was able to obey Jesus when told to go and wash in the pool of Siloam. No one took him there; he had no assistance that we are told of, but he found the pool, did as he was told, and regained his sight. That part of the story — that he was able to get to Siloam on his own — is really intriguing. When I was going to the seminary in Philadelphia, I had to take a long trolley ride down Germantown Avenue to Broad Street where I would transfer to the subway/elevated trains of the city. On the days that I took that ride in the middle of the afternoon, I frequently saw a blind man take the same trolley. He, too, got off at Broad Street, went directly to the subway entrance, down the steps, through the turnstile, out onto the platform where he, too, would wait for a train. He didn't do it by himself, however; he had a seeing eye dog, in whom he had great confidence. That dog took him to the trolley and from the trolley to the subway and saw to it that he reached his destination safely. I often wondered if the man could get around that large city on his own. I doubt it; I'm positive that he needed that dog to function as his eyes. The blind man in Jerusalem, according to the story, his eyes plastered shut by Jesus, nevertheless got to Siloam and regained his sight. His blindness was real; it was no bluff, no pretense to give him an assist in his begging.

1. He wouldn't have had a chance of ever seeing again if Jesus had not seen him and had compassion upon him. That's the first part of the story, and it has implications for us, the spiritually blind or, at best, near-sighted. He could hear — he was blind, not deaf — and he obeyed Jesus by going to Siloam and washing.

2. The once-blind man must have told the story of how he was given his sight by Jesus to everyone who would listen to him. This, of course, was too much for the Pharisees; they did not believe him for a minute, and they knew they had to do something to discredit Jesus once and for all. Perhaps they had a legal opening; after all, he healed the man on the Sabbath. They had failed to break down the testimony of the man who claimed that Jesus healed him, so they threw him out of the synagogue. They didn't know it, but they were simply condemning themselves, as all people do who deny, by living sinful lives, that Jesus is the Son of God.

3. The question that Jesus put to the man when he returned is the one he puts to us in Lent: "Do you believe in the Son of man?" He lights up our hearts and minds with his Word so that we really can say — and mean it — "Lord, I believe" — that he is the Son of God who died on the accursed tree and rose from the grave on the third day.

4. That man began to live a new life once he met Jesus, regained his sight, and believed him to be the light of the world; Lent tells us that the Lord is trying to turn us on — to him, to God — so that we might be his witnesses in the world. That's what it is all about.

A sermon on the First Lesson, Isaiah 42:14-21 — "Sing the Servant Song in Lent."

1. Sing of the patient Servant, who is about to go into action; the time has come for intervention in the affairs of the world.

2. Sing the song of the judgment that the Servant will bring upon the earth. The wicked, who will not believe and reject the Servant, will utterly be destroyed in the coming of the Servant.

3. Sing of the Servant who restores the sight of the blind and the hearing of the deaf. He does so that his servants might understand the ways of the Lord.

4. Sing the song of the Servant whose coming does indeed "magnify (God's) law and make(s) it glorious."

5. Sing the song of the Servant, Jesus Christ. The song could only be about him, our Lord.

A sermon on the Second Lesson,, Ephesians 5:8-4 — "Turned On, Not Turned Off."

1. Christians have been "turned on" by Christ through the Word and the Sacraments. Baptism is a service of illumination, a "turn on" for those who go under the water into the darkness of death and rise to the surface and the light of a new day, new life, in Jesus Christ.

Hans Reudi Weber presents a description of how baptism might have been celebrated in the early church in *The Militant Ministry*. On the Island of Rhodes, there is a mountain which has a "baptismal cross" carved into the top of it; it was there that baptismal candidates gathered before dawn on Easter. The candidates were stationed on the west side of the cross, there to undergo the final examination and exorcism. As the sun began to rise, they were led, one by one, down three steps into the water and they were asked the three-part question, "Do you believe in God, the Father Almighty, . . . and in Jesus Christ, his Son, our Lord, . . . and in the Holy Spirit?" Three times each person replied, "I believe," and each time the candidate was immersed in the water — "drowned" — at the cross-font. The newly baptized people came up out of the water just as the light of the new day was dawning, silently announcing the resurrection of the Lord. They put on their white robes, were greeted joyously by the faithful, proceeded to the church for confirmation, and joined the members of the congregation at the Table of the Lord for the first time. There was no possibility that they would ever forget the day of their baptism into the Easter faith of the Church. (Adapted from *Plastic Flowers in the Holy Water,* C.S.S.)

2. Disobedience to the commands of God and unfruitful works — *sin* — are not only unacceptable to the Lord; they are also "spiritual turn offs" which dim the light of Christ in our souls and lives.

3. Lent reminds us that it is "wake up" time, becaues the light of Christ is shining into the world. Christ is God's offer to turn us on to him and his Word forever.

Fourth Sunday in Lent

Roman Catholic	1 Samuel 16:1b, 6-7, 10-13	Ephesians 5:8-14	John 9:1-41
Episcopal	1 Samuel 16:1-3	Ephesians 5:(1-7), 8-14	John 9:1-13 (14-27) 28-38
Lutheran	Hosea 5:15—6:2	Romans 8:1-10	Matthew 20:17-28
Common	1 Samuel 16:1-13	Ephesians 5:8-14	John 9:1-41

The church year theological clue

The clue to the theme for worship and preaching this Sunday comes more from the general theme of Lent than it does from any theological content of this Sunday. Before Vatican II, the Fourth Sunday in Lent was known as Laetare Sunday, the mid-point in Lent, and was known as "Refreshment Sunday;" The purpose of this Sunday was to gather strength for the final stages of the Lenten pilgrimage. Therefore, the Introit could declare, with one of the Songs of the Pilgrims, (Psalm 122, a Psalm of Ascents), "Rejoice ye with Jerusalem, and be glad with her. . . . I was glad when they said unto me: Let us go into the house of the Lord." Lent was half over, the conclusion of the Lenten fast was in sight; there was, indeed, cause for rejoicing, because soon the death and resurrection of the Lord would be celebrated and the church would move into the glorious season of Easter. Despite the removal of the Latin name for this Sunday and the Introit/Psalm, it remains the middle of Lent, the half-way point of the journey to Jerusalem, the cross, and the tomb. In lieu of any special liturgical information from the church year, the lectionaries supply the themes for the day, with the LBW lectionary differing radically from the other three in common usage.

The Prayer of the Day — The LBW prayer is a supplication to the God who can heal and forgive so as to cleanse and renew the church for the remainder of the Lenten journey — "graciously cleanse us from all sin and make us strong." Although it could be used on any Sunday, it is appropriate for Lent and especially for the Fourth Sunday, the mid-point, of the season. It is a subtle reminder to the church that people need renewal and strength to complete the journey begun on Ash Wednesday, as well as a prayer to God asking for these blessings for all times of life.

The Psalm of the Day (LBW) — Psalm 43 — The psalm begins with a cry to God to support the cause of the psalmist and to defend him in his struggles. God, the "God of (his) strength," seems to have left the psalmist on his own in the face of those who oppress him. The relevance of the psalm for Lent and the pilgrims who kept it emerges in the verses 3-4:

> *Send out your light and your truth, that they may lead me, and bring me to your holy hill and to your dwelling; that I may go to the altar of God, to the God of my joy and gladness.*

The burden of Lent will, then, be removed and the pilgrims will be able to give thanks for what they went through to reach the cross and hear the "He is not here, but is risen, as he said" that still echoes from the empty tomb. The psalm fits quite nicely the middle of Lent, and is most appropriate as a link between the First and Second Lessons and the Gospel.

The Psalm Prayer (LBW)

> *Almighty Father, source of everlasting light, send forth your truth into our hearts*

and pour over us the brightness of your light to bring us, through our joyful participation at your altar, to your eternal dwelling on high, where you live and reign now and forever.

The readings:

Hosea 5:15—6:2 (L)

This reading provides a reminder to the pilgrims going up to Jerusalem and the cross that Lent is a penitential season that profits nothing if the people of God do not recognize, confess, and repent of their sins. The Lord does forgive and heal those who call upon him in true repentance and faith, giving them, at the end of Lent, the assurance of resurrection and new life, from the vantage point of the church, in Christ: "After two days he will revive us; on the third day he will raise us up, that we may live before him." This selection, too, is most appropriate for mid-Lent and by its typological content, which reflects the resurrection theme, virtually implores the parish pastor to preach from it and thereby enrich the Lenten experience of the people.

1 Samuel 16:1-13 (RC, E, C)

Just what this reading has to do with the other two lessons for the Fourth Sunday in Lent is difficult to discern, despite the intriguing quality of the story. Some scholars contend that the typology of this reading, in which God sends Samuel to the home of Jesse to choose, and secretly anoint, a successor to King Saul, has to be the reason that this story was appointed to this Sunday; surely, it has nothing to do with Ephesians 8 or John 9, which are the lessons selected for this Sunday by the Roman, Episcopal, and Common lectionaries. The incongruity of this choice could have been what caused the Lutherans to change all of the readings for this Sunday. But even if the typology of the anointing of David is supposed to point to Jesus' baptism and the beginning of his ministry, the lesson should be assigned to another Sunday (the Baptism of Our Lord?). If the anointing is conceived as representing the baptism that believers receive which, as noted in earlier readings, was when and how they received the light of Christ (illumination), a tenuous case may be made for combining this story with Ephesians 5 and John 9.

Romans 8 (L)

Paul's glorious statement of the status of those who are "in Christ," the believers, functions as a word of absolution, reassuring them that they have been freed from sin and death by Jesus Christ. The cross has done what the law could not do, because the flesh was too weak to keep the law and really obey its letter and intentions. Subsequently, Paul reminds the Romans that they should set their minds on the things of the Spirit and live by the Spirit, not the flesh, if they are to be pleasing to God. Paul's statements about the nature of the life that believers live indicates that it is never enough to know that salvation is by grace alone and to confess Christ as Lord; believers will be open to the promptings of the Holy Spirit and do their level best to live in ways that God will accept. It is possible to live for God because "the Spirit of God dwells in you."

Ephesians 5:8-14 (RC, E, C)

See the comments for this reading for the Third Sunday in Lent.

Matthew 20:17-28 (L)

The main reason this lesson was selected for the Lutheran lectionary is evident in the first part of the reading. It contains the announcement that used to be made at the station church of St. Lawrence-Outside-the-Walls on Septuagesima Sunday:

> *Behold, we are going up to Jerusalem; and the Son of man will be delivered to the chief priests and scribes, and they will condemn him to death, and deliver him to the Gentiles to be mocked and scourged and crucified, and he will be raised on the third day.*

There was no danger of misinterpreting the goal of the Lenten pilgrimage in those days; the statement seems to be a word that girds the pilgrims today for the final push toward Good Friday and Easter Sunday. (The reading from Ephesians appears to have been appointed to suggest how Christians ought to live as they go toward the cross and the empty tomb.)

The second part of the Gospel for the Day, with the mother of James and John interceding for them with Jesus, "Command that these two sons of mine may sit, one at your right hand and one at your left, in your kingdom," looks to the post-resurrection glory that will be Christ's and will, finally, see the Lord reigning over his kingdom. Believers are reminded that they are to be servants of the Lord, always striving to do his will in the world rather than seeking greatness and glory from God. Lent is the time to learn, or relearn, this lesson: Jesus came to serve, not to be served, and to give his life in service to God that the whole world might be saved.

John 9:1-41

See the comments on this gospel for the Third Sunday in Lent and the sermon suggestion, too.

A sermon on the Gospel — Matthew 20:17-28 — "A Glimpse of God's Glory."

In *Phoenix at Coventry,* the book explaining how he designed the new cathedral at Coventry, England, the architect, Basil Spence, wrote about his first visit to the bombed-out old cathedral:

> *As soon as I set foot in the ruined nave I felt the impact of delicate enclosure. It was still a cathedral . . . . I was deeply moved. I saw the Old Cathedral standing clearly for the Sacrifice, one side of the Christian faith, and I knew my task was to design a new one which should stand for the Triumph of the Resurrection.*

That's exactly what he did, planning and building a twenty-two foot altar table, which seems to be an invitation to the whole world to come and celebrate Jesus' death and resurrection, and including Graham Sutherland's 42' by 70' tapestry, "Christ in Glory," which hangs over the table and, in a photograph, once graced the cover of TIME magazine. The tapestry depicts the final stage of the resurrection, the ancient motif of so many mosaics in the apses of the earliest Christian churches, of the risen and ascended Lord reigning over the world until he returns again.

1. As the time of his trial and death approached, Jesus tried to prepare the disciples one last time for what was about to happen; he told them about his death and his resurrection. Beyond the cross there is good news for the whole world. That's where the pilgrims are heading **during Lent** — to the cross and past it to the empty tomb.

2. Jesus will be raised up, not only from death and the grave, but to glory in the resurrection; "for the Lamb who was slain has begun his reign" (LBW "Hymn of Praise"). James and John wanted to share in Jesus' glory, his greatness, by sitting alongside him in his kingdom; their mother pled their case. She thought they deserved those places next to Christ; apparently, they thought they did, too. Good works earn us nothing in the kingdom of God.

3. Greatness is God's to give as he chooses; service is the believer's business in the kingdom Christ has initiated. Oddly enough, beginning with the mosaics in the Church of Santa Costanza, in Rome, the church seems to have forgotten God's priorities, because Peter and Paul are pictured on either side of Jesus, not only in Santa Costanza but in most other apses, too. Those places should go unassigned, because that's not the business of individual believers nor of the church. The faithful are called to serve in love and humility; God will take care of the rest. That's a hard lesson to learn, but it is one of the key lessons of Lent.

4. By relearning about Christ's glory and humanity's role as servants, the faithful are prepared to do God's will in the world, regardless of the cost and personal sacrifice that might be required, without making any claims to greatness before God, but seeking to give him the glory due to his name.

The narrative setting of this Gospel suggests that the preacher shape it into a biblical story sermon; the above sketch would accommodate such an intention.

A sermon on the First Lesson — Hosea 5:15—6:2 — "Glory Regained and Mercy Obtained."

Hosea's prophesy could have come directly from the mouth of the Lord and the response of the believers to Jesus' death and resurrection.

1. *Glory regained* — Jesus had to go through death and rise again to return to his place of glory with the Father — "I will return again to my place" and reign until the time God has set for the Parousia. Only by dying could he be raised up to the glory of the Father.

2. *Mercy obtained* — Jesus proved himself to be loving and compassionate here on earth, equipped with the power necessary to handle any situation he encountered. He gives that power to heal and sustain people in all of the predicaments they might get into in life; the world has received mercy in his death and resurrection.

3. *Life ordained* — God has prepared places for those who love Jesus, life in the kingdom which shall last forever, and he has given them work to do as long as they remain on the earth. He ordains all of his own people for service in the kingdom. They know that his blessings are abundant and eternal, because they have already received "a foretaste of the feast to come" in the meal that celebrates the death and resurrection of Jesus.

A sermon on the Second Lesson, Romans 8:1-10 — "The Meaning of the Cross."

1. The Cross means *forgiveness* for repentant sinners, because "there is no condemnation for those who are in Christ Jesus."

2. The Cross means *death* to the old way of life, the old mind-set of living by the flesh — "to set the mind on the flesh is death."

3. The Cross means *dependence* on the Spirit of the Christ, who enables us to live in a new way, which we cannot do by ourselves — the mind-set of the Spirit.

4. The Cross means *deliverance* from that which might destroy the faithful, and the assurance that they will be with God forever, because they belong to Christ.

Fifth Sunday in Lent

Roman Catholic	Ezekiel 37:12-14	Romans 8:8-11	John 11:1-45
Episcopal	Ezekiel 37:1-3 (4-10), 11-14	Romans 6:16-23	John 11:(1-17)
Lutheran	Ezekiel 37:1-3 (4-10), 11-14	Romans 8:11-19	John 11:1-53 or John 11:47-53
Common	Ezekiel 37:1-14	Romans 8:6-11	John 11:(1-16), 17-45

The church year theological clue

The Fifth Sunday of Lent has not only lost its name, *judica,* but it has also lost its liturgical function, which was quite positive in the pre-Vatican II liturgy; it used to announce the beginning of the holiest part of Lent, the two weeks of the Passion of Our Lord. Now it is simply part of Lent, and, practically, the Last Sunday in Lent, introducing the week before Holy Week. Again, the theological, and therefore the liturgical/homiletical, clue comes more from the Gospel for the Day than it does from the theological framework of the Sunday. The Roman Church reads the story of Jesus and Lazarus, omitting the reaction of the religious leaders to the raising of Lazarus and Jesus' other miracles; the Episcopal and Common lectionaries make the reading of verses 1-17 optional, and then read the last two thirds of the story. The Lutheran lectionary offers the option of reading the entire story, including verses 1-53, or verses 47-53 without the Lazarus story. The latter selection gives sharp definition to the reasons for the development of the plot against Jesus that would cost him his life.

The Prayer for the Day (LBW) — At first reading, this prayer seems to have little to do with the other propers for the Fifth Sunday in Lent. Reflection suggests that it is meant to relate to the Gospel for the Day, John 11, and to Jesus' proclamation in it: "I am the resurrection and the life; he who believes in me, though he die, yet shall he live, and whoever lives and believes in me shall never die. Do you believe this?" Mary's answer, "Yes, Lord; I believe that you are the Christ, the Son of God," is the kind of witness that believers are expected to make in the world, thus the prayer confesses, "in our weakness we have failed to be your messengers of forgiveness and hope in the world." Logically, the petition pleads for renewal "that we may follow your commands (a major goal of Lent is to become obedient to God) and proclaim your reign of love." The good news in Jesus Christ has to be shared boldly and convincingly with the world.

The Psalm for the Day (LBW) — Psalm 116:1-18 — The psalmist could have put these words into the mouth of Lazarus after Jesus raised him from death and released him from the grave. Actually, they are the words of a poet who has been in trouble many times in his life, has prayed to the Lord, and the Lord has helped him without fail. Now, in the face of death, this person calls confidently on the Lord once more, "The cords of death entangled me; the grip of the grave took hold of me, I came to grief and sorrow. Then I called upon the name of the Lord: 'O Lord, I pray you, save my life.' " Once more, God answers his prayer and delivers him: "For you have rescued my life from death, my eyes from tears, and my feet from stumbling," and, accordingly, he can say, "I will walk in the presence of the Lord in the land of the living." As a responsory psalm to the first reading, the psalm does its work effectively, making connection to the Second Lesson and, through it, to the Gospel.

The Psalm Prayer (LBW)

> *God of power and mercy, through the Passion and resurrection of your Son you have freed us from the bonds of death and the anguish of separation from you. Be with*

us on our pilgrimage, and help us offer you a sacrifice of praise, fulfill our vows, and glorify you in the presence of all your people; through Jesus Christ our Lord.

The readings:

Ezekiel 37:1-3 (4-10), 11-14

The several lectionaries develop variations on the resurrection theme by the way that they use the First Lesson and the Gospel for the Day. The Common Lectionary calls for reading all of Ezekiel 37:1-14, while the Roman Lectionary prescribes only verses 12-14. The Episcopal and Lutheran lessons appear to be tentative, offering the preacher the choice of the entire passage as a reading and potential source of the sermon, or a reduced version of the pericope. The "dry bones" theme of Ezekiel originally spoke only of Israel living in Exile and the promise of the Lord God to bring them back from Exile in Babylon and restore their nation once more. More pertinent to Lent and Easter is the theme of resurrection in verses 12-14, "And you shall know that I am the Lord, when I open your graves, and raise you from your graves, O my people," and the theme of new life, "And I will put my Spirit within you, and you shall live . . . ." The church takes the "dry bones" prophesy, which literally had to do with the return from Exile and the restoration of Israel, to be a type of the resurrection and new life given to the faithful by Jesus Christ. The psalm picks up this theme and makes solid connection with the second reading and the gospel.

Romans 8:11-19

As a continuation of the second reading for the Fourth Sunday in Lent, this passage solidifies the resurrection theme as a reality in Christ and a hope for believers, and it also affirms the nature of the new life in Jesus Christ. The power of the Holy Spirit, which raised Jesus from the dead, has been given to the faithful — and specifically in the Sacrament of Baptism, which is implicit in this reading — and will raise up the believers to new life in the present and to eternal life at the last day. The resurrection life begins when the Spirit has been bestowed upon people in baptism and continues into the world that is yet to come. Suffering and death may try to reduce and take away this gift, but the Spirit works in human beings so that this will not happen. Those who know that the Spirit dwells in them and has given them life are able to face the future with confidence and hope.

John 11:1-45 (47-53 — Lutheran)

The story of the raising of Lazarus is intriguing and puzzling. First of all, Jesus heard the news that Lazarus was gravely ill, in danger of dying, but Jesus deliberately waited and did not go to Bethany until after Lazarus was dead. John suggests that he allowed Lazarus to die so that Jesus would be identified as the Son of God in another of the "seven signs," and so that God would be glorified. This suggests that John didn't know — and, therefore, couldn't tell — the entire story; God doesn't use people or act in this way. The story may easily be misinterpreted, because the resuscitation of Lazarus gets tied into the encounter between Mary and Jesus (above), and the story might be interpreted as a resurrection, rather than a resuscitation experience. After all, Lazarus had been in the grave for four days before he was brought forth by Jesus, but it was the same "old Lazarus," from one perspective, who would still have to die and await the general resurrection of the dead. No doubt Lazarus had a new lease on life after Jesus brought him out of the tomb; he must have looked differently at everything, and that's inherent in the story. To be brought back from death and given another chance to live alters one's perspective on life and death completely. There is no doubt that the church seeks to have the two themes in this gospel — resurrection and renewed life — sounded together as good news in the face of death, especially in the shadow of the cross. The Lutheran Lectionary highlights the result of the miracle — some people believed, others ran to the authorities to report the miracle to them; when the religious leaders heard about this latest and most powerful miracle of Jesus, they reached the decision that Jesus must die. The raising of Lazarus set the stage for the scenario that saw the Son of God nailed to a cross and left to die.

Sermons from the Gospel — John 11:1-53

(Note: Several different sermons, both in theme and shape, may be legitimately preached from this gospel, depending on: the lectionary that is followed; the theology of the church year; the purpose of Lent; one's personal theological stance; and the situation in the congregation. Several possibilities, which do not exhaust the text by any means, are sketched out below. All of them emerge from the narrative context of the text.)

I. A biblical story sermon — John 11:1-44 — "Resuscitation or Resurrection?"

Scene 1 — "Beyond the Jordan" with his disciples: the beginning of this story is enigmatic, because when he heard about Lazarus' illness, Jesus allowed him to die without even going to make a last call on him. Why should he react that way when a friend was about to die? Why didn't Jesus immediately go to Bethany? Was it necessary for Lazarus to die in order to convince the disciples of Jesus' identity as the Son of God? What is going on here? Isn't that the way it always seems to be, that God isn't around when we need him the most, and that he doesn't really seem to care about our troubles and suffering?

Scene 2 — Outside Bethany: Martha, not Mary, as might have been expected, met Jesus outside the town and almost blamed him for Lazarus' death; "Lord, if you had been here, my brother would not have died." Did she know that Jesus could have been there, perhaps in time? Why does God allow people to die, seemingly before their time? The promise of resurrection doesn't seem enough ("I know he will rise again in the resurrection at the last day."); we would like to have resurrection now — or, at least, to find some way to by-pass death, or put it off as long as possible.

Scene 3 — At the grave: resurrection or resuscitation — that's the question. Jesus sent for Mary, who, between her sobs of grief, repeated Martha's pathetic expression of faith, "Lord, if you had been here . . . ." At the grave, Jesus wept — and then, after the stone had been rolled back, he commanded, "Lazarus, come out." He did, wrapped in the embalming clothes. A miracle — of resuscitation, not resurrection. Lazarus lived again — only to face death a second time; but how different would that be — he would be able to look death in the eye and laugh after his experience, wouldn't he?

Last Sunday, I met a friend I hadn't seen for months and learned that he had nearly died of a rare illness. "Everything's different now," he said. "I was sustained by the power of the Spirit. I believe my faith is stronger now. I can look death in the eye, unafraid."

Scene 4 — On leaving the cemetery — the aftermath — some believed, but others still doubted and went to report to the Pharisees what Jesus had done. They couldn't deny the miracle, but they could reject the man; they refused to believe that Jesus was the Son of God, the Messiah. They would settle for resuscitation and, thereby, lose the resurrection. Isn't this where we come into the story, if we are interested in a Christ who primarily is able to work miracles right now? Resuscitation or resurrection — that's the question we have to answer.

The key to this type of story is the interweaving of three stories: The Story, the people's stories, and the pastor's story, so that the gospel will be proclaimed here and now. See page 115 f. of *The Song and The Story* for an example of a biblical story sermon on this text, "Grave for Sale."

II. A thematic sermon — John 11:47-53 — "The Horns of a Dilemma."

1. *The dilemma:* The lordship of Jesus has to be accepted in faith, or Jesus has to be rejected and gotten rid of once and for all. That was the predicament of the Pharisees; they might have accepted him as a teacher or a prophet, but never as the Messiah. Do we try to settle for something less than Jesus really is?

2. *The solution:* execute Jesus and he will be "out of our hair" — death is final, permanent — once you're dead, you're dead. That's it. But Jesus made a return appearance in just three days! They couldn't get rid of Jesus as easily as they thought they could — nor can we, when we attempt to banish him by indifference or absolute hostility. Jesus lives forever. He is here to stay.

3. *The resolution:* The Pharisees didn't know it, but they were playing right into the hands of God when they decided that Jesus had to die and hatched the plot to accomplish his death. Caiaphas didn't realize that he was right when he said, "it is expedient that one man should die for the people." That was God's plan, and that's exactly how it worked out; Caiaphas and the other religious leaders were used by God, but they didn't even know it. They had a hand in our salvation and the deliverance of all people. When they condemned Jesus to death, they were opening the gates of the kingdom of heaven to all believers.

III. A funeral sermon, as well as a possible sermon for the Fifth Sunday in Lent — John 11-27 — "Grave for Sale." (This is the same title as the sermon in *The Song and the Story*, but a different sermon in type and substance.)

1. Like Lazarus, we have all been here before. _____ has been here, too; he/she entered the grave in baptism, when the water was poured on him/her. We have experienced many "little deaths" in our lifetimes, haven't we? Actually, dying is but one more death, one more journey into the grave; the final one.

2. Like Lazarus, we have all come back from death; our baptism did not end in death but resulted in sharing in the resurrection of Jesus Christ. Life has been filled with many "little resurrections," too — experiencing new life after desperate illness, knowing the joy of forgiveness of our sins, welcoming life in the birth of a child almost simultaneously with the death of a loved one . . . .

3. With Lazarus, we can look forward to the resurrection through our Lord, Jesus Christ. Our "little deaths" and "little resurrections" have helped prepare us for physical death and the final resurrection. We know, with Lazarus, that we shall dwell in the house of the Lord forever. When that day comes, all of us will have a grave for sale.

A sermon on the First Lesson — Ezekiel 37:1-14 — "Dem Bones Gonna Rise Again."

1. The Capuchin order, a branch of the Franciscans, of the Roman Catholic Church, has recreated this scene in the lower level of their church on the Via Veneto in Rome. When one of their order dies, he is buried in dirt in the basement until his flesh is gone from his bones, and then the bones are added to the collection of skulls, vertebrae, and all the other bones of the body that are indeed "very dry bones." Some entire skeletons are vested in the habit of the Capuchins, seemingly keeping silent watch over the collection of bones; others are arranged in symmetrical patterns, and still others are placed in piles of skulls and other bones that seem almost to have been discarded. Their message: the bones will rise again, when God opens the graves of all people.

2. He will do this as certainly as he brought the children of Israel back from their captivity in Babylon. It is one thing to gain the release of a captive nation, but it is quite a different matter to raise the dead from their graves. God has the power to do just that — and he has promised he will do it for Jesus' sake.

3. In the interim, it is for us to thank and praise him for his gracious gift in Christ, and to tell the entire world that "Dem bones gonna rise again." That's the good news that Jesus brought into the world — and left behind after his resurrection and ascension.

A sermon on the Second Lesson — Romans 8:11-19 — "From Restoration to Resurrection."

    1. *Restoration and new life* — now — come through the Holy Spirit in baptism.

    2. *Resurrection and eternal life* — then, after death — will come through the Holy Spirit, who raised Jesus from the dead.

    3. *Renewal of all creation* — finally — will come on the last day, at the general resurrection.

    4. *Redeemed* — forever — in Christ. Live faithfully — in hope — now.

Sunday of the Passion

Roman Catholic	Isaiah 50:4-7	Philippians 2:6-11	Matthew 26:14—27:66
Episcopal	Isaiah 45:21-25	Philippians 2:5-11	Matthew (26:36-75)
	or Isaiah 52:13—53:12		27:1-54 (55-66)
Lutheran	Isaiah 50:4-9a	Philippians 2:5-11	Matthew 26:1—27:66
			or Matthew 27:11-54
Common	Isaiah 50:4-9a	Philippians 2:5-11	Matthew 27:11-54

The church year theological clue

By shortening Passiontide from two weeks to one and shifting Passion Sunday from the Fifth to the Sixth Sunday in Lent, several significant liturgical changes have been made. First, the Sixth Sunday in Lent can no longer be Palm Sunday, as it could when the period of passion stretched over two weeks and Palm Sunday was in the middle of it; Palm Sunday has to be a part, really the beginning, of the liturgy of Passion Sunday. Second, there is an attempt to return to the earlier practice of reading the story of the Passion in its entirety on Passion Sunday and three other times (Tuesday, Wednesday, and Good Friday) during Holy Week; each evangelist told the Passion story from his perspective. Third, there is a focus on the mighty — *redemptive* — acts which God performed in Jesus' passion — *his suffering and death* — during this week. Holy Saturday is really given over to the resurrection in the first service of Easter, the Easter Vigil. Clearly, the first part of Lent deals with the human predicament, with penitence, baptism, while the last week highlights God's dealing with sin in Jesus' death on the cross and anticipation of the Paschal mystery, Easter. Passion Sunday could be an occasion when there is no formal sermon in the liturgy of the word. A brief homily might be preached in the Liturgy of the Palms, if it is done at all. A dramatic reading of the Passion history, with different persons reading the dialogue of the various people involved surely is one way to deal with the mass of narrative material in the text. It is a story and should be treated liturgically and homiletically as a story.

The Prayer of the Day (LBW) — The prayer, which would be said near the beginning of the Liturgy of the Word, addresses God from the context of Holy Week: "Almighty God, you sent your Son, our Savior Jesus Christ, to take our flesh upon him and to suffer death upon the cross." The petition asks God to let the faithful "share in the obedience to your will and in the glorious victory of his resurrection." Those who dare to follow Jesus are committed to obedience to death and live in the hope of the resurrection of the Lord. The best way that people can participate in the "glorious victory of his resurrection" is through the renewal of their baptismal covenant. Baptism, as death and resurrection, brings obedience and victory together as a gift of grace.

The Psalm of the Day (LBW) — Psalm 31:1-5, 9-16 — The last word Jesus spoke on the cross, "Into your hands I commend my spirit," comes from this psalm. It points to Good Friday and the apparent end of the story. The plea of the psalmist is appropriate for the Passion of our Lord because he, like Jesus, was in desperate straights and had only God for his refuge. He calls on God for help and cries out:

Have mercy on me, O Lord, for I am in trouble . . . . my strength fails me . . . and my bones are consumed. I have become a reproach to all my enemies and even to my neighbors, a dismay to those of my acquaintance . . . . I am forgotten like a dead man . . . . For I have heard the whisperings of the crowd; fear is all around; they put their heads together against me; they plot to take my life.

126

And Jesus could have said, as he faced death on the cross:

> *But as for me, I have trusted in you, O Lord. I have said, "You are my God. My times are in your hand; rescue me from the hand of my enemies and from those who persecute me. Make your face to shine upon your servant, and in your lovingkindness save me."*

The Psalm Prayer (LBW)

> *God of kindness and truth, you saved your chosen one, Jesus Christ, and you give your martyrs strength. Watch over your people who come to you now, and strengthen the hearts of those who hope in you, that they may proclaim your saving acts of kindness in the eternal city; through your Son, Jesus Christ our Lord.*

The readings:

Isaiah 50:4-9a

The words of this passage could also be put into the mouth of Jesus who, like the prophet, knew that his mission in the world was to deliver the Word of God to the people, even if it cost him his life. Jesus, like Isaiah, knew that he would encounter opposition and would suffer the consequences of being the servant of God. Jesus, like Isaiah, was ready to obey God and receive the worst that people might give him for his willing obedience. Jesus, like Isaiah, was ready to face shame and "spitting." Jesus, like Isaiah, had made up his mind to do God's bidding and, in his case, had set his course to the cross. Jesus, like Isaiah, is sure that God will finally vindicate him and declare him righteous. Jesus, like Isaiah, could declare, "Behold, the Lord God helps me; who will declare me guilty?"

Philippians 2:5-11

Scholars today believe that Paul certainly wrote to the church at Philippi, "Have this mind among yourselves, which is yours in Christ Jesus," but that he was quoting an older hymn in the beautiful verses that follow. The first part of the hymn refers to Jesus' existence with the Father before he took on human flesh and form, "emptying" himself and taking the form of a servant. The second section speaks of his "being born in the likeness of men," and, as a human being, "humbled himself and became obedient unto death, even death on a cross." The third part tells how God has "highly exalted" him and has given him "the name which is above every name." The fourth stanza states that "at the name of Jesus every knee shall bow . . . and every tongue confess that Jesus Christ is Lord, to the glory of God the Father." Paul probably made additions to the second and fourth verses of the hymn, which have been accepted as integral parts of it. The reading, indeed, is most proper as a reading and also a preaching text for the Sunday of the Passion.

Matthew 27:11-54

The longer form of the Gospel, chapters 26 and 27 of St. Matthew, combine into a reading of such length that in some congregations, where this is read in its entirety, the people are invited to sit rather than stand for the reading of the Gospel for the Day. This is the shorter form, which is also quite long, but can be managed and incorporated into a sermon quite readily.

The story of Jesus' trial is taken up at the point where Caiaphas and the chief priests sent Jesus to Pilate to be condemned and executed. The chief question Pilate asks has to do with Jesus' royal lineage, "Are you the King of the Jews?" Pilate was amazed that Jesus wouldn't answer the charges brought against him; he knew he was innocent, was warned by his wife, "have nothing to do with that righteous man," but gave in to the crowd, released Barabbas, washed his hands, and condemned Jesus to die by crucifixion. The soldiers pressed the question of Jesus' royalty, putting a purple robe upon him and a crown of thorns, mocking him by saying, "Hail, King of the Jews," and, when they crucified him, putting a sign on the cross, "This is Jesus, the King of the Jews." Later, the chief priests joined in the cries of derision:

> *He saved others; he cannot save himself. He is the King of Israel; let him come down now from the cross, and we will believe in him. He trusts in God; let God deliver him now, if he desires him; for he said, "I am the Son of God."*

holars say that Jesus' desperate cry, "My God, my God, why have you forsaken me?," is obably the most authentic saying of Jesus from the cross; it makes the priests' taunts more nounced and final. This shorter reading ends with the centurion's statement from below cross, "Truly this was the Son of God."

processional Gospel — Matthew 21:1-11 — "The One Who Is the King of Kings."

his gospel is to be read before the Liturgy, or Procession, of the Palms, as the preliminary art of the day's worship. As the beginning of the final drama that took place in Jerusalem, needs to be articulated in one form or another — read or told, or both. The royalty theme hat Matthew sounds in this section of the story is clearly announced in the quotation he borrows from Isaiah (62:11) and Zechariah (9:9), "Tell the daughter of Zion, Behold, your King is coming to you, humble, and mounted on an ass, and on a colt, the foal of an ass." lthough he rides into Jerusalem like an ordinary person, he is accorded a greeting fitting or a king born in the royal line, "Hosanna to the Son of David! Blessed is he who comes n the name of the Lord! Hosanna in the highest!" When the people ask, "Who is this?" and the crowds answer, "This is the prophet Jesus from Nazareth of Galilee," the beginning of the end is at hand for Jesus.

A sermon on the Gospel — Matthew 27:11-54

Rudyard Kipling's story, *The Man Who Would Be King,* which was made into a movie, suggests the scope of the content and how the shape of a sermon on Passion Sunday should be structured. When Dan Dravot and Peachey Carnahan enter the legendary Kingdom of Kafiristan to seek their fortunes, it is almost like Jesus' entry into Jerusalem; they are accepted as gods, and Dan is acclaimed king, Peachey his prime minister. Dan is a benevolent ruler until he decides, against the advice of Peachey, to take a wife for warmth and companionship during the long, cold winter. The girl he picks out is resistant to his idea and bites him; he bleeds, therefore he cannot really be a god — "gods do not bleed." A revolt ensues and Dan goes to his death when a suspension bridge over a deep gorge is cut; Peachey is crucified, left to hang on the cross until he dies, but he survives snow and a cold winter night and lives to tell the whole story on his return to the story teller, Kipling. Could this be Kipling's explanation for the death and resurrection of Christ? At any rate, he had to use two persons to tell his version of the story, if that's what he was up to. The clue for the preacher who faces the task of preaching on the Sunday of the Passion is simply this: the whole story has to be told as succinctly and interestingly as possible. That's the homiletical priority of the day.

1. Begin with the triumphal entry of Jesus into Jerusalem as the sermon introduction.

2. Describe the events that led up to the arrest of Jesus; this material is so voluminous that it may take the shape of a listing, or an enumeration, of these portions of the story.

3. Retell — in a condensed version — the story of the arrest, trials, condemnation of Jesus, taking care to include the most important details in it.

4. Tell the tale of Jesus' passion and death over against the story of the resurrection.

5. Make clear the meaning of all of this for the people who observe Holy Week in anticipation of the Easter celebration.

Simply tell the passion week story. Tell it simply!

128

A homily on the Gospel for the Liturgy of the Palms — Matthew 21:1-11 — "The Triumph and the Terrible Tree."

1. Jesus entered the Holy City in triumph, seated on a lowly beast of burden — a strange sort of entry for royalty; five days later he left the city, became a beast of burden himself who carried his own cross — and the sins of the world — to Calvary.

2. He deserved every accolade he received — the shouts of Hosanna, the palm branches, the clothing strewn in his path, because he was indeed the Son of David and the Son of God. He did not deserve the taunts of the crowd, "Come down from the cross, if you are the Son od God!" He died to save all people from sin and deliver them from death.

3. His story forces all who hear it to ask, "Who is this?" — and to find the answer through the Word and the Spirit and prayer so that they may shout, "Hosanna to the Son of David! Blessed is he who comes in the name of the Lord! Hosanna in the highest!"

A suggestion for homiletical treatment of the First Lesson.

Both lessons tend to create homiletical problems for the preacher. The homiletical problem of the first reading is, simply, that it seldom is preached by itself on the Sunday of the Passion or Palm Sunday. At best, this servant song might find a place, either as an illustration or a quotation, in Palm Sunday / Passion Sunday sermons — "The Lord God has opened my ear, and I was not rebellious, I turned not backward. I gave my back to the smiters . . . . I hid not my face from shame and spitting . . . . therefore I have set my face like a flint . . . . he who vindicates me is near." A sermon on this text would see it becoming incarnate in the Suffering Servant, Jesus, and the story of his last trip to the Holy City. The prophet spoke words which could never come forth from the very mouth of Jesus as he went to his terrible death on the cross.

A sermon on the Second Lesson — Philippians 2:5-11 — "Jesus Christ is Lord."

1. In his birth and life, *Jesus emptied himself* of the godhead — vacated his place with God — and became the Suffering Servant of whom Isaiah wrote.

2. In his life, *Jesus obeyed God perfectly,* even in the face of death. His obedience brought him death instead of the benefits and the blessings that God promises to those who fulfill the law.

3. *God turned Jesus' defeat and death into a victory,* and has "highly exalted him" and given him a name — Christ — that is above every other name. Christ, the crucified and risen one, is the Lord of all.

4. At Jesus' name, every knee should bow and every tongue confess that "Jesus Christ is Lord" — and "to the glory of God the Father." That's our agenda for today — and for every day that we live on earth.

Maundy Thursday

Roman Catholic	Exodus 12:1-8, 11-14	1 Corinthians 11:23-26	John 13:1-15
Episcopal	Exodus 12:1-14a	1 Corinthians 11:23-26 (27-32)	John 13:1-15 or Luke 22:14-30
Lutheran	Exodus 12:3-8	1 Corinthians 10:16-17 or 1 Corinthians 11:23-26	Mark 14:12-26
Common	Exodus 12:3-8	1 Corinthians 10:16-17 or 1 Corinthians 11:23-26	Mark 14:12-26

The church year theological clue

Thursday of Holy Week originally was celebrated as a feast of reconciliation, long ago when sin was taken seriously by the church; the penitents, who were excluded from the congregation during Lent were brought back and joined the congregation in the sacrament. They would come to the closed door of the church, knock and seek entrance, only to be turned away by an official of the congregation. They returned a second time, knocked and were turned away again. The third time, the bishop went to the door, opened it, listened to their petition, accepted it, embraced them, and led them to the front of the nave where they were formally received back into active membership in the congregation. That kind of ceremonial would not be feasible today, because no one is expelled from the church during Lent. (Congregations want everyone they can possibly get to attend worship services during Lent.) But there are sinners in church, who have been separated from the Lord by their sin, and they need a word of forgiveness and reconciliation. Holy Thursday takes on added significance (beyond a memorial supper) when this theme is developed in the worship and preaching of Holy Thursday. The preacher has to preach both law and gospel to proclaim the Last Supper as "the feast of reconciliation" to the people.

The Prayer of the Day (the LBW supplies two) — The first collect is addressed to the Holy God, who is the "source of all love," saying that Jesus, on the night "of his betrayal," gave a new commandment ("love one another as I have loved you") to his disciples. The petition asks, "by your Holy Spirit write this commandment in our hearts."

The second prayer is related to the Eucharist — "in a wonderful Sacrament you have left us a memorial of your suffering and death," and asks, "May this Sacrament of your body and blood so work in us that the way we live will proclaim the redemption you have brought." This prayer suggests that Lent is best fulfilled when people repent of their sins, are reconciled to Christ, and serve God and human beings in love and humility. Neither prayer speaks directly about reconciliation.

The Psalm of the Day (LBW) — Psalm 116:10-17 — The first part of the psalm (verses 1-8) is most appropriate for Easter; the selection chosen for Holy Thursday is also suitable for this occasion —

> How shall I repay the Lord for all the good things he has done for me. I will lift up the cup of salvation and call upon the name of the Lord. I will fulfill my vows to the Lord in the presence of all his people.

Verse 12 is a refrain that is repeated exactly in the next to the last verse of the psalm. Verses 13 and 14 give added significance to this choice: "Precious in the sight of the Lord is the death of his servants. O Lord, I am your servant and the child of your handmaid; you have freed me from my bonds." The church has good reason to apply this text to the contemplation of the Passion and death of the Lord, especially to Maundy Thursday.

The Psalm Prayer (LBW)

> *God of power and mercy, through the Passion and resurrection of your Son you have freed us from the bonds of death and the anguish of separation from you. Be with us on our pilgrimage, and help us offer you a sacrifice of praise, fulfill our vows, and glorify you in the presence of all your people; through Jesus Christ our Lord.*

The readings:

Exodus 12:1-14

This is the account which tells of the instructions that God gave to Moses and Aaron about the Passover that he would use to soften Pharaoh's heart and bring about the Exodus of the children of Israel from Egypt. After speaking about the sacrifice of lambs, putting the blood on the two doorposts and the lintel of the door of the house in which the lambs will be eaten, God says:

> *I am the Lord. The blood shall be a sign for you, upon the houses where you are; and when I see the blood, I will pass over you, and no plague shall fall upon you to destroy you, when I smite the land of Egypt.*

The resemblance of the Passover to the institution of the Holy Communion on the night when Jesus was betrayed is obvious, which, of course, influenced the church to remember what happened on this special night:

> *This day shall be for you a memorial day, and you shall keep it as a feast to the Lord; throughout your generations you shall observe it as an ordinance for ever*

Passover, for the Jews, even today; but the Lord's Supper, the Eucharist, for Christians.

1 Corinthians 11:17-32 or 23-26

The significance — beyond the obvious description of the institution of the Eucharist by the Lord — is that numerous congregations continue to have divisions and disunity among the members, which are similar to those that were occurring in the church at Corinth. On the other hand, few congregations, if any, are confronted with the problem of gluttony and drunkenness in the worship service or the confines of congregational property, though one might discover some overeating at congregational dinners or potluck suppers today!

In the second reading, Paul tells the Corinthian congregation how the Lord's Supper is to be done and instructs them in the meaning of what they do: "For as often as you eat this bread and drink the cup, you proclaim the Lord's death until he comes." Participation in Holy Communion proclaims Christ's death on the cross as an act that gains the forgiveness of sins and reunion with God for all repentant sinners.

John 13:1-17, 34

John's account of the Last Supper portrays Jesus as the servant who is about to suffer; Christ washes the feet of the disciples so that they will understand that he came into the world as the servant who, alone, is able to deliver humanity from sin and death. To Peter's objection, "You shall never wash my feet," Jesus replies, "If I do not wash you, you have no part in me." Still not satisfied, Peter requests, "Lord, not my feet only but also my hands and my head!" Again, Jesus instructs him, "He who has bathed does not need to wash, except for his feet, but he is clean all over." The parallel to baptism in this statement may be more significant for most congregations than actual foot washing is today.

A homily based on the three lessons, with proper emphasis on the Gospel — "Christ, Our Passover, Reconciles God to Us."

This is the night on which a feast is to be kept with joy and thanksgiving; indeed, Christ, our Passover has been sacrificed for us. Alleluia!

1. Passover — Then and Now: *Then* a lamb had to be sacrificed. *Now* the Lamb of God must be slain to effect the New Passover, the reconciliation of God and his people.

2. Passover — Then and Now: *Then* the blood saved the people of Israel from death. *Now* the blood of Christ makes people clean, washes them and removes their sin:

> *There is a fountain filled with blood*
> *   Drawn from Immanuel's veins;*
> *And sinners, plunged beneath that flood,*
> *   Lose all their guilty stains.*

3. Passover — Then and Now: *Then* only the flesh was eaten; the blood was spilled on the doorway. *Now* the body and blood of the lamb must be consumed in this Passover meal. Participation in this meal completes the "washing" and renews the gifts received in baptism.

4. Passover — Then and Now: *Then* the Passover commemorates an event of the past to the Jews. *Now* the Eucharist proclaims that which is yet to come: "As often as you eat this bread and drink this cup, you proclaim the Lord's death until he comes again."

Good Friday

Roman Catholic	Isaiah 52:13—53:12	Hebrews 4:14-16; 5:7-9	John 18:1—19:42
Episcopal	Isaiah 52:13—53:12	Hebrews 10:1-25	John (18:1-40)
	or Genesis 22:1-18		19:1-37
	or Wisdom 2:1, 12-24		
Lutheran	Isaiah 52:13—53:12	Hebrews 4:14-16;	John 18:1—19:42
	or Hosea 6:1-6	5:7-9	or John 19:17:30
Common	Isaiah 52:13:53:12	Hebrews 4:14-16;	John 18:1—19:42
	or Hosea 6:1-6	5:7-9	or John 19:17-30

The church year theological clue

The evolution of the church year — and the important place that Good Friday has in it — began with the weekly celebration of the death and resurrection of the Lord; every Sunday was the occasion for celebrating the raising of Christ from the dead. When an annual celebration — Easter — of Christ's triumph over the grave came to be observed, it included Saturday and Friday; thus, Good Friday, Holy Saturday, and Easter Sunday formed the sacred Triduum, which led into the great fifty-day celebration of the Pasch. As Lent began to take shape, the Triduum changed so that it started with Holy Thursday, plus Good Friday and Holy Saturday. Today, Good Friday remembers the death of Jesus on the cross, Holy Saturday recalls the time he spent in the tomb, and Saturday night, in the Easter Vigil as the first eucharist of Easter, testifies to the reality of the resurrection. Good Friday has different content than Holy Thursday, making so-called "identical" Holy Thursday-Good Friday services liturgically and homiletically unacceptable. The Good Friday Gospel reading tells the story of the death of our Lord, Jesus Christ, at Calvary. In at least one of the special Good Friday liturgies (LBW) a sermon is optional.

Preaching on Good Friday in the Year of Matthew

The most popular Good Friday preaching tradition features "The Seven Last Words of Christ." Usually, it is done within the scope of a three-hour liturgy, beginning at noon on Good Friday, and constituting the chief service of the day. Evening services are intended to review the whole story of Jesus' suffering and death, thus the longer reading listed above; a biblical narrative is a most suitable form for preaching on this long text (John 18:1—19:42). The shorter gospel (John 19:17-30) is better suited to a thematic sermon which might bring out the theological interpretation of the death of Christ on the cross. Although the Gospel of John is appointed for years A, B, and C, it seems fitting in year A, the Year of Matthew, that a sermon might be preached from Matthew's account of the crucifixion. John's gospel, which is traditional, may have been retained, at least in part, because it contains three "words from the cross." Matthew's gospel reports only one saying of Jesus as he hung there close to death, "My God, my God, why have you forsaken me?" One reason for preaching upon this word is that scholars consider it to be the most authentic of the seven words Jesus is supposed to have said before he died.

A sermon on Matthew 27:47 — "The Darkest Moment in the Life of Jesus."

The whole business was revolting and disgusting; Jesus was "framed" for blasphemy by his enemies and doomed to death by a cowardly politician, who wanted nothing more than to keep the peace in Jerusalem during the Passover. The worst moment for Jesus came when he felt that God was not with him in this terrible experience, "My God, my God, why have you forsaken me?"

He must have cried out soon after they nailed him to the cross, or he would not have been able to speak an entire sentence as he quoted from the scriptures (Psalm 22:1), "My God, my God, why have you deserted me?" *(Jerusalem Bible)* Death by crucifixion was not for the faint-hearted, nor was it for the strong, who might have suffered the most; they might have been able to hold their bodies upright for a longer time, so that they could breathe. As executions went in those days, Jesus' didn't last very long, according to the reports. And Matthew says that he said only this one sentence before he died, "My God, my God, why have you forsaken me?"

1. Jesus was utterly alone in his death, deserted by his disciples and friends but also, he sensed, by God the Father. He really was God-forsaken. Had there been some friendly person near the cross, or had he been confident that God was there sharing in his suffering, he might have simply asked, "Why?" That's what Martin Quarrier did, in Peter Mattheissen's *At Play in the Fields of the Lord,* when he lay dying of a blow from a cross-marked machete wielded by one of the natives he was attempting to "save" in the wilderness of South America. It shouldn't have made any sense to Jesus, because it never really makes sense to us; there's an impenetrable mystery connected to the death of Jesus on the cross. Whenever we look at the Christ figure on the cross, we ask, "Why?" Why didn't he? Could it be because he had no one of whom to ask the question?

2. But Jesus really knew why he was dying a criminal's death, despite having done nothing wrong; this was to fulfill scripture and, thereby, make a radical change in the relationship of God and his people. What he didn't expect, according to Matthew (and Mark), was the complete absence of the one who had said, "This is my beloved Son, in whom I am well pleased." Did Jesus think that God would send angels to pull out the spikes and set him free? Probably not, but he did believe that he would have the comfort of God's presence as he was dying; surely, he had the right to expect that much from his heavenly Father. His death was the darkest moment in his life, not because he was dying, but because he could not sense the presence of God as death was about to claim him.

3. Jesus' last cry, at the time of his death, was a cry of surrender, when he turned over his life to the God who didn't seem to be there. The total despair that Jesus experienced had to be momentary, otherwise, he would have fought to live as long as he could. He died in the assurance that, as he had told the disciples from the words of the prophets, God would raise him from the dead. Together, his death and resurrection take the terror out of our deathtime, because our Lord will be with us as long as we live and see us through the darkest moment of our lives. We may dare to believe that God really is with us, in Christ, when we need him the most. He never lets us down, even in the face of death.

4. Jesus conquered sin in his life and destroyed the darkness of death when he died on the cross. He had to face the worst that death has to offer in order to win the victory over it. He may have cried, "My God, my God, why have you forsaken me?" — and really meant it — but before he died, he realized that God was there all the time. He is present at death, as well as in life. Each Good Friday tells us that — and we can never forget it.

The Easter Season

The Vigil of Easter

The Easter Vigil is the service that connects Good Friday with Easter Sunday. It takes place on Saturday evening or early on Sunday morning; it probably was an all-night vigil when it originated, consisting of a fast and a prayer service that culminated with the celebration of the Eucharist. Baptism became a part of the service and took place during the night as early as the beginning of the third century. By the fourth century, Easter had become the time par excellence for ministering baptism as a central feature of the Easter Vigil. The lighting of a new fire came into the liturgy by the ninth century, although a blessing for it was not created until the twelfth century. The readings, which have varied from four to twelve lessons in various places and at various times in the evolution of the vigil, were chosen from the Old Testament and the Gospels, because the celebration of the Easter Vigil illustrates the Christianization of the Jewish Passover. The Passover is merely the foundation for the Easter Vigil and the Feast, which goes far beyond the Passover. The Eucharist is the climax of the Easter Vigil and, as such, the first service of Holy Communion on Easter Sunday (or, for practical reasons, on Saturday evening).

The liturgical order of the Easter Vigil

1. The Service of Light begins with the gathering of the people outside the nave, the lighting of a new flame and the paschal candle, entrance into the church, the "lumen Christi" liturgy and the Easter proclamation, the lighting of the people's candles with the concluding liturgy.

2. The Service of Readings follows the Service of Light and, in modern practice, may vary from four to twelve lessons, all Old Testament readings, plus one from Baruch. (For example, in the LBW the twelve anciently appointed lessons are listed, along with the option of using only four lessons. In some congregations, where the option is selected, a sermon is substituted for the other eight lessons.) A response is sung after the last lesson, which had its origin as a processional hymn that was chanted as the people moved from the church to the baptistry (the baptistry was in a separate building after the fourth century).

3. The Service of Baptism is the third part of the Easter Vigil and makes contemporary not only an ancient practice but it also renews the theology of the death and resurrection of the Lord in a dramatic and meaningful manner. Baptisms ought to be administered in this service, but the renewal of the baptismal covenant by the congregation should have a central place in the vigil, even if no baptisms are performed. The Service of Baptism and, for most Christians, the renewal of the baptismal covenant, offer the most profound way of entering into the Easter celebration, because baptism involves us — personally and individually — in the Easter event in a manner that cannot be duplicated by any other liturgical practice. God gives us all of the gifts of the kingdom in Holy Baptism.

4. The service of Holy Communion, the Easter Eucharist, concludes the Easter Vigil and completes the injunction, "Let us keep the feast (of reconciliation and the renewal of his gifts to us in Christ) with thanksgiving." The movement from baptism, as participation in the death and resurrection of the Lord, to the Table of the Lord, where God's people are fed again and again, and where "as often as (they) eat this bread and drink this cup, (they) proclaim the Lord's death until he comes again," announces as nothing else can, "Christ is risen! He is risen indeed!"

In *The Liturgical Year*, Adrian Nocent, O.S.B., gives detailed information about the Vigil of Easter as well as the other festivals and seasons of the Church year.

A theme for a sermon during the Easter Vigil, based on Exodus 13:10 — 15:1a and Matthew 27:33-66 — "Jesus Christ — Passover Today."

1. Passover — God's Gift to the Jews

2. Passover — The Blood of Many Lambs

3. Passover — The Blood of the Lamb of God

4. Passover — Celebration of Life over Death

The Easter Season

Easter is the heart of the Christian year; it is also the foundation of the Christian faith, because the Lord Jesus Christ was raised from the dead on the third day, as he said he would be. Without the resurrection, our faith, as Paul said, "would be in vain." We would still be sinners, who could only look ahead to death without hope. Accordingly, it is the essential action that God the Father took, in light of the cross, to justify human beings and redeem them through the death — and resurrection — of Jesus Christ.

Easter is a day and also a season. It was celebrated every Sunday, almost from the beginning of the Christian era, as a weekly celebration of the death and resurrection of the Lord. Soon it was expanded into the "Great Fifty Days," the Pasch, and when that happened, the church year began to take shape. The gospels give the reason for the expansion in the forty-day sequence to the Ascension of the Lord, fifty days to the coming of the Spirit on Pentecost.

As a Sunday, Easter is a kind of super Sunday, gathering the content of each Sunday and concentrating it into the eighth day, The Ogdoad, the new day of creation. God has said, "Behold, I make all things new." He did, in Jesus' resurrection. As a season, it is a "week of Sundays" — seven Sundays are included in the season. These Sundays are enumerated as the Sundays of Easter, not as, in the old church year and lectionary, Sundays after Easter. It should be noted, too, that the older Latin names for the Sundays, have been discarded in favor of simply numbering the Sundays as "of" Easter. More than anything else, this emphasizes for the church today that Easter is not simply one Sunday, or even a Super Sunday; it is a fifty-day season of triumph, joy, and hope, because "Christ is risen, as he said."

The Ascension of Our Lord comes on the fortieth day *of* Easter to mark the completion of the resurrection, on one hand, and the beginning of his reign, on the other. Pentecost is the fiftieth day *of* Easter, really, because it brings closure to Easter as a season while celebrating the advent of the Holy Spirit. The festival of Christ the King, which concludes the Pentecost season, affirms again that the risen and ascended Lord will continue to reign until he comes in glory at the end of the age. That is why the Scottish liturgical scholar, A. Allan McArthur, said that Easter is not merely a seven week period of "special rejoicing," but that it is "a symbol of this whole world epoch . . . which is bounded on one hand by the Resurrection and Ascension, and on the other hand, by the Second Coming — the consummation of the Kingdom which shall have no end." *(The Evolution of the Christian Year*, p. 165.)

Every sermon stands on the foundation of the Easter event, the death and resurrection of the Lord. Gustave Wingren wrote (in *The Living Word):* "The early Christian kerygma of Christ's work in death and resurrection has demonstrated, as no other factor in human history has, that it holds the power of renewing the Sunday preaching. In analyzing the essential nature of preaching it is impossible to overlook that. The message of the cross and the resurrection is the main pillar, not only of missionary preaching, but of preaching, in general." The good news, which someone needs to hear every Sunday of the year, is that Jesus died on Calvary's cross, but God raised him up on the third day, giving us hope of forgiveness and eternal life in his loving and gracious action. Articulated, or unarticulated, the resurrection is central to all Christian preaching.

The Resurrection of Our Lord
Easter Day

Roman Catholic	Acts 10:34, 37-43	1 Corinthians 3:1-4 or 1 Corinthians 5:6-8	John 20:1-9
Episcopal	Acts 10:34-43 or Exodus 14:10-14, 21-25; 15:20-21	Colossians 3:1-4	John 20:1-10 (11-18) or Matthew 28:1-10
Lutheran	Acts 10 34:43	Colossians 3:1-4	John 20:1-9 (10-18) or Matthew 28:1-10
Common	Acts 10:34-43	Colossians 3:1-4	Matthew 28:1-10

The church year theological clue

Easter, the theological center of the church year, celebrates the resurrection of the Lord; it is also the main festival of the Christian faith. It pins the Christian faith on a preposterous event, the raising of Christ from the grave after he had been dead almost three days. Easter is the great mystery of the faith, which no one can completely fathom or understand; it must be accepted on faith, faith alone. It is the heart of the good news, the gospel of Jesus Christ, because the one who was proclaimed King of Kings and Lord of Lords at his birth is indeed the Son of God and the long-promised Savior of the world. It reminds the church that, without the reality of the resurrection of Jesus, the gospel would simply be another "idle tale;" there would be no truth in it. And without the resurrection, Jesus would merely be a misguided martyr, or a well-meaning but poor fool, who died not only cruelly, but unnecessarily. Easter gives credence to the action that God took in Jesus to redeem the world, and it supports, while deepening, the mystery of the atonement in the cross and the hope of eternal life in Jesus' resurrection.

The Prayer of the Day (LBW) — The LBW offers two prayers for Easter Day. The first speaks of — and gives thanks for — Jesus' death on the cross and how God has "delivered us from the power of death" in "his glorious resurrection." The petition is concerned with the necessity of dying daily to sin, "so that we may live with him forever in the joy of the resurrection." The underlying theology is, of course, baptismal.

The second prayer begins with a linguistic overhauling of an ancient prayer: "Almighty God, through your only Son you overcame death and opened for us the gate of everlasting life." The petition could fit any Sunday worship service, but it really speaks to the purpose of Lent and Easter, which is to renew our lives and bend them to the doing of God's will on earth: "Give us your continual help; put good desires into our minds and bring them to full effect." The content of these prayers is such that the "or" in the LBW might well be changed to "and" so that both would be offered before the readings of Easter Day.

The Psalm of the Day (LBW) — Psalm 118:1-2, 15-24 — After a rather general, but glorious, introduction, the the first two verses ("Give thanks to the Lord, for he is good; his mercy endures forever. Let Israel now proclaim, 'His mercy endures forever.' "), the middle portion of the psalm addresses quite well what God has done in the resurrection of the Lord, despite the fact that it was created for another and entirely different occasion (probably the completion of the walls of Jerusalem, under Nehemiah, in 444 B.C.). Its choice in the LBW for this day is partly because this was Martin Luther's favorite psalm:

This is my own psalm which I specially love. Though the entire Psalter and the Holy Scriptures are indeed very dear to me as my sole comfort and my very life . . . . For it has done me great service on many an occasion and has stood by me in many a difficulty when the emperor, kings, wise men and clever, and even the saints were of no avail . . . .

The psalm says what needs to be said on Easter Sunday:

There is a sound of exultation and victory . . . . The right hand of the Lord has triumphed . . . . I shall not die, but live, and declare the works of the Lord . . . . This is the Lord's doing, and it is marvelous in our eyes. On this day the Lord has acted; we will rejoice and be glad in it.

It says everything except, "Christ is risen! He is risen indeed." The Psalm Prayer takes care of that.

The Psalm Prayer

Lord God, your Son, rejected by the builders, has become the cornerstone of the Church. Shed rays of your glory upon your Church, that it may be seen as the gate of salvation open to all nations. Let cries of joy and exultation ring out from its courts to celebrate the wonder of Christ's resurrection, now and forever.

The readings:

Acts 10:34-43

By replacing the Old Testament readings for the Easter season with selections from the book of The Acts of the Apostles, the church intends to give renewed emphasis to the importance of Easter as the Great Fifty Days of the church. These readings continue to announce the Easter proclamation and to keep it prominent in the consciousness of the faithful so that by the end of the season it will be burned into their hearts and minds forever. This particular choice reveals Peter's Christology in a sermon he is purported to have preached to Cornelius and others in Caesarea after his moving vision took him there. In the sermon, he outlines the central facts of the gospel, showing how the earthly ministry of Jesus was rejected by Israel and led to his death. He declares that the resurrection is God's way of vindicating Christ in the face of his awful death on the cross. And Peter personally affirms that he and others "ate" with Jesus after the resurrection, receiving his commandment to witness about what had taken place to the whole world. In this reading, the witness of Peter and the apostles proclaims the resurrection to contemporary people, assuring the faithful that they meet the risen Christ in the meal which he began on the night before he was betrayed.

Colossians 3:1-4

This reading succinctly spells out the nature of baptism as dying with Jesus and rising with the resurrected Christ; it is, at the same time, affirming the resurrection of the Lord. Once more, the ethical nature of the new life, which is central to the celebration of Lent, finds expression in the way that believers are expected to live in Jesus Christ: "Set your minds on things that are above, not on things that are on earth," is Paul's way of expressing how the new life in Christ issues from the resurrection. He also states that the final glory of the resurrection will come with the Second Coming, when he will gather the faithful to himself.

John 20:1-9 (10-18)

John tells the resurrection story a bit differently than do Matthew, Mark, and Luke. All of them mention Mary Magdalene, but the other three Evangelists say that there were other women, whom they name, with Mary Magdalene; John has Mary Magdalene at the tomb by herself but she does not enter the tomb, as she did in the other accounts, rather, she immediately went and told Peter what she had seen. When Peter and the "other" disciple ran to see what had happened, Peter was the first to enter the tomb and to examine the grave clothes that had been left behind. When the other disciple finally entered, John says that he "saw and believed." Oddly enough, despite the fact that Jesus had told the disciples three times that he must die and rise again on the third day, John says that "as yet they did not know the scripture, that he must rise from the dead." Completely missing from this part of the story (but it is in the next sequence in which Mary stays in the garden) is the angelic presence (Matthew and Mark have one angel, Luke tells of two at the tomb) and the Easter proclamation that they made to the women (Matthew's report has the angel of the Lord giving a tomb-side speech):

> *Do not be afraid; for I know that you seek Jesus who was crucified. He is not here; for he has risen, as he said. Come, see the place where he lay. Then go quickly and tell his disciples that he has risen from the dead, and behold, he is going before you to Galilee; there you will see him. Lo, I have told you.*

According to John, the "other disciple" entered the tomb, after Peter had gone inside, saw that the tomb was empty, observed the "grave cloths" and the napkin that had been placed on Jesus' head, and "believed." He was, in John's account, the first person to believe in the resurrection of Jesus without having actually seen the risen Lord. That "other disciple" is us, who must believe without ever actually seeing the risen Lord.

The longer lesson, which was added later to the traditional reading for Easter, gives a fuller, more complete, and more satisfying story of the Easter proclamation and the first appearance — to Mary Magdalene — after his resurrection. This is necessary to any kerygmatic sermon on this text, because without it, one must preach about the empty tomb and, possibly, that one man believed when he saw it. The appearances of the resurrected Jesus are important to the story, otherwise the gospel would be supposition and superstition.

A sermon on the Gospel (the longer reading) — "What Really Happened to Jesus?"

Mary went to mourn the death of Jesus. But when she got there, the tomb in which Jesus had been buried was empty, really empty. What happened? What had become of the body of Jesus, whom they buried just two days ago? Mary had gone there to mourn and to see that all was well; she received a shock that made her wonder what had happened to the body of Jesus? It appeared that the grave had been desecrated — robbed — and that Jesus' body had been taken away during the night. She had to do something, so she did the only possible thing; she ran and told Peter about the empty tomb. That's what John really tells us in this portion of the story.

Peter lost the race to the tomb. A younger disciple outran him, looked in and saw the empty tomb, but did not enter. Peter rushed right in — as he seems to have done in every situation — and discovered the grave cloths lying where Jesus had lain, and that Jesus was indeed gone from the grave. Oddly enough, nothing is known about his reaction, but the other disciple, once he finally entered the tomb, believed that Christ had risen from the grave. Most of us, like Peter, have to have more evidence than an empty tomb or discarded death wrappings. Even the Shroud of Turin can't make believers of most of us, can it? Even if it were proved beyond a doubt to be the cloth that Christ had been wrapped in when he was taken down from the cross, that would not make it evidence of Jesus' resurrection; it would only be testimony of his death. We may even know what the scripture says about Jesus' resurrection on the third day, but who can believe it really happened?

Mary Magdalene, the mourner, did not hear the Easter proclamation, but she was the first to see Jesus. She remained in the garden, weeping, finally looking into the empty tomb, only to be see two angels who did not tell her that Christ was raised from the dead; they asked her why she was crying. "They have taken away my Lord," she replied, and just then, before they could answer, Jesus appeared to her, asking her why she was weeping and whom she was looking for. She told him, and Jesus called her by name and she recognized him, fell at his feet and tried to cling to him, but received orders to find the disciples and tell them the news of his resurrection and impending ascension. She did what true believers ought to do; she obeyed the Lord and told the good news to them as he had instructed her to do. That's how the message gets out to all the world, even to you and me, so that we know what really happened to Jesus after he was buried in the garden tomb.

A sermon on the First Lesson — Acts 10:34-43 — "Easter and God's Good Intentions."

1. God's intention in Jesus Christ is that through him the world might be saved from sin and death.

2. God's intention was to go to any length — even the death of his son — to save all people.

3. God's intention was to allow nothing — not even the death of Jesus — to interfere with his plan.

4. God's intention was to give hope and the promise of eternal life to all who believe in the resurrection of Jesus.

5. God's intention is that the whole world might know and confess that Jesus is Lord of all. Easter affirms that God made good on his intentions.

A sermon on the Second Lesson — Colossians 3:1-4 — "Life After Death."

1. Easter is about life and death: "Christ is risen! He is risen indeed!" Jesus has conquered death and the grave and made life a possibility. Life has triumphed over death.

2. Our baptism ties us into the Easter death of Jesus, because in baptism we have already died with Christ and have been "marked with the cross of Christ forever." We must die — in baptism — to experience life in Jesus now.

3. But baptism also seals us into a relationship with Christ, affirming a new covenant, that guarantees that *we are participants* — now and eternally — *in Jesus' resurrection and life after death.*

4. Our business, as reborn Christians, is to live the new life in Christ to the fullest, declaring to the world that he is Lord, and looking forward to seeing the fullness of his glory when he comes to us again on the last day.

Second Sunday of Easter

Roman Catholic	Acts 2:42-47	1 Peter 1:3-9	John 20:19-31
Episcopal	Acts 2:14a, 22-32	1 Peter 1:3-9	John 20:19-31
	or Genesis 8:6-16; 9:8-16	or Acts 2:14a, 22-32	
Lutheran	Acts 2:14a, 22-32	1 Peter 1:3-9	John 20:19-31
Common	Acts 2:14a, 22-32	1 Peter 1:3-9	John 20:19-31

The church year theological clue

Two major changes were made in the rationale of the Easter season in virtually all of the new lectionaries: the first was dropping the Latin names for the six Sundays between Easter and Pentecost, as was done in Lent. Since these names come from the introits, the psalms, rather than the gospels, and established the theoretical and real themes of the Sundays, something of Easter was often lost in the process. For example, the Fourth Sunday after Easter was *Cantate* and became known as Church Music Sunday in some parts of the church, a day to promote singing in choirs, etc. "Singing a new song to the Lord," in response to the resurrection, was lost, more often than not, in this special emphasis, which even included turning this Sunday into a day for cantatas and concerts which made spectators of the people of God. By deleting the Latin names and the singing of the introits, the gospels have been given their due. Second, by naming the Sundays "of Easter" instead of "after Easter" places strong emphasis on the Great Fifty Days, indicating that the Sundays *of* Easter are actually a *continuation of the Easter/resurrection celebration.* Therefore, Easter, as a season, has been restored to what it was in the primitive church. This almost insignificant alteration in the titles of the Sundays of Eastertide makes Easter what it should be, a seven-week celebration of Jesus' resurrection. The preaching during the Sundays of Easter focuses on *the reality of the resurrection,* including its completion in the ascension of the Lord, *and the implications of the resurrection for Christian faith and life.* "Christ is risen! He is risen indeed!" should be sounded and re-sounded on each of these Sundays. On this, the Second Sunday of Easter, Jesus' appearances to the disciples in the upper room in Jerusalem announce that the risen Lord is able to make contact and communicate with his disciples in a mysterious manner; he has seen and heard. In the future, he will be heard but not seen. Faith in the good news that Jesus is risen from the grave will come by hearing alone. Hence, the Word must be preached throughout the world, so that people will have an opportunity to hear the gospel, to believe, and to be blessed by the Lord.

The Prayer of the Day (LBW) — The rewording of this prayer is intended to give impetus to the continuing celebration of the resurrection of the Lord, but it tends to put Easter in the past rather than in the present and the future, too: "Almighty God, we *have celebrated* with joy the festival of our Lord's resurrection . . . ." To be in real harmony with the Easter season, it ought to begin, "Almighty God, we are celebrating with joy our Lord's resurrection." The petition asks God to "help us to show the power of the resurrection in all that we say and do" — in other words, to be genuine and believable witnesses of the resurrection of Christ, not only during Easter, but throughout the whole year of the Lord and our entire lives, too.

The Psalm for the Day (LBW) — Psalm 105:1-7 — This psalm connects with the prayer of the day, as well as the readings, sounding the note of thanksgiving for God's deeds and making reference to the work of witnessing to these deeds in the world — make known his deeds among the peoples." The children of God are not only to sing to him and give glory to his name, but to search for him "and his strength; and continually seek his face" by remembering "the marvels he has done, his wonders and the judgments of his mouth." The psalm can also remind those who believe in Jesus that they are children of Abraham, suggesting that their new covenant is in Christ; they are the new Israel. God is the God of the whole world, and Jesus is Lord of all, is suggested, if not actually proclaimed, in the psalm.

The Psalm Prayer (LBW)

God our Father, through the death and resurrection of your Son you have fulfilled the promise to abraham, Joseph, and Moses to redeem the world from slavery and to lead us into the promised land. Grant us living water from the rock and bread from heaven, that we may survive our desert pilgrimage and praise you forever; through Jesus Christ our Lord.

The readings:

Acts 2:14a, 22-32

When the new lectionaries began to appear early in the 1970's, there was some unanimity on the choice of Acts 2:42-47 as the First Lesson, but some of the churches changed this reading, as the list above reveals. The original lesson portrays how the church was actually living out the resurrection of Christ in daily life (the gospel was preached, a genuine community "in Christ" developed, the people "broke bread together," and they were faithful in prayer in the name of their risen Lord). The selection that most non-Roman churches have built into their lectionaries finds Peter preaching to the Israelites on the day of Pentecost, accusing them of being responsible for the illegal crucifixion of Christ, whom God had sent to do his work in the world and had identified as the Chosen One through "miracles and portents and signs." Peter also insists that David had prophesied about — and rejoiced in — the coming of the Christ, who uncorrupted by death, lives again. "God raised this man Jesus to life, and all of us are witnesses to that." *(Jerusalem Bible)* This reading affirms the Easter proclamation that Jesus is indeed risen from the dead.

1 Peter 1:3-9

This reading is a perfect selection for the Second Sunday of Easter because it refers to the resurrection of Jesus and it parallels the gospel: "without having seen him you love him; though you do not now see him you believe in him and rejoice with unutterable and exalted joy." The reader should not be surprised by this combination of themes in the content, because there is considerable scholarly opinion that suggests that 1 Peter was an Easter/baptismal homily or liturgy. The baptismal theme is clearly sounded in the first sentence after the greeting:

By his great mercy we have been born anew to a living hope through the resurrection of Jesus Christ from the dead, and to an inheritance which is imperishable, undefiled, and unfading, kept in heaven for you, who by God's power are guarded through faith for a salvation ready to be revealed in the last time.

Believers, who have been baptized into Christ's death, also anticipate in his resurrection and the new life he gives to his own. The Word and the Water — through the ministry of the Holy Spirit — have sealed the faithful into an everlasting relationship with the living Lord.

John 20:19-31

The "seeing is believing" theme, which is introduced by Thomas, who was absent when the Lord made his first post-resurrection appearance to his disciples, quite naturally gains a hearing with believers of every age. The faithful have had, ever since the ascension of Christ, to believe by the hearing the Word, the Good News, without having the benefit of actually seeing the resurrected Lord. Thomas' problem is common to all people. Who can believe the word of witnesses who lived nearly twenty centuries ago? After all, this part of Jesus' story — about his rising from the dead — is an incredible tale, even in an age that has known all sorts of medical marvels connected to death and resurrection.

But the first part of the story tends to be overlooked by the natural appeal that Thomas' honest difficulty in believing the incredible news of Jesus; resurrection has for most people. Jesus greeted the disciples with "Peace be with you," and that has remained to this day as the greeting of the risen Lord to his church, as well as the greeting of the faithful to one another. Next, he made it clear that they were not to spend the rest of their lives attempting to untangle the mystery of his death and resurrection; their task was to continue Jesus' ministry in the world — "As the Father has sent me, even so I send you." To give them power for this work, he "breathed on them, and said to them, 'Receive the Holy Spirit.'" Lastly, he gave them the authority to forgive — or retain — the sins of people to whom they would preach and witness. This part of the story is at least as important as the faith problem Thomas had and the subsequent encounter he had with Jesus.

Two sermons on the Gospel

I. John 20:19-21, 24-31 — "The Confession of a Heretic."

A couple of years ago, Dr. James Kennedy, the parish/television preacher, gave an intriguing sermon in which he made a confession to his congregation and the television audience. He apologized for bringing up "this matter" on Easter Sunday, but said that it was so important that it needed to be addressed. "I have been accused of heresy," he declared. "It is said that I have denied the resurrection of Jesus Christ." He said that is one of the most serious charges that could be made against a minister of the gospel. The truth of the matter was that "I did (deny the resurrection)" — and before an important "group of ministers." He went on to say, in this startling introduction, "My name is Thomas." In this first-person narrative sermon he moved from "Doubting Thomas," the person who said, "Unless I see in his hands the print of the nails, and place my finger in the mark of the nails, and place my hand in his side, I will not believe," to the man of faith who cried, "My Lord and my God!" That man he called "Doubt-less Thomas," the person that God would make of all of us. The text lends itself beautifully to a biblical narrative sermon.

The risen Christ can go anywhere he wants to; there is no barrier that can prevent him from communicating with his own. Neither the thickest wall, the stoutest door, nor the hardest heart, can stop the Lord from reaching his faithful people. He does it with his Word, "Peace be with you" and the report of the witnesses who say and heard him speak.

Like Thomas, people always want more than a word, a report, a tall tale; those who would believe in Jesus often desire to see him for themselves. That would make believing much simpler, more positive; human beings have to have proof, even in matters of faith: "Unless I see . . . ."

Thomas ought to be called "Fortunate Thomas," because he did get his wish; the risen Christ appeared to him and invited him to touch his wounds, and believe; his doubt immediately vanished in genuine faith. Some people have mystical experiences like that to bolster their belief in the risen Christ, but not many are that fortunate. All that most people will ever have on which to base their faith is a word, the witness of believers, the good news. We're not going to get anything more than the Word and Sacraments.

That Word will suffice; it is sufficient to wipe away our doubts and through God's grace, to plant true faith in Christ in our hearts. Otherwise, Jesus would not have asked Thomas, "Have you believed because you have seen me?" And in an afterthought, he said, "Blessed are those who have not seen and yet believe."

Believe! Believe! Christ has risen! He has risen indeed! Believe! Believe!

(For narrative and supplemental material that parallels this incident in a man who wanted to be a believer, but never reached the point where he could call Jesus the living Lord, read Loren Eiseley's autobiography *All the Strange Hours,* along with *The Night Country.* In one of his books, he said that a preacher never visited his home when he was growing up. It is unclear whether he ever attended worship services in a Christian church, although he read and knew the Bible. Was his "faith-difficulty" a matter of not hearing the Word proclaimed in the community of faith?)

II. John 20:19-24 — "Peace, Peace . . . There is no Peace."

1. The risen Lord spoke a word of peace to his church; it is a gift of the resurrection. "The peace of the Lord be with you" is always the greeting of the living Christ to his people.

2. "Peace" is a greeting that exacts a response in the form of action by the believers. Christ expects his own — all of them, every one — to be witnesses, peacemakers, who by word and deed proclaim the good news that God has given peace to the world in the risen Lord.

3. He empowers his followers to do his bidding by giving them the Holy Spirit. All Christians, in this sense, are charismatic; they can neither believe nor witness effectively without the inspiration and guidance of the Holy Spirit.

4. The church is given the care of souls in the form of power to forgive — or retain — the sins of people who claim to be believers. Through the preaching of the law, people must be brought to repentance, and through the absolution as the gospel is preached, their faith in Christ will be renewed and they will come to understand Jesus' greeting, "Peace be with you."

A sermon on the First Lesson — Acts 2:14a, 22-32 — "Peter's Plea for Repentance."

1. Any person who has lived in the midwest for any length of time knows what a "mighty wind" really is. The wind and flames that touched the people on Pentecost must have driven them out of the upper rooms into the street where they acted as if they were drunk. *They were — with the Holy Spirit.*

2. Peter, backed by the rest of the Eleven, explained what was happening and took the occasion to preach for repentance by talking about the death of Christ. "This man, who was put into your power by the deliberate intention and foreknowledge of God, you took and had crucified by men outside the law." *(Jerusalem Bible)* Every sinner participates in the crucifixion of Jesus Christ, now as then.

3. "You killed him, but God raised him to life, freeing him from the pangs of Hades." And, Peter adds, "All of us are witnesses to that." That's what the new life in Christ is all about: witnessing to the resurrection of the Lord. That's what God wants from us.

A sermon on the Second Lesson, 1 Peter 1:3-9 — "Signed, Sealed, and Delivered."

1. *Signed:* Christians are "marked with the cross of Christ forever." The cross is the sign that they have died with Jesus in baptism.

2. *Sealed:* The Holy spirit "seals" people into the resurrection of the Lord and the new life that he gives now to his believers. Through baptism, in which water is poured, the Word is spoken, and the Spirit is active, people are sealed into that relationship.

3. *Delivered:* Baptism delivers us into the hands of God for time and eternity. Christ is ours, and we are his — and at last, we are promised, the final enemy — death — will be overcome and we will see him face to face.

4. *Signed, sealed, and delivered — in Holy Baptism:* That's the Christian's condition in Christ that links the believer to God in heaven, and to the earth and the work he has for us in it.

Third Sunday of Easter

Roman Catholic	Acts 2:14, 22-28	1 Peter 1:17-21	Luke 24:13-35
Episcopal	Acts 2:14a, 36-47	1 Peter 1:17-23	Luke 24:13-35
	or Isaiah 43:1-12	or Acts 2:14a, 36-47	
Lutheran	Acts 2:14a, 36-47	1 Peter 1:17-21	Luke 24:13-35
Common	Acts 2:14a, 36-41	1 Peter 1:17-23	Luke 24:13-35

The church year theological clue

The Second Sunday *after* Easter used to be titled as *Misericordia Domini* ("the goodness of the Lord") and was known as Good Shepherd Sunday. Now it is listed as the Third Sunday *of* Easter, and Good Shepherd Sunday was moved to the Fourth Sunday of Easter, Years A, B, and C. Years A and B now feature the first appearances of Jesus, according to Luke 24; Year C employs John 21:1-14, which is the third appearance of Jesus after the resurrection. This is one way of extending the appearances of Jesus, which were called the apparitions of Jesus in earlier liturgies, beyond the so-called Low Sunday, when, traditionally, the last "appearance story" was read. (Low Sunday today, in Protestant churches, probably is connected to a drop in attendance. In liturgical practice, most major festivals, including and especially Easter, were celebrated for eight days. In the case of Easter, one of the gospel stories about Jesus' appearances was read every day of the first week after Easter Sunday, concluding with the John 20 gospel on the Second Sunday after Easter).

The present arrangement of Luke 24 for two years and John 21 on the third year of the Third Sunday of Easter keeps the resurrection theme before the people for one more week. Preaching on the triumph over the tomb, which God worked in Christ, will help the faithful *continue the Easter celebration* and, also, get their theology straight. *The risen Lord makes himself known to his own in the word* — the gospel/good news — *and the breaking of the bread.* Christ himself gives us hope in the face of sin and death.

The Prayer of the Day — There is theological reflection in the Prayer of the Day in at least one of the service books (LBW). The address to God reveals this: "O God, by the humiliation of your Son you lifted up this fallen world, rescuing us from the hopelessness of death." This prayer functions theologically by keeping the cross and the empty tomb together in the consciousness of the people, thereby preventing aberrant and shallow celebrations of Easter; it allows the cross to throw its shadow upon the empty tomb and keep the death and resurrection of Christ in proper theological perspective. The petition is kerygmatic and eschatological: "Grant your faithful people a share in the joys that are eternal." It would be appropriate on any Sunday and at almost any other time or liturgical occasion. Here it functions as an antiphon to the opening word of prayer, working in the manner of a litany, an extremely brief litany, in this case.

The Psalm of the Day (LBW) — Psalm 16 — The thought of the Prayer for the Day is given new impetus and direction in the opening sentence of this psalm: "Protect me, O God, for I take refuge in you . . . 'You are my Lord, my good above all other' " — in life and in death. The psalmist is concerned about other people and their theological and religious pursuits, acknowledging that those "who run after other gods" will find themselves in deep trouble; they will find themselves outside the aegis of God's grace. In the spirit of Easter, he continues, steadfast in the true faith:

My heart, therefore, is glad, and my spirit rejoices; my body also shall rest in hope.
For you will not abandon me to the grave, nor let your holy one see the pit. You

will show me the path of life; in your presence there is fullness of joy, and in your right hand are pleasures forevermore.

The tone of the psalm suggests that the psalmist knows that this is God's intention for all people, and that he would bring all people into a right relationship of faith with himself.

The Psalm Prayer

Lord Jesus, uphold those who hope in you, and give us your counsel, so that we may know the joy of your resurrection and share the pleasures of the saints at your right hand, where you live and reign with the Father and the Holy Spirit, one God, now and forever.

The readings:

Acts 2:14a, 36-47

The game of "musical lections," as played by the various denominations in their lectionaries, gets into high gear on this Third Sunday of Easter, but none of the lessons is totally eliminated; they are shifted around from Sunday to Sunday with additions or deletions. In the Roman lectionary, this reading was assigned to last Sunday's propers without verses 14a and 36-41. The Roman Lectionary, as well as the Common Lectionary, puts the Acts 2:14a, 22-32 lesson of last Sunday's non-Roman lectionaries on this Sunday, while the Fourth Sunday of Easter picks up verses 36-41 of Acts 2 and sets them alongside Acts 6:1-9 and 7:2a, 51-60. Thus, one of the "musical lections" is removed, but another is put in its place. Incidentally, the LBW originally had this same three-Sunday alignment of these texts.

This reading jumps from the beginning of Peter's sermon to the concluding appeal, in which he calls upon the hearers to repent and be baptized for the forgiveness of otheir sins, promising them the gift of the Holy Spirit. Three thousand persons responded, repented, and were baptized on the day we know as Pentecost. The latter part of the text, which does offer another sermon in itself, reveals what the community of believers was like in the beginning, in studying the teaching of the apostles and praising God for the miracles that were performed in Jesus' name, in daily prayer in the Temple, in sharing all things in common, and in eating together in their homes. The impact that these people made upon the world is suggested in the last verse: "And the Lord added to their number day by day those who were being saved."

1 Peter 1:17-21

All of the lectionaries agree with this choice, as well as with the Luke 24 Gospel for the Day, and use exactly the same verses. The baptismal setting, in which Peter writes to the faithful, reminds them of their participation in the new Passover (the use of "ransom" parallels the development of the Passover theology by the time of Christ and the Apostles). The writer of this book apparently knew Jewish theology, classic and contemporary, in the death of Christ, whose blood has delivered them from sin and death. Despite the assurance of salvation which they have, the faithful are to live in fear as they live in the world, just as if they were actually in exile in Babylon; they must die while the fullness of the glorious life with God is in the future. But Christians are able to live in confidence, because in the end they will experience fullness of the resurrection life as their own.

Luke 24:13-35

Luke alone heard — and wrote down for time and eternity — this beautiful story of Christ and the two disciples whom he joined on the road to Emmaus. How much of the

146

seven-or-so-mile walk he made with them is unknown, but they did not, for some reason, recognize him. Could it have been almost dark when he appeared to them, or were they so preoccupied with their own thoughts that they never really looked at him? No one will ever know! The conversation has been recorded for any and all to read, revealing how much Cleopas and the "other disciple" loved the Lord and the depth of their confusion and grief over the death of Jesus. Jesus, still unrecognized, asked them, "Was it not necessary that the Church should suffer these things and enter into his glory?" — and gave them the answer himself in a lesson on Christology. It wasn't until he accepted their invitation to dinner, and blessed and broke the bread, that they recognized him — and then he simply vanished out of their sight. They immediately walked back to Jerusalem — at a much faster pace, I am certain, than was used on their journey to Emmaus, and found the Eleven. In response to the state- ment of the people gathering with the Eleven, who said, "The Lord has risen indeed, and has appeared to Simon," Cleopas and the "other disciple" announced what had "happened on the road, and how he was known to them in the breaking of the bread." From Luke's perspective, Cleopas and his companion were the second and third people to be visited by Jesus. The whole of the story reveals how Christ makes himself known in the Word and also in the sacraments. For Christian worship to be all that it is meant to be, the liturgy needs both the reading and preaching of the Word and the regular celebration of the sacraments. The Roman Church seems to be gaining this unity more readily than the non-Roman Churches.

A sermon on the Gospel, Luke 24:13-35 — "The Stranger."

The late Edmund A. Steimle wrote and preached a sermon on this text, which he entitled "The Stranger," and included as the "title sermon" in a volume of radio sermons called, *God, the Stranger.* It is a biblical sermon cast in the narrative style that Steimle developed in his teaching and preaching career (see *Preaching the Story).* In it he interweaves his story and other human stories with the biblical account of this walk to Emmaus. The outline is simple and uncomplicated, accepting and following the story-line of the text. The sermon, as Steimle plotted it, looks like this:

1. In the introduction, Steimle calls this one of the most — and yet most puzzling — stories in the New Testament. Jesus had only been dead for three days, but they didn't recognize him.
2. "Their eyes were kept from recognizing him." He asks — and gives possible answers — "Why was this so?" He poses over a dozen questions in this half of the sermon, which also deals with why people today don't recognize the risen Christ.
3. But before the story ends, "their eyes were opened and they recognized him" (in the breaking of the bread). The second half of the sermon follows this quotation, affirming the different ways Jesus reveals himself so that people may recognize him. The homiletical high- light of the sermon is a story about a Jewish tailor, Mr. Birnbaum, who posed a difficult question for Steimle forty years ago and made him realize that Christ was revealing himself in the person of this friendly and humble Jewish tailor. Although Steimle shows how Christ reveals himself in word and sacrament, the Mr. Birnbaum story emphasizes how he makes himself known to us in other — and highly unlikely — people.
4. Steimle brings the sermon to a brief conclusion with, "and he vanished out of their sight," capping it with an appropriate quote from Fred Buechner in the last paragraph: " 'The stranger comes suddenly out of nowhere like the first clear light of the sun after a thunderstorm, or maybe like the thunder itself, and maybe we recognize him and maybe we don't.' But maybe we can reach the point where we can bless God not merely for his recognizable presence, but precisely because he is different, unpredictable, breaking away from our stultifying expectations, precisely because he does come as the stranger into our lives to give assurance and pardon and hope."

Another sermon on the Gospel — "Holy Heartburn."

The late James S. Stewart approached this text quite differently in a class on exegetical preaching which I was in many years ago. He insisted that the homiletical key to this sermon was verse 32, "They said to each other, 'Did not our hearts burn within us while he talked to us on the road, while he opened to us the scriptures?' " The preacher might use that verse as the text for a sermon on the power of the Word to reach and turn people's hearts to Christ. Such a sermon might take this shape:

1. A strange thing happened on the way to Emmaus; Jesus appeared and went unrecognized by two of his disciples, and gave them a case of heartburn.

2. He gave them heartburn by what he said to them as they walked to Emmaus; later on they said, "Did not our hearts burn within us while he talked to us on the road, while he opened to us the scriptures?"

3. He blessed and broke the bread and he became known to them; the heartburn opened their hearts and minds to his presence. He comes to us the same way in the Word and the Table Meal. Word and sacraments belong together and reveal the Christ to us.

4. We come to worship expecting him to reveal himself to us — and he does. Ours is to receive him — the risen Lord — with joy and thanksgiving — and praise God for this special gift whenever he comes to us. Pray God for a case of holy heartburn!

A sermon on the First Lesson, Acts 2:14a; 36-47 — "The Church as the Christian Community."

1. *The initiation:* Entrance into the Christian community comes through repentance and baptism.

2. *The privileges:* forgiveness of sins and the gift of the Holy Spirit to strengthen faith and bring people to spiritual maturity.

3. *The responsibilities:* to cling to God's promise in Christ and live faithfully and lovingly in the world as a special and unique community.

A sermon on the Second Lesson, 1 Peter 1:17-21 — "The 'Water Community.' "

One of the most fascinating sights in all the world comes to tourists who get to travel on the canals of Bankok, Thailand. The natives have built their homes on stilts right in the water. They literally live on the water — and from the water (dirty, as it is). They have floating markets, as well as other buildings, which make and sustain their life-style. Theirs is, literally, a "water community."

1. The church is a "water community," which lives with the Lord in its baptismal covenant. (This concept comes from acceptance of the viewpoint that 1 Peter is a baptismally oriented letter.)

2. The church is a "blood community," which knows it has been "ransomed" by Jesus' death on the cross, the New Passover.

3. The church is a "fearful community," whose members, unafraid of death, live out their lives in the "fear of the Lord" and in the hope of the resurrection at the end time.

4. The church, as a "water community," will exist and grow until that day.

Fourth Sunday of Easter

Roman Catholic	Acts 2:14a, 36-41	1 Peter 2:20b-25	John 10:1-10
Episcopal	Acts 6:1-9; 7:2a, 51-60	1 Peter 2:19-25	John 10:1-10
	or Nehemiah 9:6-15	or Acts 6:1-9; 7:2a, 51-60	
Lutheran	Acts 6:1-9; 7:2a, 51-60	1 Peter 2:19-25	John 10:1-10
Common	Acts 2:42-47	1 Peter 2:19-25	John 10:1-10

The church year theological clue

The Fourth Sunday *of* Easter, in years A and B, at least, has the biblical content that the Second Sunday after Easter used to have: namely, *Good Shepherd Sunday.* John 10 is read in all three years: Year A is assigned John 10:1-10; Year B has the original Good Shepherd Sunday Gospel, John 10:11-16; and Year C contains the last part of the chapter, John 10:22-30. The figure of the Good Shepherd was central to the symbolism of all of the ancient churches, picturing the risen Christ, ascended, sitting on a throne, Peter and Paul on either side, the other disciples often in the background and, nearly always, sheep drinking from a river emanating from the four gospels, while other sheep graze on the grass by the river. The Good Shepherd usually has a hand raised in benediction. Josef Jungmann, the noted Roman Catholic liturgical theologian and homiletical scholar, once wrote: "The ancient church knew full well why she had placed the Easter Christ and His Easter work in the apses of her basilicas, why she had proclaimed Easter so loudly, providing it with a forty-day preparatory celebration and a fifty-day aftermath, and had given the stamp of Easter to every Sunday. This played a great part in educating the Christian in the knowledge of his Christian dignity and in confirming his confidence." The Good Shepherd is the risen and ascended Lord, who will be with his church, caring for his people, until he comes again. This Sunday articulates the Good Shepherd/pastoral theology of the Gospel.

The Prayer of the Day — The LBW provides two collects for this Sunday, of which the first specifically applies to Good Shepherd Sunday: "God of all power, you called from death our Lord Jesus, the great shepherd of the sheep." After this introduction, the prayer asks God to "send us as shepherds to rescue the lost, to heal the injured, and to feed one another with knowledge and understanding." The latter part of the second prayer, "Give strength to all who are joined in the family of the Church, so that they will resolutely reject what erodes their faith and firmly follow what faith requires," is introduced by a word to God that suggests the role of the Shepherd ("you show the light of your truth to those in darkness, *to lead them into the way of righteousness"),* and could be attached to the opening address of the first prayer.

The Psalm for the Day — Psalm 23 — The Shepherd Psalm is really the only psalm that could be appointed for this Sunday. Jesus really is the Good Shepherd, really is the Lord of all, and really is the one who watches over his own in all situations, reviving the souls of the faithful, leading them in life and death so that they will, feasting at the table he has set, "dwell in the house of the Lord forever." The imagery of the psalm clearly suggests the sacraments of Baptism and Holy Communion. If the ancient churches would have had modern technology available to them, they might have had a recording of the 23rd Psalm beneath the mosaics of the Good Shepherd, playing continuously when there were no services in the churches, to call people to prayer and devotion — and preparation for the meal at the Table of the Lord — in the name of the Good Shepherd, Jesus Christ.

148

The Psalm Prayer

> *Lord Jesus Christ, shepherd of your Church, you give us new birth in the waters of baptism; you anoint us with oil, and call us to salvation at your table. Dispel the terrors of death and the darkness of error. Lead your people along safe paths, that they may rest securely in you and dwell in the house of the Lord now and forever, for your name's sake.*

The readings:

Acts 6:1-9; 7:2a, 51-60

This lection, which tells about the growth of the early church, the election of seven deacons "to serve tables," and the amazing ministry of Stephen, seems to complement the first prayer more than it does the Gospel for the Day. The portion of Acts 7 that is attached to Acts 6 tells of the part of Stephen's speech that got him into trouble with the authorities and caused him to be stoned. His miracles were apparently accepted by most of the people as acts of God, but his proclamation of the good news in the death and resurrection of Jesus Christ was too much for the religious leaders to swallow. He died, firm in the faith, with a word on his lips — "Lord, do not hold this sin against them" — that echoes Jesus' word from the cross, also reported by Luke alone, "Father forgive them, for they do not know what they are doing." Stephen's words suggest that his executioners really did know what they were doing, and he even reports that Saul fully approved of the execution.

1 Peter 2:19-25

The passage from 1 Peter picks up the theme of suffering that was introduced in the second part of the Acts reading with the stoning and death of Stephen. The Christian life, if lived fully and with positive witnessing for Jesus Christ, is almost certain to bring persecution and suffering; sometimes, the faithful will actually be put to death for their faith — *today!* Believers may very well expect to be, at the least, laughed at and ridiculed for their faith, but will have to learn, as did Stephen, to take all forms of persecution and suffering with patience. God surely doesn't desire people to suffer needlessly, particularly those who are living righteously in the faith bestowed upon them in Jesus Christ, but he is pleased when people suffer for the faith with patience, as did their Lord. Peter points to Christ's *innocent suffering and death* as the supreme example for the Christian community. Not only did he die innocently on the cross, but he "bore our sins in his body on the tree, that we might die to sin and live to righteousness." The last verse of the lection provides movement from the Acts reading to the Gospel for the Day, declaring that his wounds brought healing to the human beings of the world who were straying like sheep, but now have been returned to the one to whom they belong, the shepherd and guardian of their souls.

John 10:1-10

In these first ten verses of the beautiful Good Shepherd chapter of St. John, the person and work of the Good Shepherd, Jesus Christ, are described. In the first little parable, Jesus shows his authority and legitimacy as the Messiah to the religious leaders of Israel; it had to be heard as a challenge by them, one they couldn't ignore. In the second little parable, Christ asserts that those who have faith will hear and follow him; he will indeed be their shepherd, for they are his sheep. They "know his voice," and they cannot be led astray by false shepherds who would rob them of their faith. As the shepherd, Jesus is also the gate to the sheepfold, the door by which they must enter the kingdom of God, because there is no other way to gain entrance. Jesus' purpose in coming as the Good Shepherd, who is also the Suffering Servant in his passion and death, is to give life — abundant and eternal — to those who will have him as their shepherd and their Lord.

A sermon on the Gospel, John 10:1-10 — "A Question for the Sheep."

No one ever forgets the nursery rhymes that are learned as little children, including the one with the question in it: "Baa, baa, black sheep, have you any wool?" There is a question, which is put before all sheep, not just "black sheep," that takes precedence over this question. It is: "Sheep, do you have a shepherd?"

In the spring of the year a couple of decades ago, my family and I took a weekend drive through the highlands of Scotland. We hadn't gone very far before we saw a young lamb dead alongside the road. Soon there was another — and another — and another. Occasionally, we would see a full-grown sheep dead by the roadside. In a day and a half of driving, we counted twenty-two dead lambs and sheep, which had obviously wandered onto the narrow roads of the highlands and been hit and killed by automobiles. The reasons were obvious: there were no fences to keep them off the highway; there were no sheep dogs to be seen anywhere; not a single shepherd was in evidence during that trip. Without fences, sheep dogs, and, especially, shepherds, the sheep didn't have a chance and, when they wandered onto the highland highways, they simply perished. A shepherd would have given them the opportunity to live out their lives as God meant them to.

1. "I am the shepherd" — he said it, the one who was and is the Good Shepherd, Jesus Christ, the Lord, of whom the psalmist sang.

2. Jesus really is the Good Shepherd, who proved his right to the title, Good Shepherd, when he laid down his life for all of the sheep, to save them from sin and death and give them life abundant and eternal.

3. The Good Shepherd, the Risen Lord, "has begun his reign;" he is the gatekeeper, the "door," of the kingdom. By him alone are the sheep able to enter God's fold.

4. The shepherd gives courage and confidence to faithful followers, who know and love him as their guide and protector, as long as they live.

A sermon on the First Lesson, Acts 6:1-9 — "A Church That Is Pleasing to God."

1. The early church took care of its own; the leaders took action to care for all of the widows and children. It provides a model for the modern church. The church must be caring and compassionate, concerned about all people.

2. The church knew it was more than a social or welfare agency; the leaders and the people were regular and constant in prayer and worship; they took time for daily prayer. Their example reveals a serious defect in contemporary Christians, who are too busy to develop a devotional life.

3. The church members took their evangelism responsibilities seriously; the first evangelism program (selecting Stephen and six others "to serve tables") was developed so that the Word might be given its due by releasing the disciples for missionary work in the world. The church desperately needs to do something like this today.

4. The church pleases God when its members have the caring heart of Jesus, the prayerful spirit of the psalmist, and the evangelical zeal of Paul (this could be a sermon plan by itself).

A second sermon on the First Lesson, Acts 6:1-9; 7:2a, 51-60 — "Stones Break Bones — and Kill."

My son, daughter-in-law, and two granddaughters live in Williamsburg, Virginia, where they are members of St. Stephen Lutheran Church, which was built after a design by Thomas

Jefferson right across from the campus of William and Mary College. It is an interesting building, not in the round, but hexagonal in the floor plan, and octagonal in the clerestory windows, with a centrally located table and pulpit. The clerestory tells the story of Stephen. The church might have been named St. Stephen the Deacon, or better yet, St. Stephen the Martyr, both of which are implied by simply naming the congregation St. Stephen. Whenever I go there — or to any other church bearing the name of St. Stephen — I look for a pile of stones, sometimes thinking that the lawn ought to be littered with rocks to remind all people who enter or pass by that Stephen was the first person to die for the faith after Jesus' death and resurrection, and to impress upon them the cost of discipleship. Some of the stones and rocks ought to have "blood" — bright red paint — on them.

1. Salvation is God's free gift in Jesus, but discipleship is costly; it demands total surrender of one's time, possessions, and life.

2. Contemporary Christians, it is claimed, prefer "cheap grace;" the human thing is to claim the faith at bargain basement prices, so that being a Christian costs as little as possible. Dietrich Bonhoeffer's "cheap grace" theology was developed because he, like Stephen and the other martyrs, had learned the true cost of discipleship. Like Stephen, he paid the high cost with his life. Oddly enough, most of the stories and sermons I have heard about Bonhoeffer say lots about his theology and his ethics, but little about his martyrdom. Curious, isn't it?

3. The question for contemporary believers is simply this: Are you willing to pay the cost of discipleship, which in one way or another means giving up your life to and for Jesus?

A sermon on the Second Lesson, 1 Peter 2:19-25 — "Patience — A Precious Gift of the Spirit."

The Rite of Confirmation has been changed, to the total confusion of many long-time members of the congregations of Lutheranism, into a rite for the Affirmation of Baptism. The theology is sound, the liturgical rite is appropriate because it is built on solid tradition (and it may still be called confirmation). An ancient prayer for the gifts of the Holy Spirit is used as the Prayer of Bblessing in the rite: "Pour your Holy Spirit upon _____ _____: the spirit of wisdom and understanding, the spirit of counsel and might, the spirit of knowledge and the fear of the Lord (plus) the spirit of joy in your presence." But a serious omission is made when this prayer is substituted for the older Prayer of Blessing:

> *The Father in Heaven, for Jesus' sake, renew and increase in thee the gift of the Holy Ghost, to thy strengthening in faith, to thy growth in grace,* to thy patience in suffering, *and to the blessed hope of everlasting life.*

By the omission of "to thy patience in suffering," an important dimension of discipleship is deleted from the rite.

Fifth Sunday of Easter

Roman Catholic	**Acts 6:1-7**	**1 Peter 2:4-9**	**John 14:1-12**
Episcopal	**Acts 17:1-15**	**1 Peter 2:1-10**	**John 14:1-14**
	or Deuteronomy 6:20-25	**or Acts 17:1-15**	
Lutheran	**Acts 17:1-15**	**1 Peter 2:4-10**	**John 14:1-12**
Common	**Acts 7:55-60**	**1 Peter 2:1-10**	**John 14:1-14**

The church year theological clue

Cantate, the Fourth Sunday *after* Easter, with its theme of "sing a new song for the Lord," which came to be known and celebrated as "Church Music Sunday" in many parts of the church, finds expression on the Fifth Sunday *of* Easter. In the older liturgies, because Cantate had become a "cause" Sunday, the Easter celebration was interrupted or was lost entirely. The Cantate theme is not mentioned specifically on this Sunday, but it is set forth in the appointed Psalm for the Day — Psalm 33:1-11 — "sing for him (the Lord) a new song" and renews the response of the believers to the resurrection of Jesus Christ and continues the celebration of the great fifty days of the Pasch. The specific themes for the Fifth Sunday of Easter continue to be articulated in the readings for the day. Acts and 1 Peter speak to the mission of the church to tell the world about Jesus Christ, while the Gospel for the Day, John 14, points to the Ascension and has an eschatological cast to it, which is taken very personally by the faithful; John 14 is read — and frequently used as the text for sermons — at funeral or memorial services — because it contains precious promises made by Christ to believers.

The Prayer of the Day (LBW) — Another of the ancient prayers has been reworked to make it more acceptable in contemporary worship in the church. It is the beautiful collect for the Fourth Sunday after Easter (now the Fifth Sunday of Easter in the revision of the church year), which does not suffer too much, despite attempts to improve and modernize it. The opening sentence, it must be noted, has been altered from a statement which is meant to praise God ("O God, who makest the minds of the faithful to be of one will"), has been turned into a prayer ("O God, form the minds of your faithful people into one will").

The last sentence of the prayer has an important, if subtle, theological alteration fixed where true *joy* (in the risen Lord) may be found," rather than "(that) our hearts may there be fixed where true *joys* are found." This rewording (joy rather than joys) seems more appropriate for the Easter season, inasmuch as the resurrected Christ is the reason for the joy celebrated by the church during this time. The Fifth Sunday of Easter actually restores, especially in the psalm, the anastasial theology of Eastertide — Cantate — that had almost disappeared from the Fourth Sunday after Easter.

The Psalm for the Day (LBW) — Psalm 33:1-11 — "The Cantate Verse," verse 3, "Sing for him a new song, sound a fanfare with all your skill upon the trumpet," recalls what might have happened in the worship on Easter Sunday, when trumpets boldly and joyously announced the resurrection of the Lord to the gathered people of God. The psalmist reminds the faithful that it is only right and proper that those who have been made righteous by God should praise him for his gracious actions with their voices, with the harp, as well as with the trumpet. Harp and trumpet may be for the few, but most of the people of God can sing, or make a good attempt at praising the Lord through some sort of singing. It is not a Sunday for entertainment by a choir, organist, or orchestra, with the presentation of special music commemorating Cantate. Rather, this is a time, the psalmist declares, *for all of the people to join in singing* the new song — "Christ is risen! He is risen, indeed!" While the psalmist lists the works of creation, those who celebrate the Easter Christ will have the new creation in mind, knowing that God's work will last forever.

The Psalm Prayer
> *Lord God, through your Son you made the heavens and earth; through him you continue to accomplish the intentions of your heart. Make your chosen people witnesses of your truth among the nations and heralds of your glory in the heavens; for the sake of your Son, Jesus Christ our Lord.*

The readings:

Acts 6:1-7 (see the Fourth Sunday of Easter)

Acts 17:1-15

Saul, who in last Sunday's first reading, stood by approvingly as the Jewish mob stoned Stephen to death, has been converted to Christianity and is engaged in missionary work in Thessalonica, and Silas was with him. Newly named Paul, he preached powerfully for three weeks and won many converts with his arguments that Jesus was the Messiah, who died and rose again on the third day. He also aroused considerable hostility, so much so that a gang of men was enlisted to carry out a kind of citizen's arrest; instead, they took Jason, the man who was playing host to Paul and Silas, and some of the "brothers" to the authorities, who compelled them to post a security bond to guarantee that they would not harbor the two "Christian criminals" in their homes. Paul and Silas were whisked out of town after dark and sent to Berea, where they had a friendlier reception from the Jews. From there, leaving Silas and Timothy behind him, Paul went to Athens, and once there he sent back instructions asking Silas and Timothy to join him there. There was important work to be done in Athens, and he needed their support.

1 Peter 2:4-10

If the entire letter of 1 Peter is oriented to baptism, there is a likelihood that this passage was part of a set of theological instructions given to newly baptized members of the church. Central to all of it, and emanating from the "living stone" concept contained in it, is the basis for the doctrine of the priesthood of all believers that was so forcefully promulgated by Luther and the other Reformers. The people of God are to offer spiritual sacrifices to him in the name of Jesus Christ, to live as his holy people in the world, and to declare all that he has done for them and made of them, in Jesus Christ. The priesthood means that people have direct access to God in prayer, but not that anyone should be turned loose in the pulpit or at the table of the Lord without theological and practical training; that kind of liturgical license would threaten to undermine the gospel and the sacraments. What it does mean is that the church should worship regularly and thank God for his mercy, and "proclaim the Lord's death until he comes again," as Paul instructed the Corinthian Christians. The priesthood of all believers is exercised, too, in the ethical lives of the people, which give weight to the words of witness they offer on behalf of Christ.

John 14:1-12

Jesus was close to death when he spoke these words to the disciples to reassure them that death wouldn't end their relationship. They have been words of blessed assurance for people who are dying and facing death. Even if they weren't included in almost every funeral liturgy, they would be read anyway because of the comfort they give to believers ever since Jesus spoke and John wrote down these words. The disciples needed to hear them, for Jesus was approaching the time of his "departure;" they had to know what was going to happen. So Jesus told them that he would return to God, from whom he came, that heaven has many rooms in it, and that he was going to prepare a place in heaven for them. He also said that

154

he would come back to gather them to himself, so that they could be with him again. Thomas' question, "We do not know where you are going; how can we know the way?" elicits Jesus' singular statement about the access to God that he alone provides: "I am the way, and the truth, and the life; no one comes to the Father, but by me." And Philip's "Show us the Father, and we shall be satisfied" brings Jesus' rejoinder, "Have I been with you so long, and yet you do not know me, Philip? He who has seen me has seen the Father." and he tells them all why they have seen the Father in him; he, Jesus, has done the will of God, willingly and completely. His words prove that he is in a full and lasting relationship with the Father. His disciple are to follow his example and live out their lives in the true faith by doing works that praise and bless God in Jesus' holy name.

A sermon on the Gospel, John 14:1-12 — "A Look Beyond Death."

Jesus preached his own funeral sermon just before he died. As with all funeral meditations, it was preached for the benefit of the mourners, in this case his disciples. He knew that they were like the man who said to his nurse, a member of the same congregation to which he belonged, "Tell me about dying and death." She did, and did it so effectively that when his time came he died in complete peace and total trust. This passage is read every day in the year — at funerals — but it is proclaimed in all churches one day in the year to give blessed assurance to those who have lost loved ones to death and have yet to face death themselves.

For another approach to the use of a "John text" for a Sunday sermon or a funeral homily, see my sermon, "Grave for Sale," pages 116-120, in *The Song and the Story*. The first paragraph reads:

Some time ago, a strange classified ad appeared in a newspaper in one of our cities. It began: "Tombstone for sale," and continued, "Didn't die; don't need it." A reporter investigated and interviewed Art Kranz, the man who had placed the advertisement in the paper. Kranz told him that the tombstone had been sitting in his living room for several months, but it was not his; it belonged to his sister, who had been gravely ill with terminal cancer. An orderly person, she made arrangements for her funeral, including the purchase of a tombstone, a cemetery plot, and chose a funeral director. But she didn't die (on schedule). She recovered, asked her brother, who had a pickup truck, to move the tombstone and sell it. First, he stored it in his living room, then moved it to the front porch and ran the ad, "Tombstone for sale," in the hope of finding a buyer for it.

Jesus knew there would be an empty tomb after he died, but there would be no offer of "grave for sale;" instead, he directed the attention of his disciples — and all believers — to his gift to his own — the reality of everlasting life in God's kingdom. There is a place for all believers in the everlasting kingdom of God.

1. *Death is always a departure from this world.* It was no different with Jesus when he was nailed to the cross; he had to — and did — leave the world and his loved ones behind when he died. Jesus left the world twice; once on the cross and a second time in his ascension.
2. *Death means departure for a destination.* Jesus was convinced of that, knew that he would return to the Father's house, or he would not have given over to death on the cross.
3. *Death means reunion with the Father,* who made and rules over heaven and earth. God holds the destiny of the whole world in his hand; he intends to renew the relationship he had with people in the beginning — and have it last forever.
4. *Death leads to new life with God,* according to Jesus; the faithful have nothing to fear beyond death itself, because Jesus has given us a glimpse of eternity in his words, in

his own death, resurrection, and ascension. "He is risen! He is risen, indeed!" Here's where Cantate takes over as we sing a new song to the Lord. We can sing because Jesus has given us hope — and a new song to sing.

A sermon on the First Lesson, Acts 17:1-15 — "What God Expects of Believers."

1. When God wins people to faith in the risen Christ, he expects them to follow the example of Paul (and Silas, too) and witness to the Gospel, as the outward expression of an interiorized gift.

2. Baptism involves all of the believers in the work of the kingdom, which is taking the Gospel to the entire world — to all nations, to all people, without any exceptions. The world is the agenda for the proclamation of the good news.

3. God's servants and witnesses must expect resistance and outright opposition from some, or many, of the hearers, because the Gospel puts people in the position where they must declare, or deny, that Jesus is Lord. People hate to give up their personal gods, even for Jesus.

4. Christ has given his assurance to his witnesses that he will be with them, regardless of what they may encounter, to the end of time.

A sermon on the Second Lesson, Acts 2:4-10 — "The Priestly People of God."

1. Christians who are "marked with the cross of Christ forever" in baptism wear the mantle of priesthood, the priesthood of all believers. Every Christian is a priest, according to the text and is to offer sacrifices to God.

2. Christians are called by Christ to live the life of priests of God. All of God's people are expected to perform daily sacrifices in private prayer and devotions and by regular participation in public worship and celebration. That's a fundamental part of the priesthood of all believers.

3. Christians are directed to declare the mighty works of God in the sacrifice of Jesus Christ, the good news of Jesus' death and resurrection, by word of mouth, as well as by living obedient and holy lives in the Holy Spirit. That's another dimension of the priesthood.

4. Christians, as the priestly people of God, offer themselves as sacrifices to the Lord by dying daily to sin in repentance and rising in faith to celebrate new life in Jesus, their Lord. That's the ultimate privilege of the priesthood of all believers.

Sixth Sunday of Easter

Roman Catholic	Acts 8:5-8, 14-17	1 Peter 3:15-18	John 14:15-21
Episcopal	Acts 17:22-31	1 Peter 3:8-18	John 15:1-8
	or Isaiah 41:17-20	or Acts 17:22-31	
Lutheran	Acts 17:22-31	1 Peter 3:15-22	John 14:15-21
Common	Acts 17:22-31	1 Peter 3:13-22	John 14:15-21

The church year theological clue

This Sunday, as the Fifth Sunday *after* Easter, was known as Rogate Sunday, or Rogation Sunday, which signalled the approach to the three special days of supplication and prayer that preceded the Ascension of our Lord. In most non-Roman Churches, this Sunday became a day for prayers that had, in the minds of most people, only a limited connection with Easter; Rogation Day was a time given over to particular and pointed prayers for the fields that had been planted in the hope of an abundant harvest. Now, as the Sixth Sunday *of* Easter, the rogation emphasis has disappeared entirely from the propers; Rogation Sunday, as it was observed, no longer exists in the liturgy of the church. But rogation practices, which, of course, are good in themselves, are well established in some rural areas, and some congregations continue to bless the fields on this Sunday. This is, indeed a worthy liturgical practice, but it isn't the main purpose of this Sunday.

The Sixth Sunday of Easter points to the proximity of the Ascension on Thursday of this week. It should be a reminder to the faithful that the resurrection of the Lord is only completed when he leaves the earth and "ascends" to the right hand of God and begins his reign. It is also a sign that the Great Fifty Days of Easter are drawing to a close, and that the church must still be celebrating Jesus' death and resurrection with "Christ is risen! He is risen indeed!"

The Prayer of the Day (LBW) — Once more, an older collect has been modernized and transformed into a contemporary liturgical prayer. The LBW prayer accommodates the "rural rogation" theme, because it addresses God as the source of all good things: "O God, from whom all good things come." The petition changes course from material "good things," asking God to "lead us by the inspiration of your Spirit to think those things that are right (and good, of course), and by your goodness help us to do them." The prayer brings together good thoughts, which are inspired by the Holy Spirit but might only lead to good intentions, and ties them together with positive action on the part of the faithful. The burden of the prayer, therefore, is that those who celebrate the death and resurrection of Jesus Christ will, after his ascension, think and live the new life that he offers to all of his own.

The Psalm of the Day (LBW) — Psalm 66:1-6, 14-18 — The theme of this psalm is most appropriate for Eastertide and the Sixth Sunday of Easter. It issues a call to praise and prayer on the part of those who know that they have been richly blessed by God, and have, therefore, caught the true spirit of Rogation (which was not at all, of course, in the mind of the psalmist when he wrote it). God's name is glorious, and he is to be praised for awesome deeds he has done, not only in the Exodus, but specifically, as the Psalm Prayer suggests, in our baptism into the faith of Jesus Christ, his Son. After a rather general beginning, the psalmist becomes very personal and takes on the character of evangelical witness in the form of personal testimony: "Come and listen, all you who fear God, and I will tell you what he has done for me." He is one who has repented of his sin, been cleansed and blessed by God, "who has not rejected my power, nor withheld his love from me." In Jesus' cross, of course, he offers his love to all who will receive Christ as Lord and Savior.

156

The Psalm Prayer

Almighty Father, you brought us through the waters of baptism to the shores of new life. Accept the sacrifice of our lives, and let us enter your house, there to praise your unfailing power and love, through your Son, Jesus Christ our Lord.

The readings:

Acts 17:22-31

In this passage, Luke reports on the central happening in Paul's visit to Athens — an invitation by some of the philosophers to speak to the entire Council of the Areopagus. He not only accepted the invitation, but he demonstrated his skill as a preacher, first, in the introduction to his speech/sermon, which he began, inductively, by talking about his observation that they were very religious people and, second, by telling them that he wanted to inform them about the "unknown God" to whom they had dedicated an altar. Paul continues on common ground, mentioning that the God who has created all things does not dwell in buildings made by human hands, nor is he dependent upon human beings for anything. He tells the Athenians that he is a God of grace, who freely gives "life and breath" to everyone. Paul also tells them that this God is in charge of human history, determining the rise and fall of nations so that they might seek and find him. He completely pulled out the rug from the Greek religious system when he said, "In him we live, and move, and have our being," quoting, in support of his statement, Greek thinkers who had said, "We are all his children." After verbally pulling down their altars, he told them that God wanted people to repent of their sins, that the whole world will be judged at a fixed time, and that God has selected one to be judge. He has even raised that man from the grave. Some laughed, but others said, "We would hear more about this," and some actually believed and became disciples of Jesus Christ.

1 Peter 3:15-22

In this text, the writer of Peter continues to give instructions to the newly baptized converts, telling them that being a Christian will not be easy; they will probably undergo real persecution, not simply ridicule and laughter of the sort Paul experienced in Athens. Christians should not be defensive, when asked about the reasons for their conversion; they should have ready and honest answers, given in a kindly and considerate manner to those who might be attacking them (and even be seeking evidence on which to charge them with heresy or treason). Peter reminds them of Jesus' innocent suffering, and that if they should have to suffer, to accept it in the spirit of Jesus Christ. The remnant of a baptismal hymn, which here has been converted into a letter, mentions how Jesus, who was put to death in the body and raised to life by the Spirit, preached to lost souls before his resurrection. And Peter likens baptism to the water experience of Noah and his family, who were "saved by water." The newly baptized are to remember that Baptism is not physical washing, but the pledge of a good and cleansed conscience through the risen and living Lord, Jesus Christ.

John 14:15-21

This reading begins with a statement about obedience to the commands of the Lord Jesus Christ and, after a rather circuitous route, ends with a very familiar quotation to which is added a word of assurance: those who love Christ and obey his teachings will, in turn, be loved by the Father and Jesus Christ himself. Christ will send the Comforter, the Holy Spirit, to give hope and strength, who will mediate the Lord's presence to believers; non-believers, of course, cannot receive one in whom they refuse to believe. So it is that when Jesus left the earth, he gave his own the assurance that he would come to them in this way, because he is alive again and forever. "Because I live," he declares, "you will live also." Through the coming and indwelling of the Spirit, the faithful are joined to Christ and to the Father, who loves them just as much as Jesus, who suffered and died for them and all people. Christians who claim to believe that Jesus is the living Lord are expected to live obediently, seeking through the power of the Holy Spirit to live life on the level that he lived it. The Son and the Father surely love those who make an honest and sincere attempt at trying to be obedient and useful people of God.

A sermon on the Gospel, John 14:15-22 — "Loving Obedience."

In one of his sermons, the late Edmund A. Steimle talked about obedience to the commands of Christ in terms of Jesus' seemingly impossible edict, "Be perfect, as your Father in heaven is perfect." He insisted that to think that Jesus didn't really mean this is "nonsense." He said, *"Jesus expects us to be perfect,"* to be obedient to all of his teachings. One of the difficulties with *sola fides/sola gratia* theology is that some persons interpret this to mean that all that "saved" Christians need to do is sit back and bask in the blessed assurance that is theirs. Christians are expected to be active in the faith and to obey Jesus' teachings — not *to learn* the grace of God, but *as a response* to being freed from the law. Salvation is a free gift of God, which is not earned by obedience or striving to live perfectly. Rather, obedience is the natural activity of those who are saved by God's grace. Believers cannot obtain perfection by obedience, because their perfection is in the Lord, but they should live out their lives as his disciples in the world, in full knowledge that they are loved by the Father and the Son.

1. The cross: sign of Christ's obedience, as well as his love for people. It is — and will be forever — a symbol of that unspeakable love of Father and Son, which moved Jesus to obey the Father perfectly, thus to suffer and die on Golgotha — for us.

2. Obedience is the sign of our love for Christ. We do our best to live according to his commandments, not to win God's love, but to reflect our gratitude for the loving grace of Father and Son, who died to save us from our sins. Disobedience is the sign of self-love, of something that is less than perfect love.

3. The comforter is the mediator of the presence of Christ. The Holy Spirit brings the presence of Christ to us, assuring us that he is alive and, as the ascended Lord, still loves us. The Holy Spirit moves us to love the Lord and helps us to obey his commandments.

4. *The Father loves those who love Christ.* He makes room for them and assures them of a place in his eternal kingdom. So Charles Wesley sings and prays for us:

> *Finish then thy new creation,*
> *Pure and spotless let us be;*
> *Let us see thy great salvation*
> *Perfectly restored in thee!*
> *Changed from glory into glory,*
> *Till in heav'n we take our place,*
> *Till we cast our crowns before thee,*
> *Lost in wonder, love, and praise. Amen*

A sermon on the First Lesson, Acts 17:15-22 — "High on a Lonely Hill."

1. That's where it happened. It was on that hill in Athens where the high court met that Paul dared to preach his famous sermon which evoked laughter, curiosity, and faith. Alone on that hill, he took on the whole of Greek civilization; the religious, cultural, and intellectual dimensions of it were all represented there before him.

2. That's what happened. As did the Greeks, some people will always discount the central tenets of the Christian faith, the death and resurrection of Christ — and ridicule it. Others will wonder, and intellectually seek the Lord all their lives (as the hymn has it: "It was not I who found, O Savior true; No, I was found of thee"). And there are others who, through the power of the Holy Spirit, will believe that Jesus really is the Messiah, the Lord.

3. This is what always happens. The proclamation of the gospel always separates the sheep from the goats, the unbelievers from the believers. The self-sufficient and the hard-hearted who are offended by the gospel, find themselves in a different religious, spiritual, and theological "camp" than those, who hear the same Word, but receive it and cling to it with all the strength they possess.

4. This is what will happen. Some will never be admitted to the kingdom and will be lost forever. Others may be overcome by the Spirit in time and receive the gift of faith in Christ and be saved. Still others, who know the Lord and entrust their lives to him, will live out their lives in hope and peace. They know that God has saved them in Jesus Christ. Indeed, he has done just that.

A sermon on the Second Lesson, 1 Peter 3:15-22 — "The Light upon the Water."

This sermon is about lighting up the water of baptism, which is what the author is doing in this passage. Years ago, there originated a water and light show in Wisconsin Dells, Wisconsin, that was called "Dancing Waters." The water rose and fell and colored light was employed to add more beauty to the extravaganza. Today, a company that manufacturer lawn sprinklers has developed and marketed an undulating sprinkler that they call "Dancing Waters." There is no light show connected to its use (but imaginative homeowners could easily rig up their own nighttime extravaganza). In this text, a kind of water show takes place but it is done through the words put down in writing by Peter. He is lighting up the waters of baptism, so that the newly baptized — and all Christians — will understand what has happened to them and what the new life in Christ brings to them.

1. The baptized believers in Christ know that Jesus is Lord and hold on to him with all their hearts, minds, and souls. Faith in him is their most precious possession, coming as it does as a gift from God.

2. Christians had better know that believing in Christ as Lord does not exempt them from pain and suffering, even from persecution and martyrdom. Not every Christian will be persecuted "for righteousness' sake," and surely not every Christian will become a martyr, but every Christian should be a *confessor* — ready and willing to defend and hold on to the faith and witness to it as opportunity arises.

3. Christians can live positively, dealing patiently with persecutors and unbelievers, while attempting to win them over with the gospel, because they know the presence of the living Lord and the certainty of eternal life.

4. When the waters of baptism are lighted up, Christians know that in baptism they are better off than Noah. They are Christ's forever.

The Ascension of Our Lord

Roman Catholic	Acts 1:1-11	Ephesians 1:17-23	Matthew 28:16-20
Episcopal	Acts 1:1-11	Ephesians 1:15-23	Luke 24:49-53
	or Daniel 7:9-14	or Acts 1:1-11	or Mark 16:9-15, 19-20
Lutheran	Acts 1:1-11	Ephesians 1:16-23	Luke 24:44-53
Common	Acts 1:1-11	Ephesians 1:16-23	Luke 24:44-53

The church year theological clue

In the church year as it was formerly constituted, there were really three sub-divisions in Eastertide: first, there was the week of the "six apparitions" of Jesus, the week from Easter Sunday to its octave; second, the time of preparation for Jesus' departure in the Ascension, from the second Sunday to Rogate, the Fifth Sunday after Easter (the last three weeks of this period were marked by readings from John 16 in preparation for the Ascension of Our Lord); and, third, the time between the Ascension and Pentecost, which is the time of waiting for the coming of the Spirit (in Acts) and the conclusion of the Great Fifty Days, as well as the beginning of the Pentecost cycle.

With the ascension, the resurrection of Jesus Christ is completed; he returns to the Father who sent him into the world and begins his reign, which will continue until he returns to bring in the fullness of the kingdom of God. The Ascension of Our Lord needs to be celebrated in every parish because it is the way that the church finishes its annual celebration of the resurrection of the Lord. At the reading of the gospel for the Day, the Paschal Candle is extinguished and then, or later, moved to a place by the baptismal font, where it is lighted for each and every baptism. Ascension Day is the conclusion of Eastertide and its declaration,"Christ is risen! He is risen, indeed!"

The Prayer for the Day (LBW)

The Prayer for the Day (LBW) — The ascended Christ is mentioned in this prayer to "Almighty God," as one who "in power intercedes for us (with God in heaven)," and the petition asks that we, the church, might also "come into your presence and live forever in your glory." The old collect has content that suggests a different liturgical and theological direction, addressing the prayer to Christ, not to God the Father, as he "who didst this day ascend in triumph far above all the heavens," and asking the Lord not "to leave us comfortless," but to send the Holy Spirit, the Spirit of Truth, to us." The ascension is the final act in the triumph of Christ over death and the grave and is, therefore, a festival of great joy and celebration.

The Psalm of the Day (LBW)

The Psalm of the Day (LBW) — Psalm 110 — This has been called a messianic psalm, which describes one who is both king and priest, who will rule over Israel and his enemies, too. This one, born to be King of Israel and redeemer, stands in the lineage of David, and will reign forever (virtually nothing is said in the psalm about his religious functions as priest). The first verse, rather obviously, suggests why this psalm is appointed (in the LBW) for the Ascension: "The Lord said to my Lord, 'Sit at my right hand, until I make your enemies your footstool.' " The bulk of the psalm is interpreted to describe how God will deal with the enemies of the Messiah during the interim between his ascension and his Second Coming (from the Christian point of view).

The Psalm Prayer

Almighty God, make known in every place the perfect offering of your Son, the eternal high priest of the new Jerusalem, and so consecrate all nations to be your holy people, that the kingdom of Christ, your anointed one, may come in its fullness; and to you, Father, Son, and Holy Spirit, be all honor and praise now and forever.

The readings:

Acts 1:1-11

This continuation of the Gospel according to St. Luke is the reading that has established the festival of the ascension forty days after Easer. It offers a picture of the departure of Christ from the earth which is satisfying, but also quite disturbing. The satisfaction comes with the knowledge that Christ has completed his work in triumph and now returns to the Father; the disturbing part is the ascension itself; it is too unscientific for many persons today. Had he just disappeared, at least it would put the story into the realm of science fiction; his ascension would be seen as entrance into a new dimension of existence, which human beings do not know about or understand. Actually, that is what "returning to the Father" has to mean; Jesus, after his resurrection, lived in another dimension — his was a glorified body — but he had the power to reveal himself to people for these forty days. At the ascension, he really left this world, as Luke tells us, but with a postlude in which two angels appeared to the disciples and told them that Jesus would come back to the world in the same way that he left. The ascension affirms the start of Jesus' reign over heaven and earth, but it also points to the Parousia and his return, when he will judge the earth and rule completely over it.

Ephesians 1:16-23

This reading is a single — and rather complicated — sentence, in which Paul informs the Christians at Ephesus of his prayer of thanksgiving for them, in which he asks God to give them the "spirit of wisdom and revelation" they need to comprehend and cling to the Gospel. He devotes the last half of the sentence to a recounting of what God accomplished in Christ's death and resurrection, as well as his ascension (God "made him sit at his right hand in the heavenly places"), informing them that God has put him over everything in heaven and on earth — forever.

Luke 24:44-53

In this concluding portion of his Gospel, Luke shows Jesus teaching one last lesson, which is in the form of a review that "opened their minds to understand the scriptures" and what was said about him, including his death and resurrection. Their task, after he leaves them, is to preach repentance and forgiveness of sins "in his name" and "to all nations, beginning with Jerusalem." He also ordered them to wait for the coming of the Spirit before they began their mission. After the brief lesson, Luke tells us that he took them out to Bethany, blessed them, and then was taken up into heaven. The disciples then returned to Jerusalem "with great joy" and "were continually in the Temple blessing God."

A sermon on the First Lesson, Acts 1:1-11, and the Gospel, Luke 24:44-53 — "A Final Farewell." (See, also, "The Final Farewell" in *The Tree, the Tomb, and the Trumpet*, C.S.S., 1984)

The church has always been intrigued by the Ascension of Our Lord; in the past, it has almost been ingenious in the way that the feast has been celebrated. In some medieval churches, a figure of the risen Christ would be lifted from the floor level of the nave and taken through a hole in the roof when Luke's words — "While he blessed them, he parted from them, and was carried into heaven" — were read. In more than a few modern congregations of various denominations, the Paschal Candle is extinguished at that point and moved from a special place in the chancel area to a spot by the baptismal font. With modern electrical

162

technology and a little imagination, the possibilities of recreating the Ascension of Our Lord are viritually limitless. But problems remain with the ascension, which need to be cleared up, will not be answered until Christ returns, never to say "farewell" again. The ascension was Jesus' last farewell.

First, where did Jesus go? John Gordon's sermon (in *Resurrection Messages,* Baker, 1964) of a quarter century ago, "The Whereabouts of our Risen Lord," asks what most people consider the central question about the ascension: Where is heaven? Where did he go? That's the kind of question that non-believers, or people who are having difficulty in believing, are likely to ask. But that's not *the* question, according to the Gospel; it cannot be answered beyond the biblical evidence that "he was carried up into heaven" and "sits at the right hand of God."

Second, why did Jesus have to depart from the earth? That might very well be the question of faithful people who believe in the resurrection but still would like to see Jesus for themselves. For one thing, he would become some sort of ghost, or a good witch, who appears to some from time to time and not to others. And for another thing, faith that comes from hearing the Word with the help of the Holy Spirit would not exist, and the freedom of the will would be taken away from human beings. Of course, there would still be people who wouldn't believe in ghosts or ethereal figures, but the evidence of his resurrection would be overwhelming (as with Thomas) for those who actually saw the risen Lord. The resurrection had to be completed in the ascension; that was the final act in the drama.

Third, as the glorified Christ, he had to depart and return to the Father because his earthly work was finished. The plan was yet to be completed; seated on the throne at the right hand of God, his rule began, means that he, too, is waiting for the time when he will return and the plan will finally run its course in him. When that day comes, he will never say "farewell" again. In the meantime, Jesus turns the work of the kingdom on earth over to us.

Fourth, for now, he sends the Holy Spirit to us with power to soften our hearts, bring us to repentance and true faith, and enable us to live the "disciple-life" as long as we live and work for the good of his kingdom here on earth. That same Spirit gives us hope that death has finally been overcome, and that our inheritance in Christ is the everlasting life in the kingdom of God the Father.

Seventh Sunday of Easter

Roman Catholic	**Acts 1:12-14**	**1 Peter 4:13-16**	**John 17:1-11a**
Episcopal	**Acts 1:(1-7) 8-14**	**1 Peter 4:12-19**	**John 17:1-11**
	or **Ezekiel 39:21-29**	or **Acts 1:(1-7) 8-14**	
Lutheran	**Acts 1:(1-7) 8-14**	**1 Peter 4:12-17; 5:6-11**	**John 17:1-11**
Common	**Acts 1:6-14**	**1 Peter 4:12-14; 5:6-11**	**John 17:1-11**

The church year theological clue

The Sunday after the Ascension, as the Seventh Sunday of Easter previously was designated, was known as Exaudi Sunday and served much the same function as the Seventh Sunday of Easter does today. This Sunday is a time of *reflection on the glory* God has given Christ by lifting him up to his right hand on the completion of his work. It is also a period of *expectation for the coming of the Holy Spirit* to the church and the world to empower the church to do the work of Christ. It is also the day when *anticipation begins* for the promised return of Christ at the end of the era. It, therefore, is a Sunday on which the church gives thanks for the life, ministry, death, and resurrection of Christ that have been completed in his ascension, and a day of preparation for Pentecost, to be celebrated next Sunday. Whether it is called the Sixth Sunday *after* Easter or the Seventh Sunday *of* Easter, the purpose and function of the Sunday remain pretty much the same; only two of the lessons are different (the Second Lesson carries over, with alterations in the verses, from the old set of propers, but the First and Third Lessons are changed).

The Prayer of the Day — In the LBW, two prayers are offered instead of a single collect. The first prayer is especially appropriate during the Year of Matthew (despite the fact that the Gospel is from St. John), because it contains the central point of Matthew's Gospel: namely, that Christ has promised to be with his own forever. The address acknowledges the ascension of the Lord ("your Son, our Savior, is with you in eternal glory"), points to the coming of the Spirit on Pentecost ("Give us faith to see, that true to his promise, he is among us still"), and affirms the continued presence of Christ until the last day ("and will be with us to the end of time").

The second prayer was inspired by the Gospel for the Day (John 17:1-11) and is for unity, that the church "might be one," asking that the church might find unity in Jesus Christ, "as he is one with you." This unity is to be functional, so that the unified church, which knows "peace and concord," may carry to the world the message of your love." For liturgical emphasis, it might be well to read both prayers in the day's worship. Homiletically, they remind the preacher that both themes are theologically important and need to be preached for the spiritual welfare and growth of the people.

The Psalm of the Day (LBW) — Psalm 47 — This psalm takes up the refrain of Easter and, in a manner not intended or even imagined by the writer, makes it apply to the Ascension of Our Lord: it actually puts the people who worship on this Sunday in places beside the disciples after the ascension; they went back into Jerusalem, according to St. Luke, praising and praying, and blessing God in the Temple for the risen Lord, Jesus Christ. In its own way, the psalm brings together the approaching conclusion to Easter ("Clap your hands, all you peoples; shout to God with a cry of joy"), the Ascension of the Lord ("God has gone up with a shout, the Lord with the sound of the ram's horn . . . . God reigns over the nations; God sits upon his holy throne"), and the mood of the early church ("Sing praises to God, sing praises; sing praises to our king, sing praises'') as it waited for the coming of the Holy Spirit. Although it was composed for another and radically different occasion (the defeat of the Assyrians in the time of Hezekiah?), it is most appropriate for the Seventh Sunday of Easter, the Sunday after the Ascension of Our Lord.

The Psalm Prayer

Lord Jesus, the dominion of the universe is yours, for you have ascended on high and are seated on the throne prepared for you by the Father. Gather all peoples into your Church and make them a holy nation, a royal priesthood, your own chosen heritage, to praise and adore your divine majesty now and forever.

The readings:

Acts 1:(1-7) 8-14

It is probably a good idea to use the longer lesson as the preaching text, which includes the introduction to the book and details about the ascension and Christ's instructions to the disciples to return to Jerusalem and wait for the coming — their baptism by fire — of the Holy Spirit, because most members of the average congregation will not have attended the worship on Ascension Day, and may even have been oblivious to it. Verses 12-14 are the new portion of the lesson, and relate the story of the obedience of the disciples immediately after the ascension. The Eleven did as Jesus had commanded them, went to an upper room, and, along with ''the women and Mary, the mother of Jesus, and with his brothers,'' . . . ''with one accord they devoted themselves to prayer . . . .'' The Seventh Sunday of Easter, despite its new *of* orientation, remains — and always will be — the Sunday *after* the Ascension of Our Lord. It is the final act in the drama of Jesus' resurrection from the dead.

1 Peter 4:13-19

The writer of 1 Peter could have been given the mantle of the prophet, according to his admonition about sharing in the sufferings of Christ that were given to, in all probability, the newly baptized members of the church. Persecutions had already taken over the people who were followers of Christ, and martyrdom was a distinct possibility on the horizon of anyone's life who confessed Christ as Lord and had been baptized in his name. In the face of evil, Christians are to cling to the good, regardless of their fate; they are to accept suffering in the spirit of their Lord and, no doubt, of Stephen and probably others who, by the time this epistle was written, had been persecuted and even murdered for their faith in Christ. The text is a reminder to Christians that faith is expensive; the cost of discipleship may be too rich for our blood, when we compare our situation with that of the pioneers in the Christian Church. But with these early Christians, perhaps we can ''entrust (our) souls to a faithful Creator'' in the name of our Lord Jesus Christ.

John 17:1-11

The high and priestly prayer of Jesus Christ is taken and set down in a completely different liturgical setting than that in which it was originally spoken: the work of the Lord is now totally finished and the door to eternal life has been thrown wide open by the death and resurrection of Jesus Christ, completed in the ascension. Christ therefore — and this is the main reason that the latter half of this text is appointed for this Sunday — prays for his disciples, who were a gift from God to him. He says:

I am praying for them; I am not praying for the world but for those whom thou hast given me, for they are thine; all mine are thine, and thine are mine, and I am glorified in them.

The reading concludes on a note which is critical for the health of the church in every age and for the effectiveness of its witness in the world: "Holy father, keep them in thy name, which thou hast given me, *that they may be one, even as we are one.*" The church has but one Lord and finds its unity in him.

A sermon on the Gospel, John 17:1-11 — "A Prayer for the Faithful."

Jesus' "high priestly prayer," as it is set down in the 17th chapter of John's Gospel, is broken up into three parts and used in years A, B, and C, much in the manner that John 10 is appointed for the Fourth Sunday of Easter. The entire prayer will provide the context for each sermon,which will highlight different emphases in the text.

1. There is a touch of nostalgia in Jesus' last prayer; he is ready to — even longs to — return to the Father in heaven. He knows that the hour of his departure from this world is at hand — and he welcomes it. His work is almost done, nearly finished. He has glorified the Father in his life and ministry here on earth, but the final act of glorification is at hand.

2. Jesus, the Son of God, did a very human thing; he prayed for himself: "Glorify thy Son that the Son may glorify thee." The supreme moment of "glory" for Jesus comes in a strange way; he is glorified when he is nailed to the cross, a sign posted above his head, "This is the King of the Jews." When he is high and lifted up, the whole world has the opportunity to glorify him.

3. Jesus, about to die, prays for his followers — that God will "keep them in (his) name." The support of the faithful was important to Jesus; he knew what would happen to the believers — they would need all the help they could get. He warned them that their lives would be anything but easy; they knew — and certainly he knew — what they should expect. Christians are never promised exemption from suffering, pain, and tragedy, simply because they are Christians. But they are promised the support and comfort of God.

4. Jesus also prayed for the church and its unity. All parts of the church and all believers are one in him; that's the nature of Christ and his body — that's the way it really is, despite the efforts that are made, and have been quite successful, in fragmenting the church into small bodies of believers and exclusive sects. Jesus wants the church to recognize its unity and to live and operate within it.

A sermon on the First Lesson and the Gospel

Most congregations need to hear a sermon emphasizing the unity of the church in its Lord as central to its existence and its mission in the world. The church can only be "one," because there is only one Lord, who is "one" with the Father, as well as "one" with the church. The ascension affirms that there is but one Lord, that he reigns in heaven over his church and the world.

The Benedictines of St. John's Abbey, Collegeville, have done as much as any other group of Christians to promote ecumenicity and the unity of the church in the last quarter of a century. Ever since their great church was built at the beginning of the sixties, they have been inviting people to visit them, worship with them, study with them, and live with them for a time. They have done just about everything they could to break down prejudices and smash the barriers that separate the various denominations from each other — and they have done it because their theology has been sound and scriptural. When a group of seminarians visited the monastery and the abbey church a quarter of a century ago, one asked Father Colman Barry, noted theologian and the host for most visiting groups, "Where is your 'Mary' altar?" Father Colman immediately replied, "Back in the corner, where it belongs." (An ancient statue of the Virgin resides in a side "altar room" chapel toward the rear of the nave. There is only one altar in the nave of the church building.) A few years ago, in

166

conjunction with their university, the Benedictines established an Ecumenical Center on the campus, appointing a non-Roman Christian as director. Currently, a Lutheran pastor, Alvin Rueter, teaches the homiletics courses at St. John's University. At great risk to themselves, (possibly to be censored — or worse — by a bishop or even "Rome"), participation in the worship services of the abbey church by retreat groups, visiting scholars and pastors, and people attending ecumenical conferences, is allowed by the Benedictines. They do so because, theologically, they believe in the unity of the church. They know that the church is one, and can only be one in Jesus Christ, the Lord. Their theology demands that they witness to the unity of the church in every way they can.

1. The unity of the church is an eternal reality. In this era between the ascension of the Lord and his promised return at the end of the age, the church needs to relearn that it is, and can only be, "one" in Jesus Christ, the Lord. Baptism is the sign of that unity, which also finds expression at the Table of the Lord. Dr. Harry Whitley's every Sunday announcement in St. Giles Cathedral, Edinburgh, Scotland, comes to mind once more; it cannot be remembered or repeated too often, especially where Lutherans are concerned. There has been a radical change in many denominations since I first heard him say, "The Holy Communion will be celebrated in the Murray Aisle Chapel at 12:15. We cordially invite our visitors to join us, remembering that this is the Table of the Lord, and not the table of any one denomination." Episcopalians and Lutherans are not only gathering at each other's altar-tables; they are on the verge of establishing full communion with one another. One prays and hopes that such unity will move the whole church to acknowledge its oneness in the Lord, to gather about his table, and confess the unity of the church in him.

2. Divisions in the church — theological and denominational — are the work of people, not God. They tend to sap the strength of the church as it seeks to make its witness for Christ in the world; non-believers look at the church and — until quite recently — could not say, "See how these Christians love one another." Such divisions work their way down to the level of congregations so that there is disunity rather than unity in the Lord.

3. Ecumenicity is a sign that God has hope for the unity of the church; Christ is finally getting to his own and making them conscious of the fact that he is the Lord of the church — and that the church is one in him. I was invited to preach at a Saturday evening mass in the chapel of a Roman Catholic "house-monastery." Before he began the Eucharistic prayer, the priest-chaplain asked me, "Would you, please, elevate the cup when I elevate the bread?" He didn't even wait for an answer, but simply offered it for me to hold and to elevate at the proper time. For both of us — although we never discussed the matter — this was a response to the message of the Lord that the church is one in him.

4. With the disciples after the ascension, it is the business of the church to engage in regular and heartfelt prayer — not simply for the world, but for the church. We don't know what the prayers of the disciples and the others were after Jesus' departure, but we do know one thing that we must pray for today, the unity of the church — that God will make the church what it is, one in Christ the Lord.

A sermon on the Second Lesson, 1 Peter 4:13-19 — "The Christian Initiation Fee."

1. Jesus paid the initiation fee for becoming a Christian with his death on the cross of Calvary. No one can buy his or her way into the kingdom of God; Jesus gave his life "for many" to gain entrance into the church and the kingdom.

2. Persecution — be it in the form of verbal opposition that may take the shape of ridicule or other types of derision and/or actual physical violence — is something that Christians should be prepared to expect. Those who "follow Christ" will often receive the same kind of treatment that their Lord experienced in his ministry and death. The "noble army of martyrs" has paid the ultimate price by laying down their lives, as did their Lord, for the faith.

3. Christians must still pay a high price for being members of the body of Christ, the church. It is a price that each committed person has to pay for herself/himself in terms of faithful discipleship, stewardship of time, talents, and possessions, and work in — and for — the kingdom of God. Commitment to Christ will inevitably involve suffering in one form or another. Christians can be certain of that.

4. When suffering of any kind comes from the opponents of Christ and the church, Peter's word reminds us to accept such suffering in the spirit of the Lord, who not only reigns over us but is with us on our journey of faith to the very gates of heaven.

The Season of Pentecost

Pentecost is a *day,* a *season,* and a *cycle.* It was observed, first, as a *day,* one of the major festivals that was observed early in the history of the church and, quickly, found a place in the church year. It was the natural conclusion for the Great Fifty Days of Easter and, in due time, became the beginning of a season and a cycle of the church year that took its name. Pentecost marks the end of the first half of the year and the beginning of the second — non-festival — portion of the church year. Pentecost gives its name to both season and cycle. This was not always so.

As the third cycle of the church year, Pentecost is roughly one half of the year, and is often called "The Half Year of the Church," or (as in the LBW) "The Time of the Church." In some ways, cycle and season seem to be indistinguishable from each other; they cover the same period of time within the church year. However, the cycle is the framework of the season; it extends from the festival of the Holy Trinity to Christ the King Sunday. The season is composed of the Sundays between these two biblical and liturgical poles. Actually, Pentecost is a one-season cycle; it may have as many as twenty-eight Sundays "after Pentecost" in the years when Easter is celebrated early in April or late in March.

The Sundays after Pentecost

Pentecost is a *season of Sundays.* Sunday comes into its own in Pentecost (or Ordinary Time, as the Roman Church calls it). Sunday is the Lord's Day; at least, that's what the church has called it since the primitive age of Christianity. Sunday is always a "Little Easter," a day set aside each week to celebrate Christ's victory over sin and death; it is not the equivalent of Easter, the singular and special day of resurrection. Sunday, as the Lord's Day, is set aside to remember and celebrate Easter and acknowledge the presence of the living Lord as the church awaits his return at the end of the age. It is not the equivalent of the Jewish Sabbath, the day of rest, the seventh day; Sunday is the eighth day, the *ogdoad,* the day of new creation, when all things were made new and found a new beginning in the resurrection of the Lord. Sunday is the day when, conscious that humanity has been given a second chance by God to live responsibly in the world, prays for power to live the new life in Christ. Sunday is the day when the church gives thanks — especially in the eucharist — for all that God has done, and is doing, for us in Christ Jesus.

From a practical point of view, the season after Pentecost really has two parts, a "summer section," from the end of Easter to the mid-point of Pentecost (the end of August, usually), and a "fall portion," from Labor Day to Christ the King Sunday. Churches in North America experience a drop in attendance and activities during the summer months; they often reduce the number of worship services on Sunday, sometimes adding weekday services to attract persons who may not be able to worship on Sunday. September marks the start of "new life" in the annual life of many congregations, as people return from summer vacations or some sort of "spiritual hibernation." Attendance improves, Sunday church school begins a new year, special adult and youth programs are promoted, and soon the annual stewardship drive is shaped and put into action. All of this means that the worship, and, especially, the preaching, during these two unofficial "seasons" within Pentecost, will differ radically.

The Church Year and Lectionary during Pentecost

The church year loses much of its "influence" over the themes and theology of Sunday in Pentecost, when compared to the other two cycles of the church year, but it continues to throw its theological framework around the season and its Sundays. The theological clues and themes for the several Sundays of Pentecost come primarily from the Gospel for the

Day, rather than from the theological content of the church year, as in the Christmas and Easter cycles. The Gospels focus the attention of pastors and people upon the work of Christ in the world, but not in the same manner as the Sundays in the first half of the year spell out the kerygmatic theology of the saving events in the life of Christ. The lectionary functions differently in Pentecost than it does in the Christmas and Easter Cycles of the church year.

It is through the semi-continuous reading of the Gospel (Matthew, in this year) that Sunday themes are established. This means that the integrity of Scripture and purity of the Word are preserved, because the readings are not forced into "thematic molds" for worship and/or preaching; the Gospels establish the theme, or themes, for the Sundays. Incidentally, the semi-continuous *(semi-lectio continua)* readings begin in Pentecost approximately where they left off in Epiphany. The Old Testament lessons continue to be chosen to harmonize with, and support, the Gospel for the Day. They do not follow any "series" pattern, except for the Common Lectionary, and may come from any book of the Old Testament.

The second readings reveal a radical change from their arrangement in the other two cycles; they are appointed in a short series of semi-continuous readings, (this year, the book of Romans is assigned to sixteen Sundays after Pentecost), which generally make no connection with the first reading or the Gospel for the Day. The second readings float freely and function on their own. This, of course, creates some problems — thematic and otherwise — for worship and, particularly, for preaching. It doesn't seem to make much sense to read the second lessons, if they create "thematic confusion" for worship and never become preaching texts by themselves. What should be done about this odd phenomenon in the lectionary?

Preaching during Pentecost

Sunday preaching during Pentecost takes its thematic and theological clues primarily from the Gospel for the Year, Matthew. Sermon themes — and their development — must be from the specific Gospels (and/or the other readings). More often than not, the Gospel for the Day — in consideration of pastoral exegesis — will determine the type and the actual shape of the sermon. The texts themselves will suggest the "what" and the "how" of the preaching. Such preaching will attempt to tell the story so as to open up the Gospel in support of the faith and life of the people of God. It should encourage and undergird their "new life" in Christ.

While the second lessons, through their lack of agreement and harmony with first reading and Gospel, pose a practical problem for the preacher, nonetheless, they do present homiletical opportunities. First, there is the opportunity to acquaint people with difficult, but extremely important, books of the Bible; the second lessons suggest a teaching emphasis in one's homiletical program. Second, these readings suggest preaching series of sermons, which might have special relevance for a congregation today; many of the spiritual and practical problems that Paul addressed in Rome and Corinth and other parts of the Christian community of his time find expression in contemporary congregations and need to be addressed from the biblical — Gospel — point of view. Third, there may be some occasions when the second lessons cry out to be preached in place of the traditional Gospel on a given Sunday. These readings often speak to contemporary concerns and causes in the week-to-week life of a congregation.

The bottom line in all of this, as far as one's preaching ministry is concerned, is that one has to plan one's preaching program differently in Pentecost than in the other half of the church year. Sermons will be different, especially if the preacher has developed multi-text sermons in the festival part of the year; three-text sermons are exegetically impossible on most Sundays, but two-text sermons are always a possibility. Sermon themes emerge after exegetical study of the texts; they are not established by the content of the Sundays (except for the obvious festivals — The Holy Trinity, Reformation Sunday, All Saints Day, and Christ the King Sunday). A "Sermon series" on the Gospel according to Saint Matthew is really the "homiletical order" for the cycle and Season of Pentecost. That's the direction the remainder of this study will attempt to go.

Exegetical study of the three readings for any Sunday should not preclude working with the Prayer of the Day, the Psalmody, which changes to harmonize with Old Testament and the Gospel in Cycles A, B, and C, the Psalm Prayer, and other portions of the appointed propers. But these should be studied along with the readings to enrich one's understanding and proclamation of the Word, rather than to help determine the theme and/or the theology of a given Sunday. A study of the propers supplies an added dimension to the preparation of Sunday sermons.

The Day of Pentecost

Roman Catholic	Acts 2:1-11	1 Corinthians 12:3b-7, 12-13	John 20:19-23
Episcopal	Acts 2:1-11 or Ezekiel 11:17-20	1 Corinthians 12:4-13 or Acts 2:1-11	John 20:19-23
Lutheran	Joel 2:28-29	Acts 2:1-21	John 20:19-23
Common	Isaiah 44:1-8	Acts 2:1-21	John 20:19-23

The church year theological clue

The Day of Pentecost is the Fiftieth Day *of* Easter; it brings the Paschal Season to its conclusion and, at the same time, signals the giving of the Holy Spirit to the disciples and to the church. Pentecost is not simply a festival of the Holy Spirit, rather, it is the time for acknowledging — ten days after the Ascension of Our Lord — the powerful gift of the Holy Spirit that Christ had promised to his followers. Like Easter, it has a vigil (not observed to the same degree as the Easter vigil in either Protestant or Roman Churches) that really begins the day's celebration. For details about the Vigil of Pentecost, see: Adrian Nocent, O.S.B., *The Liturgical Year, the Book of Common Prayer, The Lutheran Book of Worship* (Minister's Desk Edition), etc. The Roman Church treats the vigil much as it does the Easter Vigil, appointing six readings (four Old Testament, one Second Lesson, and a Gospel) for the Vigil of Pentecost. The Episcopal Church employs the same texts but puts them in the setting of an "early" service or a "vigil" for Pentecost. The Lutheran Church (LBW) has four readings, of which the first two are connected by an "or," so that there are really only three readings for a vigil. Pentecost, it should be remembered, was also a Hebrew feast that preceded the Christian Pentecost, but was later altered (by A.D. 250) into a festival that celebrated the giving of the Law to Moses on Mt. Sinai, apparently to offset the giving of the Spirit on Pentecost, as the church celebrated the occasion. The coming of the Spirit marks the reversal of the confusion and disunity that sin had brought into the world; the church is unified in the Holy Spirit and, thereby, equipped for its mission in the world. Pentecost actually celebrates, too, the unity of the death, resurrection, and Second Coming of Jesus, along with the power and hope that the gift of the Holy Spirit, who has been operative in the world since it was created by God, gives to the people who belong to the body of Christ, the church.

The Prayer of the Day — Two prayers are provided in the LBW, both more theologically oriented to the themes of Pentecost than the classic Pentecost prayer. The first prayer bears some resemblance to the classic collect for Pentecost in that it mentions "our hearts" over against the "hearts of thy faithful people" in the older prayer, but the tense of the two prayers is different. The classic collect recalls the activity of God in the work of "sending to them (God's faithful people) the light of the Holy Spirit" as their *teacher,* while the modern prayer recalls the "promised *gift* of the Holy Spirit" and asks God to "look upon your Church and open our hearts to the power of the spirit." The culmination of this prayer revives memories of the Easter Vigil, as well as the Day of Pentecost, when it says, "Kindle in us the fire of your love," asking God thereby to "strengthen our lives for service in your kingdom." The theological concept of the coming of the Holy Spirit as a gift to the church is affirmed as central to the theme of the day and the meaning of Pentecost.

The second collect concentrates on another — and major — theme of Pentecost, unity through the power of the holy spirit. It stems from the Acts 2 reading with its emphasis on "many languages" and "all nations" who hear the Gospel in "one heavenly speech." The petition asks that we might be made "messengers of the good news" so that all people on earth might "unite in one song of praise." The two prayers point toward the theology of Pentecost in terms of the Holy Spirit as a gift from God to his own people and the unity that the Holy Spirit offers to the church.

171

The Psalm of the Day — Psalm 104:25-34 — A psalm that looks to the God who is the maker and creator of all things, and who is responsible for all of the good that happens on earth. God's works mirror his image in the world and fill his people with "good things." When God hides his face, the people are filled with fear, because their "breath" is taken away and they die and "return to their dust." This phrase reminds the church of Ash Wednesday and its declaration, "You are dust and unto dust you shall return;" it completes the Easter — death/resurrection — cycle that began thirteen weeks ago. And the psalm goes on to mention the work of the life-giving Spirit of God, which is why the psalm is appointed for Pentecost, of course. God sends forth his Spirit and "they are created; and so you renew the face of the earth." The same Spirit that God set to work in the world at the beginning of creation was released by God on Pentecost to accomplish a new work of creation — resurrection — in the form of the church and the preparation of the faithful for their mission on earth. So the psalmist can declare:

> *May the glory of the Lord endure forever; may the Lord rejoice in all his works . . . . I will sing to the Lord as long as I live; I will praise God while I have my being.*

The Psalm Prayer (LBW)

> *God of all light, life, and love, through the visible things of this world you raise our thoughts to things unseen, and you show us your power and your love. From your dwelling-place refresh our hearts and renew the face of the earth with the life-giving water of your Word, until the new heaven and new earth resound with the song of resurrection in Jesus Christ our Lord.*

The readings:

Joel 2:28-29

This reading is one of the lessons appointed for the Vigil of Pentecost in the Roman and Episcopal lectionaries; the Lutheran Church uses it only on the Day of Pentecost. As Joel envisioned in his prophecy, the dispensation of the Holy Spirit by God upon "all flesh," he was undoubtedly thinking only in terms of Israel. He believed that the gift of the Spirit would be given to ordinary people, as well as the ordained leaders of the godly community. Peter includes this reference in his Pentecost sermon, quoting the entire prophecy (verses 28-32), rather than just the first two verses of the text which are read in the Lutheran setting to emphasize the nature of the gift God gives in the Holy Spirit, which is offered to all faithful and receptive people by the Father.

Acts 2:1-21

The Common and Lutheran lectionaries include the story of what happened on the day of Pentecost, plus the reaction of the crowd, which concluded that the Spirit-filled disciples were drunk. The Roman and Episcopal lectionaries employ this part of the story as the First Lesson for the Day, probably because it comes as a fulfillment of the Joel prophecy, read in the Pentecost vigil. I suspect that the committee that put together the Luthern Lectionary knew that there was little chance that the Pentecost vigil, whose propers were not even included in the first edition of this lectionary, would "catch on" in the liturgical revisions of the parishes. (Oddly enough, propers for the Vigil of Pentecost were printed in the pew edition of the LBW, but the Vigil of Easter, which was already being celebrated in many Lutheran congregations was omitted from the pew edition. Propers for both the Vigil of Easter and the Vigil of Pentecost were printed in the *Minister's Desk Edition* of the LBW.) The Lutheran church reads the longer text on Pentecost so that the prophecy and fulfillment will be heard on the Day of Pentecost as God's gift to the Christian community to prepare and empower it for its task in the world.

Again, it should be noted that by using Joel as the first reading and Acts 2 as the second reading, the impression is given that Easter ends on the Seventh Sunday of Easter instead of on Pentecost. The Gospel sounds the note of the resurrection and Pentecost and corrects any such misconceptions that people might have.

John 20:19-23

This reading is, of course, the first part of the Gospel that was proclaimed on the Second Sunday of Easter, in which the Lord appeared in the upper room, greeted the disciples with "Peace be with you," showed them his hands and his side, declared "peace" a second time, outlined their mission ("as the Father has sent me, even so I send you"), and breathed on them, saying, "Receive the Holy Spirit." He also gave them the power to forgive — or retain — sins, which is a reference to baptism, because one's sins are forgiven in baptism. Despite the fact that John seems to stir up a controversy as to when the Holy Spirit came to the disciples — whether on Easter Eve or fifty days after the resurrection — the Gospel for the Day makes it clear that Pentecost is the conclusion of Easter; the resurrection of the Lord requires the ascension and Pentecost to make it complete. The Holy Spirit is a gift of the resurrection of Christ to the church to shape, empower, and send it into the world on its mission for the Lord.

A sermon on the Gospel, John 20:19-23 — "A New Act of Creation."

This Gospel takes us back beyond Easter Sunday, all the way to Ash Wednesday with its reference to the retention of sin and the inevitability of death; Ash Wednesday's first word was, "You are dust, and unto dust you shall return." The Easter greeting of the risen Lord to his church, "Peace be with you," assures the faithful that all is well, because our sins have been forgiven and we have been given new life in Christ. This is the last Sunday of Easter, but that doesn't mean that we put away the festival for another year; every Sunday has the cross and empty tomb indelibly marked upon it. This Gospel also reminds us of baptism with its "Receive the Holy Spirit . . . . If you forgive the sins of any, they are forgiven," because it is, indeed, in baptism that sin is forgiven and the new life in Christ, the life of the Spirit, begins, because Christ "breathes on us" when the Word is spoken and the Water is poured upon us. So we celebrate, today, not only the birthday of the church of Christ, but the gift of the Holy Spirit, which the Lord God bestows upon the Christian church in the same manner he gave the Spirit to the Israelites in the past. Pentecost, therefore, marks the beginning of a new era in human history, that of the Holy Spirit, who will implement Christ's work on earth "until he comes again."

1. The word of the resurrected Christ to his church and to the world, too, is "Peace be with you." The Lord, crucified on Good Friday, is alive again, and he will live forever, the "first-fruits" of the resurrection. That is why we remember and celebrate Easter at least every Sunday; Jesus, himself, speaks the good news to us in our worship, "Peace be with you."

2. The wounds of Jesus, his body and blood in the Sunday Eucharist, are evidence that his death on the cross was real enough. And we know that it was for us — and for new life — that he hung and suffered there. Jesus died so that our sins might be forgiven and we would be reconciled to God once and for all. If Martin Scorsese had really wanted to damage Christianity when he made the movie, *The Last Temptation of Christ,* he picked the wrong novel and novelist in Kazantzakis; he should have chosen one of the novels about finding the bones of Jesus, such as the former evangelist, Chuck Templeton, wrote over a decade ago. That would have attacked the central doctrine of the faith, Jesus' death and resurrection. Scorsese denies any intention to discredit the Christian faith.

3. The wind on Pentecost Day takes us back to the Garden of Eden, when God breathed on a handful of dust and created the human race. Jesus "breathed on them," the disciples gathered in the locked room, and thereby engaged in a new act of creation, one that is repeated again and again in Holy Baptism as the Spirit moves over the waters and changes the dead into living creatures again.

174

4. The witness of the faithful is spelled out on Pentecost, "See what the Lord has done for us! He has made us his own people. He can do the same for you." So the church has to go about preaching, "Repent, believe that Jesus is the living Lord, and be baptized in his holy name — and you will become a new creature, a child of God who will live forever."

A sermon on the First Lesson, Joel 2:28-29 — "God Keeps A Promise."

This text might best be incorporated into a sermon on the Second Lesson. If it isn't, it has to be preached in the context of that lesson.

1. God promised — long ago — to pour out, lavishly and generously, with no limits on his action, his Holy Spirit on "all flesh." The Spirit would be given to any and all who would receive this precious gift.

2. God declared — long ago — that a day like Pentecost would occur, when the young people would dream dreams and the elderly would see visions of his kingdom and his reign.

3. God acted — long ago — and really did "pour out his Spirit" on "all flesh." The really good news is that he continues to give the gift to the church and the faithful today. He acts to give us faith through Christ. He acts to make us new creatures in baptism. He acts and renews us at the Table of the Lord and whenever we call upon him in repentance and true faith.

A sermon on the Second Lesson, Acts 2:1-21 — "Pentecost: Then and Now."

One of the stories my paternal grandfather used to tell me when I was a little boy, was about a mid-summer storm that left him and my grandmother more startled than afraid. It wasn't the storm itself that disturbed them; they had experienced many severe storms with thunder and lightning in northeastern Pennsylvania. They lived in a "land of lightning rods" — and they had lightning rods on their home. But on this occasion, just as the storm was breaking, a strange phenomenon occurred; a "fireball," as they called it, came down the fireplace in their sitting room, which was almost in the middle of the home, moved across the room out into the hallway, past two other open doors, and went right out the front (screen) door. It scorched the screen, so that it had to be replaced. I have since wondered why my grandfather didn't keep it. It would have been a marvelous memento, perhaps a religious relic! The fireball didn't touch or hurt them, but my grandparents never forgot the experience. Deeply religious people that they were, I never learned whether they made any connections to the wind and the fire on the Day of Pentecost, but I suspect that they better understood what happened on that day after Christ's ascension to heaven. The fireball might have made Pentecost mean more to them than it ever had before.

1. Pentecost — what happened? — Through the "mighty wind" God breathed on the people in the upper room and through "the tongues as of fire" he baptized them with the Holy Spirit, just as John had prophesied about the work of Christ.

2. Pentecost — what purpose? — Through the gift of the Holy Spirit God perfected the faith of his disciples so that they would become new persons and be prepared for their mission in the world. Upon receiving the Holy Spirit, they immediately began to tell the good news to the world.

3. Pentecost — what meaning? — Through his Spirit the Lord unifies the faithful in Christ and his church. The Holy Spirit testifies that the Lord is indeed alive — now and forever. "This is the day that the Lord has made. Let us rejoice and be glad in it."

The Holy Trinity
(First Sunday after Pentecost)

Roman Catholic	Exodus 34:4b-6, 8-9	2 Corinthians 13:11-13	John 3:16-18,
Episcopal	Genesis 1:1—2:3	2 Corinthians 13:(5-10) 11-14	Matthew 28:16-20
Lutheran	Genesis 1:1—2:3 or Deuteronomy 4:32-34 39-40	2 Corinthians 13:11-14	Matthew 28:16-20
Common	Deuteronomy 4:32-40	2 Corinthians 13:5-14	Matthew 28:16-20

The church year theological clue

The Holy Trinity is a "liturgical late-comer" among the feasts and festivals of the church; officially, it has been an established feast of the church for 555 years, since Pope John XX approved of it in 1334. Its history began with the dedication of churches to the Holy Trinity in the ninth century, at least one liturgy in the tenth century, and an actual feast celebrated in the eleventh century. This festival was retained in the revised church year and the liturgy of the church by the skin of its teeth. Some liturgical theologians and "revisionists" wanted to have it deleted from the worship program of the church because it is the celebration of a doctrine, focusing on an abstraction: who has not heard — or delivered — a sermon in which the theme centered on the nature of the Holy Trinity, attempting to explain how Father, Son, and Holy Spirit are One God, how each person of the Trinity has "a complete personality but with all possessing a single divine nature?" (Adrian Nocent) Try as we will to make such theology concrete, we are almost certainly doomed to failure; the best we seem to do is in the symbols of the liturgy that attempt to picture the Trinity as a "three-in-one" God. Small wonder, in view of the abstract doctrinal theology, that so many symbols had to be created in an attempt to make concrete this abstraction. The festival might easily have been eliminated from Roman and other church year lectionaries, but it wasn't.

Something important would have been lost, if the Holy Trinity were removed from the church year, because it is a positive theological emphasis of the church upon the activity of God in the world. This is accentuated in contemporary theology and gives support to those who argued for retaining the festival in the liturgical life of the church. God the Father is creator and a redeeming God, who "so loved the world that he gave his only begotten Son . . . ." to save the world. Jesus is the "Father-lover" who loves God and humanity so much that he is willing to die to accomplish salvation for the human race. The Holy Spirit acts through the Word and the sacraments to reach the hearts and minds of people and to become incarnate in them, shaping them into the image of God. The Holy Trinity is celebrated as a festival of the divine love operative in the three persons of God, not as an occasion to attempt to celebrate the abstractions of Western theology.

The Holy Trinity remains as a festival that functions as an *octave*, not only of Pentecost, but of the entire first half of the Christian year. It sums up the work and actions of a God who has revealed himself as love in what he does as Father, Son, and Holy Spirit.

The Prayer of the Day (LBW) — Two prayers, again, are offered for the use of liturgical leaders and preachers. The first is an "action" collect that is addressed to

Almighty God our Father, dwelling in majesty and mystery, renewing and fulfilling creation by your eternal Spirit, and revealing your glory through our Lord, Jesus Christ.

The petition asks,

> *Cleanse us from doubt and fear, and enable us to worship you, with your Son and the Holy Spirit, one God, living and reigning, now and forever.*

It is something of an "action" prayer on our part, too.

The second prayer is a revision of the traditional collect for the festival of Holy Trinity; it reflects something of the theological abstraction with which the feast was celebrated in the past:

> *. . . you have given us grace, by the confession of the true faith, to acknowledge the glory of the eternal Trinity and, in the power of your divine majesty, to worship the unity. Keep us steadfast in this faith and worship, and bring us at last to see you in your eternal glory, one God, now and forever.*

This collect tends to emphasize the importance of a correct theological perspective of the Holy Trinity for faith and worship. Some pastors may want to put both to use in the worship services of the day.

The Psalm of the Day — Psalm 150 (E) — A familiar song of praise that makes a fitting responsory psalm to the first reading. It begins and ends with a "hallelujah," and every verse calls upon the people of God to "praise the Lord." He is to be praised "in the temple," and in the world he has made, too; he should be revered "for his mighty acts" and "for his excellent greatness." The last verse calls upon all who are living to worship and praise the Lord God: "Let everything that has breath praise the Lord. Hallelujah!"

Psalm 29 (L) — The psalmist issues a call to acknowledge God for who he is, "ascribe" the "glory due his name," and to worship him "in the beauty of holiness." The psalmist pictures a God who, through his "voice" is operative in the world and whose glory and might are in evidence in his power over nature. *God is in control* — even over the Great Flood — is really what the psalmist is telling the world; his might is evident in the thunder and the storms that strike the earth. He is always in control, and those who are aware of what he does through his mighty power are moved to worship him with "glory." But, the psalmist makes clear, this God of tremendous power and control is out to bless his people, not destroy them as he could, and to give them something of his power and might: "The Lord shall give strength to his people; the Lord shall give his people the blessing of peace." God's awesome power is tempered by love and mercy.

The Psalm Prayer (LBW)

> *Lord our King, your voice sounds over the waters as you reign above the flood. Help us, who are born again by water and the Holy Spirit, to praise your wonderful deeds in your holy temple; through your Son, Jesus Christ our Lord.*

Psalmody — The Roman Catholic *Ordo* appoints Daniel 3:29-33, 52-56 (deutero-canonical portions of the book), which have contributed two canticles to the liturgy of the church, the *Benedictus es* and the *Benedicite, omnia opera,* as the psalmody for the day. The *Book of Common Prayer* allows either portion of this song to be used as an alternate responsory psalm (Psalm 150 is the first choice). These selections are portions of the song that Shadrach, Meshach, and Abednego sang when they were thrust into the fiery furnace and survived without any harm. It was God who saved them, and God who, in the second section of this responsory, is praised by all his works, especially by the "pure and humble of heart."

Psalm 33:1-12 (C) — Here is a psalm that speaks mostly about God as creator and Lord of all people. It tells of the mighty acts of God and what he has accomplished through his Word. It is, therefore, a joyful song, not only recounting the reasons for rejoicing, but also for his rule over the nations. The last verse speaks powerfully on this feast of the Holy Trinity: "Happy is the nation whose God is the Lord! Happy the people he has chosen to be his own."

The readings:

Exodus 34:4b-6, 8-9 (R)

This reading was chosen, not simply to tell the story of Moses cutting two tablets of stone — for a second time — and taking them, at the instructions of Yahweh, up Mt. Sinai, but to illustrate how the Old Testament parallels the New Testament in God's revelation of himself. Yahweh is the Lord, who revealed himself as Yahweh-Lord to Moses, and who creates in Moses' being a response of true worship and prayer in the presence of the Lord. The reading shows the God of grace, mercy, and love, who is known as Father, Son, and Holy Spirit in the Christian Church.

Genesis 1:1—2:3 (E, L)

The familiar creation story is selected for the Holy Trinity to show what God is like, and to recount what he has done and how he has done it in the creation of everything that ever has been, is, and will be. God turned loose his spirit and the earth began to be what God intended; order and life came into being at his *word*. He created all that is — including human beings — with the word and the Holy Spirit. God's Word became incarnate in life and, particularly in those he made in his image. Genesis 1, therefore, gives us a story of how God acts as Father, as Word (which finally becomes incarnate in Jesus Christ), and Holy Spirit. The Good God, the God of Love, does good works in the world he has created and in the creatures with which he has populated it. It is a fitting and appropriate reading for the festival of the Holy Trinity.

Deuteronomy 4:32-40 (C); 4:32-34, 39-40 (L, alternate)

The exodus was in its fortieth year when Moses spoke these words to the people of Israel, reminding them of all that God had done for them as they neared the end of their long trek from Egypt to the land that God had promised to them. He tells them that God has spoken to them "with his voice," and that his word has accomplished for them what they could not do by — or for — themselves. The God of the Old Testament is a God who works through his mighty word to sustain, as well as create, his children in the world. He blesses the Israelites because he loves them, and they, in their turn, must fulfill his commandments, if they are to continue as the blessed people of God.

2 Corinthians 13:11-13 (R); 13:(5-10) 11-14 (E); 13:11-14 (L); 13:5-14 (C)

These are the last verses in Paul's second letter to the Corinthians, coming at the end of his discourse to them to be *perfect* in Jesus Christ. They are to live in love, peace, and unity, helping one another and, Paul promises, "the God of love and peace will be with you." Christians, he instructs them, should "greet one another with the holy kiss" in their liturgical assemblies. That is where his letter was supposed to be read; it prefaced the celebration of the Eucharist, which the closing words — "The grace of the Lord Jesus Christ, the love of God, and the fellowship of the Holy Spirit be with you all" — really began. At the same time, this greeting announces what this festival is all about — God the Father's love, God the Son's grace, and God the Holy Spirit's fellowship, or communion, with his people. God himself has created the feast of the Holy Trinity by what he is and what he has done as Father, Son, and Holy Spirit.

John 3:16-18 (R)

In this brief, but critically important, reading, the church is reminded that God's love became incarnate in Jesus Christ in order to deliver people from sin and death. Jesus came to "save" the world, not condemn it, and everyone in it; from the beginning, this meant that Jesus would have to die to accomplish God's purpose. Faith in Christ, in the form of genuine belief in his person as the Son of God and the Savior of the world, assures people that they have been saved, not condemned, by Jesus. But the refusal to believe that Jesus is Lord, Son of God and Savior of all, means "automatic condemnation" by those who reject him as their Lord.

Matthew 28:16-20 (E, L, C)

For once, the Gospel for the Day, although it was written for different people and a different time, takes up — from the perspective of the trinitarian formula — where the second reading leaves off. Both are the conclusions of writings and both spell out the nature of God as Father, Son, and Holy Spirit. This Gospel restates with the central theme of Matthew's Gospel, "and know that I am with you always; yes, to the end of time" *(Jerusalem Bible)*. This text makes it manifestly clear that the business of the church is to proclaim the good news and baptize those who believe "in the name of the Father, Son, and Holy Ghost" — and it asserts that God is with his church as it does his business.

Sermon suggestions:

Matthew 28:16-20 — "The Orders Christ Gave Us."

1. *Christians are to be "disciple-makers."* Those who receive God's gift — Jesus Christ — are to be busy "making disciples of all nations." Jesus himself has cut out our work for us.
2. *Go, tell/teach, and baptize.* That's how disciples are to be "made" in all nations. The story has to be told, the faith has to be taught, and believers have to be baptized "in the name of the Father, and of the Son, and of the Holy Spirit" — in the name of the Lord God himself.
3. *The orders are binding as long as life exists on the earth.* That's how it has been since the beginning of the Christian era, and that's how it has to be now and until the end of the age. *This is God's plan to redeem the world and restore it to himself.* Jesus has set the plan into motion at Calvary, and has given the church orders to implement the plan devised by God.
4. *The plan will be successful,* when the church obeys Christ's orders, because the Lord, who gave the church its orders, will be with his people, directing them and supporting their efforts, until the end of time.

John 3:16-18 (R) — "Jesus — The Gift God Gave Us."

1. God's love is a mystery, because he loved us so much that he gave his only begotten Son that those who believe in him might have eternal life. How could God possibly love defiant and disobedient human beings, who have made such a mess of life on earth, let alone love them enough to send his Son to die for them?

2. A radical action on the part of God was necessary to save people from sin and death — and God was willing to take that action in Jesus Christ. Jesus' cross is the sign of salvation — not condemnation — offered by God for the creatures he created in his own image. For some reason or other, God could not discard his creatures and start all over again. People are too loved by God to throw away!

3. Believe! Believe! — For that is the only way you can receive the gift — salvation — which God offers in Jesus Christ the Lord. Salvation can never be earned by human beings; it is God's gracious gift in Christ.

4. Live the life of love. The cross teaches us how much Jesus loved God, as well as how to love God in response to his gift of eternal life in Jesus Christ.

Exodus 34:4-6, 8-9 (R) — "The Return to Mt. Sinai."

1. *An obedient man.* Moses must have become quite proficient in working with stone! For the second time, he had to fashion stone tablets to take up the mountain for another meeting with God. He smashed the first set after he came down from Mt. Sinai and discovered that the people were worshiping a golden calf. If he had been like us, he might have attempted to get by with a single tablet this time; surely, the terms of the covenant would fit on one stone tablet, wouldn't they? At least, that's what the pulpit in the parish church I belong to suggests. A panel below the preacher's right shoulder depicts a tablet with a whip superimposed upon it and the Latin numerals one through ten cut into the wood. Numbers one to three are on one side, and four to ten in another column, representing the two-in-one approach to the two tablets of the law. Moses didn't attempt any short cuts; he simply did what God commanded him to do and made his way up to another showdown with God. He must have been shaking in his sandals.

2. *A bold prayer.* Once more, when he dared to call upon the name of God, Moses suddenly discovered that he was in the presence of the Lord God almighty, and he did the only thing he could do; he prostrated himself before God and worshiped him, making a plea to God on behalf of the recalcitrant children of Israel; he not only wanted them to know God's forgiveness, but to experience his presence, as well. That happened when he went down the mountain, the two tablets of the Law in his hands, and his face radiant from his contact with the Lord God.

3. *God answers to his name.* That prayer, answered positively by God in the covenant established in Mt. Sinai, has been answered again and again, specifically at one time and place in the incarnation of Jesus Christ and the new covenant God has made with us in his life, death, and resurrection. And on innumerable occasions he has come to his people through his Word and Holy Spirit, forgiving their sins and renewing that covenant in Christ again and again. Believers go up to the mountain of the Lord by gathering in his church, hearing the Word, and going up to the Table of the Lord, where he comes to them in the meal of bread and wine.

4. *A hill becomes a mountain.* Moses went up a mountain to enter into a covenant with God. Jesus went up a little hill and was nailed to a cross and, in that, established a new covenant for all people. Golgotha became a mountain peak that was higher than Mt. Sinai, because it supported a man on a cross so that all the world might see God in him and bless his holy name.

Genesis 1:1—2:3 (E, L) — "And God Said . . . ."

1. God did it: he created the world and all the life in it. The solar system and our earth did not come into existence by chance; God determined what would be created — and he accomplished his purpose and his intentions by his mighty word.

2. God held humanity in his hand — and he breathed his life-giving spirit into a bit of earth and it became a living being, made in the image of God. (2:7) God became intimately involved in the work of creation. He had to, to make people in his own image.

3. God put human beings in charge of all that he had made. The business of people on the earth is to take charge of the earth and all life on it, and administer it properly. We're doing quite well on filling the earth, but failing miserably on managing it. Did God give humanity an impossible responsibility to perform? Are we destroying rather than preserving the race? Are we doomed to fail God and ourselves? Will we self-destruct?

4. God will see to it that we do not fail; the cross tells us that. He has brought his whole being — Father, Son, and Holy Spirit — into the action he took in Jesus Christ to bring about a new creation which will last to the end of time.

Deuteronomy 4:32-40 (C) — "The One and Only God."

The festival of the Holy Trinity, according to this reading, is a day of remembrance that began with Moses' address to the people in conjunction with the giving of the Law to them. He reminds them that God has always blessed his creatures, and has especially blessed them as he brought them forth from Egypt, sustained them for forty years, and gave them the power to defeat all those who stood in their way as they moved toward the Promised Land. He declares: "Know therefore this day, and lay it on your heart, that the Lord is God in heaven above and on the earth beneath; there is no other."

1. *The God of all creation.* God is the maker of the world, of all things that are good and lasting.

2. *The God of the covenant.* God made a covenant with Israel, which he has always kept. He made a new covenant with all nations in Jesus Christ.

3. *The God for all time.* God is the one and only God, who was, is, and will be, now and forever. Worship him, the Father, the Son, and the Holy Spirit.

2 Corinthians 13:11-14 — "A Greeting Born of Experience."

1. Jesus introduced us to the fullness of God through gifts of grace bestowed upon humanity in his life, his ministry, his death and resurrection. Jesus gave everything he had to give, including his life, for our benefit and restoration.

2. God is a loving Father, who loves people enough to give his only begotten son to die for them. That's what selfless love is all about. God loves his creatures so much that, in his Son, he lays down his life that they might live.

3. Through the work of the Holy Spirit, God constantly comes to people and restores them to communion with himself in the body of Christ, the church. Through the Holy Spirit, he makes his presence known at the Table of the Lord.

4. Praise Father, Son, and Holy Spirit — now and forever!

The Second Sunday after Pentecost
Ninth Sunday in Ordinary Time (R)
Proper 4 (E, C)

Roman Catholic	Deuteronomy 11:18, 25-28, 32	Romans 3:21-25, 28	Matthew 7:21-27
Episcopal	Deuteronomy 11:18-21, 26-28	Romans 3:21-25a, 28	Matthew 7:21-27
Lutheran	Deuteronomy 11:18-21, 26-28	Romans 3:21-25a, 27-28	Matthew 7:(15-20) 21-29
Common	Genesis 12:1-9	Romans 3:21-28	Matthew 7:21-29

The church year theological clue

From this point until late in the Pentecost season, on Sundays there is only the general theological framework of the church year to provide biblical/theological clues for worship and preaching themes. Pentecost, as "the time of the church," is *eschatological;* the church worships and waits, learns and grows, and witnesses and works for the coming of the fullness of the kingdom in Jesus' promised return. On the Sundays of Pentecost, the church is counting time, not marking time, until the Lord returns. Pentecost is the annual countdown of the church, not merely to the end of the church year, but in anticipation of the Parousia, which will occur at the end of the age as determined by God the Father. The final consummation of the Gospel of the Lord, with its promise of resurrection and eternal life is yet to come. Pentecost reminds us of that and turns us into pilgrims who are assured of salvation and who are on their way to the kingdom of heaven.

The Prayer of the Day (LBW) — This prayer picks up where the Gospel of the Day left off last Sunday, and it serves very nicely as the opening collect for the Pentecost season: "Lord God of all nations, you have revealed your will to your people and promised your help to us all." The petition seeks help from God to "hear and to do what you command," and it shares this concern for obedience to God with the classic collect for this Sunday. The conclusion of a former prayer says more about God's intention than does the traditional prayer for the Sunday: "that the darkness may be overcome by the power of your light" instead of "that in keeping thy commandments we may please thee, both in will and deed."

The Psalm of the Day — Psalm 31:2-14, 17, 25 (R); 31:31, or 31:1-5, 16-24 (E); 31:1-5 (6-18) 19-24 (L) — This could very well have been the lament of one of the Christian martyrs, rather than the personal expression of pain and suffering of the psalmist. It doesn't seem to complement the first reading and the Gospel, partly because it is so personal, but also because it doesn't appear to harmonize with the readings. The last six verses of the psalm praise God for his goodness and his protection of his people who are under attack. God is with his own people, hears their prayers, and answers them. The conclusion of the psalm is appropriate to the day and the eschatological nature of the season:

> *Love the Lord, all you who worship; the Lord protect the faithful . . . . Be strong and let your heart take courage, all you who wait for the Lord.*

182

The Psalm Prayer (LBW)

God of kindness and truth, you saved your chosen one, Jesus Christ, and you give your martyrs strength. Watch over your people who come to you now, and strengthen the hearts of those who hope in you, that they may proclaim your saving acts of kindness in the eternal city; through your Son, Jesus Christ our Lord.

Psalm 33:1-22 (C) — The psalmist sings a beautiful refrain in the last half of this psalm of joy: "Happy is the nation whose God is the Lord! Happy the people he has chosen to be his own!" The latter sentiment brings forth an *amen* from all those who have heard the gospel and believe Jesus to be Lord. The cross of Christ assures us that God has looked upon his people with love and mercy — and has saved us all in Jesus. The first sentence surely is true, but one is not so certain today that God is the Lord of our nation. The way we live as a nation seems to indicate that we have many gods whom we worship and place above the Lord God Almighty, the Father and Creator of us all.

The readings:

Deuteronomy 11:18-21, 26-28 (E, L), 11:18, 26-28, 32 (R)

This reading was chosen because it sets out the consequences of keeping or breaking God's covenant in terms of blessings or curses upon those who are bound by the covenant. The setting has to do with the practice of preparing phylacteries, which were leather pillbox-like containers in which were placed four portions of the Torah (Exodus 13:1-10, 11-16 and Deuteronomy 6:4-9; 11:13-21); these were strapped to the wrist and fastened to the forehead, and attached to the doorposts of houses in a kind of cartridge. They served to remind those who wore them of the basic tenets of their faith, such as the uniqueness of God, obedience to his commands, deliverance from captivity, and the redemption of the first-born (See Gerard Sloyan's *A Commentary on the New Lectionary).*

The second part of the reading reveals the reason for the selection of this lesson on the Second Sunday after Pentecost; it contains the material about the blessings that God's people will receive if they obey God's commandments, and the curses that will come to them if they disobey the commandments of the Lord God. These blessings and curses are illustrated at the conclusion of the Gospel for the Day (Matthew 7:21-29) in the parable of the houses built on rock or sand, which spells out the fate of those who hear and obey, or who disobey, Jesus' teachings.

Genesis 12:1-9 (C)

For the next eighteen weeks, the Common Lectionary employs only two books on the Old Testament in the readings assigned to these Sundays of Pentecost: Genesis is appointed for five Sundays and Exodus is selected as the first reading for the following thirteen weeks. The second readings and the Gospels are, generally, in harmony with those of the other lectionaries. The Psalmody, as a rule, is different.

The story of the shaping of Israel's destiny begins, in this reading, with God's call of Abram to leave Haran, where he and his family had settled prematurely after leaving Ur of the Chaldeans, and to make his way to Canaan. Abram packed up his family and went to Canaan. When they had reached Shechem's "Holy Place," the Oak of Moreh, God appeared to him and told him that he would give "this land" to him and his descendants. Abram immediately built an altar to the God — Yahweh — who had appeared to him. After that, Abram travelled to the district "east of Bethel" and built another altar for the worship of God. The story concludes this way: "And Abram journeyed on, still going toward the Negeb." The conclusion of this story is but the beginning of the fuller story of God and his people of Israel.

Romans 3:21-25a, 28 (R, E); 3:21-25a, 27-28 (L); 3:21-28 (C)

This selection begins the semi-continuous reading of Romans for almost four months (sixteen weeks), and has no direct connection with the Old Testament reading or the Gospel for the Day. This particular lesson, however, does complement both Old Testament and the Gospel readings in that it states that God has fashioned "a way out" of the curses that those who have broken his commandments deserve. Grace — as the forgiveness of sins and, thereby, the renewal of the (new, baptismal) covenant with God — is a gift of the Lord God. God's blessings are not earned by obedience to the commandments of the Lord, but are bestowed freely upon people of faith. Since all "have sinned and fall short of the glory of God," there is no one who is worthy of God's blessings. Sinners are "justified by faith apart from works of law," declares Paul. God himself lifts the curse, and in that gives his blessings, "through the redemption that is in Christ Jesus." Here, indeed, Paul sets forth what he believes to be the heart of the Gospel in Jesus Christ.

Matthew 7:21-27 (R, E); 7:(15-20), 21-29 (L); 7:21-29 (C)

The conclusion of the Sermon on the Mount declares that Jesus expects his teachings to be learned and obeyed by those who claim to be his disciples. The faithful are required to do "the will of my Father who is in heaven," not to win salvation, Paul would say, but as a response to God's mercy in Christ. Here, Jesus is really talking about the final blessing that can be given to people, eternal life, because he speaks of "that day" — the "day" of his return and the judgment that will bring upon all humans who have ever lived. On the other hand, on "that day," those who have not kept the teachings of Jesus Christ will be expelled from the kingdom of the Lord God. The little parable about the wise man who builds his house upon the rock, and the foolish man who builds his house upon the sand, sums up the Old Testament reading as well as it brings closure to Jesus' last lesson in the Sermon on the Mount. The conclusion of this reading indicates that the people who heard Jesus' teachings were aware that what he said was to be taken seriously, because it came from God himself through Jesus.

Sermon suggestions:

Matthew 7:21-27, 21-29 over against the second reading, Romans 3:21-25a, 27-28 — "Building on the Rock."

"The House on the Rock" is a tourist attraction in Wisconsin that is really worth seeing. It is the epitome of Jesus' teaching; there is no way that floods can reach it and destroy it, because it is built on a high crag, many feet above the ground. The architect who designed and built it must have been a disciple of Frank Lloyd Wright, because it seems to be integral to the rock itself. The "house" is part of a complex which includes a fascinating museum and the usual souvenir shops and restaurant. It takes about a full day to see all that is offered in conjunction with "the House on the Rock." But the "house" is the central piece in the buildings and exhibits that are there. I suspect that if Jesus were living today, he would want to see it. It is his "house on the rock" par excellence. It is the "castle" of the architect who built it; and it should stand as long as the rock itself.

1. *All human beings build "sand castles"* — because they have disobeyed God's commandments rather than houses that are "built upon rock" by perfect obedience to the precepts of the Lord. Paul puts it so clearly: "all have sinned and fall short of the glory of God." No one, save Jesus Christ, is able to keep the law perfectly.

2. *"Sand castles" are doomed to fall* and be completely destroyed, even before they are built; the flood of the incoming tide — for they are usually built on beaches — quickly washes them away and they disappear forever. No matter how carefully they are designed and built, they will not stand very long. Sinners are far from the kingdom of God and have no hope of belonging to it by themselves.

3. *Castles built on rock alone will stand forever.* That "rock" is faith in Jesus Christ, believing that he is the Lord and Savior of the world, and living a life of obedient service to him and all people in the world. Good works and the effort to fulfill the law — to be perfect, as Jesus commands — are the expression of faith in Christ, and not an attempt to earn God's ultimate blessings for ourselves.

4. Build castles, but build them on the rock alone, and through Christ they will stand forever.

Deuteronomy 11:18-21, 26-28 — "Imprinted on the Heart."

Just the other day, when I was watching a professional football game, I saw a modern "phylactery" being used by, of all things, an athlete. The quarterback of the one team was a "rookie," and was playing his first regular season game. The announcers discovered the "phylactery" strapped to the left wrist of the quarterback. It wasn't the four excerpts from the Torah; it wasn't scripture, at all, and it surely wasn't a life-plan from God, spelling out the essentials of the faith, but it was a game-plan, listing the numbers and sequence of the different plays that the quarterback was to use as necessary during the football game. The television camera, on one occasion, took a close-up of the "football phylactery" so that the viewing audience could see it and comprehend how complex it really was. The quarterback was expected to follow the game-plan which, theoretically, would offer a way of winning the football game.

1. God intends that his commandments — and those of Jesus, too — should be written on the hearts of his people, permanently engraved so as to show them how to live as the people of God.

2. Dependence upon "phylacteries" . in the form of empty religious rituals, shallow "spiritual" exercises, or reliance on knowledge — gains absolutely nothing in the kingdom of God. "Surface faith," which is only skin-deep, as it were, avails nothing but rejection by God.

3. God has used a cross to write upon our hearts — and through his Spirit he gives and bolsters our faith so that we can take his commandments seriously and live them faithfully, as new creatures, in this life.

Genesis 12:1-9 — "The Father of All Families."

1. *A call and a promise.* God called Abram and promised to make his name great.

2. *The purpose of the call.* God said that Abram would be a blessing to all families. Jew and Christian would call him Father Abraham. We do so today.

3. *Unquestioned obedience.* That's how it was between God and Abram. He knew that God was the only God, and was his God, and was to be obeyed without question. Do we know and believe as much about God as did Abram?

4. *Journeying south.* Abram trusted God; he and his family went where God told them to go, claiming the land that God had promised to him and his offspring. Christ has taught us again to love and trust God — through his cross.

Romans 3:21-25a, 27-28, or Romans 3:21-28 — "Now — Now — Now."

Paul not only understood the gospel, but he also wrote and preached it from a proper theological perspective; God saves his people by faith alone, not by the works of the law.

1. When the time was right, God took action to save his people from sin and death. He did so through the incarnation, death, and resurrection of his Son, Jesus Christ.

2. He had to, because all people have sinned and "fall short of the glory of God." Not one person is able to save himself/herself. Without the cross of Christ, all persons are condemned to death and separation from God forever.

3. Faith in Christ is our only hope of salvation — only he can save us, and he has done just that. He has won the kingdom for us, and he even helps us to claim it through the power of the Holy Spirit.

4. Thank God for his gifts of grace in Jesus Christ — faith and hope and love — every day and every way that you/we can.

The Third Sunday after Pentecost
Tenth Sunday in Ordinary Time
Proper 5

Roman Catholic	Hosea 6:3-6	Romans 4:18-25	Matthew 9:9-13
Episcopal	Hosea 6:3-6	Romans 4:18-25	Matthew 9:9-13
Lutheran	Hosea 5:15—6:6	Romans 4:18-25	Matthew 9:9-13
Common	Genesis 22:1-18	Romans 4:13-18	Matthew 9:9-13

The church year theological clue

The broad, eschatological framework of the church year provides the only clue to the theme for worship and preaching on the Third Sunday after Pentecost. God's promise to bless all those who keep his commandments continues to be announced by the biblical elements assigned to the propers of this Sunday. The Gospel for the Day illustrates, as part of its theme, one example of complete and total adherence to the commands of Christ; when Jesus said, "Follow me," to Matthew, he meant it — so did Matthew, and he immediately obeyed the Lord.

The Prayer of the Day — This prayer, which was assigned to the First Sunday after Trinity in some of the pre-Vatican II propers, has been modernized and rewritten, but it retains much of the flavor of the original collect. "Trust in thee (God)" has been changed to "hope in you," reflecting the eschatological stance of the entire church year and, particularly, the Pentecost cycle/season. The petition asks for "the help of your grace," ("because in the weakness of our mortal nature we can do nothing good without you") so that we might please God in "will and deed" by keeping his commandments. The grace note of the gospel is clearly articulated in this lovely Prayer of the Day.

The Psalm of the Day — Psalm 50:1, 8, 12-15 (R); 50:1-15 (L); 50:1-24 (E) — This psalm, written by one called Asaph, spells out how God has spoken and revealed himself to his people, declaring, "Gather before me my loyal followers, those who have made a covenant with me and sealed it with sacrifice." God is not pleased by the ritualism of Hebrew worship with its animal sacrifices and burnt offerings; the earth and everything in it are God's — his for the taking ("If I were hungry, I would not tell you, for the whole world is mine and all that is in it."). But God is pleased by true worship — the utter dependence of people upon the Lord their God and the self-sacrifices they made — and the psalm commands: "Offer to God a sacrifice of thanksgiving and *make good your vows* to the Most High." A promise concludes the portions of this psalm used by the several liturgical churches in their worship: "Call upon me in the day of trouble; I will deliver you (he has, in Jesus Christ!), and you shall honor me" — by your obedience and keeping of the covenant, the psalm suggests.

The Psalm Prayer (LBW)

> *Heavenly Father, because Jesus your servant became obedient unto death, his sacrifice was greater than all the holocausts of old. Accept the sacrifice of praise we offer you through him, and help us show the effects of it in our lives by striving to do your will, until our whole life becomes adoration in spirit and truth; through your Son, Jesus Christ our Lord.*

Psalm 13 (C) — The psalmist asks four "how long" questions to God. How long: "will you forget me?"; "will you hide your face from me?"; "shall I have perplexity in my mind, and grief in my heart?"; "shall my enemy triumph over me?" He pleads, "Look upon me and answer me, O Lord my God,'' asking God to give him new life and vindication before his enemies. Nevertheless, the last two verses of this brief psalm overshadow his earlier lament, as the psalmist speaks of his trust in God, the joy he knows because God *has* helped him, and, finally, he sings praises to God for his kindness and mercy: ''I will sing to the Lord, for he has dealt with me richly; I will praise the name of the Lord Most High.''

The readings:

Genesis 22:1-18 (C)

This reading finds ''multiple use'' in the various lectionaries of the churches. It is read annually as one of the Old Testament selections of the Easter Vigil, and is assigned to the First Sunday in the Lutheran lectionary, Series B, and to the Second Sunday in Lent in Roman Catholic and Episcopalian scripture lists for Year B. The Common lectionary assigns Genesis 9:8-17 to the First Sunday in Lent, Genesis 17:1-10, 15-19 to the Second Sunday in Lent, preferring to place this reading in Pentecost as the second of the five readings from Genesis. It tells the familiar — and powerful — and *near-gospel* story of the sacrifice by Abraham of his son, Isaac. Abraham passed God's test when the Lord God commanded him to take his son to the ''land of Moriah'' and offer him there as a burnt offering; he was ready to plunge the knife into his son's breast when God intervened, commended him for his absolute obedience, and provided a ram for the burnt offering. In the gospel story, God does not intervene and the Son himself actually becomes the sacrifice offered by God — to God the Father — for the sins of the world.

Hosea 5:15—6:6 (E, L); 6:3-6 (R)

The last verse of Hosea 5 establishes the situation, in the context of the gospel, that the church is in; Jesus has ''returned to his dwelling place'' — God's right hand — and will remain there until the time when ''they acknowledge their guilt and seek my face, and in their distress they seek me.'' Israel knew the nature and character of God and could say, with Hosea:

> *Come, let us return to the Lord; for he has torn, that he may heal us; he has stricken, and he will bind us up. After two days he will revive us; on the third day he will raise us up, that we may live before him.*

This, the experience of the children of the covenant, has been repeated in the history of the Christian Church, not only in the sacrifices of the martyrs, but in the response of ordinary people to pain and suffering. ''Fickle faith,'' like that of Judah, brings down God's wrath and judgment. God desires — from Hebrew and Christian alike — ''steadfast love and not sacrifice, the knowledge of God, rather than burnt offerings.''

Romans 4:18-25

Paul was thoroughly convinced that God is a powerful God, able to do all that he promised to his people — even able to raise Jesus Christ from the dead. His belief in the ability of God to do what he said he would do was not based upon wishful thinking or empty flights of fancy; it was grounded in the past experience of the Hebrews with God, and, in this passage, on the promise God made to Abraham that he and Sarah would have a son in their old age. God took a seemingly impossible situation and turned it completely around in the conception and birth of Isaac. Thus, Paul supports his theological concept of the justification by faith alone; God is one who does those things for people which they cannot do for themselves, including reconciliation with himself and new life in the death and resurrection of Jesus Christ.

Matthew 9:9-13

All of the lectionaries bypass the eighth chapter of St. Matthew and move from Matthew 7:27 to Matthew 9:9. The apparent reason is that the church is eager to develop the story of the calling of the disciples instead of dealing with the five specific miracles listed and the "many cures" also mentioned in chapter eight, as well as the healing of the paralytic in chapter nine. It could be that the church didn't want to deal with the miracles that the Gospel says Jesus actually performed on the sick, the handicapped, and even on nature itself (stilling the storm). One could make an argument that these should be included, partly because they are reported in the Gospels, but also because — over against Romans 4 — God has done miraculous works, of which the chief display of God's amazing and miraculous power is the resurrection of Jesus Christ. Without that miracle, there would be no risen Lord to believe in!

Nevertheless, the lectionaries all move to Matthew 9:9, which tells the story of Jesus' calling of the tax collector, Matthew, to follow him. He did — immediately! That really shook up the Pharisees; they wondered about Jesus' intelligence and his wisdom. He didn't call a single Pharisee to become a disciple, but he called a despised tax-collector; that was a blatant insult. And when Jesus followed up that insult with another — by accepting an invitation to eat with tax collectors and other sinners — it was too much for the Pharisees. They simply had to "put him on the spot" by asking his disciples, who in turn must have asked him, "Why?" The final insult came in Jesus' answer:

> *Those who are well have no need of a physician, but those who are sick. Go and learn what this means, "I desire mercy, and not sacrifice." For I came not to call the righteous, but sinners.*

To the Pharisees, it must have appeared that Jesus had declared war on them, and from that point on in the gospel story they set out to win the battle by destroying him.

Sermon suggestions:

Matthew 9:9-13 — "Why me, Lord?"

Most of us, when friends learned that we were going to prepare for the ministry, have been greeted by statements of surprise, even amazement. "You are going to become a minister of the Gospel? You're going to be a preacher?" And most of us have been asked an accompanying question, "Why? What made you decide to become a pastor?" The answers to that question may be numerous, but they are all variations of one reply, "God has called me to the ministry of his church." Had anyone asked Matthew why he abandoned his lucrative job as a tax collector to follow Jesus, he could only have said one thing: "Jesus said, 'Follow me.' " He did.

1. *God's call is pure grace.* To be a minister of the Gospel of Jesus Christ — lay minister or ordained pastor — is always an act of grace on the part of God. Human beings never choose or decide by themselves to be servants of God; they simply obey and respond to his call.

2. Christ's choosing of Matthew demonstrates God's intention. Jesus came to save sinners. That's why he mingled with them, even accepted invitations to their homes. Shouldn't that give us encouragement and hope?

3. *Come, follow Christ, and do the work of the kingdom.* Christians who answer the call of the Lord and dare to follow him are to reach out for the lost and the lonely, the sick and the suffering, for all of the outcasts and sinners — in the name of Jesus.

4. *Jesus himself commands us to do this.* Love for God through Jesus Christ that expresses itself in service to humanity is what Jesus demands of those who call him Lord. He doesn't tell us why he calls us, but simply says to you and me, "Follow me!" — and he means it.

Genesis 22:1-18 — "The Supreme Sacrifice."

One of the most astounding stories of our time appeared in newspapers in Italy in 1972. Joseph Kramer, a Jew, gave a Torah scroll to a synagogue in Tel Aviv and dedicated it to his sixteen month old son, David, who had died in Latvia during World War II. Kramer broke down and cried during the ceremony — and with good reason. Almost three decades before, while he was living in Latvia, he had fashioned a bunker beneath his home for the express purpose of hiding Jews from the invading Nazi army. When the Nazis entered his town, he and his wife, their young son, and forty-five of their Jewish friends and neighbors, were hidden in the bunker. The noise of tanks and the tramping sounds of the foot-soldiers frightened the baby; Kramer and his wife did everything they could to calm the child and stop its crying, which was so loud and near-hysterical that the Nazis might have heard it and found the bunker. Desperate, Joseph Kramer did the only thing that he could do to save all those people; he put his hand across the nose and mouth of the child and smothered him. That's why he broke down when the scroll was dedicated in Tel Aviv. All of those in the bunker escaped, and some were there that day in Tel Aviv. This much is sure — none of them forgot the sacrifice that Joseph Kramer had made to save them; he must have seemed like Abraham offering Isaac to God — with the difference that Kramer completed the sacrifice of his son for the sake of others. Kramer's act was the very act of a loving God, to Christians, who gave his only-begotten Son to die for the salvation and survival of all people in the world.

1. *Unbelievable obedience.* The story of Abraham and Isaac — and a brush with death.
2. *Fantastic faith.* "God himself will provide the sacrifice." (He didn't realize what he was saying, did he? The cross tells us that.)
3. *Abundant grace.* At the last moment, God stopped the sacrifice Abraham was about to make in the death of Isaac and provided a lamb for the burnt offering. In the Gospels, of course, God's Son, the Lamb of God, becomes the sacrifice which saves us all from death. (See Bass [with Fred Kemper] *You Are My Beloved,* Concordia, for a complete sermon, "The Incredible Sacrifice," on this text.)

Hosea 5:15—6:6 — "Sacrifice — Plus . . . ."

The Joseph Kramer story has deeper significance to it than the obvious dedication of a memorial to a son who had been dead a long time; it tells the tale of a man who had done a terrible thing when God didn't seem able to help him and his friends, but who still loves God! Kramer didn't ask, "Where were you, Lord, when I needed you?" And while the deed haunted him for three decades and what he did would be in his sub-conscious mind as long as he lived, he didn't blame God for what happened; he still loved and trusted God. Awful as his action was in the bunker when he smothered his son, the gift of the Torah in memory of his son must have pleased God because it answered his word given through Hosea. Joseph Kramer not only continued to love God — "For I desire steadfast love and not sacrifice, the knowledge of God, rather than burnt offerings" — He also turned to him to be healed. He was still the servant of the Lord God.

1. *God heals every wound.* Ours is to believe it, love him, turn to him, and trust him.
2. *Love for God tends to dry up.* Hosea says it is like a "morning cloud" or the "dew that goes away early." Fickle faith is a deterrent to love and obedience.

3. *Keep our love steadfast, our faith strong.* We cannot love God as we should, nor can we live out his commandments by ourselves. Help us to believe, to love, to obey, and to live as your servants, O Lord!

Romans 4:18-25 — "The Patriarch's Lesson."

1. *Believe in God despite everything.* He is a God of mercy, love, and compassion — and has power to help and heal.

2. *Love God with all your heart.* That's what God desires of us.

3. *Entrust him with your life.* Then we can really be his obedient servants in the world.

4. *Cling to him* — to the cross — as long as you live. It's the only hope of salvation we have.

The Fourth Sunday after Pentecost
Eleventh Sunday in Ordinary Time
Proper 6

Roman Catholic	Exodus 19:2-6a	Romans 5:6-11	Matthew 9:36—10:8
Episcopal	Exodus 19:2-6a	Romans 5:6-11	Matthew 9:35—10:8
Lutheran	Exodus 19:2-8a	Romans 5:6-11	Matthew 9:35—10:8
Common	Genesis 25:19-34	Romans 5:6-11	Matthew 9:35—10:8

The church year theological clue

The eschatological stance of the church year continues to throw its theological aura around the assigned readings for the day. It insists that the call to the ministry of the church and the proclamation of the gospel began with the calling and naming of the disciples, and that the church must establish evangelism as its outward thrust and its reach into the world. The church is evangelical by the work and definition accorded it by Jesus Christ; its business is the Word of God, and particularly the good news, the Gospel of our Lord.

The Prayer of the Day (LBW) — The Gospel for the Day is responsible for the content of this prayer. It defines the church as "a new company of priests," whom God has created and called "to bear witness to the Gospel." The "priesthood of all believers" rests on this evangelical principle; not only may all of the faithful "approach the mercyseat" of God in prayer and devotion, but they also are charged with responsibility for witnessing and proclaiming the gospel in and to the world. Therefore, the prayer's petition asks God, "Enable us to be faithful to our calling to make known your promises to all the world."

The Psalm of the Day — Psalm 100 (R, E, L) — The Good Shepherd/Sheep theme is at the heart of this psalm: "Know this: The Lord himself is God; . . . we are his people and the sheep of his pasture," which suggests that it could be used on several other Sundays, too, especially as it relates to the joy and thanksgiving of the people of God. But it is the first part of the psalm that stands out in sharp relief over against the Gospel for the Day: ". . . serve the Lord with gladness and come before his presence with a song." A Gospel theme — "For the Lord is good; his mercy is everlasting; and his faithfulness endures from age to age" — has a definite eschatological dimension built into it, so that it sounds the theological motif of the Pentecost cycle/season.

The Psalm Prayer

> *God our Father, you have created us as your people and you sustain us with your hand. Help us always to give you thanks, for you alone are worthy of thanksgiving and praise and honor now and forever.*

Psalm 46 (C) — The key is in the seventh verse, "The God of Jacob is our refuge," which clearly makes contact with the first reading, Genesis 25:19-34. See the commentary on this psalm for Reformation Sunday (L) for more detailed discussion of it.

The readings:

Genesis 25:19-34 (C)

This particular story finds no place in the lectionaries of the other churches. It is the familiar story of the birth and early life of Esau and Jacob. That they were twins cannot be in doubt,

192

nor is it possible to conclude that they were identical twins; far from it, because they were as different as day and night. Isaac's wife, Rebekah, was barren for the first twenty years of their marriage, and this prompted Isaac to pray to God for the birth of a son. His prayers were answered — with twins, who "struggled with one another" in their mother's womb, according to the story. Esau was the first-born; he was covered with red hair and grew up loving the outdoors and becoming a skillful hunter. Jacob was born "with his hand grasping his brother's heel;" he was quiet, a man who loved to stay at home — and definitely "mother's boy." Isaac preferred Esau over Jacob; he was his kind of child. But, while they were still young, Jacob obtained Esau's birthright from him in exchange for a bowl of lentil soup. "That was all Esau cared for his birthright," the story teller informs us. A bittersweet story — that of Esau and Jacob — begins this way.

Exodus 19:2-8a (E, L); 19:2-6 (R)

For the first time, Moses goes up Mt. Sinai to be with God, who instructs him to remind the people of Israel what he did to the Egyptians when they attempted to foil the exodus of the Israelites, and how he "bore them (the Israelites) on eagles' wings and brought you to myself." Without the help of the Lord God, they would still be in Egypt, or they would be dead. And once more, Moses hears God call for obedience to his "voice" and the keeping of his covenant, the terms by which they would be God's "possession" among all peoples. Moses went to the elders and the people and gave them the message that God had delivered to him, and the people and their leaders promised to obey God and keep the covenant he made with them. The connection with the Gospel for the Day comes in verse 6, ". . . you shall be to me a kingdom of priests and a holy nation."

Romans 5:6-11

Paul understood the gospel in terms of a God who loved his unlovable creatures, despite their sin and waywardness; that was nothing short of amazing to him. This is his way of saying what John, later, spelled out in his gospel (3:16), "God so loved the world that he gave his only begotten Son . . . ." Through his death, all have been justified and live in hope of spending eternity in the company of God. The death of Jesus, the Son of God, has reconciled us to God, and this makes it possible to live in the hope and expectation of belonging forever to the kingdom of God. This is a brief, but very theologically important pericope; it has no thematic connection to the other readings.

Matthew 9:35—10:8

Jesus' early preaching, teaching, and healing ministry was extremely successful; he attracted great crowds of people and, as he surveyed their size, Jesus realized that there was more to do than any one man — even he — could possibly do. He pointed this out to the disciples, adding, "The harvest is plentiful, but the laborers are few; pray therefore the Lord of the harvest to send out laborers into his harvest." Without any more warning than that, the disciples were assigned to the first missionary effort; evangelism was born there and then. First, they were *called,* then they were given *authority* to cast out unclean spirits, to heal every disease and every infirmity. Now they were becoming *active participants* — not merely learners — in the ministry of Jesus here on earth. After Matthew names the twelve, listing Simon Peter and Andrew first and Judas Iscariot, "who betrayed him," last, he sent them out with a charge: "Go nowhere among the Gentiles, and enter no town of the Samaritans, but go rather to the lost sheep of the house of Israel." And, lastly, he "ordained" them to preach the good news, "And preach as you go, saying, 'The kingdom of heaven is at hand.' " Their preaching and healing ministries were to go hand in hand. And they were not to charge for their services, because they were only giving what had been given freely to them by their Lord. (Verses 9 and 10, with their injunction to take no provisions with them, but to allow — even expect — themselves to be supported by the people to whom they ministered in the name of Jesus, have been omitted, for some unknown reason.)

Sermon suggestions:

Matthew 9:35—10:7 — "The Persistent Call."

Were it not for the fact that women and older persons are accepting the call of Christ to prepare for ordained ministry, enrollment at theological seminaries in America might well be at an all-time low. Women now comprise slightly over fifty-one percent of the student body at one Lutheran seminary; second career students comprise more than thirty-five percent of the student bodies in several theological institutions, fifty percent in one. A typical near-fifty-year-old student, when asked about his decision to become a pastor, responded, "I have been wrestling with the call to the ministry almost all of my life. I finally decided that the time had come to do something about it." Obviously, the traditional source of students for the ordained ministry of the church — young men, who have just been graduated from college or university — has been drying up. Take away the women and older men and women from seminary student rosters and the church would probably be facing a very severe shortage of clergy in the next few years. The church has to be thankful for those who are answering the call to ministry, but it must ask questions and find the reasons why many persons, who ought to be applying to seminaries, are not doing so.

1. Ministry and evangelism are the business of the church. That's the way that Jesus determined that it had to be; believers had to witness and preach the good news so that the Church could become a living, growing, celebrating reality in the world. Evangelism is the never-ending business of the church, not merely another program to be planned, followed for awhile, and then put on the shelf. Every believer is called — in baptism — to be an evangelist!

2. Jesus' call to ordained ministry is a command, not merely a career choice. The Twelve, who followed the Lord and became the nucleus, the leaders, of the church, were not given a choice by Jesus when he called them to ministry. Jesus sent them out, charging them to preach to the "house of Israel," "The kingdom of heaven is at hand." Jesus ordered them to go — and they did — teaching, healing, and preaching as Jesus himself had done. Some go, some do not. Ordained leaders are critical to the mission of the church.

3. Young men and women are being called by Christ to the ordained ministry of the church. Why do many refuse to accept Jesus call, his command? Is the call to the things of the world stronger than the call to the business of proclaiming the good news to the world? (Jim Fuller, Staff Writer for the Minneapolis *Star Tribune*, wrote an article, "Will retirement be a dream come true?" [September 18, 1988] about today's baby boomers. He quotes Mark Jares, a Minneapolis investment advisor, who says, "Baby boomers have the attitude that they should have the cars, the $300,000 houses, the clothes every day, that it's not something they should wait for, or have to give up when they retire." They want what the world has to offer — *now*. A survey in California last year, showed that forty-six percent of the baby boomers expect to retire before they are sixty, another seventeen percent want to retire before they are fifty. All want to have as much and do as much after retirement as they do now. Is this the main reason for the decline in seminary enrollment by the baby boomers? Could the problem be that most of us have become materialists?

4. The concerted effort of the church, lay ministers, as well as ordained ministers, is required to evangelize the world. When all believers not only comprehend that everyone is an evangelist — and that they have no choice in the matter — evangelism will become the

main business of the church, as it should be, and the gospel will be a force to be reckoned with by the entire world. And, in the process, the faithful will discover the eternal riches of the kingdom of heaven.

Genesis 25:19-34 (C) — "The Buy-out of a Birthright."

1. *The backward twins.* Jacob and Esau were born in the wrong order; Jacob should have been born first, because he appreciated Esau's birthright more than did Esau.

2. *A birthright for a full belly.* Esau was easy to deceive because he thought more of his stomach, his hunger, than he did of his birthright, so he sold it to Jacob for a bowl of lentil soup.

3. *A buy-out by the world.* The "Life is just a bowl of cherries" attitude that many of us pursue results in the danger of a complete sell-out of our baptismal birthright, the kingdom of heaven. Can the world buy out our claim to the kingdom?

4. *The kingdom-birthright is God's gift to everyone.* Appreciate it, claim it, and cling to it in true faith forever.

Exodus 19:2-8a — (R, E, L) — "A Necessary Reminder."

1. *The ascent to Mt. Sinai.* Moses needed to reconnoiter with God, not to survey the surrounding terrain. A great human leader needed to go on a spiritual retreat — as all do, from time to time.

2. *The voice of the mountain — God.* God spoke to Moses, ordering him to remind the people that the Exodus succeeded because he put down the Egyptians. From that time right to the present day, the children of Israel have remembered and celebrated the Exodus. It is their most memorable feast.

3. Jesus said, "Do this in remembrance of me." And the church remembers another exodus — somewhere — every day of the year in the breaking of the bread.

4. An ever-lasting covenant. God made it with Israel, and Jesus makes a new covenant with us — in our baptism. Ours is to keep it and be kept by the maker of the covenant — forever.

Romans 5:6-11 — "The Bloody Reconciliation."

1. Reconciliation between God and humanity, required a bloody sacrifice. The powerful grip of sin upon the human race had to be broken. God had to be satisfied that this had happened — through a perfect sacrifice, Jesus Christ.

2. It is always Good Friday, as well as Easter, for the church. Cecil Alexander's hymn, "There is a Green Hill Far Away," has been retained for Holy Week in the LBW, but it was reduced to three verses by the deletion of the last two verses. This is one of them:

> *There was no other good enough,*
> *To pay the price of sin,*
> *He only could unlock the gate*
> *Of heaven, and let us in.*

3. Our salvation was won wholly by the blood of Jesus. Ours is to know this, to believe it, and to accept it with thanksgiving, "This is my blood, shed for many for the forgiveness of sins."

4. We rejoice and live in the miracle of his love. He loved God and us enough to die to accomplish the reconciliation of God and his people. The last verse of Alexander's hymn announces:

> *O dearly, dearly has he loved,*
> *And we must love him too,*
> *And trust in his redeeming Blood*
> *And try his works to do.*

The Fifth Sunday after Pentecost
Twelfth Sunday in Ordinary Time
Proper 7

Roman Catholic	Jeremiah 20:10-13	Romans 5:12-15	Matthew 10:26-33
Episcopal	Jeremiah 20:7-13	Romans 5:15b-19	Matthew 10:(16-23) 24-33
Lutheran	Jeremiah 20:7-13	Romans 5:12-15	Matthew 10:24-33
Common	Genesis 28:10-17	Romans 5:12-19	Matthew 10:24-33

The church year theological clue

Only the name of this Sunday, the Fifth Sunday after Pentecost, gives any theological clue from the church year; the church is moving eschatologically and continues to anticipate the last times and the return of Christ. The Pentecost cycle/season is roughly one-fifth completed today, so there's a long way to go, as well as a long time to wait for the eschaton. The business of the church continues to be proclaiming "the Lord's death" — in worship, preaching, witnessing, and working — until he "comes again," as he said he would.

The Prayer of the Day (LBW) — Liturgical revision has completely overhauled the collect for this Sunday (perhaps it was thought to be unrealistic, as well as theologically inept: "Grant . . . that the course of this world may be so peaceably ordered by thy governance, that thy church may joyfully serve thee in all godly quietness"). The prayer now is realistic ("storms rage about us and cause us to be afraid") and dependent upon God ("Rescue your people from despair, deliver your sons and daughters from fear, and preserve us all from unbelief"). It catches the theological flavor of Pentecost and, in particular, speaks to God on behalf of those who hear — and would respond to — Christ's instructions in the Gospel for the Day.

The Psalm of the Day — Psalm 69:1-18 (E); 69:1-20 (L); 69:7-9, 13, 16, 32-34 (R) — A song of the passion that is considered to be second only to Psalm 22 in the Psalter. It finds a response in the instructions that Jesus gives to the first apostles in the Gospel for the Day. Clearly, it could be put — parts of it, at least — in the mouths of many of the martyrs, who might have said:

> *Those who hate me without a cause are more than the hairs on my head; my lying foes who would destroy me are mighty . . . . Surely, for your sake have I suffered reproach, and shame has covered my face. I have become a stranger to my own kindred, an alien to my mother's children . . . . Those who sit at the gate murmur against me, and the drunkards make songs about me.*

Those who faced crucifixion, the headman's sword, or the stake could have prayed:

> *Hide not your face from your servant; be swift and answer me, for I am in distress. Draw near to me and redeem me; because of my enemies deliver me.*

There is a ring of confidence and true faith in God that runs through the psalm, and becomes the promise of victory, in the face of the anguish and suffering that the psalmist — and Jesus and the martyrs — endured on behalf of God.

The Psalm Prayer (LBW)

> *God our Father, you fulfilled the ancient prophesies in Christ's passover from death to life. Through the contemplation of his healing wounds, make us zealous for your Church and grateful for your love; through Jesus Christ our Lord.*

196

Psalm 91:1-10 (C) — "He shall deliver you from the snare of the hunter and from the deadly pestilence" is the key verse of this psalm. It is one of those psalms that many of us said, if not learned, in Sunday church school, maybe in this version (King James):

He that dwelleth in the secret place of the most High shall abide under the shadow of the Almighty. I will say of the Lord, He is my refuge and my fortress: my God; in him will I trust.

The readings:

Genesis 28:10-17 (C)

The LBW places this reading in the propers for the Second Sunday in Lent of Year/Series B; the Roman and Episcopal lectionaries omit it altogether from the Sunday lessons. It is the story of Jacob's journey from Beersheeba to Haran, with a "campout" under the stars at "a certain place." There Jacob had his dream about a ladder reaching from earth to the very heavens, with angels ascending and descending upon it. God "stood above it" and spoke to Jacob, promising him and his descendants the land on which he was lying. His descendants would multiply and be a blessing to all families on earth. And God also promised to go with him on his travels and bring him back safely to "this place." Jacob awakened from his dream and remembered the presence of the Lord; God had come to him and made a promise. His response has been recorded for all time: "Surely the Lord is in this place; and I did not know it . . . . How awesome is this place! This is none other than the house of God, and this is the gate of heaven."

Jeremiah 20:7-13 (L); 20:10-13 (R); 20:(16-23) 24-33 (E)

This could be called "The Lament of a Martyr," as it issues from Jeremiah's mouth as a result of his own persecution. Persecution became the lot of a prophets, because "the Word of the Lord," as delivered by the prophets — and later the preaching of the gospel in terms of repentance — was greeted by opposition and outright rejection of both message and prophet. This reading complements the Gospel for the Day, in which Jesus warns the disciples about the problems they will encounter when they preach the good news to the house of Israel. The "woe is me, if I preach not the gospel" is in Jeremiah's lament: "If I say, 'I will not mention him, or speak any more in his name,' there is in my heart as it were a burning fire shut up in my bones." That sort of evangelical zeal always got the apostles into serious trouble wherever they went; Paul, in particular, experienced the wrath of people who were so hard-hearted that they refused to receive the good news about Jesus Christ. God began to recruit the "noble army of martyrs" in the days of the Old Testament prophets, and that any army grew by leaps and bounds with the beginning of the Christian era.

Romans 5:12-15

For all practical purposes, this is one of those rare occasions on which a passage of scripture is read twice in one year. The first reading for the First Sunday in Lent is Romans 5:12 (13-16) 17-19; the longer reading, which includes verses 13-16, insures that the lesson would be read in Lent and in Pentecost, which is not all bad, because it has an extremely important theological message. Sin came into the world through one man's — Adam's — disobedience, and with it came death (hence, the appropriateness of this reading for Lent 1, "remember, you are dust, and unto dust you shall return"). And although sin was not "counted" until the giving of the Law, death reigned "from Adam to Moses," because, like Adam, "all have sinned and fall short of the glory of God." God's free gift in Jesus Christ reversed the course of sin and death; by the one man sin and death were overcome and "the free gift in the grace of that one man Jesus Christ abounded for many." For Paul, the gospel is the liberating force that frees us from the law, which can only condemn people to death; the gospel, therefore, and not the law, is the means of salvation that God has given to the world in Jesus Christ. God's grace is abundantly sufficient to wipe out all of our sins — and death!

Matthew 10:26-33

Jesus continues his charge to the disciples who are about to begin their apostolic ministry. He had to warn them about the opposition and outright persecution that they would experience when they attempted to preach the gospel to Israel. They would be among the first followers of Jesus to suffer death for their bold witness to the faith; they were the first recruits in "the noble army of martyrs" — and Jesus wanted them to know that they had nothing to fear. God, he was telling them, would never forget them; they were precious to him and, he told them, "even the hairs on your head are all numbered." His final word to them was simply that "every one who acknowledges me before men, I also will acknowledge before my Father who is in heaven." He also added a warning: ". . . whoever denies me before men, I also will deny before my Father who is in heaven." Tradition has it that eleven of the twelve were faithful — ten as martyrs and one, John, as a "confessor," who faced persecution, was willing to die, but was spared a martyr's death and lived long enough to die from natural causes.

Sermon suggestions:

Matthew 10:26-33 — "Marching Orders."

In less than two weeks, my wife and I will attend a high school class reunion; there is, usually, nothing special about that. This one is special, partly because half a century has gone by since my classmates and I were graduated from a suburban Philadelphia high school; many of them died, beginning with World War II, and can't attend. It will be special for me for the usual reasons, but also for a kind of hidden agenda; my wife and I will be staying in a motel with several of our classmates, one of whom I have not seen for over thirty years. This man was the Air Force colonel who led the rescue mission that was sent to bury the missionaries who were killed in the attack by the Auca Indians in South America almost thirty years ago. I intend to ask him for his story about the Aucas and the missionaries, who gave their lives as they attempted to make contact with the Aucas in order to preach the gospel to them. It is one of those stories which reminds us that the proclamation of the gospel continues to be met with distrust, hostility, and violent action — now, just as Jesus predicted it would in the first century A.D.

1. All people — of every age — need to hear the gospel of Jesus Christ. Hence, Jesus continues to give "marching order" to the faithful, commanding the church to preach the Word to all the world.

2. Resistance to the word and spirit is to be expected. Some people refuse to hear and believe, because they are enemies of God and have no faith in Jesus Christ. Most of us have something of Augustine in us, "make me a Christian, Lord, but not yet." Opposition by indifference may be the more rampant form of resistance to the gospel today.

3. Boldness is required of the church that claims to be apostolic in its creeds and actions. Jesus continues to assure his followers, who obey his command to go and preach and minister in his name, that they have nothing to fear. God, who is with them, will be faithful and receive them into eternal life.

198

4. The bold, for Christ, will overcome! God will see to that, for his will is that all shall be saved through the death and resurrection of Jesus Christ. In the end, all people on earth will have the opportunity to hear the gospel, to believe, and be saved. And the martyrs, who line the way to the very gate of heaven, will — with Bunyan — be singing, "Come in! Come in! Eternal glory you shall win."

Genesis 28:10-17 — "Ceiling Zero."

The clouds must have been very low — ceiling zero — or the ladder was very long in Jacob's dream, if the angels were ascending and descending between earth and heaven. What happened to their wings? Angels always are pictured with wings, aren't they? Are they only decorative? Or is there a species of "wingless angels?" These must have been rather common angels, nothing like the six-winged seraphs, the highest of the nine orders of angels spoken of in the Bible. Imagine, angels that had to climb from earth to heaven, from heaven to earth!

1. The angels were delivering a message to Jacob. They are primarily messengers, and in the Bible they often came to people in their dreams. They were trying to make Jacob aware of the presence of the Lord God.

2. God stood at the top of the ladder and spoke to Jacob: "I am the Lord, the God of Abraham your father and the God of Isaac . . . ." According to Genesis, God spoke for himself, instead of employing angels to convey his message to Jacob, and made his "land promise" to him and his descendants. God is still able to speak for himself — through his everlasting word.

3. Jacob really heard what God had to say! That's why he could acknowledge the presence of God; heaven was really close to the earth when he awakened from that "ceiling zero" kind of dream, and he declared, "Surely the Lord is in this place; and I did not know it."

4. Jesus made "ceiling zero" a reality for all people. Didn't he say, "he that has seen me has seen the Father"? And he has replaced the ladder with a cross, from which he was removed, placed in a grave — dead and buried — only to rise again on the third day. Indeed, in the cross, Jesus brought God down to earth so that we can say with Jacob, "This is none other than the house of God, and this is the gate of heaven."

Jeremiah 20:7-13 (E, L); 20:10-13 (R) —"The Lot of the Prophets."

All Christian preaching, be it missionary or pastoral, has to have a prophetic element in it. To preach the gospel in such a way that people are called to repentance requires one to preach the law and, in that sense to preach prophetically. Preachers/prophets, Jeremiah could tell us from personal experience, will make enemies and will be persecuted; very few people want to be called "sinners," nor do many persons feel the need to repent of their sins and change their ways, especially if they think they are "good" and "godly" people. Jeremiah may have shaped Jesus' preaching about this, according to what he said to his disciples as they were about to embark upon their apostolic ministry of preaching the Word in the world. Opposition and persecution are the lot of prophets and preachers in every generation.

1. Evangelical witnesses will encounter resistance when they speak the good news to the world. This "goes with the territory" and should be expected by lay or ordained witnesses to the gospel.

2. Some will be wounded and killed, but more will be laughed at — especially today. It may take as much as fortitude and faith to face ridicule and scorn as it does to face a sure and painful death as a martyr. More than one person has felt as did Jeremiah, when he said, "I have become a laughingstock all the day; everyone mocks me." But not God, nor Jesus Christ.

3. Zeal for the word of the Lord consumes true disciples of the Lord. With Luther, we are compelled by the Spirit to declare, "My tongue is the pen of a ready writer" — because we just have to tell the story, regardless of the consequences.

4. All will be well for God's witnesses. He has promised to deliver us from "the hand of evildoers" — and he will. Praise the Lord!

Romans 5:12-15 (R, L); 5:12-19 (C); 5:15b-19 (E) — "One for All."

Jesus is the one who died to save all people; all are dependent upon him to reach and enter the kingdom of heaven. The *death* of Christ on the cross means *life* for all who believe and are baptized in the name of Father, Son, and Holy Spirit. Eternal life comes through one man, Jesus Christ.

1. Sin came into the world through disobedience — by one man, Adam, and one woman, Eve. With Adam and Eve, *all have sinned* — and die as a consequence of sin.

2. One man — Jesus — lived in perfect obedience — without sin — and died for it. He opened the gates of eternal life for all people by being "obedient unto death."

3. Grace reigns in this sinful world. The cross tells us so. Without Christ, the world can only destroy itself.

4. Receive God's gift — life in Jesus Christ — and live the new life of loving service expected of those who have been redeemed and saved by God himself.

The Sixth Sunday after Pentecost
Thirteenth Sunday in Ordinary Time
Proper 8

Roman Catholic	2 Kings 4:8-11, 14-16	Romans 6:3-4, 8-11	Matthew 10:37-42
Episcopal	Isaiah 2:10-17	Romans 6:3-11	Matthew 10:34-42
Lutheran	Jeremiah 28:5-9	Romans 6:1b-11	Matthew 10:34-42
Common	Genesis 32:22-32	Romans 6:3-11	Matthew 10:34-42

The church year theological clue

Beyond the natural progression of the Pentecost cycle/season, with its eschatological emphasis, there is no clear and definitive clue from the church year. The insertion of these particular readings within the theological framework of the church year does, however, tend to emphasize realized eschatology as much as it does any future eschatology. The latter, of course, is always present, if only in the Eucharist with its "as often as you eat this bread and drink this cup, you proclaim the Lord's death until he comes." The church is always waiting for the return of the Lord and must, in the meantime, be about the business of obeying his commandments and completing his mission in the world. The second reading and the Gospel for the Day bring the last things into sharp perspective on this Sunday.

The Prayer of the Day (LBW) — Another classic collect has been modernized in this Prayer of the Day simply by overhauling its language. In older sets of propers, the prayer was used in conjunction with Luke 5:1-11. (The tremendous catch of fish made by Peter and his companions at the direction of Jesus, followed by Peter's confession, "Depart from me, for I am a sinful man, O Lord." Once back to land, they heard Jesus say, "Follow me, and I will make you fishers of men.") The prayer fits the readings for the Sixth Sunday after Pentecost, too, as it points to the reward ("joys beyond understanding") of those who love Jesus enough to follow and serve him:

> *Pour into our hearts such love for you that, loving you above all things, we may obtain your promises, which exceed all that we can desire.*

The eschatological note is strongly suggested in this prayer.

The Psalm of the Day — Psalm 89:1-4, 15-18 (L); 89:1-2, 15-16, 17-18 (R); 89:1-18, or 89:1-4, 15-18 (E) — This psalm is cut up and inserted into the propers mainly because it is too long to be used as a responsory in the Sunday liturgy (there are fifty-two verses in it). It does respond to the closing theme of the Jeremiah reading, which has "messianic implications" in it ("As for the prophet who prophesies peace, when the word of that prophet comes to pass, then it will be known that the Lord has truly sent the prophet"). The psalm also describes the kind of king that the Lord God, out of his steadfast love and mercy, will provide for all people on earth. In this respect, it does build a paradoxical bridge to the Gospel for the Day, in which Jesus declares, "Do not think I have come to bring peace on earth; I have not come to bring peace, but a sword." At the same time, this reading is in the context of God's promise to provide a savior-king in the line of David; Jesus is that Promised One.

The Psalm Prayer (LBW)

> *Mighty God, in fulfillment of the promise made to David's descendants you established a lasting covenant through your firstborn Son. You anointed your servant Jesus with holy oil and raised him higher than all kings on earth. Remember your covenant, so that we who are signed with the blood of your Son may sing of your mercies forever; through your Son, Jesus Christ our Lord.*

Psalm 17:1-7, 15 (C) — This is another psalm that could have been quoted by Jesus in his suffering and passion on the cross: "Hear my plea of innocence, O Lord; give heed to my cry; listen to my prayer, which does not come from lying lips . . . ." He could have cried out: "I give no offense with my mouth as others do; I have heeded the words of your lips," and prayed, "Show me your marvelous lovingkindness, O Savior of those who take refuge at your right hand from those who rise up against them."

The readings:

Genesis 32:22-32 (C)

The Book of Common Prayer and *The Lutheran Book of Worship* appoint this reading for the Twenty-second Sunday after Pentecost in Year/Series C, but the Roman Catholic lectionary omits it altogether. It gives the account of Jacobs's all night wrestling match at "the ford of the Jabbok." The "stranger" who wrestled with him had to strike him in the hip, dislocating it, in the hope of overcoming Jacob, but Jacob hung on to the "man" and, disabled though he was, he would not give up his hold. The "one" who had been wrestling with Jacob had to plead, "Let me go, for the day is breaking," and had to "bless" Jacob, changing his name to Israel, one who "would prevail against men." The "night angel" refused to tell Jacob his name, nevertheless, Jacob was convinced that he had "seen God face-to-face," and he named the place Peniel. He might easily have repeated what he said on that other occasion, "This is none other than the house of God, and this is the gate of heaven."

2 Kings 4:8-11, 16-18 (R)

This is the tale, finally, of two miracles performed for a woman of Shunem, who had been kind to Elisha, first feeding him and then, with her husband, building a spare room on the roof of their home so that the prophet might have a place to stop over. The first miracle was in the birth of a son to the woman; the second, in a section of the story that was not told, was the resuscitation of the woman's dead son. God has the power to raise the dead, not merely as resuscitation, as in the case of Lazarus, but in the resurrection of Jesus Christ, which has been promised to all who have been baptized in Jesus Christ. This reading complements the second reading, Roman 6:2b-11, which speaks of the "newness to life," which believers receive in the sacrament of baptism.

Isaiah 2:10-17 (E)

Isaiah's vision of the "last times" is spelled out graphically in the second chapter of the book that bears his name. It is an eschatological vision, which sees the power of God unleashed in the world; the mighty will be brought down and the proud will be humbled. Nothing will be able to stand against the might of God. Peace will be established when the end comes; swords will be beaten into ploughshares when the reign of God takes effect in human hearts and people learn to obey the commands of God. "Yahweh alone will be exalted, on that day, and all idols thrown down."

Jeremiah 28:5-9, 18 (L)

Jeremiah's word to Hananiah, "spoken in the presence of the priests and all the people who were standing in the house of the Lord," was a response to Hananiah's prophecy of God's promise to "break the yoke of the king of Babylon" in two years. The precious liturgical vessels would be returned as well as the king's son and all of the exiles. Jeremiah declared that he hoped this would come to pass, but reminded them all that the prophets of the past had spoken of war, famine, and pestilence against "many countries and great kingdoms." He added, looking forward to the coming of the Messiah, "As for the prophet who prophesies peace, when the word of that prophet comes to pass, then it will be known that the Lord has truly sent the prophet.

Romans 6:1b-11 (L); 6:3-11 (R, E, C)

The Easter Vigil makes use of this pericope, with its exposition of baptism as Paul understood it, as the transitional reading of the vigil. What has been prophesied in the past has happened — the human race has been freed from the curse of sin, the gospel has negated the law, and the people of God live in hope. Baptism means that we are dead to sin; this has been accomplished in Christ once and for all, and is a past action. Baptism also looks to the future when resurrection will take place; it is eschatological. In the meantime, believers are to live the new life of obedience, given them as a gift of Christ in baptism, and this means that they must die daily to sin and rise to that new life every morning. Christ's claim upon us has been made permanent for "we have been marked with the cross of Christ forever."

Matthew 10:34-42 (E, L, C); 10:37-42 (R)

These verses, which contain two blocks of material with several themes running through them, conclude Jesus' charge to the disciples as they are about to embark on their first mission. Jesus makes it very clear that the gospel forces people to make a definitive choice for or against Jesus Christ; this can very well break up families. He said:

> *Do not think that I have come to bring peace on earth; I have not come to bring peace, but a sword. For I have come to set a man against his father, and a daughter against her mother . . . and a man's foes will be those of his own household.*

A "decision for Christ" also involves taking up one's cross and following Jesus, which will have its final reward in the age to come. Three short sayings, two of which are about the reception of the evangelists, while the third is about giving a cup of water to "one of these little ones," conclude the charge and the chapter. The Roman reading concentrates on the second of these three remarks of Jesus, highlighting the second (the reception of a prophet) over against the first reading from 2 Kings.

Sermon suggestions:

Matthew 10:34-42 — "The Costly Decision."

Those who hear the gospel must, necessarily, make a decision for or against Christ, and this may very well mean the disruption, even destruction, of family relationships. To believe that Jesus is the Son of God, who says, "Follow me," demands that this is no casual decision. For most of us, it is a matter of denominationalism; one church seems to have a better understanding of the gospel than another communion, although other factors frequently enter into the choices that are made. When one member of a family joins a denomination that is foreign to the heritage of the family, relationships sometimes reach the breaking point. Sometimes each member of the family may take a different route and they don't seem to be at odds with each other. I know a family in which the father has moved from Methodist to the Unitarian faith, the mother is Church of Christ, one child has become a Roman Catholic, another a Presbyterian, and their youngest fell in love with a Jewish woman and converted to Judaism. They get along quite well, continue to be rather close to one another, perhaps because they take their religion in small doses; Christianity is a casual kind of faith for them. The really difficult decision has to do with taking Jesus seriously enough to follow him; that can — and does — break up families.

1. *A serious decision.* Those who hear the good news must decide whether or not they believe it, receive it, and are willing to place their hope in Jesus. Christianity has no room for those who choose to view the faith casually.

2. *A destructive disagreement.* The gospel is as sharp as a Toledo blade and severs relationships, as well as establishes new ones, when people decide to call Jesus Lord. One of the problems with "second career" people accepting the call to ordained ministry is that the spouse — husband or wife — may not agree with the decision. Numerous marriages break up after one partner decides that he or she is called to the professional ministry of the church.

3. *A severe demand.* Christians can never follow Jesus empty-handed; they must take up and carry their crosses, if they are to be worthy of Christ. That's just the way it is; Christianity is more than a matter of "finding one's own life."

4. *A positive denouement.* Those who face and make this serious decision, risk destructive disagreement in close relationship, respond to the severe demand of the gospel and do not attempt merely "to find their lives," will know Christ's positive promise, "he who loses his life for my sake will find it."

Matthew 10:37-42 — "Honor and Hospitality."

1. Prophets — and pastors — ought to be held in high regard. They bring the Word to the people, which is why they, in their office, should be received with esteem by the faithful.

2. Prophets — and pastors — should live up to their high calling. The Word is not only delivered in preaching, but it becomes incarnate in the life and ministry of the parish clergy. They necessarily are to model the "new life" in Christ.

3. Prophets — and pastors — and preachers, who are faithful in their work and lives, will be honored by the Lord himself. That's the bottom line, and what really should matter to the faithful servants of Christ.

Genesis 32:22-32 (C) — "The Decision."

Jacob would not have had his hip dislocated if he and the "night stranger" had been wrestling under Graeco-Roman rules, which prohibit any holds below the waist! Of course, the whole point of the story might have been lost, too. Jacob was a man of great and powerful faith, and he would not let go of his hold on God under any circumstances; he learned that God would never fail him, but he had great plans for him and the people of Israel. So God blessed him.

1. *The wrestling match.* Faith in God often is a life-and-death struggle — a kind of wrestling match with God — for people who are serious about it.

2. *Death grip.* True faith holds on to God, despite the many forms of doubt and temptation. It is a "death grip" that is blessed by God.

3. *God's decision.* The Lord blesses those who cling to him in faith, despite the struggle they have to believe and live the Christian life. His decision is always in their favor.

2 Kings 4:8-11, 14-16a (R) — "On the Reception of Prophets and Pastors."

This pericope really needs to be connected to verse 41 of Matthew 10: "He who receives a prophet because he is a prophet shall receive a prophet's reward . . . ." The past few years, a veil of distrust has hung over the clergy like a shroud and many lay people have lost, in addition to their respect for pastors, their faith. A sermon on "the reception of prophets and pastors" might be of spiritual help to the people in many congregations who are struggling with the issue of "fallen" clergy.

1. *A story of hospitality.* The Shunamite woman recognized a true man of God when she saw him. He spoke the Word of God to people of his time. He was worthy of her hospitality.

2. *Believable prophets.* They are commited to the Word they preach, and they live by the Word which has been given them by God. Their faith is Bible-based, not the result of mystical — or fanciful — experiences.

3. *Surprise guest.* Jesus himself comes to those who receive the prophets and preachers and believe the Word they deliver to people. Theirs indeed is a "prophet's reward" — the blessed assurance that they belong to God forever.

Isaiah 2:10-17 (E) — "A Fateful Vision."

This text suggests a sermon on the last things, not merely on the fall of the kingdom of Judah, which occurred pretty much as Isaiah warned it would, but on the ultimate fall of the world. As such, it would be heavy on law and light on gospel. But there is another side to the text, and gospel side, that is more implied than fully defined. This balances the first note and gives people some hope.

1. *A terrible day.* Isaiah believes that there is a time when people should "get among the rocks, hide in the dust, at the sight of the terror of Yahweh." It is a day when "human pride will be humbled," and "the arrogance of men will be humbled." A time is coming that human beings should fear; all sorts of phenomena threaten the continued existence of the earth.

2. *A glorious day.* In contrast to "the terror of Yahweh," there is also "the brilliance of his majesty" that will be in full display at the last day. God alone will be exalted on that day; all the world will know that he is the Lord and that there is no other.

3. *Comfort in Christ.* The faithful have absolutely nothing to fear, for they are the Lord's and he has promised them a place in his everlasting kingdom.

4. *Live a new life.* Live in faith, not fear, and work to save the world and all living creatures on it.

Jeremiah 28:5-9 (L) — "A Prophet's Promise."

Here in a prophecy of restoration there is a promise of long-lasting peace. Of course, Jeremiah was talking about the return of Israel from its captivity in Babylon, which makes it difficult really to comprehend the full meaning of his words.

1. *Restoration.* That was the evident message of Jeremiah to Israel; they would be released and allowed to go back to Jerusalem and their land. That's what they wanted. Don't we always want to retain, or regain, the status quo?

2. *Revival.* Jeremiah mentions that "the vessels of the house of the Lord" would be returned to their proper place — not as precious artifacts and treasures, but to be used in the proper worship of their God — a religious revival, if you will. That's what God wanted of them. Of us, too?

3. *Renewal.* God was offering Israel a new lease on life, a new beginning. He offers us new life every day, the opportunity to live out the precious gift he has given us in our baptism into the death and resurrection of the Lord Jesus Christ.

4. *Rejoice.* If the end is at hand, it will be glorious indeed, because it will mean the beginning of the reign of the Lord over all the earth and the era of lasting peace.

A Sermon on the Second Lesson, Romans 6:1b-11 — "Buried Alive."

1. *Baptism is being buried alive.* We have suffered something of the sailor's death, who goes down — still living — with his ship. Through baptism, Paul tells us, we have died with Jesus Christ. We are united with Christ forever.

2. *Baptism means resurrection.* Since we are united with Jesus in his death, we shall be united with him in his resurrection. Because he lives, we know that we, too, shall live with him forever.

3. *Baptism means new life now.* Our sin was buried with us in baptism; we are "dead to sin and alive to God in Jesus Christ." Our business is to live the new life.

The Seventh Sunday after Pentecost
Fourteenth Sunday in Ordinary Time
Proper 9

Roman Catholic	Zechariah 9:9-10	Romans 8:9, 11-13	Matthew 11:25-30
Episcopal	Zechariah 9:9-12	Romans 7:21—8:6	Matthew 11:25-30
Lutheran	Zechariah 9:9-12	Romans 7:15-25a	Matthew 11:25-30
Common	Exodus 1:6-14, 22—2:10	Romans 7:14-25a	Matthew 11:25-30

The church year theological clue

Beyond the general and continuing eschatological framework of the church year, no distinct or additional clue is provided. Pentecost remains the "time of the church," or, the season of the "life of the church." The specific themes that support and expand the *time/life* concepts of Pentecost are all provided by the assigned readings of the cycle/season and Sunday.

The Prayer of the Day (LBW) — This prayer is radically different than the classic collect it replaces. It is a prayer for peace, peace whose source is God himself in Jesus Christ — as in Jeremiah's prophecy (9:9-10) — and peace that goes into the world through the life and ministry — the witness — of those whose peace is in Jesus Chirst. It is unique in that the church asks God: "Send us as peacemakers and witnesses to your kingdom," adding "and fill our hearts with joy in your salvation; through your Son, Jesus Christ our Lord." The prayer would be fitting at the end of Jesus' charge to the twelve disciples as they embarked upon their first missionary effort, asking the Lord God to make us partners in the ongoing work of the church. It is, of course, appropriate for this Sunday, and for most others, too.

The Psalm of the Day — Psalm 145:1-2 (3-13) 14-22 (L); 145:1-2, 8-11, 13-14 (R); 145, or 145:8-14 (E) — Despite being chopped into little pieces in the Roman Catholic and Lutheran sets of propers, Psalm 145 will be recognized by most regular church-goers: "Every day will I bless Thee and praise Thy name forever and ever" (v. 2), and again, "Great is the Lord and greatly to be praised . . . ." (v. 3), and verses 15 and 16 may be the most familiar, because they are often used by Christians of all denominations in their table prayers.

> *The eyes of all look to thee, and thou givest them their food in due season. Thou openest thy hand, thou satisfiest the desire of every living thing.*

Interestingly, the Episcopal Church ends its use of this responsory psalm at verse 14. As a responsory, the psalm also accommodates the first reading —

> *Rejoice greatly, O daughter of Zion! Shout aloud, O daughter of Jerusalem! Lo, your king comes to you; trimphant and victorious is he, humble and riding on an ass, on a colt the foal of an ass. (Zechariah 9:9)*

which is included in the classic choice of gospels (Matthew 21) for Palm Sunday. The concluding verse is always appropriate: "My mouth shall speak the praise of the Lord; let all flesh bless his holy name forever and ever."

The Psalm Prayer (LBW)

> *Loving Father, you are faithful in your promises and tender in your compassion. Listen to our hymn of joy, and continue to satisfy the needs of all your creatures, that all flesh may bless your name in your everlasting kingdom, where with your Son and the Holy Spirit you live and reign, now and forever.*

Psalm 124 (C) — It is the last verse of the psalm — "Our help is in the name of the Lord, the maker of heaven and earth" — that would be familiar to many older Christians, especially to Lutherans, because it was the beginning of the people's participation in the Confession of Sins. This verse, in particular, is highlighted in the liturgical expression of this psalm.

The readings:

Exodus 1:6-14, 22—2:10 (C)

This is the first of thirteen consecutive readings from the book of Exodus. If it were included in the lectionaries of other liturgical churches, as well as the Common Lectionary, it would probably be the first time that many Christians would have heard the story of Moses' birth read publicly since their Sunday church school years. Since there are so many parallels between the Moses and Jesus stories — both born to accomplish specific "exodus tasks" for the Lord God, both threatened with death while infants and delivered so that their divine destinies might be fulfilled — it is odd that the reading is not included in all of the lectionaries. Those congregations who follow the Common Lectionary will profit by hearing again the story of Moses' birth, his rescue from the river and his adoption by Pharaoh's daughter.

Zechariah 9:9-12

In its customary identification with Palm Sunday, this reading stirs up memories of the victorious and triumphant entry of Jesus into Jerusalem. The note of joy obviously sounds on this and every Sunday of the church year, but along with that joy, today the humility of Christ in his identification with the poor and lowly leaps out at the listener. To these familiar verses are added:

> *I will cut off the chariot from Ephraim and the war horse from Jerusalem; and the battle bow shall be cut off, and* he shall command peace to the nations; *his dominion shall be from sea to sea, and from the River to the ends of the earth.* [emphasis mine]

The theme of peace, which will come when the reign of Christ is extended over all the earth at the end of time, expands in proper perspective the "peace" note of the Prayer of the Day. It also finds subtle expression in the Gospel for the Day.

Romans 7:15-25a (L); 7:14-25a (C); Romans 7:21—8:6 (E)

These three slightly different readings may be considered together, because preachers will want to read all of chapter seven and continue with Paul's theme that spills over into chapter eight. The substance of the reading is Paul's lament/confession to the Roman Church of his problem with his spiritual and unspiritual nature. He loves the Law and wills to obey it, but his unspiritual — unredeemed — self causes him to disobey it; he says, "I do not understand my actions. For I do not do what I want, but I do the very thing I hate."

208

That means, for him, that the law is good, because it convicts him of sin and forces him to admit that there is no good dwelling in him. He says, "For I do not do the good I want, but the evil I do not want is what I do;" that tells him that sin dwells within him. In short, Paul is aware that a "war" is being waged within himself, which is "making me captive to the law of sin which dwells in my members." "Who will deliver me from this body of death?" He answers his own question with, "Thanks be to God through our Lord Jesus Christ." The reading of the Episcopal Lectionary picks up where verse 25 leaves off and spells out what Paul knows to be the grace of God, because Christ has "set us free from the law of sin and death."

Romans 8:9, 11-13

The Roman Lectionary, despite the omission of Paul's lament, reads on to commend the Roman congregation for its interest in the "spiritual," "since the Spirit of God has made his home in you. In fact," he says, "unless you possessed the Spirit of Christ you would not belong to him." It is that Spirit, which raised Jesus from the dead, that gives life to "your own mortal bodies" because the Spirit lives in you. That Spirit will help to "put an end to the misdeeds of the body (and) you will live." Paul's over-arching theology would declare that the battle between good and evil, the spiritual and the unspiritual, must be fought on a daily basis by dying to sin and rising to new life.

Matthew 11:25-30

The first part (through verse 11) of this chapter is omitted because it belongs to the Third Sunday in Advent; it might also be appointed for the season of the Manifestation, Epiphany. The context of these verses is the reaction of Jesus to the recalcitrant attitude of the cities where he has performed his miracles; Chorazin, Bethsaida, and Capernaum are mentioned specifically by Jesus, and he warns them of the judgment and condemnation that will befall them. It is at that point that Matthew (and Luke) has Jesus saying, "I thank thee, Father, Lord of heaven and earth, that thou has hidden these things from the wise and understanding and revealed them to babes." Christ makes it perfectly clear that the reception of the good news is not an intellectual exercise, nor the dominion of the super-intelligent people, but is something that can best be grasped by those who are as humble and open to real faith as little children. Jesus brings the wisdom of God to the world and reveals it in himself, his preaching, teaching, and ministry to the poor and the suffering; in receiving the person, Jesus Christ, through faith, one receives the wisdom of the Lord. This is what makes the redeeming wisdom of God available to all people.

Scholars contend that both parts of this gospel are probably liturgical fragments; the first sounds like something that belongs to Johannine theology, but the second part — the invitation of Jesus, "Come to me, all who labor and are heavy laden, and I will give you rest . . . ." — is peculiar to Matthew. Where he got it, and why he alone has this lovely saying of Jesus doesn't really matter to most people who know it, because it is a precious promise that has brought, and continues to bring comfort to people in all walks of life. It seems to demand homiletical consideration on its own from this perspective.

Sermon suggestions:

Matthew 11:28-30 — "A Pastor's Heart."

From a pastoral perspective, this portion of the reading takes priority over verses 25-27; every congregation has people in attendance at worship who are looking for comfort and strength to meet the exigencies of the week that has just begun. These verses come from the pastoral heart of the Good Shepherd and are his invitation to take all their troubles to him, "lean" on him, and let him bear those burdens that are too heavy for us to carry.

1. *A pastoral invitation.* "Come to me," says Jesus to every human being who finds that life is too difficult for him/her to face any longer. "Take my yoke upon you, and learn from me." Jesus could carry on his ministry, simply because he "turned to the Lord" and, in prayer, laid his burdens upon God, who never failed him.

2. *A pastoral revelation.* "I am gentle and lowly in heart," he said. Jesus is always approachable; he is constantly available to those who call upon him in prayer when they are in need. He reminds us, "My yoke is easy, and my burden is light." His religion does not wear out people, as did the religious exercises and observances of the scribes and Pharisees; the demands of the law are a burden that we can't carry ourselves. Simple faith is all that is needed to approach Jesus in prayer.

3. *A pastoral promise.* "I will give you rest" — Jesus helps us carry our burdens, face our problems and life's difficulties, and sustains us in pain and suffering. He gives us peace of mind and heart, because we know we can entrust him with our very lives and he will never fail us.

A second sermon on Matthew 11:25-27 — "The Unique Relationship."

1. *Jesus could call God "Father."* He "knew" the Father intimately and uniquely, in a manner unknown to all other human beings. He knew that he was the Son of God, and, therefore, almost had to call God his Father.

2. *Jesus gives us knowledge of God.* He tested the love and power of God on the cross. And God did not fail him; even in death God was with him, raising him up on the third day. The Christian faith rests on the revelation of God in the life, death, and resurrection of Jesus Christ, not on any system of philosophy or metaphysics.

3. *Jesus made God available to all.* He came to save all people — the poor and disadvantaged, but also the rich and affluent; the sick and suffering, but also the well; the sad and lonely, but also the happy and contented; the blind and lame, but also those who can see perfectly and walk well — because all people need to know and embrace God as their maker and heavenly Father.

4. *Rejoice and give thanks with Jesus — and for Jesus.* Join him as he thanks the Lord for "hiding these things from the wise and understanding and (revealing) them to babes . . . ." Thank him at the table where he is host, and by the way you live, directed by his Word and sustained by his Spirit, in the world.

Exodus 1:6-14, 22—2:10 — "Pharaoh's Evil Plan: God's Prevailing Providence."

1. *The first holocaust.* At Pharaoh's order, male babies were drowned in the river because they were becoming too numerous and might be a threat to the Egyptians in time of war.

2. *The real problem.* The descendants of Abraham, after Joseph, were not allowed to become citizens of Egypt, even should they have wanted to be Egyptians; they were turned into slaves before Moses' birth, and already wanted to be free. Pharaoh would have had nothing to fear from them if they had been treated properly and fairly; they would have been loyal to Egypt, which had sheltered and sustained them in a time of drought and trouble.

3. *God had another plan.* In his providence, he would provide "a way out" of bondage — Exodus — for the children of Israel, and for that purpose he raised up a leader, Moses, who was protected by the daughter of the very man who wanted to kill all of the boy babies born to the Hebrews.

4. *God's ultimate plan.* He sent and raised up a new leader, his own Son, to lead another Exodus. He selected a young peasant girl, not the daughter of a Pharaoh, to mother him,

and he had to protect him by sending him to Egypt when a Hebrew king ordered all boy babies to be killed. He, too, set his people free in a different kind of Exodus — death and resurrection. All who want to be free of sin and death need only turn to Christ in humility and faith.

Zechariah 9:9-10 — "A Different Kind of King."

1. *A different type of prophecy.* This king would come from God himself to begin a gracious rule, which would also set God's people free. His coming is a signal for great jubilation and loud celebration. Jeremiah prophesied that a blessing, not a curse of doom, would come to all the world in this king, and that's really different.

2. *A different kind of king.* Jesus came in a lowly manner, just as the prophet said he would come. He was indeed meek and lowly, humble enough to ride upon a colt, the foal of a donkey, as he entered Jerusalem. His humility reinforced any claim to the kingship that people bestowed upon him; even his birth was lowly. His humility identified him with common humanity, not royalty. He was a different kind of king.

3. *A different sort of rule.* He came to establish peace — between God and his people, between members of families, between nation and nation. He could only do this by obeying God differently — by becoming obedient unto death, even death on the cross. Jesus' cross is the sign of peace on earth, between God and his children.

4. *A different reign.* "He will reign forever and ever," not for a few years or decades, as have all other kings and rulers. The reign, begun when they placed a crown of thorns upon his head, nailed him to a cross, and put a sign above his head — "The King of the Jews" — for all the world to see, will last to the end of time and as long as God has determined that he shall reign as King of Kings and Lord of Lords. Rejoice and shout for joy, ye righteous! He saves us and that's the difference he makes in our lives.

Romans 7:14-25a (C, L); 7:21—8:6 (E); 8:9, 11-13 (R) — "Helpless, but Not Hopeless."

I, personally, would consolidate the material included from Romans 7:14—8:13 in a single sermon and in the context of the Brief Order of Confession of my church (LBW).

1. *If we say we have no sin, we deceive ourselves.* That comes right from the lips of St. Paul; he knew himself to be a helpless and hopeless sinner. He never could fulfill his good intention, doing evil when he intended to do good.

2. *If we confess our sins,* God who is faithful and just will forgive our sins and cleanse us from all unrighteousness. He does what we cannot do for ourselves, forgiving us for the failure of good intentions and empowering us to live a new life.

3. *If we claim to be Christians,* we are to live godly lives. That's the consequence of God's actions and our faith in Jesus Christ. Christ expects Christians to say "yes" to God and "no" to Satan and sin. Through the Holy Spirit, he makes this possible.

The Eighth Sunday after Pentecost
Fifteenth Sunday in Ordinary Time
Proper 10

Roman Catholic	Isaiah 55:10-11	Romans 8:18-23	Matthew 13:1-23
Episcopal	Isaiah 55:10-11	Romans 8:18-23	Matthew 13:1-9, 18-23
Lutheran	Isaiah 55:10-11	Romans 8:18-25	Matthew 13:1-9 (18-23)
Common	Exodus 2:11-22	Romans 8:9-17	Matthew 13:1-9, 18-23

The church year theological clue

As the first third of the Pentecost cycle/season approaches its conclusion, the preacher must keep in mind that the theological framework of the season continues to be eschatological; the church continues to wait and work in anticipation of the Parousia. The Gospel for the Day, supported by the first reading, continues to provide the primary theme for worship and preaching, depending on whether or not one reads the shorter or longer lection, while the second reading continues to go its own way and sounds its own eschatological note.

The Prayer of the Day (LBW) — Two prayers are provided for this Sunday, neither of which bears any relationship to the older, classic collect used on this day. The first is so conceived and constructed as to complement, if not announce, the "seed/Word" theme of Matthew 13, the Gospel for the Day. It gives thanks to God for "planting in us the seed of your word," and asks for the power of the Holy Spirit so that we may "receive it with joy," "live according to it, and grow in faith and hope and love." Obviously, this is the prayer that should be read on this day. The other prayer has to do with witnessing to the love of God by the way we live; it will be considered in the future in conjunction with other Gospels assigned to this day.

The Psalm of the Day — Psalm 65 (L); 65:10-14 (R); 65:9-14 (E) — The last six or seven verses of this psalm, which Roman Catholics and Episcopalians use on this day, make it abundantly clear that this is a thanksgiving for an abundant crop of grain about to be harvested. It picks up the theme of the Old Testament reading that speaks of the Word of the Lord, what might be called "the seed of salvation," which will not return "empty" after it has been sown in the hearts of people. It makes a solid connection with the parable of "the Sower and the Seed" in the Gospel for the Day. The Word of the Lord will grow and bear fruit, therefore the workers in the kingdom may rejoice and give thanks. The Lutheran usage includes the first part of the Psalm, which emphasizes that it is always proper for sinful creatures to give thanks to God for the salvation he gives to his creatures — in Christ, from the perspective of the church.

The Psalm Prayer (LBW)

> *Lord God, joy marks your presence; beauty, abundance, and peace are the tokens of your work in all creation. Work also in our lives, that by these signs we may see the splendor of your love and may praise you through Jesus Christ our Lord.*

Psalm 69:6-15 (C) — A brief commentary on this psalm is included in the material for the Fifth Sunday after Pentecost.

212

The readings:

Exodus 2:11-22 (C)

Here is another first reading that is not included in the other lectionaries; it has little or no relationship to the second reading or the Gospel, except as it is an integral part of the exodus story, in which Christians and Hebrews both have a stake. It relates the incident when Moses, now a grown man, killed an Egyptian who was mistreating one of the Hebrews. He thought he had committed the deed in secret, but discovered, when he reproved a Hebrew for mistreating another Jew, that his infamy was known by the Hebrews and would soon be common knowledge and reach the ears of Pharaoh. This happened and he fled for his life to Midian, where he was kind to the daughters of Reuel/Jethro, a priest, who invited him to have dinner with them and ultimately, gave him his daughter, Zipporah, as his wife. She bore him his first son, while he was in self-imposed exile from Egypt.

Isaiah 55:10-11 (L, R)

This pericope offers insight and even corrective to any who might interpret the Gospel for the Day as an occasion to preach about the condition of the "soil" in which the Word/seed is sown. It is about the Word of God, the seed that God plants in human hearts, where it will germinate, grow, and provide harvest; it is not simply about the seed that a farmer sows in the fields, tends, and is watered by the rain and, finally, gives ripe grain for the reapers. Isaiah declares, as God's prophet, "so shall my word be that goes forth from my mouth; it shall not return to me empty." He insists that God's Word "shall accomplish that which I purpose, and prosper in the thing for which I sent it." God will not fail in his intention to save the world, especially in the work of his Son, Jesus Christ, we Christians dare to add.

Isaiah 55:1-5, 10-13 (E)

The *Book of Common Prayer* expands the first reading of Roman Catholics and Lutherans in two directions. First, it provides a preface and context for verses 10 and 11 in the form of an invitation, "Come to the waters all you who are thirsty; . . . Buy corn without money, and eat, and, at no cost, wine and milk." *(Jerusalem Bible)* God sows his seed, his Word, freely and abundantly in the world and offers it, at no cost, to all who accept his invitation. Second, there is a kind of postlude provided in verses 12 and 13 for those who have accepted the invitation and have received the Word: "Yes, you will leave with joy and be lead away in safety . . . ." Indeed, the Word of the Lord will bear fruit and feed the hunger and thirst of people who will receive God's gracious invitation to them. Verses 10 and 11 remain as the heart of the first reading for this day.

Romans 8:18-23 (R); 8:18-25 (L)

Here is a powerful reminder that God created the entire world and everything in it — the "created order" — and not just the human race. Paul recognizes that humanity is out of harmony with the created world, as well as with the Creator; the world, as well as people, is in desperate trouble because human beings have desecrated it and much of what is in it, rather than caring for the earth as commanded by God. Both human beings and the world are in need of redemption; and when people are reconciled to God, they need also be reconciled to the world. Paul not only knows that people live in hope, waiting for the redemption of their bodies at the last day, but he is also aware that they have already been "adopted" as the children of God in Christ, and are to live in harmony with the creator and his creation, in the meantime.

Romans 8:9-17 (E, C)

Roman and Lutheran pastors would do well to read this again; it provides the background and context for their second reading, 8:18-23 and 8:18-25. Paul informs the Roman Christians about the life in the Spirit; they are really living by the Spirit of God and the promise of the risen Christ, that they, too, will be raised up and know the glory of the resurrection at the proper time. They are able to live spiritual lives in the world, rather than unspiritual, because the Spirit lives in them and fosters their interest in the spiritual, the things of God, rather than those things which are unspiritual. So they are to live in hope, as well as the reality of the resurrection of the Lord.

Matthew 13:1-9, 18-23 (L, E, C); 13:1-23 (R)

In the first nine verses of this Gospel, Jesus teaches the parable about the sower, the seed, and the soil; the longer reading, be it optional or a required extension of the Gospel, adds the allegorical explanation, which most scholars believe is a later addition, or redaction, to the parable. The point of the parable is that the mission of the church — to preach the Word, plant the seed of salvation in the whole world — will succeed; the seed is strong and powerful, and life-giving. It germinates and grows in the minds and hearts of people, and causes their faith to flower and reach maturity. Jesus was teaching the disciples that despite the hostility and actual enmity which would ultimately claim his life, his mission — and theirs, too, as his disciples — will succeed. Despite set-backs and frustration from evident failures in the past (it would seem that the mission to Israel has been something of a failure, and that there is competition and a continuing debate about the authenticity of the two communities), the church — then and now — is to continue to believe this as it plants the seeds of salvation wherever the Word is preached.

Sermon suggestions:

Matthew 13:1-9 (18-23) (L); 13:1-9, 18-23 (E, C); 13:1-23 (R) — "The Seed and the Soil."

This is one of those rare Sundays in Pentecost in which the three lessons coordinate — accidentally — with each other. It seems well to link the first two readings with the Gospel for the Day.

People who hear this Gospel will react differently to it after surviving the drought of the summer of 1988. Substantial crop failures resulted, not because there was anything wrong with the seed, but because there was not enough rain to nurture the various plants and allow them to grow to maturity. Some people may think that Jesus omitted an important element in the parable of the Sower; he not only omitted rain but also sun and warmth. Others, who comprehend that the passage is talking about a plentiful harvest in the good soil where the seed was sown might think only of what might, or should have been, a bumper crop of wheat, or corn, or soybeans. Still others may make no connection between the parable and actual agriculture, preferring to take the allegorical approach which concentrates on the type of soil — human hearts, minds, and spirits — in which the seed/Word is sown. A few might comprehend that this Gospel just may be about the ultimate success of the church's mission — preaching the gospel — in the world.

1. *A supply of good seed.* That's why the Lord has given to the church in the Word, the gospel, which the church is to spread through the world. The Word/seed will germinate and grow because it is good. Isaiah knew that long before Jesus gave the parable of sower, seed, and soil.

2. *The inhospitable soil.* That's what the church often encounters when the good news is proclaimed to people. Some Christians wonder about the ability of God to reach human hearts and turn them to himself, when he is unable to guarantee an actual harvest in the fields in many parts of the world. Droughts and devastating famines occur just about every year. Numerous people cannot begin to sing:

> *We plow the fields and scatter*
> *   The good seed on the land,*
> *But it is fed and watered*
> *   By God's almighty hand.*
> *He sends the snow in winter,*
> *   The warmth to swell the grain,*
> *The breezes and the sunshine,*
> *   And soft refreshing rain.*

The trouble may not simply be in the soil; the problem may be in lack of spiritual sustenance and power, some force to keep the Word/seed growing in human hearts — "even the birds of the air."

I drove past a school the other day and noticed at least two hundred Canada geese were gathered on the grounds, obviously eating something. It finally dawned on me that they were eating newly sown grass seed; a major addition was under construction and just about finished, so the land had been levelled and seeded. I suspect there will be many bare spots that will have to be reseeded next spring.

3. *The nurture of the Spirit.* Here's where the second reading, Romans 8, comes into the picture. The Spirit of God causes the seed to germinate, to grow, and to mature in the minds and souls of human beings. The Spirit brings God's "rain" to the hearts of people, and guarantees a plentiful harvest for the Lord. Paul considers this the business of living by and in the Spirit.

4. *Plant with faith.* God's kingdom has come into the world in Jesus Christ, and it will continue to grow as the Word is preached throughout the earth; his "word . . . shall not return to [him] empty." God himself, according to Isaiah, has said this, and promised that this will come to be. And Jesus adds, with his parable, "He that has ears to hear, let him hear."

Exodus 2:11-22 — "Truth Will Come Out."

1. *Truth Will Come Out.* That's the obvious lesson in this first reading. Moses thought that no one had seen him when he murdered the Egyptian, and that he would get away with the killing. He didn't, because someone saw him and the word quickly got around the Hebrew people.

2. *Fear seeks an escape.* So it was with Moses; he couldn't cover up the murder, so he fled to the land of Midian after the truth came out; he left Egypt because he feared for his life. The truth followed him, much as it does when we commit a crime, or do something of which we are ashamed. Sinners can never fully escape the consequence of their deeds.

3. *The truth changes people.* Moses seems to have become a changed person after he arrived in Midian; he went out of his way to help the daughters of Reuel water their sheep and obtain drinking water themselves. Did he understand the consequence of his deed? Did he raise any *mea culpa* in Midian? We'll never know, but we know that we must repent and turn around when confronted by our sins.

4. *God provides a way back.* He did for Moses, or the people of Israel might be in Egypt to this day. And he does for us — in Jesus Christ our Lord — not merely back to him but into a new life, as well.

Isaiah 55:10-11 — "The Kingdom Will Come."

1. *Isaiah believed that was God's intention.*

2. *Isaiah knew it would happen.* The good seed would be planted and "watered" by God. That's why he prophesied that it would be so.

3. *Isaiah proclaimed the Word.* He knew that his work was to preach God's powerful, never-failing Word. He did just that, and gave the church an example, as well as a prophecy.

Romans 8:18-25 (L); 8:18-23 (R) — "Glory and Grace."

1. *Glory — that's what's in our future.* We may dare to expect it, and may even wait for God's future glory with "eager longing." There is a better day coming!

2. *Grace — that's what is ours right now.* We have been redeemed in Christ, and live the new life through the power of the Holy Spirit. Jesus has given us "the first fruits of the Spirit."

3. *Gospel — God has made all things new.* We can believe that, in light of his resurrection. We had better believe it, because it is — and will be — so.

Romans 8:9-17 (E, C) — "The New Life."

1. *Jesus has given us new life.* It came in his resurrection and, specifically, in our baptism.

2. *New life means new interests.* Christians are to be interested — and involved — in those things that belong to the kingdom. They have to be concerned about the spread of the good news, if they are really Christians.

The Ninth Sunday after Pentecost
Sixteenth Sunday in Ordinary Time
Proper 11

Roman Catholic	Wisdom 12:13, 16-19	Romans 8:26-27	Matthew 13:24-30, 36-43
Episcopal	Wisdom 12:13, 16-19	Romans 8:26-27	Matthew 13:24
Lutheran	Isaiah 44:6-8	Romans 8:26-27	Matthew 13:24-30 (36-43)
Common	Exodus 3:1-12	Romans 8:18-25	Matthew 13:24-30, 36-43

The church year theological clue

The eschatological framework of the church year is strengthened on this Ninth Sunday after Pentecost, not by the character or content of the church year, but by the Gospel for the Day. With its parable of the wheat and the weeds, plus exegetically subtle support in the first reading (Isaiah 44 — "Let them tell us what is yet to be" and the second reading, Romans 8:27 — ". . . the Spirit intercedes for the saints according to the will of God"), the Gospel for the Day points to the end of time when the judgment of God will be meted out upon the human race. Without the eschatological focus of the readings, the theological clue of the church year would be almost indistinct.

The Prayer of the Day (LBW) — Two prayers have been prepared and appointed to the propers for this Sunday. The first is a reworking of the classic collect for the Eighth Sunday after Trinity; in it, the language of the older prayer is modernized, the address of God has more of a "Pentecost flavor" (from "Grant to us, Lord, we beseech thee, the spirit to think and do always such things as are right" to "Pour out upon us, O Lord, the spirit to think and do what is right . . . .") and the petition is radically altered (from ". . . that we, who cannot do anything that is good without thee, may by thee be enabled to live according to thy will . . . ." to ". . . that we, who cannot even exist without you, may have the strength to live according to your will . . . .").

The second prayer sharpens the focus of the first prayer to a point with its "Turn us to listen to your teaching and lead us to choose the one thing which will not be taken from us, Jesus Christ our Lord." It might simply have been added to the first prayer as a concluding petition. It would seem fitting and proper to offer both prayers, in order, in the Sunday liturgy.

The Psalm of the Day — Psalm 86:11-17 (L); 86:5-6, 9-10, 15-16a (R); 86, or 86:11-17 (E) — "The Patchwork Psalm" is a title that could be attached to this psalm, because it is largely a conglomeration of thoughts, ideas, and petitions which have been taken from other psalms. Nonetheless, it is one of the psalms with which many congregations are familiar and portions of it, at least — possibly because they are taken from other psalms — are well known by some Christians. This is a very personal psalm, part of which found its way long ago into the public worship of the church (v. 6, "Give ear, O Lord, unto my prayer, and attend to the voice of my supplication,") but that's not the main reason why this psalm is appointed as a responsory on this day. Verse 11 picks up where the Prayers of the Day, if not the first reading, leave off: "Teach me your way, O Lord, and I will walk in your truth; knit my heart to you that I may fear your name." The psalmist reveals that he knows what God is like, and that, because of the goodness of the Lord, ("But you, Lord, are gracious and full of compassion, slow to anger, and full of kindness and truth."), he may call upon God for deliverance from evil and from his enemies. While the Roman Catholics and the Lutherans tend to follow the lead of some biblical scholars by cutting apart the psalm, the *Book of Common Prayer* gives liturgical priority to the use of the entire psalm in its proper sequence, with the option of saying or singing verses 11-17 in resposne to the first reading.

The Psalm Prayer (LBW)

> *God of mercy, when Christ called out to you in torment, you heard him and gave him victory over death. Fill us with the love of your name and help us to proclaim you before the world, that all peoples may celebrate your glory in Jesus Christ our Lord.*

Psalm 103:1-13 (C) — This psalm may be even more familiar to the faithful than Psalm 86. Almost every Christian has said: "Bless the Lord, O my soul, and all that is within me, bless his holy name. Bless the Lord, O my soul, and forget not all his benefits." The list of God's blessings and benefits, which follows, is impressive and ought to be reviewed and reflected upon by Jews and Christians alike from time to time. But the main reason this psalm has been selected for this Sunday is discovered in verse 7a: "He made his ways known to Moses, and his works to the children of Israel." This verse probably should be used as an antiphon in those parishes which recite or sing the psalms so as to draw attention to the main reason for its use as a response to the first reading.

The readings:

Exodus 3:1-12 (C)

This reading is employed by the Roman, Episcopal, and Lutheran churchs, not for the Ninth Sunday in Pentecost, but for the Third Sunday in Lent, Series/Year C. The *Book of Common Prayer* simply extends the reading three verses (3:1-15); the Roman *Ordo* appoints 3:1-8a, 13-15 for Lent 3 of Year C; the LBW skips verse 9, so that verses 3:1-8a, 10-15 are read. The selection in the Common Lectionary simply tells the story of God's call to Moses, after the death of Pharaoh, to return to Egypt and become the leader of the Israelites and secure their release by Pharaoh and start them on their forty-year trip to the promised land that was "flowing with milk and honey." The familiar story of the burning bush and the presence of the Lord God, who commanded, "Take off your shoes, for the land you are standing on is holy land," introduce the speech by God that commissions Moses for this leadership role. The churches which read this and the three to five verse extension of the story on the Third Sunday in Lent, Year C, do so because God identifies himself and gives his name to people for all time, "I am who I am," as the one who calls for a new leader, Jesus, and a new exodus that will ultimately involve all people.

Wisdom 12:13, 16-19 (R, E)

In the context of God's grace and mercy (verse 13 — "For there is no god, other than you, who cares for everything, to whom you might have to prove that you never judge unjustly . . . ."), repentance is considered to be a gift of God (verse 19 — ". . . you have given your sons the good hope that after sin you will grant repentance."). Over against the Gospel for the Day, verse 18 stands out, ". . . you govern us with great lenience." God will not destroy the wicked, according to Jesus' parable, but will allow both wheat and weeds to grow together until the harvest, when they will be separated and the evil will be banished from the presence of God. Until that time, God will spare all from the punishment they deserve. (v. 16)

Isaiah 44:6-8 (L)

The LBW replaces the reading from Wisdom with this selection from Isaiah, because it includes God's self-identification and self-description:

> *Thus says the Lord, the King of Israel and his Redeemer, the Lord of hosts: "I am the first and I am the last; besides me there is no god . . . . Is there a God besides me? There is no Rock; I know not any."*

218

At best, it is an introduction to the parable of the wheat and the weeds taught by Jesus —
"Who has announced from of old the things to come? Let them tell us what is yet to be."
— which does tell "what is to come" and "what is yet to be." It is not as specific about
the leniency of the Lord as Wisdom, and it might be a good idea, should Lutheran pastors
be preaching from this text, to include the appropriate verses from Wisdom 12 which give
specificity to the excerpt from Isaiah 44.

Romans 8:18-25 (E, C)
(Note: Roman Catholics and Lutherans appointed this text for reading last Sunday. These
are additional comments.)

This is one of Paul's "I've got a glory" sayings, set in the context of a world that "is eagerly
waiting for God to reveal his sons" and to free the whole world "from its slavery to deca-
dence, to enjoy the same freedom and glory as the children of God." *(Jerusalem Bible)* There
is a "not yet" to Paul's understanding of "glory," because the fullness of it will not become
a final reality until the end of time. In the meantime, those who have been given the "first
fruits of the Spirit" must wait patiently for that last day. Almost by accident, therefore,
this reading harmonizes with the other two lections, particularly with the Gospel for the Day.

Romans 8:26, 27 (R, L)

Verses 24 and 25 have been deliberately omitted from this reading, despite the fact that last
Sunday's second reading ended at 8:23. Guided by the work of the New Testament scholars
who insist that verse 26 really follows verse 23, the liturgical specialists simply omitted the
two verses in between verse 23 and verse 26. The pastor/preacher might want to consider
this passage in that context. Paul assures his readers that, as they "groan inwardly as [they]
wait for adoption as sons, the redemption of [their] bodies," the "Spirit helps us in our weakness . . . [and] the Spirit himself intercedes for us [the saints] with sighs too deep for words
. . . ." This suggests that there are occasions on which the first or second readings — even
both — should be read *after* the Gospel for the Day (possibly just before the sermon, depending on the preacher's choice of text or texts).

Matthew 13:24-30 (36-43)

The parable of the wheat and the weeds is tailor-made for Pentecost, although it might seem
more appropriate to the Sundays toward the conclusion of the cycle/season than about one-
third of the way through it. Thoroughly eschatological in its perspective — the judgment
will come at the end of the era — the parable gives assurance to those who attempt to live
out the faith in the righteousness of Christ, as well as giving an odd sort of comfort to those
who may wonder why the wicked seem to get away with so much in this world. The addition
of verses 36-43, which explain the parable by giving it an allegorical twist, does not make
the problem too long; it does, however, create some problems for the preacher while giving
the pastor the opportunity to preach both law and gospel by identifying — as does the explanation — reasons why people should be punished but will not be until the end of time. Thus,
there is time to reflect on one's sin and repent of it before it is too late.

Sermon suggestions

Matthew 13:24-30 (36-43) — "Judgment and Grace."

One of the most puzzling aspects of the Gospel is that God seems to allow sin to go un-
punished here on the earth. Sinners apparently can get away with committing all sorts of

evil acts without fear of punishment; perhaps some of the worst persons living know Jesus' teaching that God will allow sinners and righteous to exist together until the end of time. When the judgment comes, they will be separated, and some will receive eternal life, while others — unrepentant sinners — will be consigned to eternal damnation. The truth is that people who think they can get away with sinning don't really understand the gospel and, in particular, this parable. It is about judgment and grace, not simply about grace alone.

1. *Judgment is coming.* That's a certainty; God will separate sinners from those who have been made sinless in Jesus Christ. But the judgment will not arrive until the end of time, when Jesus will return to judge and rule the earth. God, unlike the law, does not punish evil immediately, but ultimately "wheat" and "weeds" will be separated.

2. *Grace prevails.* That's the current situation of people before God. He gives the gift of time to sinners, as well as to the righteous; sinners are given *time to repent,* while the righteous have *time to serve.* "Wheat" and "weeds" grow and exist, side by side, in the world.

3. *Grace may become judgment.* First, sinners, who have been given time to repent, may come to the conclusion that repentance is unnecessary; they don't take advantage of the grace that has been given them. Grace will become judgment for them. Second, the righteous, who observe sinners apparently "getting away" with sin not only ask "why" this is so, but may become judgmental, condemning unrepentant sinners, and even questioning the grace-plan of God. "What kind of a God allows people to get away with the sort of thing that he/she has done?" Grace can become judgment and/or judgmental, if it is misunderstood, by both "wheat" and "weeds."

4. *Repent and serve.* Repentance is a spiritual phenomenon, a gift of grace, that turns people and their lives around — toward God and the business of the kingdom, which is loving service, not judgment. Repentance is a continuing process for those who are "in Christ;" it will occur daily for the rest of their lives, so that people may live in "blessed assurance" and serve the Lord as long as they live. That's what the parable of the wheat and the weeds is all about.

Exodus 3:1-12 (C) — "Divine Directions."

God, from time to time, intervenes in the affairs of human beings in order to extricate them from impossible situations. The call of Moses — by God — to return to Egypt from the land of Midian was such an act of intervention and grace.

1. *A dramatic appearance.* God must have thought that Moses needed more than an angel, or even a burning bush, to convince him to return to Egypt; he knew it would take a personal appearance to move Moses out of Midian — so he spoke to him from the middle of a burning bush, telling him that he knew the state of the Israelites in Egypt and that something had to be done about it. Moses was the man God had chosen to gain their release.

2. *A troubling question.* "Who am I to go to Pharaoh and bring the sons of Israel out of Egypt?" Was Moses simply afraid for his life, if he returned to Egypt, despite the fact that the Pharaoh who was ruling when he killed the Egyptian was dead? Or could it have been an honest question of self-doubt? Isn't this a question that most preachers have asked themselves at one time or another: "Who am I to stand up here and preach to these people?" And other people, ordinary people, in extraordinary circumstances also ask, "Who am I to do this?" And what of Jesus? He even went so far as to pray, "If it be possible, let this cup pass from me."

3. *A personal promise.* God told Moses, "I shall be with you," and that was enough to convince him that he had to go back to Egypt. Our Lord knew that the Father was with him, and went obediently to the cross. Christ himself has promised us, "I will be with you to the end of time."

220

4. *Follow the leader.* That's what the Lord God requires of us, just as he did of Moses and the people of Israel. He gives us divine directions which we, too, are to follow without question or reservations. Follow Jesus, our Leader, as long as you live!

Wisdom 12:13, 16-19 (R, E) — "Justice — Human and Divine."

1. *Divine justice.* God is the God whose judgment is tempered by mercy. The prophets tell us so, and Jesus Christ proved God's love and mercy in his life and death on behalf of all who deserved only judgment.

2. *Human justice.* There is more law and harshness — and sometimes an absolute absence of mercy — in our attitudes toward those who have offeneded us or harmed us. That's why the heart of the Lord's Prayer is "Forgive us our sins, as we forgive those who sin against us." Repentance and the realization of God's mercy to us are the secret of human justice and mercy.

3. *Ultimate virtue.* Kindness and mercy — and withholding judgment toward others — are the genuine expressions of true repentance and faith, testimony that one is living in a right relationship with Christ and people.

Isaiah 44:6-8 (L) — "When God Speaks, Listen!"

God spoke to Moses from the midst of a burning bush; he spoke to the Israelites through his prophets. He has spoken to us through his Son and his Word.

1. *Listen to the Word of the Lord.* That's the only sure and certain way to get to know him.

2. *Hear what he has to say.* He himself tells us what he is like and what his attitude is toward us. He is the only God; there is no other. He is the God of the past, the present, and the future.

3. *Do what he commands.* Through Isaiah, he told the Israelites much the same thing that Jesus told his followers: "And you are my witnesses." That's one demand that he makes of all people who claim to know and love him.

Romans 8:18-25 (E, C) — See last Sunday's "sermon suggestions" (R, L) for this text.

Romans 8:26, 27 (R, L) — "We Never Pray Alone."

1. *We ought to pray regularly to God.* Christians know that, believe that, but too many of us don't do it. Either we don't really believe in prayer, or we don't know how to pray, or we may simply be spiritually lazy.

2. *The spirit teaches us how to pray.* That's one of his functions in our lives. That's part of what Paul meant when he said, "The Spirit helps us in our weakness." Our business is to be open to the instructions of Word and Spirit. The Spirit will transform our meager attempts at prayer into mature communication with God.

3. *The Spirit takes our petitions to God.* He prays for us, so that through the Spirit, we kneel before the presence of the Lord, who always receives our prayers.

4. *Let the Spirit take over.* That's what is asked of us, and our prayer life will be acceptable to God.

The Tenth Sunday after Pentecost
Seventeenth Sunday in Ordinary Time
Proper 12

Roman Catholic	1 Kings 3:5, 7-12	Romans 8:28-30	Matthew 13:44-52
Episcopal	1 Kings 3:5-12	Romans 8:26-34	Matthew 13:31-33, 44-49a
Lutheran	1 Kings 3:5-12	Romans 8:28-30	Matthew 13:44-52
Common	Exodus 3:13-20	Romans 8:26-30	Matthew 13:44-52

The church year theological clue

Once more the eschatological framework of the church year is reinforced by the day's readings, especially the lesson from Romans 8 and verses 47-50 of the Gospel of the Day, which speak specifically of the "end of the age" and the judgment that will come with it. Matthew's Gospel also spells out the nature of realized and present eschatology in the two little parables of the treasure and the precious pearl. Without the readings, the eschatological motif of Pentecost would be virtually indistinct on this Sunday; the readings remind us of the movement of the church through time to the last things spelled out at the conclusion of the Pentecost cycle/season and Christ the King Sunday.

The Prayer of the Day (LBW) — The introduction to this prayer ("O God, your ears are open always to the prayers of your servants") is a theological reconstruction of the classic collect, which begins, "Let thy merciful ears, O Lord, be open to the prayers of thy humble servants." The theology of the petition has also been improved by a radical reworking of the prayer itself. The older form said: "and, that they may obtain their petitions, make them to ask such things as shall please thee . . . ." The new petition prays: "Open our hearts and minds to you, that we may live in harmony with your will and receive the gifts of your spirit . . . ." These alterations make the new prayer more positively grace-oriented than the older collect, and function — especially over against Year A's Gospel — as a reminder that the kingdom of heaven is a gift from God, through Christ, to the faithful, and that life in the kingdom that is in harmony with God's will is dependent upon the power of the Holy Spirit to reach and touch the mind and reinforce the will of believers.

The Psalm of the Day — Psalm 119:57, 72, 76-77, 127-130 (R); 119:121-136 or 119:129-136 (E); 119:129-136 (L) — This psalm, regardless of which of the above selections might be followed, echoes and responds to the "wisdom motif" of Solomon's prayer in the day's first reading. It also points toward the Gospel, particularly in those verses that speak of the precedence that God's commandments should have over the things of this world:

> *Truly, I love your commandments more than gold and precious stones. I hold all your commandments to be right for me; all paths of falsehood I abhor.* (vv. 127-128)

Central to the theology of the psalm and the Old Testament reading is verse 130: "When your word goes forth it gives light; it gives understanding to the simple."

The Psalm Prayer (LBW)

> *Lord, you are just and your commandments are eternal. Teach us to love you with all our hearts and to love our neighbors as ourselves, for the sake of Jesus our Lord.*

Psalm 105:1-11 (C) — Portions of this psalm might be incorporated into the liturgy on any given Sunday, especially the emphasis upon remembering and proclaiming all of the good things God has done for his people. The latter part of this selection speaks specifically of the covenant he made with Abraham and the promise that he made to Israel, "To you will I give the land of Canaan to be your allotted inheritance." The unused portions of the psalm are a recitation of Israel's history, speaking of Moses and the Exodus following verse 26. Obviously, to use all of the psalm would be impractical; it is simply too long as a responsory. The first verses were used to highlight the identity of God: "He is the Lord our God; his judgments prevail in all the world" (v. 7), and to complement and respond to the first reading.

The readings:

1 Kings 3:5-12 (R, E, L)

Few persons have had a dream that begins to compare with that of Solomon, wherein God asks, "Ask what I shall give you," and the child Solomon, after recounting how God has shown his "steadfast love" to David and now to him, who succeeds his father David on the throne of Israel, prays: "Give thy servant therefore an understanding mind to govern thy people, that I may discern between good and evil . . . ." No prayer could have been more pleasing to God:

> *Because you have asked this, and have not asked for yourself long life or riches or the life of your enemies, but have asked for yourself understanding to discern what is right . . . . Behold, I give you a wise and discerning mind, so that none like you has been before you and none like you shall arise after you.*

Here, then, is the content of the treasure in the field and the pearl of great price pointed out by Jesus in the two little parables which introduce the Gospel for the Day. The wisdom to know God, his will, and his ways, is of greater value than anything else in life.

Exodus 3:13-20 (C)

The Roman, Episcopal, and Lutheran lectionaries appoint Exodus 3 for the Third Sunday in Lent of Year C. All three begin before verse 13, but all spill over into the beginning of this lesson from the Common Lectionary. This reading begins with God's calling of Moses to lead his people out of Egypt and his promise of Israel's deliverance from the power of Pharaoh (which is where the Roman, Episcopal, and Lutheran readings end), and directs Moses to gather the elders and the people and tell them what God will do for them. Yahweh tells Moses who he is — "I Am who I Am" — and what he will do to convince Pharaoh to free his people: "I shall show my power and strike Egypt with all the wonders I am going to work there. After this he will let you go." Psalm 105 responds perfectly to this "free-floating first reading, which really doesn't connect with either the Second Lesson or the Gospel.

Romans 8:28-30 (R, L); 8:26-34 (E); 8:26-30 (C)

The longer lessons provide the context for the three verse readings of the Roman and Episcopal lectionaries on this day; that context is the hope that the faithful have in Christ. Because he is sure that this hope is in the future, but has also been experienced in their lives, Paul dares to say to people who have known severe persecutions, "We know that in everything God works for good with those who love him, who are called according to his purpose." He could say that to the families of those who had been martyred in the name of

Christ, and even to those who might face a terrible death because they would not renounce their faith. Paul knew that the faithful would experience a different setting and a different way of life after death than they had known and had experienced in this life. But only then would they know the reality of a final glorification.

Matthew 13:44-52 (R, L, C); (the Roman Lectionary also has a short form, 13:44-46); 13:31-33, 44-49a (E)

In order to emphasize the truth of the parables of the treasure in the field and the pearl of great price as parables of the kingdom of heaven, the Episcopal Lectionary does two things: it adds two additional parables — the mustard seed and the woman using yeast as leaven (vv. 31-33) — to highlight the kingdom of heaven theme; and, the last two verses, which really speak to the work of evangelists and preachers, who always are faced with the task of interpreting the "old" Word freshly in another time and new situations, have been removed. (One might discern the influence of Reginald Fuller in the additions and, especially, in the deletion of verses 51 and 52, which might detract from the main thrust of the gospel. He would not, however, allow anyone to misinterpret the deletion, because he has shown, again and again in his writings, the importance of redaction in the exegetical/hermeneutical process.)

The first parable may trouble some readers because the man who has discovered the treasure in the field is ready to cheat the owner(s), if necessary, in order to obtain it for himself. Of course, what Jesus is getting at is that the treasure — the kingdom of heaven — is of such value that one should stop at nothing in order to gain it. The second parable — the pearl of great price — emphasizes the same truth about the kingdom of heaven; heaven is to be gained at any cost. In considering these parables for preaching, the emphasis is on the unmatched value of the kingdom of heaven for human beings, rather than on how the kingdom of heaven is obtained. The context of Jesus' life and sayings reminds us that he was a superb theologian, and that he knew that the kingdom of heaven was a pure gift of grace from God that could not be purchased, or won, or discovered, by human initiative, ingenuity, or intention. Those who have been "found" by Christ know this and cling to their most precious possession with all their might; they know their eternal destiny hangs in the balance. The faithful dare not lose what has been found to be of such value, the kingdom of heaven.

The parable of the dragnet points once more to the last things and the judgment which will happen at that time. The good and evil will be separated, with the evil once cast into "the furnace of fire; there men will weep and gnash their teeth." The implication is that the good, the righteous ones, will remain in the kingdom of heaven and know the fullness of joy that pure communion with God gives to faithful people.

Sermon suggestions:

Matthew 13:44-50 — "Go for it — the Kingdom!"

A few days ago, my wife and I spent some time with a young couple — relatives — who are enjoying all the best things there are in life. The man is a very successful salesman, who earns enough money that his wife is able to stay at home with their two small children. They have a lovely home — brand new — the usual two cars, a motorcycle, an expensive boat moored at their lake property, a tractor at home and another at their cottage, the latest in appliances and toys for grownups as well as children (two VCRs, stereo, compact disc player, etc.). The young mother was talking about her husband's work; he is considering moving from one sales position to another in which he would be working for straight commission; ostensibly, he could earn more money that way. She said: "Oh, he makes good money now, but you might as well make as much as you possibly can, don't you think?'' Rather typically, they are living for the present, for what they can accumulate and enjoy; they will do whatever they have to do to improve their already affluent life-style even more. One could conclude that their hearts are where their treasures are, despite the fact that they can see the steeple of the church where they were married, and where their two children were baptized, from their home that is high atop a hill; they never attend worship services there. Their lives and life-style seem almost to be a parable of this time, this age, which is quite a contrast from that of Jesus' parables, because their treasures are of this world, not of the kingdom of heaven.

   1. *Our most precious gift* — the kingdom of heaven. Jesus not only believed that, but he illustrated it with parables, and died to validate his teachings about the worth of the kingdom. What value do you place upon the kingdom?
   2. *Our first priority in life* — seeking the kingdom. God gives the kingdom through Jesus to those who honestly seek it and desire to receive it and enjoy the blessings and benefits now and in this life. What do you seek most in life?
   3. *Our ultimate effort* — rejoice and cling to the hope of the kingdom. Once we have received the gift of grace — the kingdom of heaven — it is for us not to lose it, but through repentance and joyful obedience, to live the new life of the kingdom as long as we live. What do you work hardest to achieve, accumulate, and retain?
   4. *Our eternal fate* — "Choose this day whom you will serve" — the kingdom of heaven or the world — because tomorrow may be too late. "Go for it — the kingdom of God."

1 Kings 3:5-12 (R, E, L) — "A Programmed Prayer."

A colleague, Wendell Frerichs, preached a memorable sermon about prayer a few years ago. He declared that there are at least three "levels" on which believers might pray: we might pray *desperately,* when life threatens to overwhelm us, and this is the lowest level of prayer; we might pray *dutifully*, because we know that, as faithful Christians, we *should* pray to God every day, and this is a higher level of prayer; and, we might pray as a *loving response* to the God of all goodness and grace, who in Jesus Christ has saved and redeemed us, and this is the highest level of prayer. In this story — a dream sequence, if you will, Solomon offers a prayer that has a touch of desperation in it, an expression of proper piety and devotion, and a prayer that attains the highest level that a prayer might reach as he surrenders his future to God in love.

   1. *Programmed prayer* — When do you pray? Do you pray at all? In what situations do you pray? What are your prayers like? Are they all on one level? What do you pray for? Are your prayers programmed primarily by what happens in your life? Are they programmed by what God has done for you in Jesus Christ?
   2. *A prayer program* — Unlike Solomon, most of us have to depend upon conscious efforts at prayer, not on dreams in which God comes to us. Prayer is a loving response to God's constant goodness and grace, not simply a spiritual resource for desperate situations, nor even a saintly habit — valid as these are.
   3. *Prayer programmed* — God himself, through his Word and his Son, teaches us to be constant in prayer, and to pray for what is of the most value in life — the wisdom of the kingdom, for a blessed life — for our loved ones, for ourselves, for all people in this world — in which we discern what is right and good and proper — and choose to live godly lives in time and for eternity.
   This reading, especially the part of Solomon's prayer which is asking for a "discerning mind . . . that I may discern between good and evil," may readily be incorporated into the sermon on Matthew 13. It would make a fitting concluding section of the sermon, possibly replacing the second and third parts of the Matthew 13 sermon. Conversely, the main

sermon might come from the Old Testament reading, bringing in the parables of the king-dom as examples of what we should give priority to in our prayers.

Exodus 3:13-20 — "The 'I Am' God."

Introduction: Retell, concisely, the story in last Sunday's reading, Exodus 3:1-12, remind-ing the listeners of what was said in the sermon.

1. God himself — "I Am who I Am" — planned and initiated the Exodus. He gave Moses authority to execute his plan. He is the one who causes all good — the saving acts — to happen in the world.

2. God told Moses what to do and what he would do. He would bring his plan to frui-tion. He knew that Pharaoh would not let the people go, even for a three-day retreat, so he promised to display his power to soften Pharaoh's heart.

3. The "I Am" God also came and revealed himself to all the world. His revelation was *in* one man — Jesus Christ — not *to* one man, and it set in motion his plan for freeing every person from sin and death. In his death and resurrection, Jesus accomplished a one-person exodus that is valid for all people and until the end of time.

4. Listen to, and believe, the Word of God — "I Am the Lord" — and become free to live forever in Jesus Christ.

Romans 8:28-30 — "Just What is Jesus Saying?" ("We know that in everything God works for good with those who love him, who are called according to his purpose." v. 28)

1. It sounds like the promise of a "rose garden," doesn't it? At least, that's how we hear these words, because we think that Christians should have no painful or unpleasant experiences in life. We all would welcome divine intervention in our affairs, at one time or another, wouldn't we?

2. God is actively at work in our lives. He turns us toward the good by supporting us in every situation we may face, changing pain into joy, suffering into glory, and defeat into victory through Jesus Christ and the presence — and prayers — of the Spirit.

3. Just what is Jesus saying? "Trust in God" — and you will come to know how God is working to change evil, pain, suffering, and anguish into good — for you and for all peo-ple in the world.

(Romans 8:31-34, included in this day's reading in the Episcopal Lectionary, will be in-corporated into the sermon for the Eleventh Sunday after Pentecost [Romans 8:35-39 — Lutheran; Romans 8:35, 37-39 — Roman *Ordo;* Romans 8:31-39 — Common Lectionary]).

The Eleventh Sunday after Pentecost
Eighteenth Sunday in Ordinary Time
Proper 13

Roman Catholic	**Isaiah 55:1-3**	**Romans 8:35, 37-39**	**Matthew 14:13-21**
Episcopal	**Nehemiah 9:16-20**	**Romans 8:35-39**	**Matthew 14:13-21**
Lutheran	**Isaiah 55:1-5**	**Romans 8:35-39**	**Matthew 14:13-21**
Common	**Exodus 12:1-14**	**Romans 8:31-39**	**Matthew 14:13-21**

The church year theological clue

With one more Sunday remaining in August, the preacher may find more of a practical preaching clue in the approach of the fall season than a theological theme in the church year. For now, the latter part of August emphasizes a kind of homiletical eschatology; in many congregations, one has been preaching primarily to the faithful few during the summer months, and soon summer will be over. Attendance will increase in the next few weeks and one's preaching may have to be somewhat different than it was during the summer. Congregations come to life in September, awakening, as it were, from spiritual hibernation during the summer months. All sorts of programs are about to begin again. Pastoral exegesis will determine what sort of preaching has to be done to speak in this situation; the preacher may have to be reminded of the eschatological movement of the church year, which is about to enter the second half of Pentecost.

The Prayer of the Day — The LBW appoints two prayers for this Sunday; neither is an evident reworking of the classic collect for the Tenth Sunday after Trinity/the Eleventh Sunday after Pentecost. The first prayer is oriented toward the "bread" theme in the Gospels for Year A (Matthew 14:13-21) and Year B (John 6:24-35); the second prayer has been designed for use with Year C and its Gospel (Luke 12:13-21). The first prayer addresses God the Father: "Gracious Father, your blessed Son came down from heaven to be the true bread which gives life to the world," and, not unexpectedly, asks, "Give us this bread, that he may live in us and we in him, Jesus Christ our Lord."

The Psalm of the Day — Psalm 104:25-31 (L) — Verses 28 and 29 pick up the "food" theme in Isaiah 55, which also finds expression in the Gospel for the Day:

All of them look to you to give them their food in due season. You give it to them; they gather it; you open your hand, and they are filled with good things.

It functions very well as a responsory to the first reading and a "separated antiphon" (the second reading separates it from the Gospel) to the Gospel for the Day.

The Psalm Prayer (LBW)

God of all light, life, and love, through the visible things of this world you raise our thoughts to things unseen, and you show us your power and your love. From your dwelling-place refresh our hearts and renew the face of the earth with the life-giving water of your Word, until the new heaven and new earth resound with the song of resurrection in Jesus Christ our Lord.

Psalm 145:8-9, 15-19 (R) — the Roman *Ordo* employs this psalm on another Sunday, the 31st Sunday of Year C (145:1-2, 8-11, 13c-14), but only two verses (8-9) are said or sung

226

on both Sundays. Those two verses read:

> *The Lord is gracious and full of compassion, slow to anger and of great kindness.*
> *The Lord is loving to everyone and his compassion is over all his works.*

Verses 16 and 17 have found considerable use in table prayers and are most appropriate inconnecting the Old Testament reading and the Gospel for the Day:

> *The eyes of all wait upon you, O Lord, and you give them their food in due season.*
> *You open wide your hand and satisfy the needs of every living creature.*

Verse 18 offers a fitting conclusion to the portions of the psalm that are used in the liturgy: "The Lord is righteous in all his ways and loving in all his works."

Psalm 78:1-29, or 78:14-20, 23-25 (E) — Both long and short versions of this psalm are most appropriate for the reading from Nehemiah, which speaks of God's faithfulness to Israel — and specifically in providing them with water and manna in the wilderness. In the face of all the good things God has done for them, which the psalmist recites, he tells how the people of Israel railed against God and asked, "Can God set a table in the wilderness?" The last two verses provide an answer, which points to the miracle of the loaves and fishes in the Gospel for the Day: "He rained down manna upon them to eat and gave them grain from heaven. So mortals ate the bread of angels; he provided for them food enough."

Psalm 143:1-10 (C) — This psalm might very well be used *before* the first reading (Exodus 12:1-14) because it is a cry to God for help in escaping the wrath of one's enemies. The reading spells out God's directions for the Passover, which will take place as God sends the final plague to soften Pharaoh's heart and convince him to allow the Israelites to leave Egypt. Its content makes it appropriate for many Sundays of the year, especially for some of the Sundays of Lent and Easter. It functions more as a gradual than a responsory, in that it is thematically compatible with the Romans 8 reading for the day.

The readings:

Isaiah 55:1-3 (R); 55:1-5 (L)

The prophet pictures the Lord God "throwing a banquet" for the nation, Israel, after the people have returned to their homeland from exile. It is eschatological in nature, a model of the meals in which Christ fed thousands of people on a few loaves of bread and a couple of fish (Matthew 14). There is also a hint of the ultimate banquet to come, of which some Christians sing (LBW) every Sunday: "This is the feast of victory for our God. Alleluia! This much is perfectly clear: the banquet is an act of pure grace, a gift from God" —

> *Ho, every one who thirsts, come to the waters; and he who has no money, come, buy and eat! Come, buy wine and milk without money and without price . . . Incline your ear, and come to me; hear, that your soul may live . . . .*

All of this adds us to a gracious invitation offered by God to "feed and drink at his table."

The Lutheran Lectionary adds two verses to the Roman *Ordo*, beginning at verse 4, "With you I will make an everlasting covenant," as the *Jerusalem Bible* puts it, "out of the favors promised to David." Israel will be God's witness to all of the nations; some will come to Israel "for the sake of Yahweh our God." And Isaiah promises, "the Holy One of Israel . . . will glorify you." The banquet celebrates more than the return of God's people to their promised land; it ushers in a new day of mission, their mission for the Lord God in the world.

228

Nehemiah 9:16-20 (E)

The context of this reading is the Feast of Tabernacles, which was instituted after the return to Jerusalem and the rebuilding of the city walls. Following the feast, there was a fast, with carefully-programmed religious activities: For one quarter of the day, the Law was read (after Ezra's example); the second quarter was spent in a "loud" confession of their sins, and it is from this confession that this reading is excised. The confession recalls the goodness of God, recounting the events of the Exodus, the giving of the Ten Commandments, and as verse 15 reads, "For their hunger you gave them bread from heaven, for their thirst you brought them water spurting from the rock . . . ." At this point, the reading declares:

> *But our fathers grew proud, were obstinate, and flouted your commands. They refused to obey, forgetful of the wonders that you had worked for them . . . . they even thought of going back to Egypt and their slavery. (Jerusalem Bible)*

God proved to be a forgiving and a gracious God, who not only forgave their "obstinateness," but also pardoned them when they fashioned — and worshiped — a golden calf. God continued to be with them for those forty years and, says the prophet, "You gave them your good spirit to make them wise, you did not withhold your manna from their mouths, you gave them water for their thirst." Since God had already done this with his people when they spent four decades wandering through the wilderness to the Promised Land, it is not unexpected that Jesus should perform a miracle of feeding those who had followed him and had nothing to eat. Although the confession goes on for seventeen more verses, this reading concludes here, at the twentieth verse, as it tells a true story but also points to another "banquet" story in the Gospel for the Day.

Exodus 12:1-14 (C)

The Roman, Episcopal, and Lutheran lectionaries appoint this reading for Holy Thursday in Year C, rather than for the near-middle of Pentecost (the Roman *Ordo* omits verses 9-10), because the events of Holy Thursday, Good Friday, Holy Saturday, and Easter Sunday combine into a Christian Passover. The reading gives details of when and how the Passover is to be initiated in Egypt to protect the first-born of the Israelites from the death that God will inflict upon the first-born of the Egyptians, just as another Pharaoh had done to the Hebrew boy babies. This was the tenth plague and was meant to soften Pharaoh's heart and, therefore, cause him to release the Israelites from their bondage in Egypt.

> *This day is to be a day of remembrance for you, and you must celebrate it as a feast in Yahweh's honour. For all generations you are to declare it a day of festival, forever.* (v. 14)

Romans 8:31-39 (C); 8:35, 37-39 (R); 8:35-39 (E, L)

The Common Lectionary reading begins where last week's lesson ended, which is also the beginning of one of the most frequently appointed and used passages of Scripture at the burial of the dead; it begins:

> *What then shall we say to this? If God is for us, who is against us? He who did not spare his own Son but gave him up for us all, will he not also give us all things with him?*

Paul declares that the dead and risen Christ, who is at the right hand of God, makes intercession for us, and that is why the Christians can face anything this life has to offer.

The other lectionaries join in with the familiar questions: "Who shall separate us from the love of Christ? Shall tribulation, or distress, or persecution, or famine, or nakedness, or peril, or sword?" Those who read and heard these words understood perfectly what Paul was saying about life and death and, no doubt, prayed that they, too, could join the Apostle when he declared,

For I am sure that neither death, nor life, nor angels, nor principalities, nor things present, nor things to come, nor powers, nor height, nor depth, nor anything else in all creation, will be able to separate us from the love of God in Christ Jesus our Lord.

The importance of this reading is the reason that it is included here in the Roman and Episcopal lectionaries, which also assign it to the Second Sunday in Lent (Roman — 8:31-34a; Episcopal — 8:31-39). It is read in the context of the opening — and continuing — word of Lent: "You are dust, and unto dust you shall return," and in the blessed assurance that Easter gives to the faithful.

Sermon suggestions:

Matthew 14:13-21 — "From Crisis to Communion."

Just two days ago, my wife and I received a letter from the wife of a former colleague and neighbor who is living in Jamaica and survived the full force of Hurricane Gilbert (September 12, 1988). She described in detail how, when the hurricane struck with "unbelievable force," half of the roof of their house was immediately ripped off and blown away. Water cascaded in from the torrential rains, and they immediately attempted to move books and bedding from the upstairs rooms to a lower floor of their home; they soon gave this up and sought shelter to save their own lives. Water, driven by the 150 mile per hour winds, was everywhere; she didn't say so, but I suspect they were praying desperately to be delivered. What occurred in Jamaica and specifically to them, made an earlier weather-related incident seem like child's play; about ten years ago, the lake they were living on overflowed and we had to sandbag their home. That was a neighborhood event, and it had — despite the seriousness of the flooding (they had to replace a furnace in the basement, which was flooded), an air of fun and joy to it; we knew that the rain was over, that we had beaten the flood, and that we had saved their home from severe damage. Coffee and food appeared from everywhere, more than enough to refresh all who participated in the filling and placing of the sand bags.

What happened in Jamaica made that earlier incident seem like child's play; there was no way to stop the water, no way to prevent wind damage. Half the houses on the island suffered severe damage, and most of the buildings at the university were also affected. But, our friend said,

We pushed water out night and day for many days, tried to prepare food for stranded guests on campus despite no water or electricity. Standing knee-deep in water our "soup" kitchen functioned and served many hungry workers. Everything we could get went into the pot — you know I have always enjoyed creative cooking — we turned our home into a soup kitchen and fed as many people as we could.

For her, the miracle of the loaves and fishes had been repeated — in a different time and in a different way. She writes:

There is a sense of camaraderie — caring and sharing on this seminary campus that we have never experienced before. We all help each other, share what we have and the one loaf of bread becomes many!

230

She indicates that they are living a miracle: "I am sure that beautiful flowers will bloom out of the rubble."

1. *The crisis — and the disciples' concern.* The people following Jesus had brought no food with them; they had nothing to eat. No one was starving, but some might faint from hunger.

2. *Christ's compassion and power* — "You give them something to eat." Five thousand men, plus women and children, were fed miraculously from five loaves and two fish. There was more than enough for all to eat.

3. *The crowd's communion* — with each other and with the Lord Jesus, who worked the miracle; "they all ate and were satisfied." Like their ancestors during the Exodus, they ate the "food of the angels," whether they realized it or not.

4. *Care for others in the future* — "And they took up twelve baskets full of the broken pieces left over." What was done with them? Were they saved for breakfast, or what? Jesus knew that the bread had future use and would not go sour like the manna in the wilderness. Is this miracle a sign that the bread of the Eucharist will never be exhausted until the feast is celebrated in heaven itself?

This incident, coupled with the contemporary story — or stories like it, and conditions in the world, suggests a narrative sermon (Steimle-style), which would see the interweaving of a biblical story and our stories to allow the text to speak to people today.

Isaiah 55:1-5 (L); 55:1-3 (R) — "The Divine Invitation."

1. *God's invitation to a "free meal"* — the heavenly banquet costs nothing, but is often valued less than the things the world offers and on which we spend our resources.

2. *God's promise* — "Incline your ear, and come to me; hear that your soul may live." There is more than food and water, milk and wine, involved here — food for the soul! I heard a young girl say on a television program that she had to go to church a couple of times a month. "Once a month," she said, "is not enough for me."

3. *God's covenant in Christ* — renews for us the covenant made with the people of Israel centuries ago, and assures us that, in his good time, he will glorify us and give us life eternal.

Nehemiah 9:16-20 — "Care and Confession."

1. The God who cares for his people — then and now.

2. The God who works wonders — then (the Exodus) and now (in the ministry of the church in the world).

3. The confession that is good for the soul — *mea culpa, mea maxima culpa!* It opens up communication between people and God, renews relationships through God's grace, and prepares people to serve God by serving others in his name.

Exodus 12:1-14 — "The Tenth Plague and Passover."

1. *Tell the Passover story* — in the context of the material that has been omitted since last week (chapters 3:21 to 11:10) — and highlight the tenth plague and the Passover. The "blood of lambs and goats" saved the lives of the first-born — and softened Pharaoh's heart so that he would let the Israelites go.

2. *Tell the passion story* — as Jesus' Passover — and ours — from death to life. Jesus' death and resurrection are Passover for us. His blood, the blood of the lamb, the only begotten Son of God, defeated Satan and obtained our release from sin and death. Weave in contemporary stories and illustrations, as necessary.

Romans 8:31-39 — "Questions and Answers of the Faith."

1. *A question for the martyrs* — "What shall we say to these things?"

2. *A question for all believers* — "Who shall separate us from the love of Christ?"

3. *A question answered* — "For I am sure that neither death, nor life, nor angels, nor principalities, nor things present, nor things to come, nor powers, nor height, nor depth, nor anything else in all creation, will be able to separate us from the love of God in Christ Jesus our Lord."

The Twelfth Sunday after Pentecost
Nineteenth Sunday in Ordinary Time
Proper 14

Roman Catholic	1 Kings 19:9, 11-13	Romans 9:1-5	Matthew 14:22-33
Episcopal	Jonah 2:1-9	Romans 9:1-5	Matthew 14:22-33
Lutheran	1 Kings 19:9-18	Romans 9:1-5	Matthew 14:22-33
Common	Exodus 14:19-31	Romans 9:1-5	Matthew 14:22-33

The church year theological clue

Little or no help is forthcoming from the church year as a theological clue for a worship/preaching theme for this Sunday. The title of the day — the Twelfth Sunday after Pentecost — is really the only reminder, suggesting how the church got to this point in the year and, for those in the "liturgical know," where we are going, Christ the King Sunday. On this "Pentecost pilgrimage," it is the business of the church to give thanks and to worship the Lord, to seek out the secrets of the kingdom, to grow in grace and faith, and to engage in the work of the righteous, which is serving and doing good to all human beings in the name of Jesus Christ the Lord.

The Prayer of the Day (LBW) — Here is another example of a classic collect being reworked to accommodate contemporary liturgical language, rather than making any theological alterations and/or corrections; the older English — "who art" . . . "art wont," etc. — is replaced with modern linguistic and grammatical forms. The address of the revised version of the prayer is almost identical to the older collect, changing the "who art always more ready to hear . . ." to "you are always more ready to hear, etc." What is intended to be a subtle theological alteration occurs in the beginning of the petition; "Pour down upon us" simply becomes "Pour upon us." But the only way that anything can be poured here on earth is "down," so there is really no important change in this wording. The word "mediation" ("through the merits and mediation of Jesus Christ") is deleted and "merits" is cast in the singular as "merit." The revised prayer reads this way.

> *Almighty and everlasting God, you are always more ready to hear than we are to pray, and to give more than we either desire or deserve. Pour upon us the abundance of your mercy, forgiving us those things of which our conscience is afraid, and giving us those good things for which we are not worthy to ask, except through the merit of your Son, Jesus Christ our Lord.*

The Psalm of the Day — Psalm 85:8ab, 10-13 (R); 85:8-13 (L) — Verse 8 of this psalm — "I will listen to what the Lord God is saying, for he is speaking peace to his faithful people and to those who turn their hearts to him" — reveals why this particular psalm was appointed for this Sunday. It virtually puts words in the mouth of Elijah, when he is hiding in the cave and seeking out the Lord God. The psalm could also be understood as a reflection on God's revelation and assurance to Elijah, despite the fact that it was undoubtedly composed for another situation, probably the return from the exile (which suggests why the Roman *Ordo* omits verse 9). It does, however, seem to have more thematic affinity to the Old Testament reading than it does to the Gospel for the Day (the miracle of Jesus walking on water, etc.), but there is a connection in the raging wind and the voice of Jesus that stilled the storm and brought calm to the lake and the disciples, just as the Voice must have done for Elijah.

The Psalm Prayer (LBW)

> *God of love and faithfulness, you so loved the world that you gave your only Son to be our Savior. Help us to receive him as both Lord and brother and freely celebrate him as our gracious Redeemer now and forever.*

Psalm 29 (E) — The Episcopal Lectionary employs a different first reading (Jonah 2:1-9) and also a different psalm than any of the other lectionaries for the Twelfth Sunday after Pentecost. In this prayer from within the belly of the great fish, Jonah cries out to God for mercy and deliverance, recounting what God had done for him on another occasion:

> *But you lifted my life from the pit, Yahweh, my God. While my soul was fainting within me, I remembered Yahweh, and my prayer came before you into your holy Temple. (Jerusalem Bible)*

The psalm picks up the confidant prayer of Jonah,

> *Ascribe to the Lord, you gods, ascribe to the Lord glory and strength. Ascribe to the Lord the glory due his name; worship the Lord in the beauty of holiness.*

Verse 3 looks to the Gospel for the Day: "The voice of the Lord is upon the waters," which might also be heard in the context of Jonah 1:15, "And taking hold of Jonah they (the sailors) threw him into the sea; and the sea grew calm again." This psalm would also function quite well as a responsory to the 1 Kings reading of the Roman and Lutheran lectionaries, because it spells out what the "voice of the Lord" can do in all of nature.

Psalm 106:4-12 (C) — This psalm, which is a psalm of national confession, acts as a response to Exodus 14's story of Pharaoh's pursuit of the children of Israel, and makes contemporary God's care and power by individualizing and personalizing the gracious action of God in delivering the Israelites by a watery defeat of the Egyptians at the Red Sea. In a petition that follows asking God to take the same kind of action — "He saved them from the hand of those who hated them and redeemed them from the hand of the enemy" — on behalf of these people, the psalm speaks to our failure to trust God in all situations. It puts us in the boat with the fearful disciples, who didn't trust the Lord while the storm raged around them. (Matthew 14)

The readings:

1 Kings 19:9a, 11-13 (R); 19:9-18 (L)

Here is the story of Elijah's taking refuge in a cave, where "the word of the Lord" came to him and asked, "What are you doing here, Elijah?" Elijah's answer detailed the perfidy of the children of Israel, who

> *have forsaken thy covenant, thrown down their altars, and slain thy prophets with the sword; and I, even I only, am left; and they seek my life, to take it away.*

First, there was a powerful wind, but God wasn't in it; next, an earthquake, but God wasn't in it, and then a fire, but the Lord was not in that, either. Finally, a still small voice spoke to Elijah, and he heard God ask again why he was there, answered God, and then received orders for his return "to the wilderness of Damascus," where he was to anoint Hazael as king of Syria, Jehu as king of Israel, and Elisha as his successor. These would do the bidding of the Lord, exterminating all of the unfaithful in the land, but sparing "seven

234

thousand in Israel, all the knees that have not bowed to Baal, and every mouth that has not kissed him.'' This reading was chosen because it looks to the Gospel for the Day and recognition of Christ as the Son of God by the disciples after he had entered the boat and calmed the storm.

Jonah 2:1-9 (E)

When the terrified sailors threw Jonah into the sea in the hope of saving themselves (1:15), the sea grew calm and for the first time in their lives they were in fear of Yahweh. Jonah, meanwhile, had been swallowed by the great fish, which had been sent by God to effect his rescue, and during the three days and nights he prayed this prayer to God. Again, there is a connection with the Gospel for the Day, and it could be Peter, not Jonah, saying,

> *The waters surrounded me right to my throat, the abyss was all around me. The sea-weed was wrapped around my head . . . . But you lifted my life from the pit, Yahweh, my God. While my soul was fainting within me, I remembered Yahweh, and my prayer came before you into your holy Temple.*

The parallels to the story in Matthew 14 are striking, if not completely obvious and, sometimes, in contrast to the images created by the Jonah story.

Exodus 14:19-31 (C)

The three different first readings in the Roman/Lutheran, Episcopal, and Common lectionaries, illustrate the fact that there are many Old Testament stories that harmonize with the Gospels for the Day, while retaining their own integrity. This story, which tells the familiar tale of the crossing of the Red Sea by the Israelites and the drowning of Pharaoh's army (''not a single one of them was left,'' v. 28), stands on its own merits and ought to be included in the preaching regimen of every pastor at some time; it is crucial to the success of the Exodus and vitally important to the Christian faith, as well. And the story does make a connection with the Gospel, focusing in on Jesus' deliverance of Peter from drowning in the Sea of Galilee, while saving all of the disciples from a watery grave. In some ways, it is the most appropriate of the three readings when placed alongside the Gospel for the Day, which shows the power and concern of Yahweh working in the person of Jesus Christ, his Son.

Romans 9:1-5

Paul must have known of some anti-semitism in the congregation at Rome, and this prompted him to write about the Jews, as he did: ''What I want to say is this: my sorrow is so great, my mental anguish so endless, I would willingly be condemned and be cut off from Christ if it could help my brothers of Israel, my own flesh and blood.'' He goes on to tell why they are so important: God adopted them as sons, gave them the covenants, the Law, and the religious rituals; he made promises to them. Not only are they descended from the patriarchs, but Jesus also comes from their lineage. Those who love Christ should appreciate the uniqueness of the relationship between Isaiah and the church, deal with Jews in love, and, Paul would insist, work for their conversion to the Christian faith.

Matthew 14:22-33

It was between 3 and 6 a.m. that Jesus appeared to the disciples during a heavy gale, walking on the water so that he seemed like a ghost. He had sent the crowds away, and probably was still attempting to deal with the news about the beheading of John the Baptizer, which could have been the reason that he sent the disciples out on the lake by themselves while he went into a solitary retreat. Jesus reassured them that he was no ghost, which prompted Peter to test him out by asking Jesus to let him walk on the water. As most people know, he lost his faith after a few steps, began to sink, and had to call to Christ to save him. He did, verbally chastising him for his lack of faith. They reached the boat, got into it, and the wind stopped blowing. This prompted a confession from the disciples, "Truly you are the Son of God." Matthew, most scholars would agree, was using this story to speak to his congregation; the boat represents the church, the gale is the persecution they are experiencing, which Jesus will see them through. He wanted to bolster their faith in Christ, the Son of God, to help them face and conquer in Christ the terrible trials of the faith that had come to them.

Sermon suggestions:

Matthew 14:22-31 — "A Ghost, A Wizard, or A Savior?"

Ray Bradbury, in *The Stories of Ray Bradbury*, tells a tale ("Invisible Boy") about a lonely old woman and a young boy, Charlie, whom she wants to have as her own son. She is a witch, a magician, and a sorcerer of sorts. Once, when his parents were out of town, he went to visit her; she decided to keep him for her own, saying to him, "My son, you are my son, for all eternity!" Charlie ran off, locked himself in an abandoned cabin and wouldn't come out. She tried her magic potions on the door lock to no avail, offered him all sorts of bribes, if he would come out, and finally got a response by promising to make him invisible. Bradbury says of her,

> *She had long ago realized that her miracles, despite all perspirations and salts and sulphurs, failed. But she had always dreamt that one day the miracles might start functioning, might spring up in crimson flowers and silver stars to prove that God had forgiven her pink body and her pink thoughts and her warm body and her warm thoughts as a young miss. But so far God had made no sign and said no word, but nobody knew this except the old lady.*

Actually, her potion failed, but she was able to convince Charlie that he was invisible and played a sort of game with him for several days, convincing him, when time came for him to go home, that he was becoming visible again. With a shout he ran off, and she was by herself; he really was invisible, but she was sure that he was close enough to her to engage in conversation that really was all one-sided. Her intended miracles still did not work.

1. Jesus ran the risk of being called a magician, as well as a ghost, when he walked on the water to the boat. His miracles really did work; he could heal the sick, give sight to the blind, make the deaf hear, and he had just recently fed thousands of people with five loaves and two fishes. But to walk on the water? He had to be some sort of a magician to accomplish that miracle. He was the greatest magician of which there were many in the ancient world (according to Morton Smith in *Jesus the Magician*). He didn't have to — couldn't — *pretend* that his miracles, even walking on water, were real. They were.

2. Oddly enough, the disciples didn't consider him to be a magician working his greatest feat of magic, a genuine miracle, walking on the waves of a surging sea. They said, "It is a ghost!" Perhaps it was because the incident happened at night that they called him a ghost, but whose ghost was this coming across the water? Surely, not that of Jesus, because he was not yet dead and risen. Did they suppose that they were seeing the ghost of John the Baptizer, who had so recently been executed? A single sentence calmed them down, "Take heart; it is I; have no fear," — but Peter needed more and asked to be included in the

236

miracle, "Lord, if it is you, bid me come to you on the water." Jesus said, "Come," and he did, only to begin to sink — apparently he couldn't swim — and had to be saved by Jesus Christ. Peter is so much like we are; he wanted proof that Jesus really was who he said he was, the Son of God.

3. They could have called him "magician" when he and Peter reached the boat, but they didn't; the disciples simply said, after the wind and waves calmed down, "Truly you are the Son of God." That's the person who comes to us in the Word and the sacraments of the church. If we expect him to come to us primarily as a miracle-worker and a magician, he may very well seem like the old lady, whose miracles didn't work. If we think of him as one who comes as a kind of ghostly presence, instead of the resurrected and reigning Lord, we may miss him altogether. If we listen to the Word, he comes to us most often, as he did to Elijah, in a still small voice that brings peace and calm to us in every situation and enables us to declare, "Truly you are the Son of God." And that is enough for him and for us.

1 Kings 19:9-18 (L); 19:9a, 11-13a (R) — "That Still Small Voice."

Every pastor has encountered someone who has said, "I don't have to go to church every Sunday; I find God out in the woods, or on the lake, or in the mighty acts of nature. That's really all I need." They're a bit like Carl Broberg's famous hymn:

O Lord my God, when I in awesome wonder
Consider all the works thy hand hath made,
I see the stars, I hear the mighty thunder,
Thy pow'r throughout the universe displayed.

1. *That was not the way it was with Elijah.* God came to him in a still small voice, not in the storm, the thunder, the wind, or the earthquake. That's the way he comes to us, too. The still small voice reveals God in Christ to us and prompts us to sing, "How great thou art! How great thou art!"

2. *In the still small voice, God refreshes our souls.* He gives us, as he did Elijah, meaning, purpose, and direction for our lives. It makes the story of God's love and Jesus' sacrifice dear and precious to us, as Broberg rightly states it:

But when I think that God, his Son not sparing,
Sent him to die, I scarce can take it in,
That on the cross my burden gladly bearing
He bled and died to take away my sin.

3. *That still small voice will become a mighty shout when Jesus returns.* It will be heard all over the earth, so we dare to sing:

When Christ shall come, with shout of acclamation,
And take me home, what joy shall fill my heart!
Then I shall bow in humble adoration
And there proclaim, "My God, how great thou art!"

Then sings my soul, my Savior God, to thee,
How great thou art! How great thou art!
Then sings my soul, my Savior God, to thee,
How great thou art! How great thou art!

Jonah 2:1-9 — "A Whale of a Tale."

1. What a fish tale! Jonah was plucked from the sea — by God's grace — and by a great fish. He would have drowned, had it not been for the great fish; Jonah didn't have the power to walk on the water. Our salvation comes in sinking beneath the water — and dying — in Baptism — our fish story.

2. The belly of the whale. No one prayed under more different circumstances. Jonah went through a kind of conversion experience in the stomach of the great fish and, after that, offered his prayer of thanksgiving to God. But is that any stranger than praying from a cross, "Father, forgive them, for they know not what they do?" Surely, he hears our prayers of confession and helplessness — "Out of the depths have I cried to thee, O Lord."

3. The tail of a whale. Jonah must have remembered God's command to go to Nineveh and preach repentance while he was "in the belly of the whale." Just to make sure, God told him what to do again, after the fish deposited him on the beach. He did as God commanded him. The question is, will we?

Exodus 14:19-31 — "Saved by the Waves."

1. God's final act in leading the children of Israel out of Egypt occurred at the Red Sea. When Pharaoh changed his mind and broke his word, sending his army after the Israelites, God provided a safe passage through the sea. Water, since then, has provided deliverance — in Baptism — and is a blessing to human beings.

2. God doomed Pharaoh's troops to a sailor's death. They were wiped out to a man when the wind shifted and the walls of water closed in upon them. God uses water to defeat Satan and to release his people from sin and death, but we receive life, not death, when the water covers us in baptism.

3. God's deliverance opened up the future of the Israelites. They were free at last to make their way to the land promised to their fathers. "He that believes, and is baptized, shall be saved" — forever; Baptism gives us a future in the everlasting kingdom of God.

Romans 9:1-54 — "A Put-down of Prejudice."

1. Anti-Semitism reared its ugly head in the early Christian church, and that grieved the heart of St. Paul. Then, as now, it grieves the heart of God himself, for the Jews are still his chosen people. Like it or not, Jesus was a faithful Jew.

2. The church is the new Israel, and it has descended from the old Israel. The patriarchs, the prophets, and the kings are our heritage, too. Don't ever forget that without them we wouldn't be Christians.

3. God is the God of both the old and new Israel. He would have them be one in his love — and in Jesus Christ our Lord. Prejudice against the Jews, which has led to persecution, even the Holocaust, must go.

4. Bless the Lord and love one another — for all he has done to make the two Israels into one.

A congregation in which I was invited to conduct a kind of pre-Lenten retreat began Lent with the Seder as an evening meal on Ash Wednesday. The Eucharist followed, and thus the two traditions were brought together in the exodus-journey of Lent that culminates at the cross and the empty tomb. The people in that congregation are very much aware of the relationship of the New Israel to the Old and are attempting to foster positive relationships between Christians and Jews in their town. I think they understand quite well what Paul was talking about in this reading.

The Thirteenth Sunday after Pentecost
Twentieth Sunday in Ordinary Time
Proper 15

Roman Catholic	Isaiah 56:1, 6-7	Romans 11:13-15, 29-32	Matthew 15:21-28
Episcopal	Isaiah 56:1, (2-5) 6-7	Romans 11:13-15, 29-32	Matthew 15:21-28
Lutheran	Isaiah 56:1, 6-8	Romans 11:13-15, 29-32	Matthew 15:21-28
Common	Exodus 16:2-15	Romans 11:13-16, 29-32	Matthew 15:21-28

The church year theological clue

The phrase used in the title for the day, "after Pentecost," reminds the church and its preachers that the journey to Christ the King Sunday is roughly half-completed. The Holy Spirit is still at work in the church, bringing people to the Lord, undergirding the faith of the believers, and inspiring the people of God to devote themselves to good works and loving service in the name of Jesus Christ. Of itself, the church year "theological framework" has little direct influence upon the worship and preaching of the church; the near-Advent of fall (September is at hand), with the promise of new beginning in all phases of church life, places emphasis upon pastoral and practical theology in the weeks ahead. One's preaching ministry should go into high gear, theologically, because it is around Labor Day that the new year of the church is really about to begin.

The Prayer of the Day (LBW) — The traditional and classic Collect for the Day gives way to a new, and rather simple, Prayer of the Day, which might be fitting on any Sunday. It addresses the God who has "given great and precious promises to those who believe." The petition, however, is attuned to the Gospel for the Day, Matthew 15:21-28, the healing of the Canaanite woman's daughter by Jesus: "Grant us the perfect faith which overcomes all doubts, through your Son, Jesus Christ our Lord." There is more of a theological/hermeneutical clue in this prayer than there is in the church year framework. The emphasis is on the gift of faith that only God can give people, rather than on the healing miracle which Jesus accomplished, according to the Gospel for the Day.

The Psalm of the Day — Psalm 67 (E, L); 67:2-3, 5-6, 8 (R) — The Roman, Episcopal, and Lutheran churches also assign this psalm to the Sixth Sunday of Easter, Series C, primarily as a song of thanksgiving, on that occasion for the resurrection of the Lord about to be completed in the ascension. It is a psalm that was originally giving thanks for a successful harvest ("The earth has brought forth her increase; may God, our own God, give us his blessing" — v. 6), but is used in Pentecost to remember all the blessings which God has poured out upon his people. It is also a psalm that, in older translations, will be very familiar to regular church-goers:

> *May God be gracious to us and bless us and make his face to shine upon us, that thy way may be known upon earth, thy saving power among all nations. Let the peoples praise thee, O God; let all the peoples praise thee!*

Since the psalm is only seven verses in length, the thanksgiving theme can hardly be lost if it is said or sung as a responsory to the first reading by the people and, as the psalm prayer suggests, directs attention to the blessing God offers all people in Jesus Christ.

238

The Psalm Prayer (LBW)

> *Father, through your power the earth has brought forth its noblest fruit, the tree of the cross. Unite all people in its embrace, and feed them with its fruit, everlasting life through Jesus Christ our Lord.*

Psalm 78:1-3, 10-20 (C) — As a responsory, this psalm speaks to the whole history of Israel, as well as to the specific situation in the first reading, Exodus 16:2-15, which is the account of the near-rebellion faced by Moses and Aaron when food was scarce in the wilderness:

> *They tested God in their hearts, demanding food for their craving. They railed aginst God and said, "Can God set a table in the wilderness?"* (vv. 18, 19)

Since the reading recounts how God did just this by providing meat and manna for the people, this psalm seems more functional as a kind of introit rather than a responsory to the first reading. It does, of course, open up a larger question about what God is able to do today, in the light of the miracle in the Gospel of the Day, which enables it to be used as an appropriate responsory to the first reading.

The readings:

Isaiah 56:1, 6-7 (R); 56:1 (2-5), 6-7 (E); 56:1, 6-8 (L)

This reading has been chosen because it points to the way that God has offered himself and his blessings, to all people — and, in the Gospel for the Day, to a humble Canaanite woman of great faith — in Jesus Christ. It has to do (v. 1) with the post-exilic response of God's people in doing works of justice and righteousness in the expectation that the salvation of God — in the Messiah — will soon come. But it also looks to the role of "foreigners" in the worship of the Temple, stating that if they love the Lord, keep his laws and the covenant, they will be accepted in the Temple; their sacrifices will be pleasing to God. The intention of God — "for my house shall be called a house of prayer for all peoples" — was connected by Mark to the very cleansing of the Temple by Jesus. This reading connects with the Gospel for the Day and supports Jesus' action in healing the daughter of the Canaanite woman of faith.

Exodus 16:2-15 (C)

A month and a half had passed since the Israelites had left Egypt; they were now in the wilderness of Sin, between Elim and Sinai, and provisions obviously were nearly depleted. They seem to have forgotten that what God had done in gaining their release from their bondage in Egypt, the ten plagues and the crossing of the Red Sea, were far behind them. They wanted to know where God was as they passed through the wasteland; would he, could he, help them? They had been much better off in Egypt, at least, some said they had all they needed to eat; their bellies were full back there in Egypt. Yahweh informed Moses what he would do — how he would provide meat and bread for them every day; Moses ordered Aaron to inform the people and, true to his word, God sent them quail for meat and manna — "the bread of the angels" — for their daily bread. The quail they recognized and gathered for their dinner, but when they saw the manna on the ground, they asked, "What is that?" Moses replied, "That is the bread Yahweh gives you to eat." God answered their question through his servant, Moses, in a way that satisfied their hunger and their doubts.

Romans 11:13-15, 29-32 (R, E, L); 11:13-16, 29-32 (C)

Paul seems to have given up on the mission to convert the Jews to Christ, and he is convinced that the primary thrust of his ministry is with the Gentiles. There are, of course, at least two difficulties with his outlook: his sense of the impending return of Christ was myopic, because he believed that the return of Christ was close at hand; and he thought he could make the Jews jealous by offering, as Matthew puts it, "the children's bread to dogs." That salvation and eternal life are irrevocable gifts from God is quite evident to Paul; after all, he has clearly articulated the doctrine of justification by faith through grace in this same letter. Although there is a hint of "greater good because of evil" in his "God has consigned all men to disobedience, that he may have mercy upon all," he is really talking about the condemnation that comes to those who break the Law; no one can keep the Law perfectly, thus God offers mercy to all people in Jesus Christ.

Matthew 15:21-28

The plea of the Canaanite woman to Jesus, "Have mercy on me, O Lord, Son of David; my daughter is severely possessed by a demon," is one of the touching incidents in the ministry of Jesus. But Matthew makes several changes from the similar story told by Mark, the most important of which is his acknowledgement of her faith, "O woman, great is your faith!" Matthew shows his audience, Jewish Christians, that it is the woman's faith that made her prayer acceptable to Christ; he doesn't make as much of the miracle as does Mark, but simply asserts that the healing in Jesus' words, "Be it done for you as you desire" took place on schedule — immediately. Her continual cry of "Lord, help me" reached the very heart of Jesus and her faith moved him to appreciative and compassionate response, because it came out of a gift that God had already given, her faith. This Gospel picks up the thread of God's concern for all people in the first and second readings and other propers for the day and his desire to gather them all to himself in his Son, Jesus Christ.

Sermon suggestions:

Matthew 15:21-28 — "A Long Distance Miracle."

Four decades ago, an inner-city Episcopal Church in Philadelphia was engaged in a weekly healing ministry that took the shape of two worship services. One was at noon and the other late in the afternoon of the same day, Thursday. Dr. Alfred Price, the pastor of the congregation, had long been impressed with the various healings that had been accomplished by Jesus in his ministry, and by Jesus' statements that "whatsoever you shall ask the Father in my name, he will give you." He learned the healing power that comes from God during a congregational crisis in which the choir became a hot-bed of discord; in desperation, one Sunday morning he called them together, formed a circle, had them join hands, and prayed for peace and harmony. The rift in the congregation was healed, and everything began to change for the better. Since that prayer/healing service "worked" it led to the development of the healing ministry and the regular healing services in which people came to the altar rail during a liturgical service, hands were laid on their heads and they were prayed for, with the result that many miraculous healing occurred; some people, however, were not cured of their maladies. The rector said that he did not possess the healing power; it came from God and was channeled through him to the sick or infirmed persons; faith, or the lack of it, seemed to have very little to do with the healing, faith didn't *work* the healings that took place; people some distance away, who were prayed for by request, often were healed, many of them didn't even know the prayers were being requested, and raised, on their behalf. The healing services, which were begun in the 1940's, continue to be held in many Episcopal and other denominational churches to this day, because many pastors and their people have faith that God can — and does — heal his children of their various illnesses and infirmities. Any person of faith, regardless of denomination or lack of it, is welcomed at such healing services.

1. *This is the story of a long-distance healing.* It was accomplished by Jesus at the request of a distraught mother — a persistent, non-Jewish woman, whose child was "demon-possessed." Jesus healed the girl without even seeing her or touching her, but the heart of this Gospel is not the long-distance miracle; it is the faith of the Canaanite woman. How could she have such faith? Where did she get it? After all, she was not one of God's chosen people.

2. *God is the source of faith, as well as life.* He gives faith in himself to all people who will accept it. It is his intention that the good news should be preached to all people, so that all might know him to be a God of love and believe and trust him with all their hearts. Christians and Jews do not have a corner on faith; God means all people to know him and live by faith in a hostile world.

3. *God respects genuine faith which clings to him in hope.* God gives people faith which enables them to stand up to impossible odds in life, because he has love and compassion for his people; he is the sole source of all faith and hope. Human beings cannot bring themselves to believe and trust in God by their own initiative any more than they can make themselves love God and his Son, Jesus Christ. God never turns his back on those who believe and trust him in good faith; to do so would be to reject the gifts that he has given to his own. He brings healing of one sort or another to those who pray to him in faith.

4. *Jesus performed a miracle* — but the real miracle of the story is the great faith of the woman, who kept begging Jesus to heal her daughter because she had faith in him as one who had come from God and had power to heal. That miracle — faith — is one of the good gifts that God has given us so that we might live confidently in the world and be of service to God and other human beings. Faith — great faith — is the long-distance miracle that God gives to the world. Receive it and exercise it, in the name of Jesus Christ.

Isaiah 56:1, 5-7 (R); 56:1 (2-5), 6-7 (E); 56:1, 6-8 (L) — "For All People."

1. *A prophet's perception:* God wants all people to know and believe that he is God, the only God; he wants to bring them into the kingdom.

2. *A prophet's pronouncement:* God's "holy house" is meant for all people; he has built, through his servant Israel, a "house of prayer for all peoples."

3. *A prophet's plan:* God will gather a peculiar people — the children of Israel, and the "outcasts," to himself. This is the mission that Jesus has given to the church in the world.

Exodus 16:2-15 (C) — "A Heavenly Hand-Out."

1. *Times were tough in the wilderness.* Things were so bad that some wanted to return to Egypt, but there was no going back. God knew what his people were suffering in the wilderness.

2. *God kept the faith.* He stepped into the picture, just as he had done in Egypt and at the Red Sea; he gave them bread and meat, just enough for each day of their journey. It was enough; it never ran out.

3. *He has prepared a table for us.* He knows our need and feeds us with his Word, with bread and wine, the body and blood of one who said, "This is my body, given for you . . . This cup is the new covenant of my blood, shed for you and for many for the forgiveness of sins." "Take and eat," says the Lord, "Take and drink." This food and drink will sustain you forever; it will never run out.

Romans 11:13-15, 29-32 (R, E, L); 11:13-16, 29-32 (C) — "The Gifts of a Good God."

1. *God's call and gifts are intended for all people.* The Jews first heard the gospel, but it was soon preached to the Gentiles, too; God wanted it that way.

2. *Good because of goodness.* There is some truth in those lines of Frederick Faber's hymn, "Greater good because of evil, Larger mercy through the fall," but the central theme is, with Paul, "There's a wideness in God's mercy . . . ." The cross of Christ tells us that.

> *For the love of God is broader*
> *Than the measures of man's mind,*
> *And the heart of the eternal*
> *Is most wonderfully kind.*

3. *Repent and receive the gifts of God.* Forgiveness and eternal life come to those who repent of their sins. "All have sinned and fall short of the glory of God." All people must repent — every day — and receive the gifts anew. Forgiveness lasts a lifetime, but it has to be renewed daily.

4. *Share the gifts.* Each of us is called to do just that, according to Jesus Christ. There are enough for all.

The Fourteenth Sunday after Pentecost
Twenty-first Sunday in Ordinary Time
Proper 16

Roman Catholic	Isaiah 22:15, 19-23	Romans 11:33-36	Matthew 16:13-20
Episcopal	Isaiah 51:1-6	Romans 11:33-36	Matthew 16:13-20
Lutheran	Exodus 6:2-8	Romans 11:33-36	Matthew 16:13-20
Common	Exodus 17:1-7	Romans 11:33-36	Matthew 16:13-20

The church year theological clue

Summer is over, and fall has begun with its return of people to the churches and their activities, and the church is now entering the last quarter of the church year. Informed people will realize that about two and a half months remain in the Pentecost Cycle/Season. They are also aware that such things as Rally Day, Installation of Church School teachers, programs and retreats involving the young, the women, and the men of the churches are getting under way. Halloween decorations and cards are appearing in the stores, reminding people that Reformation Day and All Saints Day are soon at hand and that Thanksgiving Day is just behind them. A few people will remember what Pentecost is all about; they are ready to complete the pilgrimage through Pentecost to Christ the King Sunday and, the following week, the First Sunday in Advent. The sacred and secular years have a way of coming together in this part of Pentecost. They often combine to influence the themes that emerge from the readings for one's preaching ministry.

The Prayer of the Day (LBW) — The address to God in this prayer could just as well have been used with the readings last Sunday, because it speaks of the effort of God to reach out to "all nations" with the intention of calling people into his kingdom. But the petition points to the Gospel for the Day, not only as God "gathers disciples from near and far," but especially in conjunction with the petition, "count us also among those who boldly confess your Son Jesus Christ as Lord." It is here that the theme for the day, according to the Gospel, is introduced.

The Psalm of the Day — Psalm 138 (E, L); 138:1-3, 6, 8 (Note: The Roman *Ordo* uses almost the same portions of this psalm on the Fifth Sunday in Ordinary Time and the entire psalm on the Twentieth Sunday in Ordinary Time of Series C. The *Book of Common Prayer* appoints the entire psalm for Proper 20 of Series C. The psalm has only nine verses.)

While this is clearly a song of thanksgiving for something God has done, the scholars can't agree on the occasion and reason for this thanksgiving; some see it as a response to Isaiah's vision of God in the Temple, others would go so far as to call it a psalm of David linked to the beginning of the royal line that God has established in him. Clearly, it is a song of thanksgiving and praise for the God who has demonstrated his love and faithfulness to Israel. It speaks of a time when

> All the kings of the earth will praise you, O Lord, when they have heard the words of your mouth . . . . Though the Lord be high, he cares for the lowly; he perceives the haughty from afar . . . . O Lord, your love endures forevever; do not abandom the work of your hands.

From the standpoint of the Gospel, God's purposes for all people will ultimately find fulfillment in Jesus Christ.

244

The Psalm Prayer (LBW)

> *Lord God, you keep the proud at a distance and look upon the lowly with favor. Stretch out your hand to us in our suffering, perfect in us the work of your love, and bring us to life in Jesus Christ our Lord.*

Psalm 95 (C) — Those familiar with the ancient liturgies of the church will recognize the first seven verses of this song as the *Venite exultemus.* It begins,

> *Come, let us sing to the Lord; let us shout for joy to the rock of our salvation. Let us come before his presence with thanksgiving and raise a loud shout to him with psalms.*

But the last four and a half verses, beginning at 7b, reveal the reason that this psalm was appointed as a responsory to Exodus 17:

> *Oh, that today you would harken to his voices! Harden not your hearts as your forebears did in the wilderness, at Meribah, and on that day at Massah, when they tempted me. They put me to the test, though they had seen my works.*

The psalm concludes with a recitation of God's displeasure "with this generation" and his determination that none of those who started the Exodus would complete it; a new generation would enter into the land promised to their fathers.

The readings:

Isaiah 22:19-23 (R)

This is the second of two oracles spoken by Isaiah against Shebna, who was steward and master of the palace of the king. The charge against him and his fate are spelled out in the first oracle, 22:15-18; his position had gone to his head, and he had attempted to set himself up as one of the royal family by carving out a tomb for himself where only they could be buried. The second oracle, the first reading for this Sunday, tells of his dismissal from office and the appointment of Eliakim in his place:

> *I invest him with your robe, gird him with your sash, entrust him with your authority . . . I place the key of the House of David on his shoulder; should he open, no one shall close, should he close, no one shall open. (Jerusalem Bible)*

Jesus went even further than that in the Gospel for the Day, saying to Peter,

> *And I tell you, you are Peter, and on this rock I will build my church, and the powers of death shall not prevail against it.* I will give you the keys of the kingdom of heaven, and whatever you bind on earth shall be bound in heaven, and whatever you loose on earth shall be loosed in heaven. [RSV emphasis, mine]

Isaiah 51:1-6 (E)

This is a portion of one of the assurances given to the people of God in what has been called, "The Book of the Consolation of Israel" (chapters 40—55). It is a reminder to Christians, as well as to the Jews, that they are to "consider the rock from which you were cut. Consider Abraham your father and Sarah who gave you birth." It also contains the assurance that God will have mercy upon his own people and turn the desolation they have known into a new Eden. His Law and his justice will prevail, and his "salvation shall come like the light, (his) arm shall judge the peoples." The last verse of the reading highlights this eschatological note:

> *Lift up your eyes to the heavens, look down at the earth. The heavens will vanish like smoke, the earth will wear out like a garment, and its inhabitants die like vermin, but my salvation shall last forever and my justice have no end. (Jerusalem Bible)*

The "rock" reference, rather obviously, is the reason this reading was chosen for this day.

Exodus 6:2-8 (L)

God identifies himself to Moses in this pericope and informs him of what he will do for the children of Israel, because he has heard their "groaning" in their bondage in Egypt, and because he has remembered his covenant with them. Moses is to tell them two things: the Lord will *bring them out of bondage,* will redeem them "with an outstretched arm and with great acts of judgment," will take them again "for my people," and will be their God so they will know that the Lord is God by his deliverance; and the Lord God "will bring (them) into the land which I swore to give to Abraham, to Isaac, and to Jacob." He is able to do this because he is the Lord — and they will know it.

Exodus 17:1-7 (C)

The Roman and Episcopal lectionaries appoint this pericope as the first reading for the Third Sunday in Lent to complement the Gospel (John 4) of Jesus and the Samaritan woman he met at the well. The reading picks up the tale of the Israelites as they travel from Sin to Rephidim, going from a bad situation to a worse one; there is no water here to drink, so once more they put God to the test with their complaining. Yahweh told Moses to take the elders with him and his rod, and to go to Horeb and strike the rock in the presence of the elders, and promised that water would come forth. Moses did as God commanded and water poured forth to slake their thirst. He named the place Massah and Meribah, because they had put God to the test and asked, "Is God with us, or not?"

Romans 11:33-36

No one will ever know if Paul could sing, but he certainly knew how to compose a doxology, and this is one of the best examples he has left us; he almost breaks into song as he writes, "O the depth of the riches and wisdom and knowledge of God! How unsearchable are his judgments and how inscrutable his ways!" As a theologian, he admits that complete knowledge of God is beyond him; he will never know God's mind the way he would like to, and Paul knows this. He also knows that there are occasions when all one can do is worship God and sing his praises and acknowledge the mysteries of the faith in the liturgy of the church. "For from him and through him and to him are all things. To him be glory forever. Amen." On this note, he ends this first section of his letter to the Romans.

Matthew 16:13-20

When Matthew took over this account from Mark's Gospel, he changed it radically. He has Peter answering Jesus', "But who do you say I am?" with "You are the Christ," adding, "the Son of the living God." Scholars seem to be convinced that this is a post-resurrection redaction, and not anything that Peter said in his years with Jesus. In Mark, Peter's answer is played down, and Jesus proceeds to tell the disciples about his impending fate in Jerusalem;

246

his suffering, death, and resurrection will occur to fulfill Scripture. In Matthew, Jesus reacts positively to Peter's answer, and he is commended and praised as the one on whom the church is to be built and the one to whom the keys of the kingdom are entrusted, as well. Only after he has said these things does Jesus proceed to talk about what will happen to him in Jerusalem, eliciting Peter's objection and Christ's rebuke, "Get behind me, Satan!" All preachers should be able to preach on the first half, or so, of this reading, "You are the Christ, the Son of the living God." The second half, about building the church on the Rock, Peter, and the giving of the keys to him, will require reflection and meditation to think through the theological problems inherent in the man Peter and the Petrine office, as well as the matter of whether or not the keys of the kingdom are invested in a particular office or the whole church. (See Matthew 18, especially verse 18, addressed to all the disciples.)

Sermon suggestions:

Matthew 16:13-20 — "The Choice."

The set of questions that Jesus puts to Peter are fundamental, indeed, and the second one — "Who do you say that I am?" — must be answered by everyone who hears the good news. One's eternal destiny depends, to a large degree, on how one answers this question.

1. *The opinion poll:* "Who do people say that I am?" In Jesus' day, the choice was between various of the prophets — John the Baptizer, Elijah, Jeremiah, or some other prophet. Healer/magician and teacher, answers that people might give today, were not even considered.
2. *The personal interrogation:* "Who do you say that I am?" What really matters is how each person who has heard the story of Jesus answers this question. Is he simply a man chosen by God to announce God's reign and will, who is sent to call people to repentance and renewed faith? Or is he the Christ, the Son of the living God? Jesus puts this question to each of us.
3. *The blessing:* Assurance that God has spoken to us and has saved us in Jesus. That's what Peter received, plus the responsibility of building up the church and exercising with mercy and compassion the office of the keys of the kingdom. Every Christian participates in the first command, the upbuilding of the body of Christ, the church, and has, at least, the responsibility to ascertain that the office of the keys is being properly administered.
4. *The difference:* Jesus charged the disciples to tell no one that he was the Christ; Jesus has charged us to tell the whole world.

The manner in which the preacher opens up and emphasizes Jesus' charge to Peter as the Rock and as the keeper of the keys has to, of course, be determined mostly by the needs of the congregation. Point 3, above, may have to be expanded so as to comprise most of the sermon. Since the rest of the story is the Gospel for the Day next Sunday, it may be well to plan a two-part sermon for the Fourteenth and Fifteenth Sunday of Pentecost. Sermon 1 could be on "The Question," and Sermon 2 could be about "The Answer."

Isaiah 22:19-23 (R) — "The Keys to the Kingdom."

1. *The office of the keys is to be taken seriously.* It has to do with forgiveness and new life, matters which cannot be glossed over lightly because they have to do with the eternal destiny of human beings. In the movie, *Lady Mobster,* the tragic heroine of the story, who has discovered the identity of the man who killed her parents and her husband, goes to her brother, Paul, a priest, to make her confession. When she refuses his counsel and asserts that she is going to kill the man, he tells her, "I cannot absolve you," and she goes away — unforgiven — to her fate. Father Paul took the office of the keys so seriously that he could not even offer forgiveness to his own sister. It must have broken his heart.

2. Clergy and laity alike must face their responsibilities in the office of the keys. The unworthy clergy, according to Isaiah, are in jeopardy of losing their office and, with unrepentant laity, may lose their salvation.

3. Confession and absolution must be taken seriously by the faithful. They have to do with one's eternal destiny. Each one of us must learn how to say *mea culpa,* receive the blessing in absolution, and turn around to live a new life.

Isaiah 51:1-6 (E) — "On This Rock."

1. Abraham and Sarah are the rock on which the faith in God is built. Peter comes later as the rock, the foundation, of the Christian church. The roots of the Hebrew and Christian faith are deep indeed.

2. The Word of the Lord has established the rock. God called Abraham and Sarah, the patriarchs and the prophets, Peter and Paul and all of the Apostles. He calls and speaks to you and me, through his Word, just as he has spoken in the past.

3. God's plan for his people will endure to the end of time. Isaiah said it, Jesus affirmed it, and he will complete it at the last day.

4. Come, Lord Jesus! Come, quickly!

Exodus 6:2-8 (L) — "A Divine Announcement."

1. Item number one: God announced to Moses that he was aware of Israel's bondage in Egypt and would take action to set the people free and lead them out of Egypt.

2. Item number two: God announced to Moses that he would lead the people of Israel into the land he had promised to Abraham, Isaac, and Jacob that he would give them.

3. God's hidden agenda: God would, in time, free his people from the burden of the Law, renew his covenant with them, and seek to bring all people into his kingdom through Jesus Christ, the Son of the living God.

Exodus 17:1-7 (C) — "Is God For Us?"

1. That was the question of the children of Israel during the Exodus. There was no water for them, their families, or their cattle, at Rephidim. "Why did God bring us out of Egypt — to die of thirst?" Several excellent stories about thirst in the desert are included in Antoine de St. Exupery's *Wind, Sand and Stars.* See, particularly, the end of the "Prisoner of the Sand" chapter.

2. Afraid for his life, Moses sought out the Lord. He simply asked God what he should do, and the Lord answered him. God told him what to do; he did it — struck the rock in the presence of the elders — and there was water — and life.

3. Is God with us, or against us? That's our question, too. He has answered the question in Jesus Christ and the church. The water that has come from the rock, the church, in baptism, assures us that he is with us — and will not fail us — no matter what happens in life.

Romans 11:33-36 — "Glory to God."

1. Glory to God in the highest. He is our God, and his ways are beyond our understanding. He is God, and his mind can never fully be known by human beings.

2. Glory to God in the lowest. He has revealed himself to us in his Son, Jesus Christ, our Lord. In him, the greatest mystery of all — the cross and resurrection for our salvation — is set before us. God became a human being, born as the babe of Bethlehem, to die and rise again for our sake.

3. Glory to God — forever. He really does have the whole world in his hands; we can understand that, have hope for life in Christ, and express our faith by giving him the glory he deserves.

The Fifteenth Sunday after Pentecost
Twenty-second Sunday in Ordinary Time
Proper 17

Roman Catholic	Jeremiah 20:7-9	Romans 12:1-2	Matthew 16:21-27
Episcopal	Jeremiah 15:15-21	Romans 12:1-8	Matthew 16:21-27
Lutheran	Jeremiah 15:15-21	Romans 12:1-8	Matthew 16:21-26
Common	Exodus 19:1-9	Romans 12:1-13	Matthew 16:21-28

The church year theological clue

Had the plan of the Joint Liturgical Group in Great Britain, which set an agenda for reforming the church year, been followed in the American churches, the Advent prayers might have come at a very propitious time in the life of the churches, the beginning of September. The Joint Liturgical Group had suggested extending the Sundays before Christmas back far enough that the holy history of the faith might be read annually. While there is something to be said for such a plan, something would also be lost; the eschatological mood of Pentecost would be down-played, at best. As the life of the parishes is "stirred up" in September, it is well to keep before the people the movement toward Christ the King Sunday and the last things. The life of and in the Spirit prepares us for that, as well as for contemporary living.

The Prayer of the Day — The suffering of Christ is noted — and thanks is given to God that his Son "chose the path of suffering for the sake of the world." As it has been composed for the new lectionary, it points to, and reflects what is in, the Gospel for the Day, in which Jesus informs his disciples of the fate that will befall him in Jerusalem. It also spells out our response to his command to "take up our cross and follow him": "Humble us by his example, point us to the path of obedience, and give us strength to follow his commands; through your Son, Jesus Christ our Lord."

The Psalm for the Day — Psalm 26 (E, L) — It is rather evident that this is the plea of a person who has been falsely accused of some evil deed. This person seeks vindication from God, who alone is able to judge the thoughts, sayings, and actions of human beings. It is so idealistic — some have called it self-righteous — that it really only could be offered up to God by one man, Jesus Christ, the sinless one. The psalm speaks for him: "I have walked faithfully with you . . . . I have hated the company of evildoers . . . . I will wash my hands in innocence, O Lord." The psalmist goes on to say: "Lord, I love the house in which you dwell and the place where your glory abides." He also speaks against false accusations, as were made by Christ: "Do not sweep me away with sinners, nor my life with those who thirst for blood, whose hands are full of evil plots, and their right hand full of bribes." Only Jesus could really declare, "As for me, I will live with integrity; redeem me, O Lord, and have pity on me. My foot stands on level ground; in the full assembly I will bless the Lord."

The Psalm Prayer

Lord Jesus, Lamb without stain, image of the Father's glory: Give us the strength to avoid sin and be faithful to you always. Lead us to the place where God dwells in his glory, that we may praise him with joy among his saints now and forever.

Psalm 63:2-6, 8-9 (R) — The thirst for God, as the psalmist perceives it, is as intense as the physical thirst of those who are passing through "a barren and dry land where there is no water." (like Rephidim ?). God is able to — and does — quench the thirst of those whose souls are tortured by their longing to know God. The psalmist knows that God can be found, and one's spiritual thirst can be assuaged, by those who throw themselves upon the mercy of God, because God is constantly seeking out his own people to claim them and bless them. The cries of the faithful are heard by God; they can say, in true faith: "My soul clings to you; your right hand holds me fast." The Roman *Ordo* also appoints this psalm for the Twelfth Sunday in Ordinary Time, Series C.

Psalm 114 (C) — The psalm takes up the story of the first reading, recounting how God solved the troubles of the Israelites when they put him to the test during the Exodus: "When Israel came out of Egypt, ... Judah became God's sanctuary and Israel his dominion." The recitation of God's actions at the Red Sea and in the mountains and hills picks up the story of what happened at Rephidim in the last two verses:

> Tremble, O earth, at the presence of the Lord, at the presence of the God of Jacob,
> who turned the hard rock into a pool of water and flint-stone and into a flowing spring.

The psalm makes an excellent response to the first reading, Exodus 19.

The readings:

Jeremiah 20:7-9 (R)

These are the words of a true prophet, a man who has been completely captured by the Word of God, not by an inflamed imagination or personally induced inspiration. True to form, the prophet of the Lord has become a butt for those opposed to what he says in the name of God, as the prophet himself remarks, "I am a daily laughing stock, everybody's butt." *(Jerusalem Bible)* The prophets, who base their pronouncements upon the Word of the Lord, usually become the object of scorn and derision and, if hated enough, may even be put to death, as Jesus remarked, "Jerusalem . . . killing the prophets . . . ." In the New Testament, the martyrs took their places alongside the prophets, testifying to God the truth of his Word by laying down their lives in the name of Jesus Christ.

Jeremiah 15:15-21 (E, L)

Here is the word of a prophet who has suffered miserably at the hands of the people of God. He has been doing his best to serve the Lord and his Word, but all he has received is reproach from those he has come to lead back to God. So the prophet complains to God for himself and, no doubt, speaks on a different level for the community which finds itself at odds with God and suffering because it has not really attempted to be faithful to the Lord God. Oddly enough, the prophet, who seems to have lost faith in God, actually turns to the Lord God in his prayer and, in return, hears a word of blessing from the Lord God: "If you return, I will restore you, and you shall stand before me." He hears the promise of God's support in whatever trials and persecutions he may have to endure in life, which is what Christians have learned to expect from the Lord. Final deliverance is promised to the prophet, his community, and, in light of the gospel, to faithful Christians. Jeremiah might have been speaking for Jesus, too, in what he had to endure, and what God had promised him in the face of persecution, suffering, and death — resurrection on the third day: "I will deliver you out of the hand of the wicked, and redeem you from the grasp of the ruthless." This reading, therefore, lays a biblical foundation for the Gospel for the Day and Jesus' prediction of what will happen to him. It also points to Jesus' words on the cross, "My God, my God, why have you forsaken me?"

250

Exodus 19:1-9 (C)

Once more, the Israelites were on the move, this time from Rephidim to Sinai, after God had slaked their thirst with water from a rock split open by Moses' rod. For the first time, Moses met God on Sinai, and Yahweh addressed Moses and instructed him to remind the people of the things he had done for them in bringing them out of Egypt and leading them through the wilderness. If they keep the covenant with God, they will be his peculiar people, and also a kingdom of priests, who offer their sacrifices to him, not only in formal worship but in their daily lives. The Roman *Ordo* employs part of this reading, vv. 2-6a for the Eleventh Sunday in Ordinary Time, or the Fourth Sunday after Pentecost, Series A; The Episcopal and Lutheran lectionaries appoint Jeremiah 19:2-8a for the same Sunday. Additional comments on this reading may be found in the commentary for the Fourth Sunday after Pentecost. Jeremiah 19:3-8a, plus verses 16-20b, is also one of the four first readings of the Vigil of Pentecost, series B; the Episcopal and Lutheran lectionaries also appoint Exodus 19:1-9 for the Vigil of Pentecost.

Romans 12:1-2; 12:1-8 (E, L), 12:1-13 (C)

Long before the new lectionaries began to appear, it occurred to me that, on many occasions, the second reading, or the Epistle for the Day, ought to be read *after* the Gospel for the Day, because it frequently had a "now hear this and do this" quality about it. The first two verses of the Roman lection from Chapter 12 of Romans, suggests such an approach:

> *I appeal to you therefore, brethren, by the mercies of God, to present your bodies as a living sacrifice, holy and acceptable to God, which is your spiritual worship.*

The faithful are not to be "conformed to this world," but are to be "transformed by the renewal of (their) mind." They are to show in their lives "what is good and acceptable and perfect." For most Christians, this begins in the liturgy, but it also has to be done in the way one lives every day. The Episcopal and Lutheran lectionaries expand the reading so as to spell out the kind of humility which becomes those who belong to the body of Christ, recognizing that the members of the body have different functions, all of which are important to its welfare. Christians, too, have different gifts — prophecy, service, teaching, exhortation, contributing, giving aid, acts of mercy — which should be used in the name and service of Christ. The Common Lectionary expands the second reading to include those things Paul writes about in verses 9-13 — love for the good and loving respect for each other, untiring work for the Lord, spiritual earnestness, hope that generates a positive spirit, steadfastness when trials come, continual prayer, sharing with the saints, and making hospitality a priority of their lives.

Matthew 16:21-26 (L); 16:21-27 (R, E); 16:21-28 (C)

This reading, a continuation of last Sunday's Gospel, in which Peter makes his great confession and Christ responds with praise and the announcement that the church will be built upon this "Rock" and that the keys to the kingdom will also be given to him (and the church), is treated separately because it includes Jesus' announcement of his impending death in Jerusalem, as well as Peter's objection and subsequent rebuke by Jesus. The "then" in the RSV connects the two sections of this story; the second part finds Jesus saying that his followers must take up their crosses and follow him, and that "whoever loses his life for my sake will find it," plus two related questions. Matthew reveals in his reading Jesus' concern for the church and his conception of its discipleship in the world. The Roman *Ordo* includes the eschatological prediction (v. 27) about the return of Christ, and the Common Lectionary adds (v. 28) Jesus' announcement that some will still be living when he comes again.

Sermon suggestions:

Matthew 16:21-26, 27, 28 — "Death and Life."

1. *Born to die.* That is the fate of every person, of course, but Jesus was born to die a special death in order to reconcile God and his people, thereby accomplishing the salvation of all who believe and are baptized. Peter, like most of us, couldn't understand why Jesus had to die and tried to dissuade him from allowing this to happen.

2. *Dying to live.* Jesus had to die in perfect obedience to God, not simply to fulfill the scriptures, but to reveal the power and love of God in his resurrection. He had to die as a human being so as to be raised up to new life at the right hand of God and, thereby, complete the mystery. He also had to put down Peter — rebuke him severely — if he were to do God's will.

3. *Living with death.* That's the fate of each disciple, who, Jesus said, is "to take up his (her) cross and follow me." The cross makes its mark upon the manner in which we live in the world as we attempt to follow Jesus; it calls for total surrender of one's life to Christ and ready sacrifice — even literally — of one's life for the Lord. The sacrifice of one's ambitions, dreams, and intentions, along with one's time, talents, and possessions, on behalf of the Lord — a living sacrifice — may be more difficult than actually dying as a martyr for Christ; such sacrifice is a kind of slow and often agonizing death in which we find life.

Jeremiah 20:7-9 (R) — "Divine Seduction."

1. That's what Jeremiah experienced; God had seduced him into being his spokesperson, his prophet. It was his making, not his downfall.

2. Ridicule and rejection, not shame, were his lot. He found himself an outcast from the people he meant to warn and save.

3. God's Word — a fire in the heart. He couldn't help himself, despite derision and persecution; he had to go on prophesying in the name of Yahweh, even if it cost him his life. In this, he preceded Jesus, whom God called with, "You are my Son, in whom I am well pleased," and who suffered and died not simply for the sake of Israel, but to save the whole wide world.

Jeremiah 15:15-21 (E, L) — "The Prophet's Complaint."

1. *The complaint of a faithful prophet.* Jeremiah believed that God had let him down and abandoned him to those who rejected the Word of the Lord.

2. *Faithful even in his complaint.* When he might just as well have cursed God or turned away from him, the prophet prayed to God in faith, much as Jesus seemed to be doing when he said, on the cross, "My God, my God, why . . .?"

3. *The promise of a faithful God.* Yahweh said to the people, and to us, as well as to Jeremiah, "If you return, I will restore you, and you shall stand before me . . . ." What more can anyone ask of God?

Exodus 19:1-9 — "Preparation for a Summit Meeting."

(See the sermon suggestions for this text in the material for the Fourth Sunday after Pentecost. A variation is suggested below.)

1. *On the way again — from Rephidim to Sinai.* The Israelites always seemed to be going from wilderness to wilderness, from one bad situation to another that was worse. What a strange way to prepare for a summit meeting with God. Unfortunately, life tends to be like that for many people.

2. *God speaks again — he was still with them.* The people of Israel felt only the absence, rather than the presence, of God when they were in trouble. Like them, we doubt God's concern and even his ability to come to our aid, and we test him. God assured Moses — and us, in Jesus — that he will attend the summit; he is always present.

3. *God trusts again —* That's what sacred history, before and after Jesus' ministry, continues to tell us. His presence in his Word makes a positive summit meeting possible — at Sinai, for Israel — and at Golgotha, for us.

Romans 12:1-2 (R); 12:1-8 (E, L); 12:1-13 (C) — "The Christian's Offering."

1. *The Christian life-style — sacrifice.* Paul understood what Jesus was talking about when he said, "Take up your cross and follow me." For him, the Christian life was a living sacrifice.

2. *Transformed by the Word, not conformed to the world.* That's how the Christian life-style is shaped and is validated by Christ. The Christian life is cruciform in all of its dimensions.

3. *Fruits of faith and humility — service.* The secret of the Christian life-style lies in faith and genuine humility, wherein one finds the strength and persistence to use one's gifts — whatever they may be — in the service of God and his people. The Christian's offering to God is himself/herself.

The Sixteenth Sunday after Pentecost
Twenty-third Sunday in Ordinary Time
Proper 18

Roman Catholic	Ezekiel 33:7-9	Romans 13:8-10	Matthew 18:15-20
Episcopal	Ezekiel 33:(1-6) 7-11	Romans 12:9-21	Matthew 18:15-20
Lutheran	Ezekiel 33:7-9	Romans 13:1-10	Matthew 18:15-20
Common	Exodus 19:16-24	Romans 13:1-10	Matthew 18:15-20

The church year theological clue

The eschatological framework of the church year remains in place, but it does little or nothing to reveal any theological clue for worship and preaching or any specific theme for this Sunday. The church year does exert biblical and homiletical influence, however, in continuing to set aside September 21 as St. Matthew's Day. Those who have been preaching on the Gospel of St. Matthew may wish to take advantage of the opportunity to connect the man and his message in a sermon.

It might be even more helpful, if one were to preach about the gospel writers just before one began preaching on the Gospels they have written; in such a case, the festival of St. Matthew, Apostle and Evangelist, would have been celebrated a year ago, and St. Mark and St. John should be preached this year. St. Mark's Day poses a "time problem" inasmuch as it occurs on April 25th; too much of a time lapse would occur before the beginning of Series B Gospels on the First Sunday of Advent, December 2, 1989. St. John's Day, which occurs on December 27 might shape the sermon on the First Sunday after Christmas. St. Luke's Day falls on October 18, which makes the timing quite propitious for preaching about his Gospel shortly before Series C begins in 1990. At any rate, these four festivals for the four evangelists join the minor festivals of the saints and martyrs in sounding "kerygmatic accent marks" during the church year. (See Bass, *The Renewal of Liturgical Preaching,* p. 144.)

The Prayer of the Day (LBW) — As the Prayer of the Day, this collect reveals little or no connection with the prayer generally associated with this Sunday in the past. The older prayer was offered on behalf of the church; this one suggests, of course, that the church is also praying for itself, beginning, "Almighty and eternal God, you know our problems and our weaknesses better than we ourselves . . . ," and concluding, "In your love and by your power help us in our confusion and, in spite of our weakness, make us firm in faith; through your Son, Jesus Christ our Lord." The old collect spoke more specifically of cleansing and defending the church, because "it cannot continue in safety without thy succor . . . . ," and asked God to "preserve it evermore by thy help and goodness . . . ." It could have been assigned to Reformation Day; the new prayer better accommodates this Sunday's readings.

The Psalm for the Day — Psalm 119:33-40 (E, L); or, 119:33-48 (E) — This extremely long psalm is used on several Sundays of the church year; it fits into the themes of many Sundays. The section selected for the Sixteenth Sunday after Pentecost accommodates the theme in the first reading and the Prayer of the Day quite well, praying, "Teach me, O Lord, the way of your statutes, and I shall keep it to the end. Give me understanding and I shall keep your law; I shall keep it with all my heart." It is the prayer of an individual that is meant, in worship, to refer to and include all the people of the church in its response to the first reading and the movement toward the second reading: "Behold, I long for your commandments; in your righteousness preserve my life."

The Psalm Prayer (LBW)

Lord, you are just and your commandments are eternal. Teach us to love you with all our hearts and to love our neighbor as ourselves, for the sake of Jesus our Lord.

Psalm 95:1-2, 6-9 (R) — The "liturgically familiar" will recognize these six verses as belonging to the *Venite* that has been sung at Morning Prayer, or Matins. The first part of the psalm forms an inventory; the second part is an injunction to the people to "bow down and bend the knee, and kneel before the Lord our Maker" — not simply in thanksgiving but in repentance. Within the last half of the psalm is an exhortation to the people: "Harden not your hearts, as your forebears did in the wilderness at Meribah, and on that day at Massah, when they tempted me." At the very conclusion, Yahweh says, "So I swore in my wrath, 'they (who had tested him and disobeyed his commandments) shall not enter into my rest.' " Most liturgical churches do not include the last four and a half verses in the *Venite,* which may be why the Roman *Ordo* omits verses 3-5 and assigns verses 6-9 as the major part of the responsory psalm.

Psalm 115:1-11 (C) — The people of Israel could have joined in singing this song when Moses came down from Mt. Sinai after his meeting with God: "Not to us, O Lord, not to us, but to your name give glory; because of your love and because of your faithfulness." Indeed, the Lord God has shown himself to be patient and kind, merciful and just, in his dealings with his people, particularly when they tested him again and again in the wilderness of Sin, Rephidim, and Sinai. As they stood at the bottom of the mountain covered with smoke and fire, felt the ground shaking, heard the thunder by which God answered Moses, and, finally, the trumpet, they could say with assurance, "Our God is in heaven; whatever he wills to do he does." And this is a fitting responsory to the part of the Exodus story told in Exodus 19:16-24.

The readings:

Ezekiel 33:7-9 (R, L); 33:(1-6) 7-11 (E)

The Episcopal Lectionary includes the optional reading of the first six verses of this chapter, simply because they offer a parable about the role of the prophet in Israel, and verses 7-9 set out concretely the responsibilities and consequences that one who understands the role of the prophet must face up to. It pictures the prophet as a watchman, who must be on the lookout for the "sword" — the enemy — and warn the people when the enemy is coming. The people will die if the watchman fails to do his duty; he will also be held responsible for their death. If he warns the people but they do not heed his warning and die, it will be their own fault; he will be absolved, because he has done what he is supposed to do. The reading seems more suited to a clergy conference than it does for a Sunday morning service. In short, prophets and preachers must, above all else, be faithful in their calling. The eternal destiny of human souls — their own included — depends on it.

Exodus 19:16-24 (C)

Moses had already made two trips up Mt. Sinai. In the first meeting he had with Yahweh he received instructions for his message to the people. He is to gather them together and remind them of all that God has done for them in bringing them out of Egypt and through the wilderness. If they obey his commands, they will be his people. After Moses went down and told the people of his encounter, they promised, "All that Yahweh has said, we will do." Moses had to go up Sinai a second time with that message and Gold told him to go down and assemble the people so that they could hear him speak in the thunder when he addressed Moses on the mountain. They prepared themselves, washed their clothes, abstained from sexual relations, and on the third day they were ready and gathered at the foot of the mountain. From there, they saw the mountain covered with smoke, felt the thunder as God gave additional instructions to Moses. He was to go down and get Aaron and bring him — only him — up the mountain. Anyone else who crossed the boundaries prescribed by God and marked by Moses, and set foot on the mountain would die. With that, Moses went down and talked to the people once more.

Romans 13:1-10 (L, C); 13:8-10 (R)

The Lutheran and Common lectionaries, which spell out the civic responsibilities of Christians, are joined by the Roman Lectionary at verse 8. The theme of the reading changes, at that point, from emphasis upon obedience to the law of the land to the attitudes and actions of people who claim to be Christians. Paul declares that all of the commandments of God — against adultery, murder, stealing, and coveting — are summed up in a single commandment: "You shall love your neighbor as yourself." (Leviticus 19:18) He says, "Love is the one thing that cannot hurt your neighbor; that is why it is the explanation of every one of the commandments."

Romans 12:9-21 (E)

In this pericope, Paul continues to outline the ethical behavior of believers as they respond to the grace of God that they have received in Christ Jesus. Now he is talking about genuine love, about spiritual integrity, and about allowing love to dominate one's relations with all sorts of people, enemies as well as friends. He insists that Christians must not seek revenge on those who offend or hurt them, but should in all things allow love to shine through in their relationships with others. He ends this section with:

> *If your enemy is hungry, you should give him food, and if he is thirsty, let him drink. Thus you heap red-hot coals on his head. Resist evil and conquer it with good. (Jerusalem Bible)*

Matthew 18:15-20

Since the seventeenth chapter of St. Matthew contains his account of the transfiguration story plus a second announcement by Jesus of his impending passion and death, one has some idea of why the gospel selections skip from 16:26 to 18:15. But the main reason is simply that this material belongs with the content of chapter 16, which becomes very clear when one reads, "Truly I say to you, whatever you bind on earth shall be bound in heaven, and whatever you loose on earth shall be loosed in heaven." The focus upon Peter has now been shifted to the church, which shall not only develop a procedure for settling disputes among the faithful, but must also exercise its responsibility for the Office of the Keys. God is surely with his church when the people worship, but he is also present when they gather for any reason in his holy name. Individual members of the church and countless congregations might have been spared much pain and anguish, if they had taken this Gospel more seriously than they did. This Gospel shows the love of God in operation.

Sermon suggestions:

Matthew 18:15-20 — "The Right Way."

As I write this, three prominent citizens — a judge, a car dealer, and an attorney — of a town in our state are being accused of being drug dealers and, as a result, have been severely castigated by the citizens of the town and the area. The difficulty is that they have not been accused by the police, nor openly by any group of individuals; their assumed guilt has been thrust upon them by some person, or persons, by way of gossip and rumor. No one seems to know who has started the vicious gossip, but friends, acquaintances, and various public officials have begun to step forward and defend them, condemning, at the same time, the efforts of the persons who are making the apparently unfounded charges against the trio. One of the rumors has it that drugs are hidden in new cars when they are delivered, handed over to the attorney, who passes them on, while the judge covers up the entire operation when anyone gets caught by the law-enforcement agencies. The awful thing about the accusations is that they seem to be totally unfounded, but there will have to be some kind of a legal investigation before the gossip and rumors will be silenced and the three men justified before their community.

1. Jesus took human relationships quite seriously. He realized that all manner of disputes took place within the community of the faithful, and that accusations are best made in face-to-face meetings of the individuals involved rather than by gossip and rumors. He could have been speaking about his own experience when he said, "If your brother has anything against you, go and tell him his fault, between you and him alone." This was Jesus' better way, including his additional agenda for settling such disputes. (In the *Faculty Handbook* of the institution in which I teach, there is a section on this subject — for faculty and administration, students, and staff — which follows Jesus' teaching almost exactly.)

2. Congregations have been given this "better way" by Jesus. And most would be healthier if they accepted Jesus' teaching about relationships within the congregation. In too many congregations, such disputes and disagreements are never settled; if they are severe enough, those involved often leave the congregation and move to, or even start, another church. The better way is God's way, because it is founded on love for one another, in the name of Christ.

3. To follow Jesus' dictum means that two things will happen in the church: Christians who really love one another will manifest their concern through open and direct communications with each other in times of disagreement or controversy; the congregation will also take seriously the whole business of discipline — "binding and loosing" people who have sinned — in the spirit of Christian love.

4. The presence of Christ makes possible resolution and reconciliation among Christians — "For where two or three are gathered in my name, there am I in the midst of them." He generates the necessary love for one another to make resolution of problems and reconciliation happen between people who love him and one another.

In some congregations, a sermon on the latter part of the Gospel for the Day — church discipline — might have to be developed from a different point of view, depending on the congregation and pastoral exegesis. It could be that the most suitable sermon would be textual, and would be developed from the last verse.

Matthew 18:20 — "Christ and the Congregation."

1. In any Christian group, large or small, the presence of Christ is guaranteed: "Where two or three are gathered in my name, there am I in the midst of them."

2. Christian business — worship or whatever, even the discussion of accusations and the arbitration of disputes — takes place in his presence. Awareness of that changes the tone and spirit of services and meetings of all kinds.

3. Jesus will make the occasion worthwhile and valid, when business and worship are conducted in his name. His promised presence assures us of that.

Ezekiel 33:7-9 (R, L); 33:(1-6) 7-11 (E) "The Watchman and The Warning."

1. The prophet is God's watchman in the world. He — and the parish preacher, too — speaks God's Word at his behest. As parish prophet, the pastor preaches the Law to sinful human beings.

2. The watchman's own salvation is always at stake. God holds preachers responsible for what they say and for what they do not say to people. Preachers who ignore the Law in their sermons place their own lives in jeopardy.

3. The warning is gospel-oriented. Preachers, along with prophets, need to reveal God's heart: "I take pleasure, not in the death of a wicked man, but in the turning back of a wicked man who changes his ways to win life." It is God, who says through his preachers and prophets, "Come back, come back from your evil ways. Why are you so anxious to die, House of Israel?" *(Jerusalem Bible)*

Exodus 19:16-24 — "The Staging of a Spectacular."

1. *God promised a spectacular at Mt. Sinai.* He gave Moses instructions on how it was to be set up for his people. (Our Lord did much the same thing when he faced suffering, death, and resurrection.)

2. *Three to get ready.* The spectacular would occur on the third day; they had three days to get ready, and that was enough. (It was not so with the disciples and friends of Jesus when he was crucified, despite the fact that he had told them he would rise on the third day.)

3. *The mountain moved.* That's what it seemed like, at least. Covered with fire and smoke, lightning and thunder punctuating the shroud of clouds, a trumpet sounding, and an earthquake, the mountain "moved" — they knew that God was there, speaking to Moses in their presence. (What of the garden tomb, the earthquake that moved the stone, and the presence of angels in the empty tomb — and the risen Lord?)

4. *The people kept their distance.* Only Moses and Aaron could ascend Mt. Sinai; people and priests had to remain at the bottom of the mountain, if they were to live. That was enough. (Only a few saw the risen Lord; the rest of us find life "at a distance" from Christ. But that is enough, because he is intimately close in the bread and the wine.)

Romans 13:1-10 (L, C); 13:8-10 (R) — "Duty and Love."

1. Christian duty, according to Paul, is obeying the law of the land. He believed rulers were God-given, and should be respected, obeyed, and even honored. His theology cost him his head.

2. Civil disobedience is a necessary "evil." That's how Paul might look at it. The "living sacrifice" of Christians, even in their death martyrs, might be more powerful than disobedience and open defiance of the law. The church was built on the blood of the martyrs, as well as the blood of Christ.

3. Love for God and people should determine how one does one's Christian duty. The bottom line, according to Paul, is "Love is the fulfilling of the law."

The Seventeenth Sunday after Pentecost
Twenty-fourth Sunday in Ordinary Time
Proper 19

Roman Catholic	Sirach 27:30—28:7	Romans 14:7-9	Matthew 18:21-35
Episcopal	Sirach 27:30—28:7	Romans 14:5-12	Matthew 18:21-35
Lutheran	Genesis 50:15-21	Romans 14:5-9	Matthew 18:21-35
Common	Exodus 20:1-20	Romans 14:5-12	Matthew 18:21-35

The church year theological clue

September 29th marks the celebration of another minor festival, St. Michael and All Angels. The last line of the second reading, Revelation 12:12, supports the eschatological perspective of Pentecost, because it announces that he (Satan) "knows that his time is short." Without the theological input of the readings for St. Michael and All Angels Day to supplement the readings of the Seventeenth Sunday after Pentecost, the eschatological framework of the church year would be almost imperceptible at this point in Pentecost. The readings, during most of the Pentecost Cycle/Season, have to reestablish and support the theological themes of the church year, or they will be completely lost, and "lectionary preachers" may lose their "theological" direction. The lesser festivals tend to supplement the other readings, and prove to be helpful in the exegetical/homiletical endeavor.

The Prayer of the Day (LBW) — The content of this prayer seems to have been influenced by parts of several collects that were formerly in use. It also appears to have been shaped by the Gospel for the Day, Matthew 18:21-35, which includes the parable of the unforgiving debtor. In contrast to the man in the Gospel, who had received the forgiveness of a huge debt but wouldn't show the same mercy to a man who owed him an insignificant amount of money, the prayer speaks out: "O God, you declare your almighty power chiefly in showing mercy and pity." The gracious response of the faithful, in which they show love, mercy, and forgiveness to others, is connected to the glory of God in this prayer: "Grant us the fullness of your grace, that, pursuing what you have promised, we may share your heavenly glory; through your Son, Jesus Christ our Lord." The love of God for people, which was incarnate in Jesus Christ, is what motivates and determines our actions toward others.

The Psalm for the Day — Psalm 103, or 103:8-13 (E); 103:1-4, 9-12 (R); 103:1-13 (L) — The first thirteen verses of this psalm are quite well known among the faithful — in addition to the thirteenth verse:

3

Bless the Lord, O my soul, and all that is within me, bless his holy name. Bless the Lord, O my soul, and forget not all his benefits. He forgives all your sins and heals all your infirmities. (verses 1-3)

Verse 13 declares, "As a father cares for his children, so does the Lord care for those who fear him." The rest of the psalm might not be as familiar as these verses, but verse 20 renews the "Bless the Lord" note of the first two verses in an interesting and liturgically timely manner: "Bless the Lord, you angels of his, you mighty ones who do his bidding and hearken to the voice of his word." Two more "Bless the Lord" injunctions return the psalm to its opening theme, "Bless the Lord, O my soul." The psalm takes the worshiper — and the preacher — full circle in God's grace and goodness.

The Psalm Prayer (LBW)

Lord, you have compassion for the sinner, as a father has compassion for his children. Heal the weakness of your people and save us from everlasting death, that with the saints and angels *we may praise and glorify you, Father, Son, and Holy Spirit, now and forever.* [emphasis mine]

Psalm 19:7-14 (C) — Here is another responsory psalm that not only is very familiar to people who know the Psalms, but is also a fitting responsory to the first reading (Exodus 20). The beginning of the psalm, which is so well-known and even memorized by some Christians — "The heavens declare the glory of God, and the firmament shows his handiwork" — is probably omitted because it fits last Sunday's reading (the spectacular at Mt. Sinai) more specifically than it does this week's lesson. Verse 7 provides a most appropriate response to the reading:

The law of the Lord is perfect and revives the soul; the testimony of the Lord is sure and gives wisdom to the innocent. The statutes of the Lord are just and rejoice the heart; the commandment of the Lord is clear and gives light to the eyes.

All of this, and the ensuing verses, lead to the prayer which is so familiar to preachers: "Let the words of my mouth and the meditation of my heart be acceptable in your sight, O Lord, my strength and my redeemer."

The readings:

Sirach 27:30—28:7 (R, E)

This reading from a deutero-canonical book, which often is simply called Sirach, was one of those readings included in the first lectionary proposal for the LBW that was later removed and replaced by another First Lesson. The book was written in Hebrew by Jesus ben Sirach, around 180 B.C., and was discovered by his grandson some fifty years later, who translated it into Greek, "for the benefit especially of those who, domiciled abroad, wish to study how to fit themselves and their manners for living according to the Law" (from the translator's foreword to the book). The excerpts from chapters 27 and 28 were chosen for the first reading because they complement the Gospel for the Day. Verse 4, chapter 28, asks — over against the unforgiving debtor — "Showing no pity for a man like himself, can he then plead for his own sins?" At the end of the reading, this exhortation is given: "Remember the last things, and stop hating, remember dissolution and death, and live by the commandments."

Genesis 50:15-21 (L)

The LBW replaced the Sirach reading with a concrete example of forgiving others who really owe you a very large debt. Here is the story of Joseph's brothers, who are afraid that Joseph will exact vengeance upon them after their father's death. They put words in the mouth of a messenger, whom they sent to Joseph:

Your father gave this command before he died, "Say to Joseph, Forgive, I pray you, the transgression of your brothers and their sin, because they did evil to you." And now, we pray you, forgive the transgression of the servants of the God of your father.

This caused Joseph to weep and to tell his brothers, when they came seeking his forgiveness, "Fear not, for am I in the place of God?" In a way, he traced the whole business of their selling him into slavery to God:

> *As for you, you meant evil against me; but God meant it for good, to bring it about that many people should be kept alive, as they are today. So do not fear; I will provide for you and your little ones,*

he assured them. The story is quite compatible with the parable of the unforgiving debtor in Matthew 18:21-35.

Exodus 20:1-20 (C)

The Roman and Episcopal lectionaries place most of this reading (20:1-17) on the Third Sunday in Lent, Year B; the Lutheran Lectionary assigns 20:10-17 (18-22) to the same Sunday in Lent. This reading, of course, enunciates the Ten Commandments given to Moses and the people of Israel by Yahweh. These "tables of duty" — the first table to God, the second to one's acquaintances and neighbors — are valid for Christians, as well as Jews, but no person is able to keep and fulfill them, with the exception of Jesus Christ. He alone kept them perfectly, and was without sin. The Ten Commandments, try as we will to obey them perfectly, cause us to recognize our sin and our need for forgiveness; the righteousness of Jesus Christ saves us in the face of the condemnation thrust upon us by the decalogue.

Romans 14:5-12 (E, C); 14:5-9 (L); 14:7-9 (R)

The original plan for the Lutheran Lectionary was almost identical to the Roman reading, but, later, the reading was expanded to begin at verse 5; the Common Lectionary accepted this alteration to the Roman *Ordo* and proceeded to add verses 10 and 11 to the lesson. The latter addition makes the reading compatible with the Gospel for the Day, inasmuch as it ends on the note, "we shall all have to stand before the judgment seat of God," implying that we shall be judged by God for our attitudes and actions toward other human beings. The reading begins with a plea for tolerance among the "mixed-bag" of Christians — Jewish and Gentile Christians, who had different worship practices and patterns — in Rome. Both groups are reminded that we are all related to each other in Jesus Christ, who not only is the Lord of the living, but of the dead, as well. All Christians "belong" to Christ, and have been forgiven by God through Jesus' death and resurrection — and in baptism — and should acknowledge that in their relationships with each other.

Matthew 18:21-35

Once more, in this set of readings, the absolute necessity of forgiving one's neighbors and one's enemies of their sins comes to the forefront in the parable of the unforgiving servant. To forgive as we have been forgiven, in the name of Jesus Christ, is required by the Lord our God. Those who have received the assurance of the forgiveness of their sins from their heavenly Father, but refuse to forgive people who have hurt or offended them, will certainly lose the gift of grace — forgiveness — which is promised to them. Christians are to share all the gifts that God has given them with others, and forgiveness is by no means the least of these; it is the warrant of salvation in Jesus Christ. To keep and retain this gift, the Christian, in short, must give it away. That's what Jesus is saying in this parable; failing to share the gift of forgiveness will result in having it taken away from any unforgiving person.

Sermon suggestions:

Matthew 18:21-35 — "Forgiveness — the Key to the Kingdom."

When a person has been injured or offended by another person, a choice must be made; one must curse that person or bless that person. One's eternal fate hangs in the balance, according to Jesus' teaching in this parable.

There is a family I have known for two and a half decades; the husband, an airline pilot, once was the key figure in a parabolic sermon I preached, called, "The Garbage Man." He was concerned about his family, about his neighbors — near and far — in the world, about ecology, and his relationship with God. For years all went well with him and his family, but then, for some reason, he began to drink and before long was in danger of losing his job. A pilot-friend, who was aware of the drinking problem, told his wife to get in touch with the company doctor; she did, and managed to get her husband into a counseling program that saved his job and, at that time, his life. But the husband resented her "interference" in his life; his love turned to hatred, and before long they were divorced. Nothing could persuade him that what she had done, she had done to help him; he told her that he would never forgive her and that he would hate her as long as she or he lived. Now, some years later, he is losing a battle with cancer; she has done what she can to support him — neither, incidentally, has remarried — but he remains adamant and will not forgive her for the good she intended which he counted as evil. He had been the one who had done hurt to the other person, to his wife; she forgave him this, but he will not forgive. Soon he will die and, according to Jesus, he will die — barring repentance on his death-bed — unforgiven.

1. Forgiveness is the key to the kingdom of God. It is a totally unmerited and unearned gift of God in Christ to repentant sinners. It is necessary to admittance to the kingdom of God.

2. To retain the gift, forgiven sinners must give it away. Only the forgiving sinner, who prays, "Forgive *me*, as I forgive others," has the hope of retaining the gift. Lose the gift and you lose the assurance and hope of belonging to the eternal kingdom of God.

3. Forgive, as you have been forgiven. That's the dictum of Jesus Christ to you and me. That's the way we demonstrate that our love for God and people is genuine and sincere. We love and forgive, because he first loved and forgave us.

Sirach 27:30—28:7 (R, E) — "Ultimatum."

1. God is opposed to unbridled anger by his people. Anger breeds hatred, and hatred breeds vengeance, and vengeance — "I'll get even at any cost" breeds the destruction of human beings; it stands in the way of reconciliation and life.

2. "Vengeance is mine, says the Lord." He means, "Mine and mine alone." Most of us can't understand that, probably because we really don't believe it. We expect a person to hate his or her enemy, not love and forgive — as ben Sirach and Jesus insist — that person or persons. (When Michael Dukakis was asked what he would do, if his wife were attacked and raped, many people — among them Christians — were outraged, simply because he vented no emotion, showed no signs that he would hate the person, and gave a rather unemotional and academic answer that suggested forgiveness.)

3. God's ultimatum — forgive your enemy — stop hating, because your eternal destiny, after death, may be lost.

Genesis 50:15-21 — "A Godly Man."

1. Joseph was a godly man. He loved and forgave his brothers for their terrible sin of selling him into salvery, when the human thing to do would be to punish them when he could. Instead, he forgave them.

262

2. He had an inhuman God. He knew God to be loving and forgiving in a manner unknown among human beings. God is unique, in this respect; he forgives freely when he could condemn sinful and recalcitrant people. A "human god" would not send his Son to be crucified for the forgiveness of sins.

3. Joseph had no choice — nor do we. Joseph said, "Fear not, for am I in the place of God." God is the one who ultimately judges sinners and dispenses the punishment they deserve. Our business is to forgive, or we are in danger of losing his gift — forgiveness — through Jesus Christ.

4. Godly people are forgiving people.

Exodus 20:1-20 — "Ten for the Kingdom."

1. God established a covenant at Sinai. Moses was his man, and God worked through him on Mt. Sinai.

2. God put "teeth" — commandments — in the covenant. The two tables of the Law tell how people should live and act toward God, and how they should behave toward other people. These commandments are necessary to the covenant.

3. God expects his people to obey the commandments and keep the covenant intact. Sin — disobeying God and ignoring his covenant — condemns human beings and banishes them from God's presence. Sin denies that God is really God.

4. Jesus perfectly kept the commandments. Cling to him and the cross — and live in the new covenant, which he established through his death and resurrection.

Romans 14:5-12 (E, C); 14:5-9 (L); 14:7-9 (R) — "A Christian Community."

1. *The church is a community in Christ.* He is the one thing, the one person, we all have in common; he makes the church a real community, a world-wide community, in himself.

2. *The church is a loving community.* The faithful will live in, and express to others, the loving relationship which God has established in Jesus and his church. Christians are related to each other in the love of God.

3. *The church is an eternal community.* It is composed of believers who have been saved by Jesus Christ; in this life, we belong to the Church Militant, and in heaven, we will be transferred to the Church Triumphant. Christians are related to each other forever. Paul tells us so, just as he did the Roman congregation.

4. The church is to live in the love of God here on earth. Maybe the world will be able to say again, "See how these Christians love each other" — and they just may want to be part of the Christian community.

The Eighteenth Sunday after Pentecost
Twenty-fifth Sunday in Ordinary Time
Proper 20

Roman Catholic	Isaiah 55:6-9	Philippians 1:20c-24, 27	Matthew 20:1-16
Episcopal	Jonah 3:10—4:11	Philippians 1:21-27	Matthew 20:1-16
Lutheran	Isaiah 55:6-9	Philippians 1:1-5, (6-11) 19-27	Matthew 20:1-16
Common	Exodus 32:1-14	Philippians 1:21-27	Matthew 20:1-16

The church year theological clue

Although the church year eschatological framework remains in place on this Sunday, it would continue to be almost imperceptible without the influence of the readings for the day. In particular, it is the Gospel for the Day, the parable of the "householder," who goes out to the market place again and again to hire day-laborers to work in his vineyard, that casts the eschatological note of the gospel, as well as the church year, in sharp focus over against the unmerited grace of God, who calls people into the kingdom in Jesus Christ. Once more, it is the Gospel for the Day, with the other readings, that articulates the biblical/theological clue for the day's worship and preaching.

The Prayer of the Day (LBW) — This prayer was prepared with Matthew's parable of the householder, who hired servants to work in his vineyard, in mind. It addresses God this way: "Lord God, you call us to work in your vineyard and leave no one standing idle," clearly reflecting the content of the parable spoken by Jesus. It asks God to "Set us to our tasks in the work of your kingdom, and help us to order our lives by your wisdom; through your Son, Jesus Christ our Lord." The Prayer of the Day reveals the fact that for most Sundays *three* collects are needed, if the prayer is to have any real significance over against the Gospel for the Day. Any relevance for the Gospels for Years B and C has to be understood as strictly accidental; this prayer was obviously composed with one Gospel, primarily — Matthew 20:1-16 — in hand. It fails to articulate fully, however, the grace of God in calling us and giving us life in his kingdom by concentrating on the "work" we are to do in the kingdom in the petition.

The Psalm of the Day — Psalm 27:1-13 (L) — The Lutheran Lectionary sets this psalm into the propers for the Third Sunday after the Epiphany, Series A, as well as the Fourth Sunday in Lent, Series B. The first verse of the psalm is central to its use on those two Sundays: "The Lord is my light and my salvation; whom then shall I fear? The Lord is the strength of my life; of whom then shall I be afraid?" This theme fits this Sunday, too, but the last verse speaks more to the Gospel for the Day: "You have been my helper; cast me not away; nor turn away your servant in displeasure."

The Psalm Prayer (LBW)

> *Gracious Father, protector of those who hope in you: You heard the cry of your Son and kept him safe in your shelter in the day of evil. Grant that your servants who seek your face in times of trouble may see your goodness in the land of the living, through your Son, Jesus Christ our Lord.*

Psalm 106:7-8, 19-23 (C) — The choice of this psalm as a responsory to the first reading, Exodus 32:1-14, could hardly be improved upon; it fits the theme of the reading, echoing how Israel forgot what God had done for them at the Red Sea and, especially how they later made and worshiped a golden calf. The latter portion of the selection is pertinent:

> *They forgot God their Savior, who had done great things in Egypt, wonderful deeds in the land of Ham, and fearful things at the Red Sea. So he would have destroyed them, had not Moses his chosen stood before him in the breach, to turn away his wrath from consuming them.* [emphasis, mine].

Psalm 145, or 145:1-8 (E); 145:2-3, 8-9, 17-18 (R) — This psalm finds its way into the propers of the day no less than five times: three times in Series A, once in Series B, and once in Series C, of the Roman *Ordo*; it is also used twice in Series A and once in Series B, of the Episcopal Lectionary. Verses 7 and 8 are central to its choice on this occasion:

> *They shall publish the remembrance of your great goodness; they shall sing of your righteous deeds. The Lord is gracious and full of compassion, slow to anger and of great kindness.*

Verse 9 emerges in the longer form of the psalm in the Episcopal Lectionary, as well as in the Roman *Ordo*: "The Lord is loving to everyone and his compassion is over all his works." The psalm is an excellent choice as a responsory to the first reading.

The readings:

Isaiah 55:6-9 (R, L)

Here is another example of a multiple-use reading, which is cut up into little segments so as to function in harmony with the Gospel for the Day. The reading, as previously commented on, issues an invitation to the eschatological banquet God has prepared for them that loved him. It calls upon people to find God while he is near and may be found; the wicked are asked to turn back to God in true faith and repentance, and God will have mercy on them. God, sings Isaiah, "is rich in forgiving," and reminds us, "my thoughts are not your thoughts, my ways are not your ways — it is Yahweh who speaks." The Gospel for the Day magnifies this truth in Jesus' parable of the householder.

Jonah 3:10—4:11 (E)

After Jonah preached to the people of the city of Nineveh, an amazing thing happened: they repented of their sins and all of the people put on sack cloth and ashes, and God relented and did not destroy them. Jonah couldn't understand why God would not destroy them for their past sins; he was so angry with God that he told him that he was ready to die. Unable to reason with Jonah, God taught him a lesson as he sat outside the city watching and waiting to see what would happen; God caused a castor-oil plant to grow up and shelter him, and Jonah rejoiced. But when God made the plant wither, he was angry, and this prompted God to say:

> *You are only upset about a castor-oil plant which cost you no labor, which you did not make grow, which sprouted in a night and has perished in a night. And am I not to feel sorry for Nineveh, the great city, in which there are more than one hundred and twenty thousand people who cannot tell their right hand from their left, to say nothing of all the animals.*

Apparently, Jonah learned a lesson about God's love, and grace, and mercy, that all of us need to learn.

Exodus 32:1-14 (C)

Moses remained on Mt. Sinai too long for the people of Israel; they not only thought he was not going to return, but they also lost faith in God once more. Accordingly, they asked Aaron to make a god for them out of their gold, and he did, fashioning a golden calf, which they worshiped. Had it not been for Moses, who pleaded with God to have mercy upon them, God would have utterly destroyed them at Sinai. Moses' plea was based on all that God had done for them; why throw this away, when the people might yet be saved? God stayed his hand, as Moses requested of him, and gave the children of Israel yet another chance, which they did not deserve and had no reason to expect.

Philippians 1:1-5, (6-11) 19-27 (L); 1:20-24, 27 (R); 1:21-27 (E, C)

The second readings for the next four weeks will come from the Letter to the Philippians. For this reason alone, it is important to read the entire letter — and in the light of modern scholarship, which sees this as a probable compilation of three little letters sent by Paul to the congregation in Philippi while he was in prison, either in Rome or in Ephesus. In this selection, Paul, especially if he is in Rome, shows that he is aware that he may be martyred in the name of Jesus, and he is hopeful that he will be delivered by prayer. But he declares that "now as always Christ will be honored in my body, whether by life or by death," adding that wonderful thought, "For to me to live is Christ, and to die is gain." After concluding these thoughts about the fate ahead of him, he exhorts the Philippian congregation:

> *Only let your manner of life be worthy of the gospel of Christ, so that whether I come and see you or am absent, I may hear of you that you stand firm in one spirit, with one mind striving side by side for the faith of the gospel.*

He offers that same advice to all Christian congregations today.

Matthew 20:1-16

Today, Jesus would have to rework his parable about the man who went out to hire day-laborers to work in his vineyard; it would be too easily misunderstood as a story that seems to denigrate the worth of labor and, at the same time, puts down labor unions and the benefits they have gained for the working person. He would have to tell it so that people would understand that he was talking about the graciousness of God and his love, which prompts him to seek out all people and give to everyone, no matter what the duration of their faithfulness to God, the gift of the kingdom. The parable teaches one lesson, if connected to the first reading (Isaiah and Jonah, too) — "my thoughts are not your thoughts," says the Lord. It also informs people that they ought to rejoice that God gives everybody access to the kingdom in Jesus Christ, instead of being concerned that those of us who are long-time Christians should receive "something more" for their/our faithfulness and labor on behalf of God. This is a Gospel that is primarily about, as Paul perceives it, the truth that people are saved by faith through grace, not by their works or labor for the Lord.

Sermon suggestions:

Matthew 20:1-16 — "A Strange and Loving God."

In his autobiography, *All the Strange Hours*, Loren Eiseley tells his most poignant personal story; it is about the death of his father, which made a lasting effect on his life (see "One Night's Dying" in *The Night Country*, an account of how he became an insomniac the night that his father died. This other story of his father's death suggests, in part, *why* he became an insomniac.) Eiseley's father, suffering from incurable cancer and in terrible pain, was in and out of a comatose state for some time before he died. Eiseley's step-brother, whom he had not seen for years was summoned and arrived before their father died. When told that his first son was there, the comatose father seemed to respond, grasped his hand, and even smiled a bit. Eiseley was deeply hurt by this, because his father had not responded to him, the loving and faithful son, who had shared so much with his father; close to tears, he had to leave the room, go out in the hall, where his emotions took over and his resentment poured out.

The setting and the plot of the story are different, but the drama and the human emotions — resentment and selfishness — between this incident in the life of a man who went on to become a famous scientist and writer are essentially the same as in the parable Jesus told about the landowner/householder and the laborers he hired to work in his vineyard. Eiseley reacted to his brother's return and his father's apparent response about the same way as did those who were hired first who thought they should be paid more than those who worked only an hour of the day.

1. *A story about the goodness and grace of God.* Jesus' parable has nothing to do with the business world or labor/management relationships (which has to be articulated again, in most congregations). Our immediate reaction to the story — that it is unfair — simply proves that we have not really understood and/or accepted the nature of the gospel as a gift freely given by God in Jesus Christ. (This Gospel might well be preached on Reformation Sunday.)

2. *A story of law, as well as gospel, in action.* The parable shows most of us for what we are — unrepentant sinners, who deserve judgment instead of grace. We have not always:

a. Loved God for his goodness, as we should;
b. Really loved our neighbors as ourselves;
c. Accepted the fact that salvation comes by grace, not by works; don't we really believe that we earn entrance into God's kingdom by our works?
d. Appreciated the hope of heaven and the security that we have enjoyed in being numbered among the faithful in the church;
e. Understand that God loves all people and needs them as much as we need him. (Wouldn't the landowner have lost some of his grape harvest, if a supply of laborers had not been available? Note: This theme can backfire, theologically, if not treated with care; it is only suggested by the parable, but certainly is a biblical and gospel theme. It remains that the workers needed the landowner more than he needed them.)

3. *Resentment has to be replaced by repentance.* Our selfishness, when we resent people who are late-comers to the kingdom, or have received gifts from God that they have not earned, condemns us again. Ours is to appreciate what our gracious God has given us in Baptism and in the church, and to "whistle while we work" in the kingdom of God, rejoicing in the promise and hope of heaven he has given us — and *all people* — in Christ.

4. *Praise God from whom all blessings flow!* Thank him for his goodness and grace and joyfully do the work of othe kingdom of God.

Isaiah 55:6-9 (R, L) — "The Table is Ready."

1. God has set a table in heaven for those who don't deserve his company or grace. God is different.

2. God invites all to his table; acceptance is given by repentance and faith. The feast in heaven is offered to all, but pardoned sinners are certain to be there.

3. Christ, through baptism into his death and resurrection, provides "banquet garb" — forgiveness and the promise of life at the heavenly table.

4. Seek the Lord — he is near and may be found right now! Come to the table today and enjoy a foretaste of the feast to come.

Jonah 3:10—4:11 (E) — "The Happy Ending."

1. The impossible mission: to move the people of Nineveh to repentance through the preaching of the Word. That was Jonah's mission and the business of the church in the world.

2. A completed mission. Jonah managed to preach to the whole city. They listened, heard, and repented in sackcloth and ashes. Preaching of the law and gospel *does* bear fruit. You can depend on it.

3. The happy ending. Nineveh was forgiven and delivered from destruction. So it is with Christians and the church of Jesus Christ.

4. Heaven is ours. Repent and rejoice daily.

Exodus 32:1-14 (E) — "An Antidote for Apostasy." (See, also, a sermon on this text, "The Keeper of the Covenant," in Bass, *Great Stories of the Faith*)

1. A familiar story — making gods out of our gold. We have perfected an old technique today and mastered the business of apostasy.

2. The tragic consequence — losing God and losing the kingdom of heaven. There is but one God and he is better than all the gold in the world. Christians, with the apostles of old, ought to know and believe this.

3. The antidote — Moses' prayer on behalf of the recalcitrant children of Israel. It took Jesus' prayers on the cross — "Forgive them . . . . It is finished" — to provide the antidote for our sinful apostasy.

4. Christ has saved us from he death we deserve — at the cost of his life. Cling to the cross — the antidote for apostasy — and live!

Philippians 1:1-5, (6-11) 19-27 (L); 1:20-24, 27 (R); 1:21-27 (E, C) — "Partnership in the Gospel."

1. *A godly partnership.* Christians are partners, not only with Paul, but through the gospel with Jesus Christ our Lord.

2. *A costly partnership* — The gospel is freely given and freely received, but partnership in the gospel can be a costly business. It demands faith, loyalty, industry, compassion, and, not the least, courage; partnership in the gospel can cost one's life (it always does, one way or another).

3. *A profitable partnership* — The benefits of believing and witnessing to the Gospel of Christ, as partners with Paul and all Christians, is the assurance that God will support those who enter into the partnership and see them through the very gates of heaven.

4. *An enduring partnership* — It will last to the end of the age, and then will begin the final meeting of all who have been partners with Paul, the apostles, and all of the faithful in Jesus Christ and in the gospel.

The Nineteenth Sunday after Pentecost
Twenty-sixth Sunday in Ordinary Time
Proper 21

Roman Catholic	Ezekiel 18:25-28	Philippians 2:1-11	Matthew 21:28-32
Episcopal	Ezekiel 18:1-4, 25-32	Philippians 2:1-13	Matthew 21:28-32
Lutheran	Ezekiel 18:1-4, 25-32	Philippians 2:1-5 (6-11)	Matthew 21:28-32
Common	Exodus 33:12-23	Philippians 2:1-13	Matthew 21:28-32

The church year theological clue

As the church enters the last week of Sundays in the church year, the theological framework — eschatology — is renewed by the readings, particularly by the Gospel for the Day with its emphasis upon divine authority and repentance. The Gospel-context for this week's worship and preaching is the events that occurred after Jesus entered the Holy City to the day now called the Sunday of the Passion, or Palm Sunday. But the theme of today's worship takes the church all the way back to the beginning of Jesus' public ministry, to his baptism and the voice from heaven that declared, ''You are my beloved Son, in whom I am well pleased,'' and to the subsequent message which he preached, ''Repent for the kingdom of heaven is at hand.'' (Matthew 4:17) The church year is drawing to a close, and it is most appropriate to sound the theme, ''Repent,'' and, also, ''the kingdom of heaven is at hand.''

The Prayer of the Day (LBW) — The new prayer apparently draws from several older collects, such as ''keep us, we beseech thee, from all things that may hurt us, . . .'' (Nineteenth Sunday after Trinity/Twentieth Sunday after Pentecost), and could become the prayer of people who truly repent of their sins:

> *God of love, you know our frailties and failings. Give us your grace to overcome them; keep us from those things that harm us; and guide us in the way of salvation.*

Obliquely, it speaks to the Gospel for the Day, with its note of Jesus' authority and the call to repent and obey the Word of the Lord.

The Psalm of the Day — Psalm 25:1-9 (L); 25:1-14, or 25:3-9 (E); 25:4-9 (R) — When one has considered the Gospel in the context of the church year's eschatological framework, one can understand how this psalm is used on other Sundays of the year, and especially on the First Sunday in Advent, Series C, by the Roman *Ordo* and the Lutheran Lectionary. These could be the words of a truly repentant person, long ago or now, who prays:

> *Remember, O Lord, your compassion and love, for they are from everlasting. Remember not the sins of my youth and my transgressions; remember me according to your love and for the sake of your goodness, O Lord.*

That this person is aware of the love and mercy of God is evident, because the psalm is replete with statements about God's graciousness, mercy, and patience in dealing with unfaithful human beings. Verse 10, not used in the Roman or Lutheran propers, is especially pertinent: ''For you name's sake, O Lord, forgive my sin, for it is great.'' That could be the cry of a Jew, who has broken the old covenant, or a Christian, who has sinned and needs to have the new covenant in Christ, and in Baptism, renewed. It could be the word of either of the two sons in Jesus' parable.

The Psalm Prayer (LBW)

Lord our God, you show us your ways of compassion and love, and you spare sinners. Remember not our sins; relieve our misery; satisfy the longings of your people; and fulfill all our hopes for eternal peace through your Son, Jesus Christ our Lord.

Psalm 99 (C) — Here is another selection which was not included in the Roman *Ordo* but is appointed for use on the Last Sunday after the Epiphany (E) and/or The Transfiguration of our Lord (L); it might also have been included in the propers for Christ the King Sunday. It is especially appropriate in conjunction with the first reading, Exodus 33:12-23, of the Common Lectionary. Verses 6 through 8 reveal how this psalm responds to the reading about God's anger — and Moses' plea for mercy — after the "golden calf incident," especially in these words:

Moses and Aaron among his priests, . . . called upon the Lord . . . . O Lord God, you answered them indeed; you were a God who forgave them, yet punished them for their evil deeds.

The readings:

Ezekiel 18:1-4, 25-32 (E, L); 18:25-28 (R)

Ezekiel took sin very seriously. He was aware of the "shaking of the foundations" of Israel's institutions, and appears to be conscious of the fact that a major factor in this disintegration was the lack of individual responsibility in taking the covenant seriously and attempting to keep it in good faith. The sins of people were destroying the life of God's chosen people, and Ezekiel called upon the people to repent of their sins — to face up to their lack of responsibility, as individuals before the Lord God, to repent, and seek God's pardon of their transgressions. He perceived that God would forgive their sin, renew them and his covenant with them, and judge them according to their new, not their old, ways of living. The addition of verses 1-4 (E, L) was made because it declares that the lives of all people — "father's life and the son's life" — belong to God; this points to the parable of the father and the two sons. The extension on the end of the reading gives a powerful conclusion to the lection:

House of Israel, in future I mean to judge each of you by what he does — it is the Lord Yahweh who speaks. Repent, renounce all your sins, avoid all occasions of sin! Shake off all the sins you have committed against me, and make yourselves a new heart and a new spirit! Why are you so anxious to die, House of Israel? I take no pleasure in the death of anyone — it is the Lord Yahweh who speaks. Repent and live! (Jerusalem Bible)

The parable of the father and the two sons beautifully illustrates this word of the prophet; it is one of the most appropriate first readings in the lectionaries, and it almost insists on inclusion in any sermon on the Gospel for the Day.

Exodus 32:12-23 (C)

This is the last in the series of first readings from the book of Exodus; there were no less than thirteen lections taken from Exodus. Any congregation where these lessons have been read as the basis for a preaching series should be richer for the experience and ought to have deepened its understanding of the Exodus, as well as its implications for the Christian faith.

In this reading, a continuation of last Sunday's lesson, God has informed Moses about the golden calf and threatens the people of Israel with destruction. Moses pleads with God to have mercy upon them, and God agrees to withhold his wrath, sending Moses to deal with the people. Moses descended with the two tablets of stone, which contained the commandments of God, was met by Joshua, and proceeded toward the camp. The noise they heard sounded like a battle to Joshua, but like chanting to Moses; the people were worshiping their new god. Moses angrily smashed the two stone tablets and demanded an explanation from Aaron, who told how that it all came about because they thought Moses would never come down from the mountain, and they were certain that God had forsaken them. Moses, in the section beyond the pericope, straightened them out in a hurry with a bloodbath executed by "the sons of Levi." Only then was the way open for reconciliation with the Lord God.

Philippians 2:1-5, or 2:1-11 (R); 2:1-5 (6-11) (L); 2:1-13 (E, C)

Here is a plea from Paul to the congregation at Philippi to be like-minded in all things, unselfish in everything, counting "others better than yourselves." They are to have "this mind" among themselves, because it is a gift from Christ, their Lord, to them, hence their business is to exercise this gift of love from the Lord. The longer form of the lesson includes the great Christological hymn, which most scholars believe existed before Paul; he quoted it and made some additions to it. Its primary use in the lectionary is on the Sunday of the Passion, Series C, where it identifies Jesus as the One who existed before he was born "in the form of God," and though he was of equal status with God, he "emptied himself, taking the form of a servant, being born in the likeness of men. And being found in human form he humbled himself and became obedient unto death . . . ." Paul probably added, "even death on a cross." The hymn goes on to tell how God gave him

> the name which is above every name, that at the name of Jesus every knee should bow, in heaven and on earth and under the earth, and every tongue confess that Jesus Christ is Lord,

with Paul probably adding, "to the glory of God the Father." Hence, this lection is theologically "loaded" for the pastor who may be preaching from the second readings. The first section, or the short form, lends itself as a response to the repentance theme of first reading and the Gospel for the Day.

Matthew 21:28-32

Taken by itself, the little parable about the man who had asked his two sons to go out and work in the vineyard — one refused but later changed his mind — repented — and obeyed his father; the other agreed but did not go — might be interpreted on the level of ethics. But placed as it is within the story of the last days of Jesus' public ministry, it has a completely different meaning. Matthew rightly puts it in the context of the question about his authority and the unwillingness of the religious leaders to accept him and his message while the prostitutes and tax collectors eagerly accepted him. He probably could never have resolved the question of his authority to teach and preach the good news to the satisfaction of the religious establishment, so he called upon them to repent, echoing through the parable the first message which he preached, taking up where John the Baptizer left off: "Repent, for the kingdom of heaven is at hand." And, in the process, he justifies John:

> For John came to you in the way of righteousness, and you did not believe him, but the tax collectors and harlots believed him; and even when you saw it, you did not afterward repent and believe him.

Matthew could easily have added, "Repent, for the kingdom is at hand." God did just that at the cross and the empty tomb.

Sermon suggestions:

Matthew 21:28-32 — "Mirror, Mirror . . . in the Font."

At first glance, this reading seems to have little or nothing to do with us; we are certainly not to be numbered with the chief priests and the elders of Jerusalem, the people to whom Jesus addressed the parable, and we surely can't be counted with the tax collectors and prostitutes, although we claim to believe in Jesus, as they did. When all is said and done, however, we know that we need to hear the parable and realize that it does affect us, because we are in dire need of repentance and the reassurance that comes to us in knowing that God forgives us of our sins.

1. Like it or not, there are too many times in our lives when we act too much like the religious leaders who opposed Jesus and rejected the good news. Like them, we claim to be true believers, but our lives give us away as backsliders in the faith, who declare their allegiance to God in church on Sunday, but live differently on Monday and the rest of the week. We say, "I will," but we don't engage in the business of the kingdom — claim it in faith — most of the time.

2. The rebellious son is our model. He refused to go into the vineyard, but later changed his mind — repented — and obeyed his father's command. He shows us that the Christian life begins with hearing a message, changing one's mind about one's attitude toward God and the kingdom, and then going out to live as a servant of the Lord. Repentance leads from a change of mind to a new life-style — in Christ.

3. The cross is a constant reminder of God's invitation to claim the kingdom of heaven in and through Jesus Christ. It makes a silent statement, telling us that the kingdom of heaven is close at hand, and calling on us to repent of our sin and spiritual stubbornness, and to surrender to the will of God in true faith and obedience.

4. There's a mirror in front of the empty cross; it is the reflective surface of the water in the font. Look in the mirror every day — and live. What do we see, rebellious and disobedient people who refuse to change our minds and lives, or repentant Christians, who admit our sinful — and helpless — condition before God and honestly repent of sin?

In Ray Bradbury's *The Martian Chronicles,* the final scene shows the last father from earth taking his children down to one of the silver-surfaced canals of Mars to show them the Martians. When one of the children says, "Where are the Martians?", he simply points down to the water of the canal, where they see only their own images reflected back to them and says, "There are the Martians." The font tells us that we, who were unworthy sinners, have been forgiven in Jesus Christ, and — with him — will live forever in the eternal kingdom of God.

Ezekiel 18:25-28 (R); 18:1-4, 25-32 (E, L) — "The Move from Death to Life."

1. *Death warning* — Those who turn away from God and sin are doomed to death, according to the prophet. He speaks before it is too late. That is the prophet's role.

2. *Life offer* — Sinners, who repent of their sinfulness and turn their lives around, receive the forgiveness of their sins and the promise of eternal life. Both prophet and Son of God speak good news.

3. *Absolution guaranteed* — Only the Son of God could guarantee people that God does not want anyone to perish; his death and resurrection affirm it.

4. *Turn about and live* — The prophet promises life to those who repent; Jesus will deliver it.

272

Exodus 33:12-33 — "An Explosion Averted."

1. God was about to blow his top when Israel made and worshiped the golden calf. He was angry enough with the people to write them off and destroy them. It was just a matter of time, and there wasn't much time left.

2. Moses, with his plea, defused the wrath of God that was about to explode and destroy his people. He vented his own anger by smashing the tablets and, later, grinding up the golden calf, but Aaron intervened and saved the Israelites from the full force of Moses' rage.

3. God made some of the Israelites pay the price of their sin. Some lost their lives, but all of them learned another hard lesson on the way to the Promised Land.

4. Forty years in the wilderness to freedom; forty years in the tomb to new life.

Philippians 2:1-11 (R); 2:1-13 (E, C); 2:1-5 (6-11) (L) — "How Christians Are Different."

1. *They think differently,* for they have been given the mind of Christ. Therefore, they are of one mind.

2. They act differently, for they have been infused with the love of the Lord. They put others ahead of themselves.

3. *They hope differently,* for they have caught a glimpse of the kingdom of heaven in Jesus Christ.

4. *They pray differently,* for they know that Jesus is Lord, and that his name demands that they "bend the knee" in true faith to the Lord, looking for the time when they will be united with him forever.

The Twentieth Sunday after Pentecost
Twenty-seventh Sunday in Ordinary Time
Proper 22

Roman Catholic	Isaiah 5:1-7	Philippians 4:6-9	Matthew 21:33-43
Episcopal	Isaiah 5:1-7	Philippians 3:14-21	Matthew 21:33-43
Lutheran	Isaiah 5:1-7	Philippians 3:12-21	Matthew 21:33-43
Common	Numbers 27:12-23	Philippians 12:21	Matthew 21:33-43

The church year theological clue

Without the readings assigned to this day — and to this part of the cycle and season — the eschatological clue of the church year would be quite indistinct. The readings, particularly the Gospel for the Day, with its setting as one of Jesus' teachings during Holy Week, point beyond Jesus' suffering and death to the last things, when God shall hold everyone accountable for his/her deeds and life-style. Veteran preachers, who have journeyed through this portion of the church year in the past, will be attuned to the increasing sound of the eschatological note as the final weeks of Pentecost are about to begin. Those not so experienced in church year/lectionary preaching should be alert to the mounting eschatological intensity that reaches its climax on Christ the King Sunday.

The Prayer of the Day (LBW) — Many of the prayers assigned to the various Sundays of the church year ought to be called "shoe horn" prayers, because they have been written apart from the propers — or in conjunction with one set of the three year readings — and then have been forced into position where they are to function for all three years. This prayer is, indeed, a very timely prayer, aligning contemporary people with those of the past ("O Lord Jesus, you have endured the doubts and foolish questions of every generation . . . .") and speaking to our need for forgiveness and grace ("Forgive us for trying to be judge over you . . . ."), while addressing us, in light of the Gospel for the Day, ("and grant us the confident faith to acknowledge you as Lord.") as people who may still be rejecting the Lordship of Jesus Christ. It also has reference to verse 3 of the first reading: "And now, O inhabitants of Jerusalem and men of Judah, judge, I pray you, between me and my vineyard."

The Psalm of the Day — Psalm 80:8, 11-15, 18-19 (R); 80, or 80:7-14 (E); 80:7-14 (L) — Here is the cry of a nation that is in deep trouble, pleading with God to deliver the people from the mockery and ridicule of their neighbors, and to "restore us, O God of hosts; show the light of your countenance and we shall be saved." The psalmist paints a picture of Israel as "a vine out of Egypt," which God proceeded to plant, uprooting other nations in the process. But outsiders have picked its grapes and "the wild boar of the forest has ravaged it, and the beasts of the field have grazed upon it." "Turn now," the psalmist prays, "O God of hosts, look down from heaven; behold and tend this vine; preserve what your right hand has planted." Verse 16 contains a reminder of the gospel and of the need Christ will have of the Father's loving support in the future: "Let your hand be upon the man of your right hand, the son of man you have made so strong for yourself." Clearly, this is a psalm of deliverance for Israel, which obliquely appears to apply to Jesus' situation in the Gospel for the Day as well as Holy Week.

The Psalm Prayer

> *Lord God, you so tend the vine you planted that now it extends its branches even to the farthest shore. Keep us in your Son as branches on the vine, that, rooted firmly in your love, we may testify before the whole world to your great power working everywhere; through Jesus Christ our Lord.*

Psalm 81:1-10 (C) — What might almost be termed "a call to worship" marks the beginning of this psalm, which establishes the spirit of joy and thanksgiving that should characterize all true worship of God. No one can be certain about the exact origin of the psalm; some scholars contend it was connected to Passover, others insist that it was related to the Feast of Tabernacles — it would fit either liturgical occasion, and most other worship services, as well. The brief review of the sacred history of Israel spells out God's promises and his gracious actions toward his people, along with their ingratitude and infidelity. Once more, the issue of the "golden calf" is raised — "There shall be no strange god among you; you shall not worship a foreign god" — and a reminder of who their God is and what he has done for them: "I am the Lord your God, who brought you out of the land of Egypt and said, 'Open your mouth wide, and I will fill it.' " He did just that for the Israelites, feeding them with manna, the "bread of the angels," in the wilderness; he feeds us now on the body and blood of his Son, Jesus Christ.

The readings:

Isaiah 5:1-7 (R, E, L)

The prophet starts out singing a rather lovely song about a man and his vineyard, only to pull the rug out from under a whole nation when he addresses the people of Jerusalem and calls on them to judge between him and his vineyard. After he has told what the God has done *for* Israel, Isaiah proceeds to tell what God will do *to* Israel in light of the "wild grapes" that Israel has produced. There is no mistaking of whom the prophet is speaking:

> *For the vineyard of the Lord of hosts is the house of Israel, and the men of Judah are his pleasant planting; and he looked for justice, but behold, bloodshed; for righteousness, but behold, a cry!*

Has the "new Israel," the church done any better than the original Israel? We have to keep that question in mind when we read and preach the Gospel for the Day. The song of Isaiah takes on a bitter taste when one reads the parable about the man who established a vineyard, rented it out to people, only to have them beat and kill his servants and, finally, his son, so they could take over the vineyard for themselves.

Numbers 27:12-23

When God commands Moses to climb a mountain and look at the land he has promised to Israel, he informs Moses that he will never enter the Promised Land — he is soon to die. Moses asks God to choose a new leader to take the people of Israel on the final stage of their forty-year journey. God directs him to single out Joshua, lay hands on his head and anoint him, then take him before Eleazar the priest and the "whole community," making it clear to them that they must follow his commands and complete their trek from Egypt to the Promised Land. When Moses did as God had ordered him to do, Joshua was established as his successor, and the stage was set for the conclusion of what has come to be known as the Exodus.

Philippians 3:12-21 (L, C); 3:14-21 (E)

The readings from Philippians make one aware of the disagreements between denominational committees who, along with biblical scholars, were involved in the selection process. In this choice, only the Roman *Ordo* stands by the original second reading for this day; the other three major lectionaries retreat to chapter three, possibly because it contains some of the best loved passages in the New Testament. For example, verse 10 was employed in a baptismal service of the Lutheran *Service Book and Hymnal,* in conjunction with the pastor's making the sign of the cross on the forehead of the child, or children, being baptized: "Receive the sign of the holy Cross, in token henceforth that thou shalt know the Lord, and the power of his resurrection, and the fellowship of his sufferings." Paul tells the people at Philippi, "but this one thing I do, forgetting those things which are behind, and reaching forth unto those things which are before, I press toward the mark for the prize of the high calling of God in Christ Jesus." Again, he says, "Let us therefore, as many as be perfect, be thus minded . . . . Be followers together of me, and mark them which walk so as ye have us for an example." The last verse has found its way into the funeral service: "we look for the Savior, the Lord Jesus Christ, who shall change our vile body, that it may be fashioned like unto his glorious body, according to the working whereby he is able even to subdue all things unto himself." *(King James Bible).* In short, he offers himself as an example of Christian hope and godly living, urging them to join him in his pilgrimage to the eternal kingdom of God.

Philippians 4:6-9 (R)

This reading, the original selection of the Roman *Ordo,* (Philippians 4:4-8, is the Lutheran variation) was in the first published lectionary prepared and published by the Inter-Lutheran Commission on worship in 1973, only to be changed to the Philippians 3 reading when the *Lutheran Book of Worship* was finally published in 1978. The 4:6-9 lection has been expanded to 4:4-13 on the Twenty-first Sunday after Pentecost in the LBW and the Episcopal Lectionary in the *Book of Common Prayer;* the Common Lectionary uses 4:1-9 on the same Sunday. Since these readings are more inclusive, the reader is asked to refer to the comments on next Sunday's second readings from this chapter of the letter to the congregation at Philippi.

Matthew 21:33-43

Unique among Jesus' parables in Matthew, this familiar parable is an allegory which most people have heard and have come to understand. God is the one who establishes and owns the vineyard, Israel, ruled over by religious leaders who persecute, even kill, the prophets, and finally murder the Son of God, Jesus, to guarantee their ownership of the vineyard. Matthew has, of course, reinterpreted an earlier parable for his congregation, adding, beyond his allegorization, the reference to Isaiah 5 in verse 33 of the pericope, and verse 34 at the conclusion: "Therefore I tell you, the kingdom of God will be taken away from you and given to a nation producing the fruits of it." This reading, which Matthew has put in the context of Holy Week, sets the stage for the "eschatological finish" of Pentecost as the church draws near to Christ the King Sunday.

Sermon suggestions:

Matthew 21:33-43 — "Truth and Consequences."

The window of my study looks out and up toward a stand of an old cottonwood trees on my next-door neighbor's property. From my desk, I can see a nest which a pair of squirrels is busy enlarging. It wasn't there last winter, and I didn't see it until the leaves began to fall from the trees. They carry mouthsful of leaves up to the nest, disappear inside, and before long, reappear and repeat the procedure over and over again. What is unusual about this is where the pair of squirrels built the nest; it is not on a solid limb of a tree, or in the bend where a tree and limb are joined, but is in a tangle of vines coming down from one of the cottonwood trees. How could the squirrels not realize that the nest is in a most precarious location? Why wouldn't those squirrels sense that the whole thing could be toppled to the ground by a strong wind, or even by the weight of a heavy snow storm? The nest seems to be hanging in the air, suspended almost by a thread that might snap at any minute, so that all the efforts of the squirrels would be in vain. I have to wonder — even imagine — if members of the squirrel colony hadn't warned the squirrels that built this nest that they were in danger of losing their home, maybe even of losing their young. That's the truth of this situation, *and* the consequence is that they might lose everything. That's the situation in which the religious leaders and others who have rejected Jesus Christ — and put him to death — find themselves.

1. Jesus, the Son of God, is the savior of the world; that's the truth of the gospel. He really has come into the world to give us security and hope of life eternal. We really do have to decide the truth of whether or not he is the Son of God.

2. All who refuse to receive him as Lord are in jeopardy of losing the kingdom of heaven; that's the consequence of denying that Jesus is the Son of God, the Promised One. If he is an imposter, he only got what he deserved when they beat him and crucified him, didn't he?

3. Our problem is that we call Jesus, Lord, but put him on the back-burner of our lives. Our electric cook top, in our kitchen, has five burners; two large, two medium, and one quite small burner — a modern "back burner," which is almost never used. That's where we put Jesus, I'm afraid. We wouldn't think of crucifying him, would we? But putting him "on reserve" is simply a manner of crucifying him again, isn't it?

4. Accept the truth about Jesus — and live. That's the consequence of trusting God's Word and the promptings of the Holy Spirit. Because he lives — again and forever — we have a sure and certain hope of life now and forever through him, our Lord.

Isaiah 5:1-7 (R, E, L) — "High on a Fertile Hill."

1. That's where God built his vineyard. He gave it to a people of Promise, and the vineyard should have flourished and produced fruit — a peculiar people — for the Lord. Instead, it produced wild grapes — disobedient and ungodly people — for the owner of the vineyard.

2. The production of "wild grapes," instead of loving and obedient service to God, must be puzzling to God. He expects us to be faithful to him in all that we do, thereby producing a good harvest — not a new cross — for Jesus.

3. Just as God took the vineyard away from Israel because it produced "wild grapes," so he does to those to whom he gave the kingdom of heaven in Jesus Christ. God is merciful and kind and just, but he cannot act against his own character and will. The cross of Calvary rips up the vineyard, condemning those who reject or neglect Jesus, just as surely as it reconciles the faithful to God.

4. The faithful are the "pleasant planting" of the Lord today; they produce "fruit" high on the hill that was made fertile by the cross of Christ. And the heart of God rejoices in them.

Numbers 27:12-23 — "Clean Sweep."

(See, also, the sermon, "The Penalty for Betraying God's Trust," in *Great Stories of the Faith,* for another approach to preaching in this text.)

1. A clean sweep — That's what God did to the leadership of the people of Israel to prepare them for entrance into the land promised to them. Moses, along with Aaron and the older leaders, were taken by death, according to God's plan, for their spiritual shortcomings and sins. The punishment for sin is death, even in the church today.

2. A new leader waits in the wings. Moses learned — the hard way — that no one is indispensable to the work of the kingdom of God, and that God has a way of calling the people whom he wants to have leadership roles in the life of the people of God. Sometimes these leaders are surprising choices (Pope John XXIII, for example).

3. The right leader often accomplishes miracles, especially when he/she builds on what has been done before. Joshua did just that, providing a fresh start for the children of Israel just when they needed it the most. New leadership often makes the ordinary seem extraordinary, even miraculous.

4. Renewed, rather than replaced. That's the way that God would have had it, would have it still — on the part of both pastor and people, and under the supreme leadership of the Son of God, Jesus Christ our Lord.

Philippians 3:12-21 (L, C); 3:14-21 (E) — "Trouble in the Church."

1. *Trouble within.* The church has always known trouble from within as well as trouble from without. The trouble from within — as Paul sees it — is at least as dangerous to the faith as is the trouble from without; it may be more insidious in the way it affects the faithful.

2. *Philippi revisited.* That's the story of many congregations, in whom proud people step forth as leaders and formulate their own theological opinions, often to the spiritual detriment of others. Modern "enthusiasts," who think that they have already attained perfection and preach a theology of glory, can do extreme harm, causing all kinds of disharmony, in the congregation.

3. *Cruciform reorientation.* That's what is required constantly in every congregation that has known internal strife of one sort or another; all must die "in Christ" and rise — daily — to new life in Him, if the church is to be harmonious and profitable to the Lord.

4. *The best is yet to be.* That's the promise of Christ to the faithful, as Paul understood it, in the final resurrection, when we enter into a totally new and glorious existence with our Lord. Cling to the cross; the fullness of the kingdom is worth waiting for!

The Twenty-first Sunday after Pentecost
Twenty-eighth Sunday in Ordinary Time
Proper 23

Roman Catholic	Isaiah 25:6-10	Philippians 4:12-14, 19-20	Matthew 22:1-14
Episcopal	Isaiah 25:1-9	Philippians 4:4-13	Matthew 22:1-14
Lutheran	Isaiah 25:6-9	Philippians 4:4-13	Matthew 22:1-10 (11-14)
Common	Deuteronomy 34:1-12	Philippians 4:1-9	Matthew 22:1-14

The church year theological clue

If there are any chips out of, or cracks in, the eschatological framework of the church year — which admittedly becomes quite brittle by itself at this time of the year — they are restored by the readings of this Sunday. These lections point to the last things and, specifically in the first reading and the Gospel for the Day, to the incredible feast over which our Lord will preside in the new heaven and the new earth. "This is the feast of victory for our God, for the Lamb who was slain has begun his reign. Alleluia!" It would be well if every congregation could sing this hymn of praise on this Sunday.

The Prayer of the Day (LBW) — The prayer does bear some resemblance to a number of the collects for the Trinity/Pentecost Cycle/Season in the older worship books, but it does little to highlight the eschatological motif and movement of this latter section of Pentecost. It praises God, the source of every blessing, because his "generous goodness comes to us anew every day." The petition has three thoughts: "By the work of your Spirit lead us to acknowledge your goodness" (which we have just done); "give thanks for your benefits;" and, "serve you in willing obedience." The latter note, in particular, is sounded in many of the older collects for Trinity/Pentecost.

The Psalm of the Day — Psalm 23, (R, E, L) — Most people will associate this psalm with the funeral liturgy or, in the case of the more liturgically informed, the Fourth Sunday of Easter, or Good Shepherd Sunday. The Lutheran Lectionary lists Psalm 23 for all three years on Good Shepherd Sunday (the Roman *Ordo* and the *Book of Common Prayer* do not place it in Series C, at all); the Roman and Episcopal lectionaries use it on the Fourth Sunday of Easter, Series C, while only the Roman Church assigns Psalm 23 to Christ the King Sunday, Series A. The Roman and Lutheran lectionaries both place Psalm 23 in the middle of Pentecost, Series B. Oddly enough, the only use of the psalm in Series C occurs in the LBW, for Good Shepherd Sunday. The original assignment of the psalm to this Sunday obviously was to highlight God's graciousness, "You spread a table before me . . . you have anointed my head with oil, and my cup is running over." The LBW emphasizes the eschatological theme in verse 6, "Surely your goodness and mercy shall follow me all the days of my life, and I will dwell in the house of Lord forever."

The Psalm Prayer (LBW)

Lord Jesus Christ, shepherd of your Church, you give us new birth in the waters of baptism; you anoint us with oil, and call us to salvation at your table. Dispel the terrors of death and the darkness of error. Lead your people along safe paths, that they may rest securely in you and dwell in the house of the Lord now and forever, for your name's sake.

Psalm 135:1-14 (C) — Here is a song intended to be sung in the worship of the Temple, and undoubtedly meant to be sung antiphonally. It may be well to do it that way, rather than read it responsively, as so often is the custom in our churches. It speaks of — and praises — the God whom the children of Israel know, acknowledging his power to "do whatever pleases him" in the world, and his goodness toward Israel during and after the Exodus. The climax, as used in this lectionary, is reached in verse 14: "For the Lord gives his people justice and shows compassion to his servants."

The readings:

Isaiah 25:1-9 (E); 25:6-9 (L); 25:6-10 (R)

In this reading, Isaiah reiterates an older image — that of the eschatological banquet "for all peoples," — and places it on a mountain. His prophecies about the future — that God "will swallow up death for ever, and the Lord God will wipe away tears from all faces, and the reproach of his people he will take away from all the earth" — influenced the writers of the New Testament, especially the person who wrote the Book of Revelation (see, chapter 21, where part of this passage is quoted). Isaiah understands that God alone will make all of this possible, and that all human beings can do is wait in hope: "We have waited for him; let us be glad and rejoice in his salvation." Jesus might have had Isaiah's "banquet prophecy" in mind when he constructed and delivered the parable of the wedding feast given by a king for his son. At any rate, the reading from Isaiah is compatible with the Gospel for the Day and may well be combined with it in a sermon.

Deuteronomy 34:1-12 (C)

The story of the Exodus, especially the part that Moses played in it as the man whom God came to know "face to face," ends with this reading about his death. From Mt. Nebo and the "peak of Pisgah," God showed Moses all the land which he had promised to Abraham, Isaac, and Jacob and their descendants. After allowing Moses to see the land, God told him once more that he could not enter and occupy it; at one hundred and twenty years of age, and still a very vital human being, Moses died and was buried — by Yahweh himself — in a valley of the land of Moab. His grave was never found, which may explain why Peter, James, and John could identify Moses (and Elijah, too) when Jesus was transfigured on another mountain. After Moses' death, Joshua assumed command, for which he had been ordained by Moses on behalf of God, and the people obeyed him and were led into the promised land and the conclusion of their forty-year journey from Egypt to their ultimate homeland.

Philippians 4:1-9 (C); 4:4-13 (E, L); 4:12-14, 19-20 (R)

The eschatological banquet is near, according to this part of Paul's letter to the church at Philippi, for he says, "the Lord is very near." He expects the return of Christ to be imminent, but he was wrong in expecting this to happen in his lifetime; humans might expect the Parousia, but only God — and not even the risen Christ — knows when this will happen. In the meantime, Paul tells the faithful that they must be ready, and he gives a formula for positive preparation:

Finally, brothers, fill your minds with everything that is true, everything that is noble, everything that is good and pure, everything that we love and honor, and everything that can be thought virtuous or worthy of praise. (Jerusalem Bible)

280

They are to "keep doing all the things that you learned from me . . . and have heard or seen that I do." Then, he assures them, "the God of peace will be with you." In all of this, Paul could be said to be describing the proper garb for the feast that God is preparing "for those who love him." The remainder of the reading spells out the lessons he has learned as one who has known both suffering and joy in the work of the kingdom and has been "able to do all things" in the God who has strengthened him. "I know how to be poor," writes Paul, "and I know how to be rich." And he knows how to show gratitude to those who have provided financial and other support for his ministry. He is convinced that God will reward the Philippian congregation for its generosity and love toward him.

Matthew 22:1-14 (R, E, C); 22:1-10 (11-14) (L)

In this parable, it is Jesus who pictures the messianic feast, promised by God, in the context of a king's banquet for his son's wedding. Oddly enough, the invited guests refuse his hospitality (the religious leaders of the Jews are the ones Jesus is indicating for their failure to embrace him and the kingdom that he has ushered in); some made excuses and went about their day-to-day business, but others mistreated and killed some of his messengers, moving the king to give orders to his troops to go out and destroy "those murderers" and to burn their cities. Undaunted, the king tells his servants to go out and find guests and invite everyone they find to the wedding; this they do, filling the banquet room with guests.

The last part of this parable, which is considered to be a separate parable (hence the parenthetical division of it from the rest of the text in the LBW) is most puzzling. One man didn't have a wedding garment — we aren't told why — and the king, when the man is unable to give any explanation for his improper garb, has him thrown out — bound hand and foot — "into the outer darkness," where "men will weep and gnash their teeth." From our perspective, the king's action seems totally unfair, because the man simply may not have the time or the money to obtain, and change into, the proper attire. The last sentence — "For many are called, but few are chosen" — binds the two parables together, despite the fact that it is probably the addition of a redactor. Those who refuse the invitation or are not properly prepared will be cast out of the kingdom; the "chosen," who are ready for the banquet will be admitted to the kingdom of heaven.

Sermon suggestions:

Matthew 22:1-14 — "The Unacceptable Turn-down."

What was wrong with those people, who were invited by the king to his son's wedding feast, that they refused to accept the personal invitation delivered to them? Why would they turn down the opportunity to dine in the presence of the king, at his table? What did they have to do that was so pressing that they could not take the time to attend the banquet? Does all of this reflect on the king — was he a tyrant, a cruel and vicious despot — or does it reflect on the invited guests? Does the fact that he had the improperly dressed guest bound and thrown out of the feast suggest that the king was a bit of a hard-line dictator? Weren't they actually rejecting the king himself when they turned down his invitation?

In the television special, "The Man who Lived at the Ritz," about the Nazi Hermann Goering's stay in Paris, an American artist who is also a resident of the Ritz Hotel is hired by Goering to evaluate his pilfered art for its authenticity and to make certain that none of the other Nazi leaders diverts any of his holdings to themselves. The artist becomes a spy for the underground when he observes Nazi cruelty at work in Paris, and sees it especially in Goering. But he wins the Nazi's confidence, so much so that Reichsmarshall takes his face in his hands and tells him that he is "my son." Several scenes depict lavish banquets put on by Goering for the Nazi officers and their friends; no invited guest would have dared to refuse the Nazi's invitation. Oddly enough, the American goes to none of these; he always has something else to do — usually some activity for the underground — only to be found out at last, arrested and denounced by Goering, taken out to be killed by a train, where he is rescued — unwittingly — by Dr. Goebbels, who wants to employ him to oversee his confiscated art collection. Of course, the American escapes, joins up with the underground, and reappears, with his love, at the end of the movie when Paris is liberated in August, 1944.

Was the king, in Jesus' parable, that sort of megalomaniac, whose invitation should have been refused, or was he a good and beneficient ruler, who really wanted his people to celebrate his son's wedding with him?

1. In Jesus' life and death, God set the table for the promised banquet in the kingdom of heaven. Indeed, everything has been prepared and the banquet can begin any time that God decides to start it.

2. Through prophets and preachers God has sent out invitations to his people. He really does want all of his people present at this feast, which will see death swallowed up by life, sorrow taken over by joy, and tears dried up by the laughter of those who attend the banquet in the presence of the Lord himself.

3. Those invited should accept the invitation for what it is worth. There is nothing in this life that is more valuable than knowing that one's soul has been delivered from sin and death, and that one has been invited into the kingdom of heaven. (Isaiah 25 speaks to this part of the sermon.)

4. Get ready for the feast — right now — by discerning what really matters in life — one's thoughts, values, priorities, joy and suffering, by which the presence and power of God have been discerned — and holding on to them in fidelity and truth. (Paul's letter to the Philippians informs this section of the homily.)

Isaiah 25:1-9 (E); 25:6-9 (L); 25:6-10a (R) — "A Plan for a Feast."

1. God has planned a great feast at the end of time for all people. He has announced it through his prophets, preachers, and his Son, Jesus Christ.

2. God has made all the arrangements for the banquet of life. In human affairs, the arrangements are turned over to a caterer or banquet manager, who is responsible for "bringing it all together" and making certain that the plans are all fulfilled.

3. Only God could make the arrangements, because he plans to wipe away all tears, reverse the death process, and reconcile people to himself forever.

4. The day of the banquet has dawned in Jesus Christ. It is time to get ready, because "This is the Lord; we have waited for him; let us be glad and rejoice in his salvation."

Deuteronomy 34:1-12 — "The Peek from the Peak."

1. *The view from the peak.* God showed Moses all of the land which he had promised to the people of Israel, and which they were about to enter. After forty years of pilgrimage, it must have been a magnificent view for Moses, but it was hardly more than a "peek" at the promised land.

2. *Disappointment and death.* God would not allow Moses to enter the promised land; instead, he was doomed to die — and be buried by God himself in a grave that has never been found. (The tombs of the patriarchs, in a Moslem mosque in Hebron, will always be incomplete without Moses.)

3. *Jesus and the kingdom of heaven.* Unlike Moses, Jesus has preceded us into the kingdom, which he saw so clearly as he hung on the cross, and has prepared a place for us all.

4. *Jesus, Joshua and journey's end.* God's will was done when the children of Israel, led by Joshua, entered, conquered, and occupied the promised land. God has been equipping us, in Jesus, for the life of the kingdom from the beginning to the end of our lives.

282

Philippians 4:1-9 (C); 4:4-13 (E, L); 4:12-14, 19-20 (R) — "Swan Song."

1. Death is almost at hand for Paul; that means — to him — that "the Lord is near."

2. Paul is ready to die; he knows that God and the people have supported him in his ministry.

3. He is convinced that God "will supply every need" of those who believe in him and trust him.

4. Give God the glory, forever and ever.

The Twenty-second Sunday after Pentecost
Twenty-ninth Sunday in Ordinary Time
Proper 24

Roman Catholic	**Isaiah 45:1, 4-6**	**1 Thessalonians 1:1-5a**	**Matthew 22:15-21**
Episcopal	**Isaiah 45:1-7**	**1 Thessalonians 1:1-10**	**Matthew 22:15-21**
Lutheran	**Isaiah 45:1-7**	**1 Thessalonians 1:1-5a**	**Matthew 22:15-21**
Common	**Ruth 1:1-19a**	**1 Thessalonians 1:1-10**	**Matthew 22:15-22**

The church year theological clue

Since this Sunday will fall on the first Sunday in November in 1990 — and it doesn't really matter whether it is celebrated as the Twenty-second Sunday after Pentecost or All Saints Sunday, or even as one of the Sundays in the annual stewardship campaign in many congregations — the eschatological framework of the church year will be obvious for those who are liturgically informed. The climax of the church year — Christ the King Sunday — is only three weeks away; on that Sunday and on into Advent, the "final things" will be put before the people of God in the liturgy, the readings, and the sermons that are delivered. In many congregations celebrating the Twenty-second Sunday after Pentecost, stewardship concerns will crowd out the celebration of All Saints Sunday, clearly dictating the choice between remembering all of the saints and the readings of this Sunday in Pentecost. Even so, the eschatological emphasis of the church year becomes more obvious and considerably stronger on this day. The life of the Lord is "on the line" in the Gospel reading, and the last things are just out of sight.

The Prayer of the Day (LBW) — The new collect is concerned with God's self-revelation to all the world in and through Jesus Christ ("in Christ you have revealed your glory among the nations"). A little play on two words — "preserve" and "persevere" — highlights the two-part petition of the prayer ("preserve the works of your mercy," and the second part continues, "that your Church throughout the world may persevere with steadfast faith in the confession of your name . . . ."). The prayer does speak, rather directly, to the heart of the Gospel for the Day, "Render unto Caesar the things that are Caesar's, and unto God the things that are God's."

The Psalm for the Day — Psalm 96:1, 3-5, 7-10 (R); 96, or 96:1-9 (E); 96 (L) — A fitting response to God's revelation to Cyrus, and his use of the king to free Israel from its exile in Babylon, is made in this psalm. But it goes beyond Cyrus the king; it makes clear that the intention of God, as in the latter part of the first reading, is that all the world shall know that he, and only he, is God. The psalmist puts words in the mouths of all who have heard about God, his goodness, and his powerful and merciful deeds: "Sing to the Lord a new song; sing to the Lord, all the earth." All people and nations are to bless the Lord, praise his holy name, and declare him as the only God, superior to the idols of the heathens, for he is the Creator, Sustainer, and Redeemer of all that is and will come to be. The eschatological theme of Pentecost is sounded in the last verses: "Then shall all the trees of the wood shout for joy before the Lord when he comes, when he comes to judge the earth. He will judge the world with righteousness and the peoples with his truth." It is important to the theological content of the day to include these last verses in any sung or spoken rendition of the psalm.

The Psalm Prayer (LBW)

> *Lord Jesus, the incarnate Word, when you consented to dwell with us, the heavens were glad and the earth rejoiced. In hope and love we await your return. Help us to proclaim your glory to those who do not know you, until the whole earth sings a new song to you and the Father and the Holy Spirit, one God, now and forever.*

Psalm 146 (C) — Naomi would hardly have been singing this song when she set out for Bethlehem after the death of her husband and her two sons in a little more than a decade of residence in Moab. Though her plight might have led her to feel sorry for herself, her trust in her God might have led her to thoughts such as these. Verse 6b speaks of God's blessing to the Israelites, because he gave "food to those who hunger." And, later, verse 8b adds, "he sustains the orphan and widow," which speaks to the situation of Naomi and her two Moabite daughters-in-law.

The readings:

Isaiah 45:1, 4-6 (R); 45:1-7 (E, L)

That God moves in mysterious ways to accomplish his will is borne out in this reading, in which he reveals himself to the Persian, King Cyrus, for the purpose of enlisting him in his cause of liberating his people from their exile in Babylon. He uses a heathen ruler "for the sake of my servant Jacob, and Israel my chosen." But God's revelation is also for Persia's sake and for the blessing and benefit of all people, because God, who made the heavens and the earth, still has the whole world in his hands: "I am the Lord, who do all these things." In this respect, the first reading looks to the Gospel for the Day and Jesus' answer to the religious leaders when he was asked about paying taxes ("Give to Caesar the things that are Caesar's, and to God the things that are God's"), as well as to the Thessalonian congregation which, as next week's reading indicates, had become citizens of the kingdom while they were still citizens of Greece and under Roman rule.

Ruth 1:1-19a (C)

This is the tragic tale of a refugee couple and their two sons, who leave Bethlehem for the land of Moab in time of famine, only to have the father die soon after their arrival in Moab, followed in about ten years by the deaths of the two sons. Naomi, left a widow with two Moabite daughters-in-law, the widows of her sons, as her only relatives in that strange land, decided to return to Bethlehem, when she heard that God had reversed the famine so that there was enough food again. The tragedy is alleviated when Ruth, who with Orpah was urged to stay with her people, begged her mother-in-law to take her with her, voicing her love in that beautiful speech: "Entreat me not to leave you or to return from following you; for where you go I will go, and where you lodge I will lodge; your people will be my people, and your God my God. . . ." After Orpah goes back to her family and Naomi and Ruth arrive in Bethlehem, the story becomes more complicated, replete with intrigue, scheming, and even the hint of seduction, but in this reading it is the lovely twist to a tragic story that occupies our attention. (This reading finds a place in the lections for the Twenty-first Sunday after Pentecost, Series C, of the Episcopal and Lutheran lectionaries.)

1 Thessalonians 1:1-5a (L); 1:1-5b (R); 1:1-10 (E, C)

The letter to the church at Thessalonika is probably, according to most scholars, Paul's first epistle and the first book of the New Testament to be written, probably at Corinth, about A.D. 50, and sent back to the young congregation after Paul received a first-hand report from Timothy about the state of that community of Christians. Paul assures them that he remembers them regularly in his prayers, thanking God for them and asking the Lord to support the steadfastness of their faith, hope, and love "in our Lord Jesus Christ." He wants them to know that God has chosen them, not only in word, "but also in power and in the Holy Spirit and with full conviction." It would seem, from this introduction to his letter, that the church at Thessalonika had gotten off to a good start and is flourishing in the faith. This letter, as the Ruth story, gets more complicated as it unfolds.

Matthew 22:15-21

The plot to get rid of Jesus, even if it means putting him to death, continues to thicken in this pericope that Matthew has included in the events of what we call Holy Week. The religious leaders, scribes and Pharisees, will not give up their attack on Jesus, shameless people that they were, but continue to harrass him verbally so as to trap him in his own words. For one thing, they were testing Jesus about his orthodoxy when they asked the question about paying taxes to Caesar, and, on the other hand, some scholars suggest that they might have been attempting to settle a question among themselves about what constituted genuine orthodoxy and who were truly God's people. Once again, Jesus outsmarts them, asking them for a coin, looking at it, then questioning, "Whose image is this (on the coin)." To their answer, "Caesar's," he makes the "two kingdom" reply, "Render to Caesar the things that are Caesar's, and to God the things that are God's." Clearly, Christians are to be subjects of the state, obeying its laws and honoring its leaders, but they are also citizens of the kingdom of God, and they owe him their highest loyalty. Christians are relearning, of late, the importance of differentiating between — and acting upon, sometimes in civil disobedience — these two citizenships.

Sermon suggestions:

Matthew 22:15-21 — "Dual Citizenship."

Christians, as well as Jews, have dual citizenship; they are citizens of the state in which they were born and reside, and they are subjects of the kingdom of God. The question is, simply put, "Which citizenship should have priority in our lives?" The answer that Jesus gave suggests that citizens have responsibilities to both; he didn't really, in this instance, settle the question in a manner that really pleased the Pharisees; he simply told them that they have responsibilities, which they must face and meet, to the state and to the kingdom of God. Christians must pay their taxes and be good citizens, and — from the standpoint of Christian stewardship, if one so interprets Jesus' "(render) to God the things that are God's" — give the proper measures of time, talents, and treasures to the business of God's kingdom.

The matter of dual citizenship in the modern world took a new and different twist in the elections in Israel at the end of October, 1988. The Likud party, orthodox Jews, and fundamentalists, according to one Israeli citizen, gained a majority in the Hebrew parliament. Some Jews in Jerusalem, obviously from other parties and resentful of how the Likud gained so much power, said:

> *Thousands of Americans (Jews) hold dual citizenship in the United States and in Israel. Many, if not most of them, made the trip from the United States to Israel in the last week, simply to vote in the election; after they voted, they went back to America. This was the reason that the Likud was elected.*

The resentment raised the fear that the ultra-conservative Likud theologians would impose their beliefs and their rigid obedience of the Torah upon the citizens who really live in Israel, suggesting that there will be real trouble if this happens. Civil disobedience in Israel may break new ground should the Likud get anything resembling total control of the government. A couple of weeks after the election, the Likud sprang a surprise upon Jews all over the world, threatening to expel all persons, especially converts, from Judaism who had not become Jews under Orthodox rules and regulations. The outcome of this threat remains in the future.

1. *Flag and cross:* These symbols announce our dual citizenship in the United States of America and in the kingdom of God. We are to honor the flag and what it stands for by

286

obeying the laws, paying our taxes, and participating in the good things done by the state. We are to revere the cross, worship the Lord and live out our lives in faith, hope, and love as Christians.

2. *Cross or flag:* Which takes precedence in the lives of Christians? This much we know: we will be in deep trouble if we don't pay our taxes, and may wind up in jail if we break the laws meant to protect us and others. What of the kingdom and the church: are our Christian responsibilities optional, especially when it comes to giving of our time, talents, and treasure to the work of the kingdom?

3. *Flag or cross:* Are civic responsibilities, mandatory and elective, to be put on the same plane as our Christian obligations? If so, doesn't that diminish our citizenship in the kingdom? In the final analysis, doesn't the cross have to supercede the flag, because the kingdom of God embraces all nations, for God is King of Kings, and isn't the ultimate fate of all people in his hands? If so, what place does civil disobedience play in our lives?

4. *Hold high the cross:* Be a good citizen by paying your taxes, obeying the laws of the land, and working for the benefit of others. But hold up the cross by your thankful and loving response to God's goodness in your total stewardship, which builds up the church in the world, even if it, at times, means standing in opposition to the state and the very powers of this world when the state and its leaders fail to function in ways that are pleasing to God and beneficial to its citizens.

Isaiah 45:1, 4-6 (R); 45:1-7 (E, L) — "What a God!"

1. *Wonder worker:* That's what God is and always has been, from the creation of the world right up to the present time. He made and sustained his people, liberated his chosen ones from Egypt and Babylon. He delivers all people from the consequences of sin and death.

2. *Mysterious and mystifying:* God is mysterious, he has always kept people at a distance. He is both hidden and revealed, but no one has seen him, except in Jesus Christ. Yet God is equally mystifying, because he does things in strange ways, at times — using Cyrus to free Israel from Babylon, for example. And he uses the death of his Son, Jesus Christ, to free us from death and the grave. That's mystifying, indeed.

3. *Weal and woe:* God is in charge of all that happens, and rejoices in our welfare and supports us in times of sorrow and need. He is the Lord our God, mysterious and mystifying, but always concerned about us and available when we call upon him, especially in the name of Jesus Christ our Lord. Our God is unique in all the world.

4. *Worship and work:* That is our business as citizens of the kingdom of God.

Ruth 1:1-19a — "Return of a Refugee."

1. *Refugees:* That's what Elimelech, Naomi, and their two sons, Mahlon and Chilion, were when they left Bethlehem and went to live in the land of Moab. There they found welcome and a new way of life.

2. *A new tragedy:* Naomi's life took a turn for the worse when Elimelech, her husband, died; life in Moab became impossible when her two sons died a decade later. There was no future for her in Moab; she had to return to Bethlehem.

3. *A loving daughter:* That's what the daughter-in-law, Ruth, became, going all the way to Bethlehem with her. Her love mirrors the love of Jesus for his Father, which takes him on an awful journey, to the cross.

4. *A new life:* Naomi found a new life, which wouldn't have been hers to the same degree without Ruth's presence and love if she had returned by herself. This, too, has overtones for the Christians, who cannot know forgiveness and new life apart from Jesus Christ.

(See, also, the sermon on this text, "Round Trip to Bethlehem," in Bass, *Great Stories of the Faith*.)

1 Thessalonians 1:1-5a (L); 1:1-5b (R); 1:1-10 (E, C) — "From Resurrection to Parousia."

That's the spiritual journey that Paul travels with the members of the church at Thessaloni-ka in these few little verses of his letter to them.

1. *Peace:* He greeted them with the *pax*, the peace, which is the greeting of the risen Lord to his church when it is assembled in his name. Pass the peace of the Lord!

2. *Power:* Through the word which Paul preached and taught to them and the Holy Spirit, they received the power to believe the good news and become children of God, members of the body of Christ. Receive the power of the Word and the Holy Spirit.

3. *Profit:* Their lives, which gave proof that the Lord had come to them and was work-ing in them, proved to be profitable to the Lord and to the growth of his kingdom. They became witnesses for Christ in their community. Respond to the power in gratitude, faith, and good works, and be profitable to God, yourself, and the kingdom.

4. *Parousia:* The church at Thessalonika came to know the fullness of the good news. Their Lord not only forgave their sins and promised them eternal life, but he also declared that he would come again. With them, we pray: "Come, Lord Jesus! Come, quickly!"

The Twenty-third Sunday after Pentecost
Thirtieth Sunday in Ordinary Time
Proper 25

Roman Catholic	Exodus 22:20-27	1 Thessalonians 1:5-10	Matthew 22:34-40
Episcopal	Exodus 22:21-27	1 Thessalonians 2:1-8	Matthew 22:34-46
Lutheran	Leviticus 9:1-2, 15-18	1 Thessalonians 1:5b-10	Matthew 22:34-40 (41-46)
Common	Ruth 2:1-13	1 Thessalonians 2:1-8	Matthew 22:34-46

The church year theological clue

In older Lutheran Lectionaries, the readings for the last three Sundays, no matter how many Sundays there were in the Trinity/Pentecost season, all dealt with eschatological themes and the last things; they warned the church of the impending conclusion of Pentecost, as well as the Parousia. That sort of warning — that the end of the year and the end time are approaching — is not sounded in the new lectionaries (with the exception of The Lutheran Church — Missouri Synod's *Lutheran Worship*), but it probably is not needed. When the numbering of the Sundays after Pentecost reaches, "twenty-plus," and when All Saints' Sunday is behind, and when the Gregorian calendar is approaching the middle of the month, Christ the King Sunday and Advent, with their unmistakable announcements of the Parousia, are close at hand. An "eschatological shift" is actually made on the Twenty-fourth Sunday after Pentecost, so this is the last Sunday of Pentecost wherein the eschatological framework of Pentecost may seem to be indistinct. The Gospel for the Day pictures Jesus as the "supreme law-giver," who reinterprets the Ten Commandments for all time and for all people. It has to do with the love of God and people as the key to the kingdom of God.

The Prayer of the Day (LBW) — This revision of a classic collect has been shifted from the Thirteenth Sunday after Trinity/Fourteenth Sunday after Pentecost to this Sunday, partly because it has a deep concern for the ultimate things of God ("increase in us the gifts of faith, hope, and charity"), but also because it anticipates what the Gospel for the Day has to say about the love of God and human beings ("and that we may obtain what you promise, make us love what you command," that is, to love both God and people). The theological clue for this day's worship surfaces in this "theme prayer" before it emerges in today's Gospel; it recognizes that human beings cannot generate love, whether it be for God or people, and that only God can move human hearts to love for him, his will, and for love like his that embraces all other persons in the world.

The Psalm of the Day — Psalm 18:1-3, 46, 50 (R) — Here is a song of thanksgiving, possibly written by David after a military victory, which might be used on any, or many, worship occasions. Those excerpts from the psalm which are intended to be a responsory to the first reading don't accomplish their task very well, except for the first line of the first verse ("I love you, O Lord my strength"). That portion of the psalm — in the context of the entire psalm — attests to the fact that the writer loves the Lord God with all of his heart, soul, and mind in response for all that God has done for him. For him, the good, gracious, and powerful God has become a lovable God, and he can do nothing else but respond to God's loving actions with a declaration of his own love for God.

Psalm 1 (E, L) — A most fitting response to both Exodus 22:21-27 and Leviticus 19:1-2, 15-18, emerges in this psalm, which talks about people who have lived righteously, obeying the dictates of God, because "their delight is in the law of the Lord, and they meditate on his law day and night." Such people are richly blessed by God ("like trees planted by streams of water"); they will endure and receive God's full blessing in the judgment, but the wicked are doomed to perish at the end of time.

The Psalm Prayer (LBW)

Lord God, in your loving wisdom you have set us beside the fountain of life, like a tree planted by running streams. Grant that the cross of your Son may become our tree of life in the paradise of your saints, through Jesus Christ our Lord.

Psalm 128 (C) — The third verse of this six-verse psalm reveals why it was chosen as a responsory to the first reading about Ruth's impending involvement with Boaz, who ultimately married her: "Your wife shall be like a fruitful vine within your house, your children like olive shoots round about your table." The problem is that Ruth doesn't actually marry Boaz until chapter four of the story, and she doesn't bear a son, Obed, who was the grandfather of David, until the very end of the tale. But the psalm is a rather good description of Boaz, a good and righteous man who only wanted to do what was right for Ruth and her mother-in-law. He was a man who "feared the Lord" and was, in return, blessed by God.

The readings:

Exodus 22:20-26 (R); 22:21-27 (E)

The first reading was chosen to complement the Gospel for the Day with its emphasis upon whole-heartedly loving other persons as much as you love yourself. It spells out part of the code of laws and gives concrete examples of some of the ways that one should demonstrate love for God in one's relationships with other people. It could very well be read in the pulpit, after the Gospel for the Day, especially if one is preaching from this text.

Leviticus 19:1-2, 15-18 (L)

Again, this reading has been chosen because, in concrete ways, it calls for positive loving actions toward other people by those who claim to love God. It is the source of Jesus' sayings in the Gospel for the Day, defining one's responsibilities toward one's neighbors clearly and carefully. The last verse was actually quoted by Jesus in his response to the question of the lawyer: "but you shall love your neighbor as yourself." It emphasizes the importance which Jesus gave to the fact that people who claim that they love God must demonstrate that love by their attitude and actions toward the people they know and interact with every day of their lives.

Ruth 2:1-13 (C)

Once Naomi and Ruth were settled in Bethlehem, after their trip from Moab, Ruth asked Naomi's permission to go out and glean in the fields wherever an owner would be kind enough to allow her to follow the reapers. By chance, she made her way into the fields of Boaz, a relative of her late father-in-law, Elimelech, who asked his foreman about her identity and, when he had learned who she was, gave her a warm greeting, told her to stay in his fields, and warned his male servants not to harm her. In answer to her question about his goodness toward her, he told her that he knew what she had done for Naomi, and invited her to have "bread and wine" with him. Ruth had "found favor" with an important man and one who would make a considerate husband.

1 Thessalonians 1:5b-10 (R, L)

In the continuation of his address to the members of the church at Thessalonika, Paul reminds them that he and his companions tried to be an example of Christian living for them, commending them on their positive response at being "imitators of us and of the Lord." In their Christian faith and life style, they acquired the reputation of exemplary Christian living and influenced other people of Greece by renouncing the worship of idols and accepting the good news in Jesus Christ. They heard the gospel, learned of Jesus' death and resurrection, and lived in expectation of his imminent return. Paul couldn't ask any more than that of them.

1 Thessalonians 2:1-8 (E, C)

Somehow, through the grace of God and the power of the Holy Spirit, Paul and his companions got the courage to preach the good news to the Thessalonians, despite the terrible treatment they had received from the people at Philippi. He reminds them that they were not attempting to deceive anyone, nor were they trying to raise money for themselves. God had chosen them and had given them the mandate to preach the gospel of Jesus Christ, not to please people, not to gain honor and glory for themselves, but to fulfill the will and intentions of God. Paul declares that they have come to know and love the Thessalonians so well that they not only wanted to turn over the gospel to them but the "whole lives," as well. His picture of the congregation at Thessalonika is positive and appealing in this part of his letter to them.

Matthew 22:34-40 (R); 22:34-40 (41-46) (L); 22:34-46 (E, C)

In this pericope, Jesus stops the questions and the attempts of the scribes and Pharisees to entrap him in his teachings once and for all. The lawyer who went to him, hoping to trip up Jesus with his question, "Teacher, which is the great commandment of the law?", received an answer provided by scripture itself in Jesus' "You shall love the Lord your God with all your heart, and with all your soul, and with all your mind. This is the great and first commandment." He also received a lesson that he hadn't asked for when Jesus continued, "And a second is like it, You shall love your neighbor as yourself. On these two commandments depend all the law and the prophets." By itself, this two-fold answer, in which Jesus connected two parts of the law contained in the Bible, was enough to silence him, but when Jesus asked the question, "What do you think about Christ? Whose son is he?", and engaged them in the ensuing dialogue about Christ as David's son, he silenced them completely and once and for all when he asked, quoting scripture, "If David calls him Lord, how is he his son?" The only course of action open to them was to get rid of him, and they proceeded to do just that.

Sermon suggestions:

Matthew 22:34-40 (R, L) "The Two Dimensions of the Law."

Jesus really believed that the two dimensions of the law — loving God with all of one's heart, soul, and mind, and loving one's neighbor as oneself — really belong together and are inseparable. He proved that he loved God by becoming "obedient unto death" and entrusting his life and his mission to the Lord at the cross and the tomb. Most of the martyrs have similarly died for the faith, proving therein their love for God; they comprise part of the army — one great company — in the noble army of martyrs, beginning with Stephen, most of the Apostles, and a growing legion of people who loved the Lord enough that they were ready to lay down their lives in the name of the Son of God. That kind of love may be enough, in the case of the martyrs and confessors of the church, but it may not suffice for the rest of us who have never been threatened with torture or death for Jesus' sake.

The second dimension of the law carries equal force for most of the children of God. If we say we love God, we must demonstrate that love in our relationships with other people, our neighbors — perhaps even laying down our lives on their behalf. Jesus' first word on the cross was, "Father, forgive them, for they do not know what they are doing." He died, demonstrating to the world not only his love for God, but his love for other people. Every October 17, I remember the Beatification of Father Maximilian Kolbe in St. Peter's Basilica — my wife and I were there. He was one of the martyrs of the Auschwitz, who loved other people so much that he took the place of a condemned man in the concentration camp, a man who had a wife and two sons in the camp. When Father Kolbe had been the leader of a one-thousand person Franciscan religious community outside of Warsaw, the Nazis refrained from arresting him, despite his open opposition to them, for a considerable period of time; they obviously didn't want him to become a martyr, a symbol of innocent suffering for the Poles. But after they finally arrested him and put him in Auschwitz, they insulted and mistreated him, and he might easily have become a martyr for the faith. An escape from Auschwitz by one man changed all of that; ten men were chosen by the officer in charge and doomed to die for the escape of one man. When one of the ten cried out, "I have a wife and children," Father Kolbe immediately stepped forward and asked to take the man's place in the infamous "Hunger Bunker" of Auschwitz; he offered himself as one who was willing to die a martyr's death for another human being. He loved his neighbor more than he loved his own life, because he loved the Lord with all his heart, soul, and mind.

1. Love for God and people is the spontaneous response of Christians to the sacrifice of Jesus on the cross. The cross of Christ frees persons from the threat of the law, and it also makes new creatures out of people who are able to love God and each other.

2. Godly love is more than mere emotion. It is emotion that is informed by knowledge of God's good and gracious actions toward his creatures in the Garden of Eden, in the beginnings of Israel, from Egypt to Calgary to wherever we are in his world. That is the kind of love that will really be two-dimensional — toward God and toward people. That is the love that puts self-love in proper perspective.

3. Christian love is expressed in positive actions toward God and people. Those who profess to love God worship him and serve him. Those who really love God love his people, too, and express their love for others by their words and deeds. Love goes into action, or it is incomplete and/or defective. Christian love is active, or it is not genuine love, at all. It is giving oneself to others — in the name of Jesus Christ.

4. God, in Jesus and through Word and Spirit, enables us to love as we should. Without God's help and initiative, we could not hope to have a well-rounded and two-dimensional love that would result in loving actions toward God and his people; we might still love ourselves more than we love God and other people. We know that "we love, because he first loved us," and that is what, finally, makes true love possible.

Exodus 22:20-26 (R); 22:21-27 (E) — "The Other Side of the Law."

1. God has decreed that his people must love one another, as well as love him.

2. Care of strangers, widows, orphans, and the poor is a demonstration of God-like love. It reminded the Israelites — and us, as well — that they were "strangers" in a foreign land, "widowed and orphaned," and really poor, at one time.

3. Godly people will love and care for others the way that God has cared for them — in the Exodus and the Promised Land, and in the cross of Jesus Christ.

4. Loving care and actions offer proof that our professions of love toward God are genuine.

Leviticus 19:1-2, 15-18 (L) — "What It Means to be Holy."

1. Holiness begins with God, who alone is holy. His actions — love, mercy, justice — express his holiness to people.

2. Holiness involves the people of God. Their lives are to reflect God's holiness, which they cannot generate on their own or by themselves.

3. Holiness expresses the goodness of God in human relationships. It takes the concrete form of concern, kindness, mercy, forgiveness, and generosity toward people in need or in deep trouble.

4. Holiness is God's love in action in his people's lives. Made holy — whole — by the Lord their God, the children of God live in obedience, faith, hope, and love.

Ruth 2:1-13 — "A Twist to the Tale."

1. The plot thickens. Once Naomi and Ruth are settled back in Bethlehem, Ruth secures permission of Naomi to go out into the fields "to find favor" with a man, who will be kind enough to allow her to follow his reapers to get food for Naomi and herself.

2. A stroke of luck. She chooses a field in which to glean, that, it turns out, belongs to Boaz, a relative of her late father-in-law, Elimelech. This seems to have been, according to the story, a lucky choice.

3. Protection and food. Ruth found favor, indeed, with Boaz, who gave her protection in the fields and guaranteed — through orders to his foreman — that her work would be worthwhile, her gleaning sufficient for her and Naomi's needs.

4. Bright prospects. That's what really came out of the incident; she found sufficient favor in the eyes of Boaz that, before long, she became his wife.

1 Thessalonians 1:5b-10 (R, L) — "The Power in Example."

1. Paul and his companions offered the Thessalonians an example of Christian faith and life.

2. Moved by the Word and the Holy Spirit, the Thessalonians became imitators of that Christian life-style.

3. Their new life-style — a combination of faith, hope, and loving action — deeply moved other Greeks and became an example of the new life in Christ for them.

4. The story went out to all of their world. This shows us how they, and we, in one way, participate in the work of the gospel in all the world.

1 Thessalonians 2:1-8 (E, C) — "An Explanation for an Effective Mission."

1. Jesus decreed that the good news should go out to all of the world. That is behind all of Paul's evangelistic and missionary activity.

2. God himself chose and called Paul and his companions to preach the Word to all the world. He sent them to the Thessalonians with the good news.

3. Christian preaching, whether in Thessalonika or anywhere in our world, is done to please God, not people. That's why preachers, missionaries, and other witnesses for Christ may dare to face resistance and outright opposition to the good news.

4. Preaching, witnessing, and ministry bring their own reward to God's people. God's approval is more important than any amount of money that full-time evangelists and missionaries might be paid. That's how it is and always will be in service of God and the gospel.

The Twenty-fourth Sunday after Pentecost
Thirty-first Sunday in Ordinary Time (R)
Proper 26 (E, C)

Roman Catholic	Malachi 1:14a—2:2b, 8-10	1 Thessalonians 2:7-9, 13	Matthew 23:1-12
Episcopal	Micah 3:5-12	1 Thessalonians 2:9-13, 17-20	Matthew 23:1-12
Lutheran	Amos 5:18-24	1 Thessalonians 4:13-14 (15-18)	Matthew 25:1-13
Common	Ruth 4:7-17	1 Thessalonians 2:9-13, 17-20	Matthew 23:1-12

The church year theological clue

If a congregation happened to be following the readings listed in *Lutheran Worship*, the Lutheran Church — Missouri Synod's revision of the Roman *Ordo* and the LBW lectionary, the people would have caught the eschatological clue last Sunday; the *Lutheran Worship* lectionary follows the older Lutheran practice of abandoning the numerical progression of the Sundays in Pentecost and assigning the same three sets of readings — always eschatological — for the last three Sundays of Pentecost. The LBW accomplishes almost the same thing by assigning eschatological readings to the Twenty-fourth Sunday after Pentecost and any Sundays following up to Christ the King Sunday in Cycle A; the LBW takes Matthew 25:1-13, and places it on this Sunday. This choice — in this year only — along with the other lections, makes an "early eschatological announcement" that clearly strengthens the eschatological framework of the church year. It insists that the last things need to be considered by the church. The people of God must constantly be aware that their pilgrimage is taking them to the end of the era and to the fullness of the reign of Jesus Christ over heaven and earth.

The Prayer of the Day (LBW) This prayer clearly announces the "last things" in the good news, which the church is to remember and celebrate; it is specifically "tailored" for the Matthew 25:1-13 Gospel of the Day, the familiar story of the ten maidens "who went to meet the bridegroom." It declares: "Lord, when the day of wrath comes we have no hope except in your grace . . . ." The petition pleads: "Make us so to watch for the last days that the consummation of our hope may be the joy of the marriage feast of your Son, Jesus Christ our Lord." The eschatological theme of the remainder of Pentecost, therefore, surfaces in the liturgy on the Twenty-fourth Sunday after Pentecost every year (in the LBW), simply because there is only one Prayer of the Day that has been prepared for the three years of the lectionary.

The Psalm of the Day — Psalm 131:1-3 (R) — A repentant priest or Pharisee could have composed this psalm: "O Lord, I am not proud; I have no haughty looks." In this respect, it "works" as a responsory to the first reading. It also strikes an eschatological note, which is compatible with one of the last Sundays in the church year, in the concluding verse (3) of this very brief psalm: "O Israel, wait upon the Lord, from this time forth forevermore."

Psalm 43 (E) — Here is a psalm that fits perfectly into the context of the Gospel for the Day, one of Jesus' teachings during the week that led up to his condemnations and crucifixion. The psalmist could have been composing words for Jesus' prayer to God, when he prayed desperately, "Give judgment for me, O God, and defend my cause against an ungodly people; deliver me from the deceitful and the wicked." The familiar lines, "Send out your light and your truth, that they may lead me, and bring me to your holy hill and to your dwelling," take on new meaning in the light of Calvary and the tomb. Jesus could say with the psalmist, "Put your trust in God; . . . who is the help of my countenance and my God" — even, and especially, in the face of death.

Psalm 63:1-8 (L) — As a responsory to the first reading, this psalm doesn't seem to work, but it is relevant to the theological concerns of people who are conscious that the last things are close at hand. It is also suited to people who are in any sort of trouble, as surely as the psalmist was: "O God, you are my God; eagerly I seek you; my soul thirsts for you, my flesh faints for you, as in a barren and dry land where there is no water." The goal of the Christian pilgrimage is suggested in the psalmist's words, "Therefore I have gazed upon you in your holy place, that I might behold your power and your glory." With praise and thanksgiving — and more than a mere measure of hope — the psalmist throws himself upon the mercy of God in true faith and love. In this, he offers the Christian a model of eschatological piety.

The Psalm Prayer (LBW)

Heavenly Father, creator of unfailing light, enlighten those who call to you. May our lives proclaim your goodness, our work give you honor, and our voices praise you forever; for the sake of your Son, Jesus Christ our Lord.

Psalm 127 (C)

The first half of Psalm 63 might make a better responsory to the first reading of the Episcopal lectionary because it picks up the "darkness" theme of Micah 3:5-12 with its harsh prediction: "The sun will set for the prophets, the day will go black for them." Psalm 127 offers a corrective for the corruption of the priests and Pharisees, which surfaces once more in the Gospel for the Day, and in Jesus' lament over Jerusalem (at the end of Chapter 23): "Unless the Lord builds the house, their labor is in vain who build it. Unless the Lord watches over the city, in vain the watchman keeps his vigil." After a word of hope at the end of verse 3, the psalm becomes more specifically addressed to the blessing that comes with children.

The readings:

Leviticus 1:14b—2:2b, 8-10 (R)

The warning of God's messenger (Malachi means "my messenger") to the priests, who instituted new practices in the worship of God after the return from exile, also speaks to the priests and Pharisees of Jesus' time, who corrupted the worship of God even more. Malachi makes a connection to the importance of the teaching function of those who are called and ordained to the service of God, and in this he addresses contemporary clergy about an essential ingredient in their ministry: "The lips of the priest ought to safeguard knowledge; his mouth is where instruction should be sought, since he is the messenger of Yahweh Sabaoth." Too many clergy of Malachi's day had "strayed from the way" and had caused many to stumble; they had destroyed the covenant of Levi; for this, they will be reviled by the people and judged harshly by the Lord God.

Micah 3:5-12 (E)

Here is another warning — and a condemnation by God — to the prophets, who have failed to function in the ways that properly fulfill the duties of their office as servants of God and, as Micah speaks for the Lord God, "who lead my people astray." Like the prophets against whom Jesus speaks in the Gospel for the Day, they are concerned with their own welfare, and care little for the well being of the people. Micah tells them,

And so the night will come to you: an end of vision; darkness for you: an end of divination . . . . Then the seers will be covered with shame, the diviners with confusion; they will all cover their lips, because no answer comes from God.

The least that they can expect is that their office will be rendered ineffectual by God, and, as a result, Jerusalem will become "a heap of rubble, and the mountain of the Temple a wooded height."

Amos 5:18-24 (L)

For some reason, the original first reading assigned to this Sunday, Zephaniah 1:14-16, with its insistence that "The great day of the Lord is near, near and hastening fast," was replaced with this lection from Amos 5, which also refers to "the day of the Lord." Micah is convinced that there will be "trouble for those of you who are waiting so longingly for the day of the Lord." It will be a day of darkness, "all gloom, without a single ray of light." There must be harmony between the things that are done and said in worship and the lives of the people outside of the Temple; that will be pleasing and acceptable to God. Those who make false idols of any kind for themselves are doomed to exile from the kingdom of the Lord God. Amos speaks to the people as well as to the priests and other religious leaders — then and now.

Ruth 4:7-17 (C)

One could anticipate that the story of Ruth and Boaz would turn out this way; he would come to appreciate and love her, and take her for his wife. He did just that, making his declaration publicly before the elders and "all the people" of Bethlehem. After she became his wife, Ruth gave him a son, Obed, who was the father of Jesse, David's father. Ruth, through this involved story that has some elements of a modern soap opera in it, became the great-grandmother of King David, which is one of the reasons that the lovely story of Ruth's fidelity to Naomi is included in the Old Testament. This is not just another touching tale of devotion and love; it has a godly purpose built into it.

1 Thessalonians 2:7-9, 13 (R); 2:9-13, 17-20 (E, C)

The context of this reading is Paul's appreciation of, and thanksgiving for, the people of Thessalonika, who received him and his companions and heard the good news with genuine joy. He reminds them that God has chosen Paul, Silvanus, and Timothy to preach to the Thessalonians, entrusting the good news to them, and that their preaching has sought to glorify God, not themselves. He reminisces about how hard they worked — Paul as a tent-maker — to support themselves so that they would not pose a financial burden upon the community. He also speaks of their message as the Word of God, and commends them to receive it eagerly; that Word was God's message, not human wisdom or invention. And the Word was beneficial for the Thessalonians, because they received it eagerly for what it is — *the Word of God* — and, apparently, with prayer and thanksgiving. Paul spells out a concise summary of his theology of preaching in the middle of these readings, and then goes on to tell the Thessalonians how much he and his companions want to return and see them again, assuring them that they are their "pride and joy." This chapter reads like a religious love story, and it must have moved the people of the Thessalonian congregation quite deeply, because they knew the circumstances in which Paul was writing to them.

1 Thessalonians 4:13-14 (15-18) (L)

I know a man who, when he is invited to any sort of a buffet supper — be it meager or bountiful — selects his food on what he calls his own theory: "I skip the preliminaries and get to the good stuff." He will bypass appetizers, salad, and even fruit, and move along the tables to the meats and vegetables — and desserts — that have been prepared and spread before the guests. The committee that selected the readings of the LBW might be accused of operating on that principle, inasmuch as they bypassed all of chapters two and three of this letter and moved to the last five verses of chapter four, which had the better theological content for this Sunday. But it was not a matter of counting chapters two and three unimportant or of lesser value to contemporary congregations, rather it was to accommodate the obvious shift to an emphasis on the last things and to sharpen the image of the Second Coming of Christ the King at the end of time. In this lection, Paul assures the Thessalonians that God will take to himself, "through Christ," those who have already died. They will be raised up from the grave and received by God before those who are still living. All this will happen when the Lord returns with "a cry of command, the archangel's call, and with the sound of the trumpet of God."

This reading, it will be noted, changes from the system of thematic harmony of first reading and Gospel of the Lutheran Lectionary, with the second lesson "floating freely" in semi-contiuous short-courses, back to the theological compatibility of all three readings of the first half of the church year.

Matthew 23:1-12 (R, E, C)

In this chapter of Matthew, Jesus' attack on the scribes and Pharisees begins emphatically in his address to "the crowds," but continues to pick up steam as the chapter progresses. He regards the office of the scribes and Pharisees quite highly; they are the keepers of the Hebrew tradition, because "they occupy the seat of Moses." This means that their teachings should be heard and followed by the people, but the trouble is that their lives do not match their teachings. In short, Jesus sees them as hypocrites who say one thing but do another. They are religious "showboats," who want to be seen and honored by people for their religiosity; they demand, in one way or another, that they be addressed respectfully, even reverently, as rabbi. Jesus then turns from the crowds to the scribes and Pharisees and speaks directly to them, teaching that they should not insist on being called rabbi, or master, or father, or teacher, for those titles are reserved for the Father and the Son. From verse thirteen to the end of the chapter, Jesus gives the religious leaders example after example of their hypocrisy, ending with his prophecy about the persecution of those whom he will send to them, and his touching lament for Jerusalem.

Matthew 25:1-13 (L)

In some of the old single series lectionaries, especially in the Lutheran lectionary, with its last three Sundays so clearly oriented to the last things, this Gospel was appointed for the Last Sunday after Trinity; it follows that it should be appointed for one of the concluding and thematically eschatological Sundays — in the LBW lectionary — of Pentecost. It reminds us again of the wedding feast and the ten young maidens, five of whom were wise, who had enough oil for their lamps, and five who were foolish, and had to go out and buy additional oil when their lamps went out. At any rate, those who were wise enough to bring a sufficient amount of oil to see them through the night until the bridegroom arrived were received by him and given entrance to the feast; the others were locked out, despite their pleas of, "Lord, lord, open to us." "Truly," Jesus told them and all others who are not prepared adequately for his Second Coming, "I do not know you." His "Watch therefore, for you know neither the day nor the hour'' puts us all on the alert, attuned to the Word and Spirit, which supply ''oil'' for our ''lamps'' in sufficient, even abundant, measure.

Sermon suggestions

Matthew 23:1-12 (R, E, C) — "Preaching and Practice."

In the center of yesterday's Minneapolis *Star Tribune*, there was a two-page advertisement. On the first page, in 3½ inch print, were the two words, *"we practice;"* the other page carried three words, *"what we preach."* The ad was placed by Group Health, Inc. Their message was, "Group health leads the way in quality care," on the first page, listing all the different specialties and the physicians and dentists who offer quality health care in them. The photographs of eight physicians and one dentist, most of whom were department chairpersons, along with their credentials, were published with the names of staff doctors and dentists. Under *"what we preach,"* Group Health's ten-point program for "quality assurance," was printed out on the rest of the page. Point #2 caught my eye; "Every physician is reviewed by fellow physicians." In effect, that was what Jesus was doing in his attack on the scribes and the Pharisees; they failed his review — miserably!

1. Preachers, like the Pharisees and scribes before them, are the protectors and proclaimers of the Christian tradition. The people should expect — and demand — that they preach the Word of God and nothing else.
2. People are to hear the Word gladly. The words of God come to his people through the words of human beings, who speak, under the pressure of prayer and the Holy Spirit, what has been given to the church in the witness of the apostles and the Scriptures.
Recently, I heard about a powerful politician who attended a local church on a Sunday, some years ago, when the pastor was preaching about the tragedy that was occurring in Vietnam. The report is that he was offended and never again went back to that church. Was the offense commited by the preacher? Did he preach something other than the gospel? Or was the problem in what the politician heard, or even in how he heard the gospel speaking to, even condemning his support of the war in Southeast Asia? Since I didn't hear or read the sermon, I am not in a position to answer these questions, but the situation points up the necessity for preaching that is faithful to the gospel *and* hearing the Word in the spirit of prayer and humility.
3. We all need to practice what we preach. All of us are witnesses for Christ in the world, and it is incumbent upon us — clergy and laity — to live out the gospel of our Lord in everything that we say and do. (Jim Bakker and two of his associates were indicted for fraud on the day that this was revised.)
4. Then, the Lord will declare, "Well done, good and faithful servants."

Matthew 25:1-13 (L) — "Jesus will return."

Some years ago, my family and I had a strange experience on a visit to Europe. A long-time friend of mine was living in a foreign country, and we had told him and his wife that we would be in Europe the next summer; this resulted in an invitation, "Be sure to come to visit us." We promised that we would, and later indicated that we would be there during the second week of August. When we arrived in the city, I called my friend at his office; he hadn't remembered that we were coming and, with his family, had made plans to go out of the city the next day. Embarrassed, he asked us to go out to their home for dinner that evening, but things got even more complicated when he couldn't reach his wife, who was doing some last minute shopping for their trip. When we arrived, expecting to be served dinner, he was out scurrying around, attempting to find a store open where he could buy something for supper. The whole evening was almost a disaster, and proved to be embarrassing for all of us. Not only that, but my family and I didn't get anything to eat until we returned to our hotel. They weren't prepared for our visit, despite the fact that we had told them when we were coming.

1. "Prepared" Christians hear, know, and keep, the word of the Lord. They are the ones who always have a sufficient supply of "oil" for their lamps, prepared for Jesus' return.

2. Unprepared Christians hear, but do not really know or keep the Word of God. Their supply of "oil" is dangerously low and may run out at any time. They may not even think about the promised — and sudden — return of the Lord.

3. Christians are involved in a lifetime of preparation. We are always "becoming" the people of God. Hearing and doing the Word is our business, and we have to do both as long as we live. That's what the Christian life is all about.

4. Hearing and keeping the Word is the way that we watch for the coming of the Lord. Matthew still says — to us — "Watch therefore, for you know neither the day nor the hour."

Malachi 1:14—2:2b, 8-10 (R) — "The Father and the Covenant."

1. Yahweh is our mentor. He has made a covenant with us with Christ, just as he did with Abraham and the people of Israel.

2. God is the Father of Jew and Christian. That's what we had better remember all of our days.

3. Keepers of the covenant. That's what he expects all of us to be through the power of the Word and Holy Spirit.

4. Keep the faith and love one another. God will accept that.

Micah 3:5-12 — "Corruption and Condemnation."

1. Corruption among the clergy: a field day for the prophet — corruption brings condemnation by God himself.

2. Corrupt clergy become contemptible in the eyes of the people of God. Do all of us corrupt the relationship we have with God? Are we all guilty?

3. Either/or — renounce sin, or the whole community will be in jeopardy.

4. Repent and live again as children of God.

(Both of these texts accomodate the theme of the unfaithful scribes and Pharisees, and might be incorporated into sermons on Matthew 23.)

Amos 5:18-24 — "A Day of Darkness or Deliverance?"

1. A time of reckoning is coming for God's people. All will be held accountable for the way they have lived.

2. It will be a day of darkness or a day of deliverance. Which will it be? The choice is ours; we can bring judgment and destruction down upon ourselves and our world.

3. Fidelity and obedience. Those are what God expects from people who claim to love him. Godly people will work for the "good" and for peace among all people.

4. The faithful have nothing to fear — in this life or at the end of it.

Ruth 4:7-17 — "The Happy Ending."

1. Ruth and Boaz apparently did "live happily ever after." That's the jist of this last chapter in the intriguing story of the young Moabite woman. She became the wife of Boaz, and this was pleasing to God.

2. God had plans for Ruth. She was to bring new blood into the Hebrew nation through the birth of a son, Obed. He would be the father of Jesse, making Ruth the great grandmother of King David and matriarch of the line which Jesus claimed as his own.

3. Jesus could claim Ruth as an ancestor. Her story must have been told to him by his mother, Mary, before he learned to read the sacred scriptures.

4. Through Jesus, we too are related to Ruth. Ours is to learn her story and to live lives that are open to the leading and direction of God the Father.

1 Thessalonians 2:7-9, 13 (R); 2:9-13, 17-20 (E, C) — "Lessons for Preachers and People."

1. The people of God need to remember how kindly God has dealt with them. With the Thessalonian Christians, we recall the good news that has been given us in Christ. God has been good and merciful to us.

2. The preachers have to remember that they have been called to be pastors as well as preachers. A pastor is to treat the people the same way that God does — patiently, kindly, and compassionately — and to preach the Word faithfully and fearlessly.

3. Both people and pastors live by the Word of God. He is the source of the life we share in the name of Jesus Christ. The gospel means deliverance for us all.

1 Thessalonians 4:13-14 (15-18) — "Delivered by A Death."

1. Christians need have no fear of death. They have been delivered by Jesus' death — and resurrection — from the bonds of sin and death.

2. Christians hope — We have God's promise that God will raise the dead, just as he raised the Lord from the tomb and corruption.

3. Christians dare to live by that hope. God has made room for the living and the dead in his eternal kingdom

4. Christians expect to meet the Lord when he returns and raises the dead to be with him. That really gives us comfort in the face of death.

The Twenty-fifth Sunday after Pentecost
Thirty-second Sunday in Ordinary Time
Proper 27

Roman Catholic	Wisdom 6:12-16	1 Thessalonians 4:13-14 (15-18)	Matthew 25:1-13
Episcopal	Amos 5:18-24	1 Thessalonians 4:13-18	Matthew 25:1-13
Lutheran	Hosea 11:1-4, 8-9	1 Thessalonians 5:1-11	Matthew 25:14-30
Common	Amos 5:16-24	1 Thessalonians 4:13-18	Matthew 25:1-13

The church year theological clue

It is in the gospels and the other readings assigned to this Sunday that one hears the message that the "end times" are coming and the Lord will return to usher in the fullness of the kingdom of God. This note culminates in Christ the King Sunday, the last Sunday of Pentecost and of the Church year, too; it spills over into the first Sundays of Advent and the new church year. There is a kind of call to spiritual perception and understanding at the end of Pentecost that becomes a call to action at the beginning of Advent; the movement is from a type of Maranatha prayer in Pentecost — "Come, Lord Jesus, come quickly" — to a summons to make ready for the coming of the Lord — "Be alert at all times." These last Sundays of Pentecost connect the end and the beginning of the year so that the year takes the shape of a circle — continuous and complete.

The Prayer of the Day (LBW) — The mood of the prayers of Advent finds expression in this prayer, which even begins the way that three of the Advent collects address God:

Stir up, O Lord, the wills of your faithful people to seek more eagerly the help you offer, that, at the last, they may enjoy the fruit of salvation; through our Lord Jesus Christ.

Suitable for Pentecost or Advent, it reveals the continuum that exists between the last few Sundays of Pentecost and the Sundays of Advent. The prayer really is a petition to God, asking for the power of the word and the Holy Spirit to motivate the faithful to turn and cling to the things of the Lord.

The Psalm of the Day — Psalm 90:12-17 (L) — Most liturgies assign this psalm to the funeral service, for rather obvious reasons. Most of us know the heart of it: "The span of our life is seventy years, perhaps in strength even eighty; yet the sum of them is but labor and sorrow, for they pass away quickly and we are gone." (v. 10) The first part of the psalm is omitted and the Psalm for the Day begins at verse 12, probably to connect it to the last things, rather than to death: "So teach us to number our days, that we may apply our hearts to wisdom." In this way it extends the thrust of the Prayer of the Day and expands its message for our lives.

The Psalm Prayer (LBW)

Eternal Father of our mortal race, in Jesus Christ your grace has come upon us: For his sake, prosper the work of our hands until he returns to gladden our hearts forever."

Psalm 63:1-7 (R) — A lament of this kind could only come from a people who live in arid lands and are familiar with the conditions of the desert: "my soul thirsts for you, my flesh faints for you, as in a barren and dry land where there is no water." But the psalmist touches the lives and experiences of all devout people, when he declares that God's "loving-kindness is better than life itself." This, therefore, is a psalm that faithful Christians may recite with genuine enthusiasm.

Psalm 43 (E) — The Episcopal Church, more than most other denominations, tends to use entire psalms, either as responsories or as devotional acts in themselves. Sometimes this psalmody may become quite lengthy, but this is not the case with Psalm 43; it is only six verses long. *Judica me, Deus,* as it is titled from the first verse, ("Give judgment for me, O God"), has found its way into various services of the church and into its music as well (for example: "Send out your light and your truth, that they may lead me" (v. 3) finds expression in an anthem that most church choirs have sung). The conclusion is appropriate for this part of Pentecost: "Put your trust in God; for I will yet give thanks to him, who is the help of my countenance, and my God."

Psalm 50:7-15 (C) — Here is a word for the Lord God that reminds the people of Israel that Yahweh is their God, and that he is gracious and merciful — and always will be — to them. God's call to his people reminds them to do two things: First, "offer to God a sacrifice of thanksgiving," and, second, "make good your vows to the Most High." Those who claim to love God and offer him thanks for his blessings as their "sacrifice of thanksgiving" are required to prove their love for God by faithful and obedient lives outside the formal worship services of the church.

The readings:

Wisdom 6:12-16 (R)

This excerpt, which is considered to be the conclusion of the first part of the book by some scholars, the beginning of the second section by others, glorifies wisdom and reveals the secret of attaining it. It takes the shape of an exhortation to seek wisdom, and if not actually written by Solomon, it is certainly of the mind and spirit of Solomon. The message for all people who love and fear God is simply that they seek that "eschatological wisdom," which puts all of life in proper perspective. It is an appropriate reading for this part of Pentecost.

Amos 5:18-24 (E), 5:16-24 (C)

Had this reading begin at verse 14, it would have been much more complete: "Seek good and not evil, so as that you may live, and that Yahweh, God of Sabboth, may really be with you, as you claim he is." The children of Israel, who long for "the day of the Lord," are called upon to "let justice flow like water, and integrity like an unfailing stream" as they await the "Lord's day." The word of the Lord is most appropriate for all Christians to heed as they await the final day, the last times. (See, also, the Lutheran reading for Pentecost 24.)

Hosea 11:1-4, 8-9 (L)

The writer tells, concisely and in his own way, the history of the People of Israel before the Lord their God. Theirs is the tale of a covenant accepted but broken again and again over against the faithfulness of a God who will not give up on his people. What he says also applies to Christians who, in baptism have entered into an everlasting covenant with God; they are saints but also sinners and need to die and rise daily with Christ. Because they are "sealed with the Holy Spirit and marked with the cross of Christ forever," they live in the blessed assurance of God's faithfulness and abiding love for them, and this gives them everlasting hope.

1 Thessalonians 4:13-18 (R, E, C) — See the Lutheran reading for Pentecost 24.

1 Thessalonians 5:1-11 (L)

Paul, as he has done so many times in his letters, sounds the eschatological note, declaring that the "day of the Lord will come" and, drawing on Jesus' parable (Luke 12:39f.) "like a thief in the night." He was positive that the Lord would return at a time determined by the Lord God, and that Christ's second advent would catch most people by surprise and unprepared. Therefore, he warns the people of Thessalonika to be alert, ready for the immanent return of the Lord, reassuring them that they, who are "sons of light and sons of the day," have nothing to fear. Their business, in the hope of the Lord's Parousia, is to keep on what they are doing, building up one another in the faith of Jesus Christ.

Matthew 25 (R, E, C) — See the Lutheran Reading for Pentecost 24.

Matthew 25:14-30 (L)

This second parable of this very "eschatologically-rich" chapter teaches the Church to do the work of the Lord, rather than simply clinging to the faith and waiting around for the return of the Lord without doing anything. Christ expects his Church to appreciate the gifts he has given to his people and use them in the work of the kingdom during the time between his ascension and his Second Coming. He also reveals that he will be their judge upon his return, separating the profitable servants from the unprofitable ones, according to their production, or lack of it, on behalf of their Lord. Those who love and fear the Lord — and prove to be profitable servants — will be rewarded by the Lord; the others will be discarded ("into the outer darkness; there men will weep and gnash their teeth").

Sermon suggestions:

Matthew 25:1-13 (R, E, C) — See the sermon suggestion from the Lutheran reading for Pentecost 24.

Matthew 25:14-30 (L) — "In the Meantime . . . ."

"The Madonna of Medjugorje," a town in Yugoslavia, is the title of a television documentary about the daily "apparitions" of the Virgin Mary on a hillside to a group of young girls. The Virgin continues to appear to them, even when a priest has to hide them to protect them from the anti-Christian forces in their country. But the news of the vision of Mary, once it got out, has resulted in the hope of seeing the Virgin Mary, who has promised that he will come to the world once more. But some Christians, in various parts of the world and almost every year, like the pilgrims on the hillsides in Yugoslavia, do gather in all sorts of places to await the return appearance of Jesus Christ. It is one thing — and a proper thing — to expect the Christ to fulfill his word and return to the earth at the end of time, but it will do little or no good to spend our time anticipating, and waiting for, the Lord's Second Coming without doing the work he has given us to do in the interim. It will be unprofitable and downright dangerous, according to Jesus' parable, simply to sit around expecting the Second Coming without engaging in the work of the gospel.

1. The Christ, who has begun his reign, will ultimately return to claim the earth and bring in the fullness of the Kingdom. Jesus was positive about that. He expects Christians to believe this — *in the meantime.*

2. The Lord has bestowed his gifts — through the word and the Holy Spirit — upon his church, so that the faith may be enriched and the Gospel may be preached to the ends of the earth — *in the meantime.*

3. Christians, in preparation for their Lord's return, faithfully engage in the work he has given the church to do. Theirs is to be an active faith, in the hope of heaven — *in the meantime.*

Wisdom 6:12-16 — "A Word to the Wise."

1. Wisdom — in the matters that count in life — is of critical importance to the people of God. To be wordly wise is insufficient for believers.

2. The necessary wisdom — to identify and choose what is really important in life — is available to all believers in the good news of Jesus Christ.

3. Those who are really wise in the ways of God will constantly ready themselves for the return of their Lord by hearing the Word and trusting the Lord.

Amos 5:18-24 (E), 16-24 (C) — See the sermon suggestion for this text for Pentecost 24 (L).

Hosea 11:1-4, 8-9 (L) — "A Covenant Reaffirmed."

1. Remember — the God of the Covenant with the people of Israel keeps that Covenant, despite their infidelity and sinfulness. God's Covenant is forever.

2. Repent — God's unfailing love for his people is one of the great mysteries of the faith. Instead of destroying his children and giving it up as a bad job, God continues to love them as his own.

3. Respond — the cross of Christ is God's announcement to the world that he has reaffirmed and renewed his Covenant with his people.

4. Remember — repent — and respond to the love of the Lord our God in Christ Jesus, the Lord.

1 Thessalonians 4:13-18 (R, E, C) — See the sermon suggestion for this text on Pentecost 24 (L).

1 Thessalonians 5:1-11 (L) — "Surprise Visitation."

Nothing is more surprising — and disturbing — than to return to one's home after spending an evening away from it, only to discover that a thief has entered and ransacked the home and stolen precious possessions. An acquaintance, whose home was burglarized one night, spoke of feeling like she was actually violated. No one expects to find his or her home invaded; the burglar comes silently and unexpetedly. Paul affirms the words of Jesus, who declared that his return would be sudden and surprising.

1. Surprise! Surprise! That's how the Second Coming of the Lord will take place. It will be sudden and startling. But he will return, as he promised.

2. Unlike the "thief in the night," he will not slink away in the darkness but will be visible and will do those things that bring in — not diminish — the fullness of the Kingdom.

3. Christians will be prepared, when they live in "the light of the day" — faith, love, and the hope of salvation.

4. "Come! Let us walk (and work) in the light of the Lord."

The Twenty-sixth Sunday after Pentecost
Thirty-third Sunday in Ordinary Time
Proper 28

Roman Catholic	Proverbs 31:10-13 19-20, 30-31	1 Thessalonians 5:1-6	Matthew 25:14-15 (16-30) short form
Episcopal	Zephaniah 1:7, 12-18	1 Thessalonians 5:1-10	Matthew 25:14-15, 19-29
Lutheran	Malachi 2:1-2, 4-10	1 Thessalonians 2:8-13	Matthew 23:1-12
Common	Zephaniah 1:7, 12-18	1 Thessalonians 1-11	Matthew 25:14-30

The church year theological clue

The readings assigned to this Sunday's liturgy continue to highlight the eschatological framework of the worship and work of the People of God, emphasizing that not only is the end of the church year close at hand, but that the Parousia is closer than ever before. In most years, however, this Sunday's eschatological announcement will be "silent," because Easter will not occur early enough for this Sunday's propers to be included in the calendar of the church. Many of the eschatological themes of these readings, however, are made on other Sundays in the several churches of Christendom; they belong to that category of readings which might be called "musical lections," because they are used differently and on different Sundays of Pentecost by the liturgical churches.

The Prayer of the Day (LBW) — A forceful eschatological prayer, which asks God: 1. To "so rule and govern our hearts and minds through your Holy Spirit;" 2. that "keeping in mind the end of all things and the day of judgment;" 3. "we may be stirred up to holiness of life here and may live with you forever in the world to come." It looks past the Second Coming to the very last things, which will be ushered in by the return of Jesus Christ the Lord. The Advent emphasis on being "stirred up" by the Holy Spirit finds its way into this prayer, too.

The Psalm of the Day — Psalm 131 (L) — This is one of the Psalms of Ascent, which could have been said within the confines of the Temple and in conjunction with the Passover celebration. It is a statement by a person who is genuinely humble, whose soul is "quiet" within him, because he "waits for the Lord" with simple and uncomplicated faith. The last verse of this very brief psalm calls upon Israel to "wait upon the Lord, from this time forth forevermore," thereby making it appropriate for use with this set of eschatological propers.

The Psalm Prayer (LBW)

> *Lord Jesus, gentle and humble of heart, you promised your kingdom to those who are like children. Never let pride reign in our hearts, but let the Father's compassion embrace all who willingly bear your gentle yoke now and forever.*

Psalm 128:1-5 (R) — This particular Psalm of Ascent places its emphasis on the happiness that peole who know the Lord and obey him enjoy in this life. It suggests, in light of the Gospel promises, that all such people will know God's blessings "all the days of (their) lives." The eschatological note is not as clearly sounded in this psalm as it is in Psalm 131.

Psalm 90 (E) — See the comments on this psalm for Pentecost 25 (L).

Psalm 76 (C) — Here is a psalm that sings of God's mighty power, displayed in an incredible victory over Israel's enemies, which God engineered at one time or another. The psalmist also tells of the absolute judgment of God, which strikes fear into the hearts of mere mortals, and of God's intention to "save all the oppressed of the earth." So he declares to the faithful, "Make a vow to the Lord your God and keep it."

The readings:

Proverbs 31:10-13, 19-20, 30-31 (R)

Just why this reading was selected for this particular Sunday toward the end of Pentecost is difficult to ascertain. It presents the picture of a truly beautiful woman, a virtuous woman, who keeps the faith in the way that she lives. Perhaps this selection is meant to mirror the church as it waits — in true faith and love — for the coming of the Lord and the last things. It doesn't fit very well with the other readings for this Sunday.

Zephaniah 1:7, 12-18 (E, C)

The Lutheran Lectionary included Zephaniah 1:14-16 for Pentecost 24, when it was first published. Later, for another unexplained reason, it was replaced by the selection from Amos (5:18-24). This reading spells out God's judgment and the immanence of the day of the Lord; it contains a warning for all people who reject the power and authority of the Lord God. For them, it will be "A day of wrath, that day, a day of distress and agony, a day of ruin and of devastation, a day of darkness and gloom, a day of cloud and blackness, a day of trumpet blast and battle cry against fortified town and high corner-tower." No one will be able to stand before the might of God on the day of the Lord.

Malachi 2:1-10 (L)

This reading might better be appointed for a clergy conference, or retreat, because it spells out in vivid detail God's warning to his priests and urges them to be faithful in their teaching ministries. It was probably selected for this Sunday to highlight the three questions in verse 10: 1. "Have we not all one Father?" 2. "Did not one God create us?" 3. "Why, then, do we break faith with one another, profaning the covenant of our ancestors?" It stands in sharp contrast to the picture Paul paints of a faithful ministry for the church at Thessalonica in the second reading for this day.

1 Thessalonians 5:1-6 (R); 5:1-10 (E); 5:1-11 (C) — See the comments on this lesson for Pentecost 25 (L).

1 Thessalonians 2:8-13 (L) — See the comments on this reading for Pentecost 24 (R, E, C).

Matthew 25:14-30 (R, C); 25:14-15, 19-29 (E) — See the comments on this reading for Pentecost 25 (L).

Matthew 23:1-12 (L) — See the comments on this reading for Pentecost 24 (R, E, C).

See the comments made on part of this reading in the Roman Lectionary for Pentecost 24.

Sermon suggestions:

With the exception of the Zephaniah lesson of the above readings, the suggestions are included on the same Sundays as the comments.

Zephaniah 1:7, 12-18 — "The Terrible Day of the Lord."

Human beings will be able to flaunt their freedom in the face of God for just so long, then will come the terrible day of the Lord. The picture that is painted for the world, Matthew 24, of "the great tribulation of Jerusalem" comes almost directly from the Old Testament, and Zephaniah (as well as other writers), as Jesus speaks of that terrible day. Jesus perceived that the day of the Lord's judgment and deliverance would break into time with his return; then the last days, with all of their terror and tragedy, as well as deliverance, will become a reality.

1. God's warning to the world: a day of judgment and punishment is coming.

2. It will be a terrible day for the wicked and ungodly; unbelievers will suffer for their rejection of God.

3. Jesus, however, gives hope to the world. He will deliver his own from judgment and punishment into the peace of the everlasting kingdom.

Christ the King
(Last Sunday after Pentecost)
Thirty-fourth Sunday in Ordinary Time
Proper 29

Roman Catholic	Ezekiel 34:11-12, 15-17	1 Corinthians 15:20-26, 28	Matthew 25:31-46
Episcopal	Ezekiel 34:11-17	1 Corinthians 15:20-28	Matthew 25:31-46
Lutheran	Ezekiel 34:11-16, 23-24	1 Corinthians 15:20-28	Matthew 25:31-46
Common	Ezekiel 34:11-16, 20-24	1 Corinthians 15:20-28	Matthew 25:31-46

The church year theological clue

The very title given to this Sunday by the Roman *Ordo* and the LBW lectionary, Christ the King, firmly reinforces the eschatological framework of the church year, closing the gap between the Ascension of Our Lord and the end of the Pentecost cycle/season. All of the Sundays between the Ascension and Christ the King Sunday reflect the fact that in the Ascension Jesus has begun his reign. In the LBW liturgy, the traditional hymn of praise may be replaced by "Worthy is Christ," with its verse, "For the Lamb who was slain has begun his reign," on the Sunday after the Ascension and ought to be sung on various, if not all, Sundays throughout Pentecost and, of course, on Christ the King Sunday. The second reading enunciates clearly the theme of the day: "For he must reign until he has put all his enemies under his feet." (The *Jerusalem Bible* translation reads, "For he must be King until he has put all his enemies under his feet.") He must reign until the appointed time when he will come again and usher in the fullness of the kingdom of God. Then, his reign will extend over heaven and earth.

The Prayer of the Day (LBW) — The new prayer is intended to speak to the theme of Christ the King for all three cycles/series of the church year: "Almighty and everlasting God, whose will it is to restore all things to your beloved Son, whom you anointed priest forever and king of all creation . . . ." The petition asks that all people on earth, "now divided by the power of sin, may be united under the glorious and gentle rule of your Son, our Lord Jesus Christ." The Gospel for the Day in all three cycles of the church year identifies different aspects of Jesus' kingship; John 18:33-37 (Year B) has Christ saying to Pilate, "My kingdom is not of this world," and "I am a king," while Luke 23:35-43 (Year C) tells of the sign that Pontius Pilate attached to the cross, "This is the king of the Jews." Matthew 25:31-36 — today's Gospel — contains the eschatological promise of Christ's reign; he will come again "in his glory, . . . and he will sit on his glorious throne." Then, according to Matthew, the judgment of all nations and all people will occur, with banishment for some and fulfillment (The *Lutheran Worship* lectionary calls this Sunday "Fulfillment Day") in resurrection and eternal life for others. In the meantime, Paul says it best: "He must reign until he has put all his enemies under his feet."

The Psalm of the Day — Psalm 23:1-3, 5-6 (R): 23 (C) — Please see the comments on this psalm for Good Shepherd Sunday, the Fourth Sunday of Easter, Cycle A. It is especially appropriate as a responsory to the first reading from Ezekiel, with its Shepherd/sheep imagery. It is also raher surprising that the Episcopal and Lutheran lectionaries did not give Psalm 23 a place in today's propers. The 23rd Psalm picks up many of the details and, to some degree, expands the imagery of David as the "one shepherd" appointed by God to the one who says, "I am the Good Shepherd."

Psalm 95:1-7 (E); 95:1-7a (L) — Episcopalians and Lutherans will recognize this psalm as the *Venite* that is sung in Morning Prayer; it is also appointed, in a slightly different arrangement of verses, for the Twenty-third Sunday in Ordinary Time of the Roman *Ordo*, Cycle A. Please see the comments on Psalm 95 that were made for that Sunday.

The Psalm Prayer (LBW)

Almighty God, neither let us go astray as did those who murmured in the desert, nor let us be torn apart by discord. With Jesus as our shepherd, bring us to enjoy the unity for which he prays; and to you be the glory and the praise now and forever.

The readings:

Ezekiel 34:11-12, 15-17 (R); 34:11-16, 20-24 (C); 34:11-16, 23-24 (L); 34:11-17 (E)

It was while the children of Israel were in exile in Babylon that the prophet announced that God would take over the role of "shepherding" his people. The former kings of Judah had neglected this function in their relationships with their subjects, which is why God had to insert himself into the picture. Like a shepherd tending his flock, he will seek the lost and bring back the strayed by enabling the Israelites to return to the Promised Land once again. In other words, God himself is going to take charge and he will "bind up the crippled, and . . . strengthen the weak, and the fat and the strong I will watch over; I will feed them in justice." A new shepherd/king will be set over them; he will be responsible for carrying on the work of God with his people. Out of this new line, God will ultimately send the Good Shepherd, who will seek out the lost and save the strays on behalf of God. The judgment theme, verse 17 f., which tells how the good sheep will be separated from the bad, leads into the Gospel for the Day, wherein Jesus says, "he will separate them one from another as a shepherd separates the sheep from the goats, and he will place the sheep at his right hand, but the goats at the left." Jesus, the Good Shepherd, ultimately will have the responsibility of "shepherding" in the name of God the Father.

1 Corinthians 15:20-28 (E, L, C); 15:20-26, 28 (R)

Paul gives a neat summary of the gospel in the earlier verses of this chapter, insisting that Christ has been raised from the dead and questioning those who claim that there is no resurrection of the dead. Without Jesus' resurrection, there is no life after death, nor is there any hope or comfort. But, Paul declares, Jesus has been raised from the dead, the "first fruits of all who believe." He also knows that the resurrection is connected to the return of the Lord, who must reign "until he has put all of his enemies under his feet." When that day finally comes, all people, including the Son, will be "subjected to him who put all things under him, that God may be everything to every one." The verse, "For he must reign until he has put all his enemies under his feet," is where the connection may be made to Christ the King Sunday in a sermon. This is another time during Pentecost when all three lessons are in harmony with each other; it is also one of those occasions when the second reading ought to follow the Gospel for the Day.

Matthew 25:31-46

This pericope is an announcement of the last things that are to occur, although it is often called the parable of the sheep and the goats, really of the separation, or judgment, of the sheep and the goats. "When the Son of man comes in his glory" suggests, as Jesus did in other sayings, that the return of the Lord will occur at some unknown time in the future. But it will happen; Jesus believed so, as did Matthew and Paul, the apostles, and most people in the early church. A judgment will occur, "the separation of the sheep and the goats," according to whether or not people have received Jesus' messengers and the Word they preached, the good news of the risen and reigning Christ. Jesus himself will dispense God's justice on that occasion, which will mean eternal life for those who receive and believe the gospel, and eternal punishment for those who hear the Word, reject it, and by doing so repudiate Jesus Christ as their Lord and Savior. Until that time, the battle between good and evil, between believing or rejecting the good news and the risen Lord, will continue unabated.

Sermon suggestions:

Matthew 25:31-46 — "When Jesus Christ Returns."

Many years ago, a pastor friend led his congregation in building a new church. It was contemporary, but not too contemporary to be, as one critic of modern architecture put it, contemptible. It happened to be a Lutheran church and one appointment in it generated a considerable amount of discussion and some negative criticism; it was the large cross, really a crucifix, over the altar table. Most Lutheran church buildings, at that time and in that part of the country, did not have crucifixes on, or above, their altars; they didn't want to be confused with Roman Catholic churches. This congregation not only dared to have a crucifix in front of the people, but it was a different kind of a crucifix from those usually seen; it was a fully vested figure of the risen Lord superimposed on the cross, and with the marks of the nails visible in hands and feet. It was an announcement that Jesus had conquered death and risen from the grave. There was one thing more of importance; the Christ had a crown upon his head. He was not only the risen Lord, but also the Good Shepherd, and the Shepherd/King of the New Testament. In time, as people came to accept the symbolism of their *Christus Victor*, they came to appreciate it and today connect it to Paul's, "For he must reign until he has put all his enemies under his feet."

When Christians began to build their places of worship, a mosaic was placed above every altar depicting the risen Lord, sitting upon a throne, Peter and Paul on either side of him, usually holding a book in one hand and an orb in the other. Josef Jungmann wrote:

> *The ancient church knew full well why she had placed the Easter Christ and His Easter work in the apses of her basilicas, why she had proclaimed Easter so loudly, providing it with a forty-day preparatory celebration and a fifty-day aftermath, and had given the stamp of Easter to every Sunday.*

Even more, this mosaic reminded the faithful that the reign of the Lord has begun and will continue to the end of time; in the meantime, he is present with his people when they gather in his name and come to the table at which he is the host. Most churches, Roman and Protestant, have neglected that symbol of the risen and reigning Lord, which could be a constant reminder to the people of God to pray to the Lord whose victory and presence are celebrated, "Come, Lord Jesus! Come, quickly!"

1. His heavenly reign will end; his rule over all the earth will begin — when he returns. The congregation of which I am a member has a painting of the risen and reigning Christ over its altar. Every Sunday is Christ the King Sunday in that parish, whether or not the people are cognizant of it. Christ the King will return at the appointed time.

2. He will come with power and glory. The whole earth will know his presence and he will establish lasting peace — when he returns.

3. He will return a shepherd as well as King of Kings. He will judge all people and separate the sheep from the goats — when he returns.

James Russell Lowell's poem/hymn, "Once to every man and nation" (Hymn 547), was included in the *Service Book and Hymnal* (1958) of the American Lutheran Church and the Lutheran Church in America. The first verse reads:

> *Once to every man and nation*
> *Comes the moment to decide,*
> *In the strife of truth with falsehood,*
> *For the good or evil side;*
> *Some great cause, God's new messiah,*
> *Offering each the bloom or blight,*
> *And the choice goes by forever*
> *'Twixt that darkness and that light.*

Interestingly, two lines were omitted — the original lines seven and eight of the poem. They are one of the reasons that the poem/hymn was included in the hymnal; they express the judgment theme of the Gospel for the Day, despite the fact that "some great cause" is substituted for Christ the King. These lines were part of a hymn in an earlier hymnal.

> *Parts the goats upon the left hand,*
> *And the sheep upon the right.*

The entire hymn/poem was eliminated from the *Lutheran Book of Worship*, apparently, for theological reasons.

4. He will grant eternal life to the good, the sheep, but eternal punishment to evil persons, the goats — when he returns.

5. Believe in the Word, fulfill it, and pray now — instead of when he returns. He will return, you know.

Ezekiel 34:11-12, 15-17 (R); 34:11-16, 20-24 (C); 34:11-16, 23-24 (L); 34:11-17 (E) — "God as the Shepherd-King."

1. He is deeply concerned about the welfare of his sheep. God loves and cares for his people the way that a good shepherd cares for his/her sheep, and the way that the church should be concerned about all people. God really loves us, you know.

2. He is ready to rescue his own people and set them free from bondage — the bondage to sin and death, as well as a living death in captivity and exile. He actually seeks the lost, brings back the strays, cares for the disabled and the weak, and watches over the faithful. He sets an example for the church in caring for those in trouble or need of any kind.

3. He dispenses justice and mercy to all of his people. He does not desire the loss and destruction of people, because he has created them and they are his forever. He teaches the church the worth of each person, and shows that Christians should be loving and forgiving persons, who offer absolution to sinners rather than demanding retribution.

4. He has set up a shepherd in the line of David, even Jesus Christ, the Good Shepherd, who will be responsible for the sheep forever.

1 Corinthians 15:20-26, 28 (R); 15:20-28 (E, L, C) — "The Unending Reign."

1. Jesus' reign has indeed begun — it began with his resurrection and ascension to the right hand of God.

2. It will continue until all of his enemies are converted and reconciled to him.

3. Christ will return and raise the dead and grant eternal life to the dead and the living.

4. He will rule the earth as God wants it to be ruled, and God will be God to everyone who has ever lived on the earth.

5. Christ will reign forever and ever.

Reformation Sunday

Lutheran   **Jeremiah 31:31-34**   **Romans 3:19-28**   **John 8:31-36**

The church year theological clue

Virtually all Lutheran calendars and lectionaries make provision for the celebration of Reformation Day, cognizant of the fact that it is necessary to move the festival from October 31st to the previous Sunday, unless, of course, October 31st falls on a Sunday. Most Lutheran churches continue to observe Reformation Sunday, despite the good and growing relations with the Roman Catholic Church, which have developed with the onset of the ecumenical movement following Vatican II. But the tone of Reformation worship services has changed markedly, speaking to the need for a continuing reformation in the whole Catholic Church; ecumenical concerns, which confess the scandal of the denominational divisions in the church, are among the highest priorities of a "Reformation Today." The common interest in biblical studies, as well as theological discussions between the churches of Christendom, support such a continuing reformation today. Vatican II sparked interest in ecumenical worship services, often sponsored in alternate years by Roman Catholic and Protestant congregations.

The Prayer of the Day (LBW) — An older collect has simply been rewritten using modern

language to highlight one of the basic emphases of the Lutheran/Protestant reformation, the authority of the sacred scriptures. It is, in a way, a "demanding" prayer, for the address includes a request: "Almighty God, gracious Lord, pour out your Holy Spirit upon your faithful people." The key phrase follows, one of Luther's concerns, which was expressed in his hymn, "Lord, Keep Us Steadfast in Your Word:" "Keep them steadfast in your Word," followed by, "protect and comfort them in all temptations, defend them against all their enemies, and bestow on the Church your saving peace . . . ." The final portion, asking for "peace" in the church, also expresses one of Luther's original intentions, namely, that the church would be reformed, not divided into a multiplicity of churches.

The Psalm of the Day — Psalm 46 — This is really the only psalm that Lutherans could

use as a responsory, or the Psalm of the Day, on Reformation Sunday. Luther's love of this psalm prompted him to write his hymn, "A Mighty Fortress is Our God," which has been widely acclaimed and employed in various worship services; recently, I heard a Roman Catholic radio program introduced with the use of this hymn. In many respects, it does speak to the situation of the whole church in the world, which is under attack from the forces of secularism, materialism, and indifference. When combined with "A Mighty Fortress," it is often used as a preaching text for Reformation Sunday.

The Psalm Prayer (LBW)

> *Lord God, our refuge and strength, when the restless powers of this world and the waters of hell rise up against your holy city, watch over it and keep it safe. By the river that flows from the throne of the Lamb, purify this new Jerusalem as your chosen dwelling, for you are with us, our stronghold now and forever.*

The readings:

Jeremiah 31:31-34

Older lectionaries assigned 1 Samuel 3:19—4:1a to Reformation Day, or Sunday, but the LBW has moved the Jeremiah text from the First Sunday in Advent to Reformation Day.

All of the lectionaries now place Jeremiah 31:31-34 as the first reading on the Fifth Sunday in Lent, Cycle B, which is probably where it should be, because it mentions the new covenant that God will make between himself and his people. This "second use" of Jeremiah 31 makes Reformation Day into a festival which celebrates the renewal of the covenant God has made with his people, particularly in the life and death of Jesus Christ. Jeremiah, speaking for God, tells how reformation and covenantal renewal will come about: "I will put my law within them, and I will write it upon their hearts; and I will be their God, and they shall be my people." This speaks to the reality of the continuing reformation in the church. He also touches on the ecumenical hope of the day:

And no longer shall each man teach his neighbor and each his brother, saying, "Know the Lord," for they shall all know me, from the least of them to the greatest, says the Lord; for I will forgive their iniquity, and I will remember their sin no more.

Romans 3:19-28

This reading could not be replaced in the LBW, or any other Lutheran lectionary, because it speaks so directly to one of the cardinal doctrines of the Reformation and Lutheranism, justification by faith through grace. No one can be justified by good works, by the keeping of the law, in the opinion of Paul, because all have sinned and fallen short of the glory of God. God exhibited his righteousness in the death and resurrection of Jesus Christ, giving redemption as a free gift to any and all who will receive the forgiveness of their sins and their salvation in Jesus Christ. Faith alone, not works, justifies human beings in the eyes of God, and that faith is freely given to all who will receive it through the Lord Jesus Christ. There is, according to Paul, no way that anyone can win, or earn, his or her own deliverance from sin and death and entrance into the kingdom of heaven. Unless God gives these gifts, they are completely beyond the realm of attainment by those who seek to be godly people.

John 8:31-36

Here is another of the traditional readings for Reformation Day/Sunday. Its great appeal is, partly, that it describes the situation that Luther and the Reformers found themselves in in their dispute with the Roman Catholic hierarchy; more importantly, it builds on the Romans reading and informs people that by "continuing in my (Jesus') word" they, first, become disciples of Jesus, and, second, will be set free from sin and death by God's own truth. Salvation and redemption cannot come to people simply by their claim to be children of God; only those who are set free by Jesus Christ can know complete freedom from the forces of evil and darkness — from sin; without the truth of God in Jesus and his word, human beings really have no hope of heaven.

Sermon suggestions:

John 8:31-36 — "The Reformation Continues."

A Roman Catholic — Jesuit — professor of theology in Rome, suggested to me in a conversation, that since, as he put it, we believed "the same things about the gospel," I should do two things: visit a Roman cemetery, if I wanted to find out what Roman Catholics believe about the resurrection of Jesus Christ (see the All Saints' Day sermon in this work); and, visit the Church of Il Jesu, the principal church of the Jesuit order in Rome. I knew what I was supposed to see in the cemetery, and I discovered that Roman Catholic cemeteries in Italy are planned so as to continue the evidence of the hope of resurrection held to by the early Christians. But I didn't know exactly what it was he wanted me to see at Il Jesu.

Taken there by another professor, I saw the tomb of Ignatius Loyola with its *bas relief* depiction of Loyola in the pulpit pointing at a group of people. The caption read, "Loyola condemning Luther, Calvin, and the other heretics to hell." I also noticed that the main altar of that church had been replaced by a simple table at which the Eucharist was celebrated. When I attempted to find out more about Il Jesu, I discovered the reason it was built the way it was (with a single nave, no ambulatory, but six small chapels directly attached to the nave) to accommodate preaching. I learned Il Jesu was built over a thirty-year period which spanned the Council of Trent, and it was built so that every person in the place could hear the preaching of the Word. Of course, that meant polemical preaching in the late sixteenth century, but today it means the proclamation of the pure gospel. The reformation that has occurred in the Roman Church has seen Il Jesu's preaching-oriented intention purified and spread to every Roman church in the world so that the truth of the gospel might be preached to all people. My Jesuit friend wanted me to see Il Jesu and reach that conclusion for myself, and in the light of the biblical and homiletical reforms of Vatican II. The reformation continues, based on the Word of God and, specifically, the gospel of our Lord Jesus Christ. In him and his word, there is the truth of God himself.

1. *The Reformation continues.* It has been renewed, under the influence of Word and Holy Spirit, by what has happened in the Roman Church, as well as in Protestantism, especially by the common interest in biblical studies.

2. *The Word is central.* Through the preaching of the Word, God's truth, declaring forgiveness of sins in the sacrifice of Jesus Christ, God gives his good gifts of deliverance from sin and eternal life to his people. That's the main business of the church, and what it has to be about.

3. *Freedom will last.* The people of God are, as the familiar spiritual has it, "Free at last," but the freedom we have in Christ is freedom that will last — forever! "If the Son makes you free, you will be free indeed."

4. *Thank God for that freedom.* "Thank God Almighty that we're free at last" by witnessing to, and supporting in every way possible, the proclamation of God's freeing Word in the world.

Jeremiah 31:31-34 — "Renewal Through Reformation."

1. *Needed: a new covenant.* The old covenant had been broken, and Jeremiah predicted that the time was coming when God would make a new covenant with his people.

2. *Christ and the new covenant.* It was Jesus, although he doesn't name him specifically, that Jeremiah was expecting to establish the new covenant; in Jesus, God did just that.

3. *The fate of the new covenant.* It, like the first covenant, was desecrated by the faithful. Reformation of the church was, and is, needed to renew the last covenant God will make with his people.

4. *The new covenant renewed.* God does it, as he did in the past. By writing his law upon the hearts of his people he becomes their God once again. As this happens, all people will "know the Lord" for who he is and receive the forgiveness of their sins (which destroy the covenant).

Romans 3:19-28 — "The Hardest 'Pill' to Swallow."

1. *Salvation by grace.* Justification by faith through God's grace is "the hardest 'pill' to swallow" for most people. We want to think, and often really believe, that we earn, or work, our way into the kingdom of God. Not so.

2. *God's great giveaway.* God gives away the kingdom of heaven — entrance into it — in Jesus Christ, his Son, our Lord. And he gives it to sinners, who believe and repent of their sins.

3. *That's what reformation is all about.* It forces us to face up to our sins, repent of them, and, as the church, be renewed by God himself.

4. *The hope of heaven is ours again.* "The hardest 'pill' to swallow" is the one that cures and saves us. And we are able to be the church once again, a true community of the faithful that witnesses and works in the world in the name of Jesus Christ.

All Saints' Day

Roman Catholic	Revelation 7:2-4, 9-12	1 John 3:1-3	Matthew 5:1-12
Episcopal	Ecclesiasticus 44:1-10, 13-14	Revelation 7:2-4, 9-17	Matthew 5:1-2
Lutheran	Isaiah 26:1-4, 8-9, 12-13, 19-21	Revelation 21:9-11, 22-27 (22:1-5)	Matthew 5:1-12
Common	Revelation 7:9-17	1 John 3:1-3	Matthew 5:1-12

The church year theological clue

All Saints' Day is one of those days in the church year calendar that many congregations ignore, simply because they don't know what to do with it. It began and developed naturally out of the annual commemoration of the deaths of individual martyrs, beginning with the apostles. Saints' days found their way into the worship of the church before the church year took much shape; many saints' days were in place by A.D. 200, preceding most elements of the church year, except Easter and the fifty-day Pasch, plus Sunday as a weekly celebration of the death and resurrection of the Lord. In time, there were so many saints' days that an All Saints' Day was established to remember and honor all of them. All Souls' Day was later added (on November 2) to pray for "ordinary" saints. Most non-Roman denominations have, officially, combined All Saints' Day and All Souls' Day into a single festival; practically, the same thing has happened in the Roman communion. For most churches today, All Saints' Day is set aside for remembering and commemorating all those people who have died in the faith during the past year; there is no separation of saints and martyrs from all other Christians who have died in the faith. William How's hymn, "For all the saints who from their labors rest," is really the "text" for the celebration in many of the churches where All Saints' Day is observed. Instead of keeping the feast on November 1st, many churches will place All Saints' Day on the first Sunday in November, making it All Saints' Sunday. The day as currently structured is really the celebration of the reality and totality of the Church Triumphant and the Church Militant. The observation of All Saints' Day, therefore, needs to go beyond the bounds of the local congregation and this time, and even of any cemetery, to take in all saints and martyrs of the past, as well as the present. From this perspective, All Saints' Sunday is a day of thanksgiving for all who have been made members of the body of Christ, the church, and of hope for all who have departed this life in the faith, as well as for the living who hope to move in time from the Church Militant to the Church Triumphant.

The Prayer of the Day (LBW) — The language of an older collect for All Saints' Day has been altered linguistically and theologically. The intention of the verb in the first sentence remains much the same as it was, "Almighty God, whose people are *knit* [italics, mine] together in one holy Church, the body of Christ our Lord," from "O Almighty God, who hast knit together thine elect in one communion and fellowship in the mystical body of thy Son, Christ our Lord," but neither specifically mentions Baptism as the action of God which knits together all people and gives them hope of heaven. The older collect has God as the subject who does the "knitting," which is more evangelical and theologically stronger than "whose people are knit together in one holy Church." The eschatological intention of the new prayer ("Grant us grace to follow your blessed saints in lives of faith and commitment, and to know the inexpressible joys you have prepared for those who love you . . .") highlights the totality of the church as the body of Christ in much the same manner as the older collect. It is a prayer for the living as well as for the those who have died in the Lord.

316

The Psalm for the Day — Psalm 24:1-65 (R) — Whether or not this psalm was composed to give thanks and praise to God after the return of the Ark of the Covenant from the Philistines in the days of Eli is a moot question. Nor is the familiar opening of the psalm ("The earth is the Lord's and all that is in it, the world and all that dwell therein") intended to place it on Thanksgiving Day. Rather, it is from verse three onward that the psalm addresses All Saints' Day, and does it quite effectively: "Who can ascend the hill of the Lord and who can stand in his holy place?" The psalmist answers his own question this way:

Those who have clean hands and a pure heart, who have not pledged themselves to falsehood, nor sworn by what is a fraud. They shall receive a blessing from the Lord and a just reward from the God of their salvation.

Psalm 149 (E) — One of many psalms that could have been chosen to respond to the first reading, this psalm does encurge the living saints: "For the Lord takes pleasure in his people and adorns the poor with victory." It continues: "Let the praises of God be in their throat," which certainly is proper for All Saints' Day. From verse 6b through verse 9, the psalm takes on an unseemly tone:

and a two-edged sword in their hand; to wreak vengeance on the nations and punishment on the peoples; to bind their kings in chains and their nobles with links of iron; to inflict on them the judgment decreed; this is glory for all his faithful people. Hallelujah!

The business of the saints is to live out the gospel in true faith and proclaim it to all the nations, not judge them and utterly destroy them.

Psalm 34:1-10 (L) — Numerous psalms could have been selected for this occasion, but this one was chosen because it speaks so perfectly to the situation of the saints of God in verse 9: "Fear the Lord, you that are his saints, for those who fear him lack nothing." The opening verses,

I will bless the Lord at all times; his praise shall ever be in my mouth. I will glory in the Lord; let the humble hear and rejoice. Proclaim with me the greatness of the Lord,

direct the people to the gracious and powerful actions of God, which have not only delivered his people from sin, but also from the relentless grip of death. The psalm is so attuned to All Saints' Day worship that it would be fitting to use the whole psalm as a responsory to the first reading.

The Psalm Prayer (LBW)

Lord, graciously hear us, for we seek you alone. Calm our bodies and minds with the peace which passes understanding, and make us radiant with joy; through your Son, Jesus Christ our Lord.

The readings:

Revelation 7:2-4, 9-12 (R)

When this vision was set down by the apocalyptic writer, it was as much for the encouragement of those who might soon suffer martyrdom as it was to assure them that those who had already died as martyrs had been "washed in the blood of the Lamb." Martyrdom, to the writer, was not simply dying for the Lord; it was a participation in the redeeming act of Christ on the cross, joining him in his obedient sacrifice at Calvary. Martyrdom carried with it the assurance that those who were executed for the faith would soon experience all the joys of heaven itself. This chapter and other parts of "The Book of Revelation" continue to give encouragement to Christians, not because they have died as martyrs, but because they have been washed clean in Baptism and have received the Sign of the Holy Cross upon their foreheads. Used as a first reading in the Roman *Ordo*, it is also, with the addition of verses 13-17, the second reading in the *Book of Common Prayer* lectionary.

Ecclesiasticus 44:1-10, 13-14 (E)

Selected for its use on the "combination" All Saints'/All Souls' Day, this makes a beautiful and fitting tribute to *all* of the saints, those whose names have been set down in the records of the church as worthy of remembrance and praise, and for those whose names have been entirely forgotten. It reminds the church the God receives all of the faithful on his own terms, and his way of judging may be entirely different than ours. But it remains for the church to celebrate all people who have died in the faith — at least on one day in the year — and not simply to single out special persons for remembrance and thanksgiving without acknowledging the continuing existence in the community of faith of those who were "little saints" — or appeared not to be saints at all.

Isaiah 26:1-4, 8-9, 12-13, 19-21 (L)

Portions of the apocalypse of Isaiah, which was probably written a century later than his prophecies, look to a day when "*Thy* [italics, mine] dead shall live, their bodies shall rise. O dwellers in the dust, awake and sing for joy!" Truly, as the prophet sings, "We have a strong city," and LBW "Thou dost keep him in perfect peace, whose mind is stayed on thee, because he trusts in thee." This first reading surely is in harmony with All Saints' Day, speaking to it some six and a half centuries before Christ's words, death, and resurrection gave new meaning to the life, death, and resurrection of the dead.

Revelation 7:9-17 (C)

The above comments, with the omission of verses 2-4, apply for this first reading.

1 John 3:1-3 (R, C)

The writer of this "catholic" epistle continues to speak to the church today, and especially on All Saints' Day. He does not give us a picture of what heaven will be like, but assures Christians that they are "children of God" and that, in the kingdom of heaven, they will be "like him, because we shall see him as he really is." All he knows is that eternal life is a certainty for those who believe in Jesus Christ, and that this means that the children of God will be united with him somehow, some time in the future. This reading, therefore, encourages the church to be faithful, as were the saints of all ages, and to know that God will see them through life's trials and tributions, and even conquer death itself. That is all we have to live by, and it is enough.

Revelation 7:2-4, 9-17 (E)

See the comments on this reading printed above.

Revelation 21:9-11, 22-27 (22:1-5) (L)

In this apocalyptic writing, which was written some seven and a half centuries after Isaiah's apocalypse for Christians who were suffering under severe persecutions, the writer renews the image of the "strong city," in which an apocalyptic feast would take place. It is a city without a temple, because its "temple is the Lord God the Almighty and the Lamb." God's glory will fill it with continual light; there will be no night in this city, but it has no need of sun and moon. Its gates shall always be open, but nothing unclean shall enter to enjoy the feast, "but only those who are written in the Lamb's book of life." The longer reading, which tells of the river of life and the tree of life, also announces that "his servants shall worship him," and makes the promise that "they shall see his face, and his name shall be on their foreheads." God will truly be the light of all people, and he shall reign forever and the feast will have no end.

Matthew 5:1-12

There can be little doubt that Jesus was addressing the beatitudes to his disciples, who, at his call and direction, had left everything — homes, families, friends, work — in order to follow him. His "blessed are's" assures them that he knows their sacifices and devotion, and that they will be recompensed in the kingdom of heaven. Therefore, after enumerating the "blessed's" and the promises, he declares,

> *Blessed are you when men revile you and persecute you and utter all kinds of evil against you falsely on my account. Rejoice and be glad, for your reward is great in heaven, for so men persecuted the prophets who were before you.*

The first part of each beatitude is descriptive of the situations of the disciples, while the second part spells out the blessings that will come to them — and the faithful of every age — in the kingdom of heaven.

Sermon suggestions:

Matthew 5:1-12 — "Saints Alive."

It took me nearly eight years before I think I began to understand what All Saints' Day is about. Some twenty-five years ago, my wife, children, and I spent six weeks traveling in Europe in conjunction with a sabbatical leave from seminary teaching. In Edinburgh, we had seen a painting of St. Sebastian, bound to a pillar, awaiting death by the archers' arrows. In museum after museum on the continent, we saw additional paintings of Sebastian, most of which depicted him with arrows sticking out from varius parts of his anatomy. This experience prompted me to write later, "if all the portraits of St. Sebstian were superimposed upon one another, St. Sebastian would look like a pin cushion." In Rome, the experience in art museums took a new twist when, one afternoon, we found ourselves in front of the Catacomb of St. Sebastian out on what remains of the Appian Way. After a tour of the catacombs, led by a friar, whose deep voice was most appropriate for a tour of this city of the dead, which was once the temporary burial — and hiding — place of the bodies of Peter and Paul, as well as the tomb of Sebastian. At the end of the tour, we emerged by a different route and found ourselves in the Church of St. Sebastian; the church is really his tombstone. Part of the meaning of All Saints' Day, especially in conjunction with the suffering and martyrdom borne by the spiritual descendants of the disciples, became clear to me and I grasped more fully the concept of the Noble Army of Martyrs and the Church Triumphant.

A few years later, a trip outside of Rome to the Campo Verano, the "active" cemetery of Rome today, brought All Saints' Day into even clearer focus. There we discovered that catacombs beneath the 4th century church, which still holds the remains of St. Lawrence, reach out like fingers in all directions from the church. Above them are an old cemetery, in which every grave is above ground, ready for the resurrection, and a new high-rise mausoleum, which maintains the motif of the catacombs in the building. People were everywhere in both cemeteries, placing flowers on the graves, inspecting the photographs of their loved ones on the graves, cleaning small crypts and old family mausoleums, all in conjunction with and preparation for the celebration of All Saints' Day. It struck me that the Church of St. Lawrence Outside-the-Walls was actually the tombstone of the entire cemetery, below and above ground, and that for the first time in my life I had seen how the Church Triumphant and the Church Militant are both part of the body of Christ. (For additional details of these experiences and their relationship to All Saints' Day, see Chapter IX of *The Renewal of Liturgical Preaching*, and a sermon for All Saints' Day in *Telling the Whole Story*.)

1. *The saints are alive* — in heaven as on earth. All belong to the body of Christ, some to the Church Triumphant and others of us to the Church Militant. Christ gives life and hope — his blessing — to all.

2. *The martyrs kept the faith alive.* They have passed on the faith to us in the church at great sacrifice ("blessed are they") to themselves, even dying with and for Christ, whose Word and Spirit sustained them as they do us, too.

3. *The faith keeps saints alive today.* Sustained by Word and Spirit, their work of witness and worship (the "blessed are's" of discipleship) gives evidence that they live by faith and, even today, some people will be called upon to die as martyrs for the faith.

4. *Saints live in hope.* The ultimate promise of reception by God the Father in heaven is hope, as it was that of all the saints and martyrs who have belonged to the body of Christ. The saints are really alive!

Revelation 7:2-4, 9-12 (R); 7:2-4, 9-17 (E); 7:9-17 (C); — "Marked for Time and Eternity."

1. A population explosion will occur in heaven. People of all races and nations will be there. With John, we can be certain of that. Jesus has made this possible.

2. The sign of the cross will be on every forehead. Only those who die in the sign of faith, according to John, live in the assurance of entering heaven. Baptism "marks" us for time and eternity as the children of God.

3. Eternal life will really be heavenly. Hunger and thirst will be wiped out, pain, anguish, and uncertainty will be eliminated, and "God will wipe away all tears from their eyes."

4. Heaven, the abode of the saints, is worth waiting for. Sealed by the Holy Spirit and marked by the cross of Christ forever, we can wait for that day with assurance and hope.

Isaiah 26:1-4, 8-9, 12-13, 19-21 (L) — "The City Where the Dead Shall Live Again."

1. *A city for the living.* That is Isaiah's vision of the future. Heaven is the city of God, where salvation will finally be realized as abiding with God forever. It is for those who live in faith, the only people who are really "living."

2. *A city for the dead.* There they will come to life again, by the grace and power of God. In that city, God himself will raise up the dead and give them life eternal. Jesus' words to the repentant thief will become a reality for us, "Today you shall be with me in paradise."

3. *A city with an open gate.* "There was no other good enough to pay the price of sin, He only could unlock the gate of heaven and let us in." (Cecil Frances Alexander) Jesus' cross props the gate open — for all, forever.

4. *"Come in! Come in! Eternal glory you shall win."* So sang John Bunyan after he had caught a vision of heaven close to that of Isaiah's. Amazingly, through baptism and faith we can enter it before we die.

1 John 3:1-3 (R, C) — "What We Can Know About Death."

1. We know right now that we are children of God. God loves us, especially in Jesus, and that gives us hope.

2. We know very little about heaven itself. Even Jesus could tell very little about it, but he could assure us that "In my Father's house, there are many rooms . . . . I go to prepare a place for you, . . . that where I am, you may be also."

3. We know enough to give us comfort and assurance. We shall be like God, and that is really all we have to know about death and life after death.

4. We live, therefore, by faith, not by knowledge alone. Jesus and the apostles taught us that. Faith alone, through the grace of God, tells us all we need to know about death and heaven.

Revelation 2:9-11, 22-27, (22:1-5) (L) — "The City Without A Temple."

1. There is no temple in the city of God. One of the things that struck me about "Main Street, USA" in Disney World, is that it had everything but a church building. Without realizing it, the creators of this entertainment center may have been, in a way, building the City of God, which has no Temple or church buildings in it.

2. God, Father, Son and Holy Spirit, will be present, reigning over the city. Those who receive eternal life and enter the City will be able to adore God and give, first-hand, the glory that is due his holy name.

3. The Lord God will be light and life for the inhabitants of his City. His reign will go on forever and ever — to the blessing and benefit of those whom he has redeemed in Jesus Christ our Lord.

Thanksgiving Day

Lutheran   Deuteronomy 8:1-10   Philippians 4:6-20,   Luke 17:11-19
                                         or 1 Timothy 2:1-4

The church year theological clue

The liturgical clue comes from the secular calendar rather than the church year — with an assist from the liturgy itself, which celebrates the death and resurrection of our Lord as Eucharist, or thanksgiving. The occasion often falls between the last two Sundays of the Pentecost cycle/season, since it comes on the fourth Thursday of November annually. The Eucharist celebrates the gift of redemption and eternal life through Jesus Christ; thanksgiving celebrates God's gifts in the goodness of creation. Thanksgiving, therefore, calls for *preaching to function as a creation eucharist*, which might properly be followed in the worship service with the actual Eucharist. Thanksgiving, from this perspective, calls for a kind of eucharist in "two kinds" — not just bread and wine, but preaching and communion. The sermon will proclaim God's gracious acts in creation, and the communion gives people an opportunity to respond with thanksgiving to the Lord who has saved us all and is present in the *thanksgiving feast* of the eating of bread and the drinking of the fruit of the vine.

The Prayer of the Day (LBW) — The prayer for a Day of Thanksgiving is simply a reworked collect that was appointed for A Day of General or Special Thanksgiving in the previous *Service Book and Hymnal*. It is more simplified in form, but the content is virtually the same as it was before, acknowledging God's goodness which "comes to us new every day. The prayer offers this petition to God the Father: "By the work of your Spirit lead us to acknowledge your goodness, give thanks for your benefits, and serve you in willing obedience; through your Son, Jesus Christ our Lord." This petition contains what might be called a three-point eucharistic sermon: the goodness of God's creation; thanksgiving for God's gifts as a "first-step response; loving obedience expressed in service to God and humanity as a "second-step" response.

The Psalm of the Day — Psalm 65 (LBW) — Several psalms begin with a call to the people to "give thanks to the Lord, for he is good, for his mercy endures forever" — or a similar expression of thanksgiving. Psalm 118, for example, begins with two repetitions of this invitation to the people, concluding at verse 26 with "Give thanks to the God of heaven, for his mercy endures forever." Any number of other psalms might have been selected for a Day of Thanksgiving, but Psalm 65 was chosen because it announces the physical and spiritual reasons that people have for giving thanks to God better than most of the other psalms. It declares: "To you that hear prayer shall all flesh come, because of their transgressions. Our sins are stronger than we are, but you will blot them out." Later, the psalm speaks of how God "visits the earth," watering it, preparing the grain, softening the ground and blessing its production: "You crown the year with your goodness, and your paths overflow with plenty." Although it reverses the natural order of God's benefits and puts salvation before creation, the content is so rich that no harm is done to the thanksgiving theme; rather, it is enriched.

The Psalm Prayer (LBW)

Lord God, joy marks your presence; beauty, abundance, and peace are the tokens of your work in all creation. Work also in our lives, that by these signs we may see the splendor of your love and may praise you through Jesus Christ our Lord.

322

The readings:

Deuteronomy 8:1-10

The last verse of this passage, which calls upon the people of Israel to remember how God led and blessed them, fed them with manna in the forty-year trek through the wilderness, bringing them, at last, into the promised land, applies the thanksgiving theme to this particular age. The years spent in the wilderness were a time of testing, in which God sought to teach the Israelites that human beings do not "live by bread alone, but . . . by everything that proceeds out of the mouth of the Lord." The promised land is

> *a good land, a land of brooks of water, of fountains and springs, flowing forth in valleys and hills, a land of wheat and barley, of vines and fig trees and pomegranates, a land of olive trees and honey, a land in which you will eat bread without scarcity, in which you will lack nothing . . . .*

The last verse brings the message originally given to Israel home to contemporary Americans: "And you shall eat and be full and you shall bless the Lord your God for the good land he has given you."

Philippians 4:6-20

The first two verses of this text (which involves at least two of the three letters Paul had written to the congregation at Philippi, combined into this single letter) call the people of God to a prayer service in which they will give thanks to the Lord for his blessings. After urging the Philippians to think about the things that are true, honorable, just, pure, lovely, and gracious, he tells them to *do* them as servants of Jesus Christ. He wants them to live out the sacrificial faith of the cross in their daily lives, as he has, to complete their mission in the world. God will be with them in every situation they encounter. He declares: "I have learned the secret of facing plenty and hunger, abundance and want. I can do all things in him who strengthens me." As a good Jew, too, who is grateful for their support of his ministry, Paul assures them, "And my God will supply every need of yours according to his riches in glory in Christ Jesus. To our God and Father be glory forever and ever. Amen."

1 Timothy 2:1-4

Set as it is on Thanksgiving, this passage redirects the prayers of the church from God's care and provisions in the many blessings he has given his people to "supplications, prayers, intercessions, and thanksgivings for all men, for kings and all who are in high positions . . . ." Paul was convinced that kings and rulers were servants of God who were to be honored — and even remembered in their prayers — by human beings. In our country and time, it is a reminder to give thanks that there are people willing to serve in leadership roles in our world, and to ask God to bless them and help them fulfill their efforts to serve God by serving their fellow human beings. This text calls for a different note in our thanksgiving services; people are to give thanks — and pray for — the elected officials of this land.

Luke 17:11-19

This reading is assigned to the Twenty-first Sunday after Pentecost, Year C, as well as to a Day of Thanksgiving. In Pentecost, when combined with readings from Ruth and 2 Timothy, it emphasizes faithfulness rather than the gratitude obvious in its reading on Thanksgiving Day. The incident also has "messianic meaning," because cleansing of leprosy was

324

tantamount to receiving salvation from God. In this setting — Thanksgiving — the story of the ten lepers, only one of whom returned to give thanks to Jesus when he was cleansed, highlights the theme of gratitude to God for all of the blessings that he has given to his own people. That the man who returned and prostrated himself before Jesus, praising him and giving him thanks, was a Samaritan, illustrates how God gives his blessings, including salvation, to all people; this man had no additional gift, evident in his spontaneous return to Jesus and his expression of thanks for the miracle that had occurred in his life — he reconized the source of his healing and wanted to be close enough to Jesus to express his gratitude for the gift.

Sermon suggestions:

Luke 17:11-19 — "Gratitude and a Gift from God."

In his book about the Mayflower Company adventure, *Saints and Strangers*, George F. Willison tells how the first Pilgrim landing party in 1520 saw some Indians and pursued them in the hope of making contact and replenishing their supplies; the voyage from England to New England had taken sixty-days. Unsuccessful, they made their way back to the Mayflower, stopping long enough in a field where they had seen some strange mounds, to dig up a number of them, discovering that they contained the seed corn of the Indians. The party helped themselves to the corn, returned to the ship, where a prayer of thanksgiving was offered to God for providing them with the corn. Willison says that it wasn't an act of God, but that it was outright thievry; they simply stole the corn from the Indians — and gave God thanks for it. That prayer, before their actual landing some distance away, was really the "first thanksgiving," preceding the harvest which saw them celebrate the twenty-acre crop of corn with the Indians from whom they had stolen it. At least, they realized that the goodness of God in his creation had given the Indians a supply of food that was bountiful enough to give them hope and a future, even though they had taken it without permission.

In Luke's story, the Samaritan who had been healed knew that God had given him a gift through Jesus Christ, and he just had to return and thank the Giver as best he could. He really had an additional gift in the informed motivation which sent him back to the Lord to worship him in what proved to be true faith ("your faith has made you well"); he knew he needed to give thanks — and he returned and did what he had to do. That's what Thanksgiving is all about — genuine gratitude.

1. A man with a grateful heart. Here is the model for all people who have any inclination to give thanks to the Lord "for he *is* good, and his mercy endures forever." The Samaritan was so overwhelmed by his good fortune that he prostrated himself before Christ when he returned. He knew he had received a gift of creation in his healing and renewed life. So have we, perhaps in a different way.

2. Questions for the community. Jesus asked three questions — probably of the Samaritan; after all, who else would have known that all ten lepers were cleansed? But today there are questions for the entire community of faith. On Thanksgiving Day — and every Sunday, as well as every single day, do we acknowledge the presence of the Lord with thanksgiving?

3. Christian thanksgiving is actually an expression of faith in God for creation and salvation. On one hand, we thank God for the gift of life and for all that sustains and enriches it; on the other hand, we thank him for redeeming us from sin and death through the life, death, and resurrection of our Lord.

4. Christ renews people with thankful hearts. He constantly assures us that the faith he has actually given us makes us whole again. His response to our thanksgiving is, "Rise and go your way; your faith has made you well (whole)."

Deuteronomy 8:1-10 — "The Good Land."

The preacher might want to read the above mentioned *Saints and Strangers* before proceeding with the development of this sermon. The pilgrimage of the Mayflower Company was only sixty-six days, not forty years, but it was fraught with peril and the danger of death all the way. Reaching the New World in safety was indeed a reason for thanksgiving — and they knew it and did it. When they established their first settlement and experienced the "corn harvest," they had another reason for thanksgiving, and the Indians, from whom they stole the corn, were the invited guests. God was still with them — and they were grateful enough to give him the praise and thanks due him.

1. God's goodness is evident in his creation. The earth really is the Lord's — and the fullness of it. All life — and its sustenance, too — comes from God as a continuing gift of creation. The Israelites were reminded of this by God — through Moses, first, and his prophets and preachers ever since.

2. Americans have been blessed abundantly. God has given us more than enough food to sustain us; we could provide food for much of the world by ourselves. This is our cause for thanksgiving today.

3. Care and share. Our business is to care for others, as Christ has cared for us, and also to care for the earth (see Joseph Sittler's volume of sermons, *The Care of the Earth, and Other Sermons.*) Thanksgiving is caring enough to thank God, to care for the earth, and to share what we have with other people.

4. Give thanks, for God is good. He creates us, feeds us, and saves us, through Christ our Lord. God is our reason for celebrating thanksgiving on this special day, and on every day we live, as well.

Philippians 4:6-20 — "Thankful People."

1. People of God are people of faith. They have learned to trust the Lord their God for all that they need to live now and in eternity.

2. People of God pray to God. They raise their supplications to the Lord — with thanksgiving — because they know what God has already done, and will continue to do, for them. They are thankful for all of his gifts to them.

3. People of God live in peace. They are sustained by their God-given faith and know the "peace of God, which passes all understanding," because they have hope in the Lord.

4. "Come, you thankful people come." Raise a prayer of supplication to God for all people — and do it with thanksgiving.

1 Timothy 2:1-4 — "A Universal Thanksgiving."

1. Pray for all people. That's Paul's advice to Timothy. God has made all and is the God and Father of everyone, whether or not they know it, and whether or not they admit it and worship him.

2. Pray that all people will come to know the truth. The truth about God is what they need to know; it is crucial knowledge, because it has to do with existence in eternity as well as time. The truth sets people free.

3. Pray that all people will be saved. God would have every single person on earth in his everlasting kingdom. All people are subject to him — rulers of people as well as the people themselves. He is the Lord God of all.

4. Pray with thanksgiving. Thank God for his continuing acts of creation and for his salvation in Jesus Christ our Lord. Pray that all people might share in the blessings of the earth and the benefits of the kingdom of God.

DATE DUE

JUN - 8 1994			
JAN 23 '97			

DATE DUE

			Printed in USA